MICROSOFT OFFICE 365 FOR BEGINNERS

9 in 1. The Most Comprehensive Guide to Become a Pro in No Time |Includes Word, Excel, PowerPoint, OneNote, Access, Publisher, Outlook, OneDrive, and Teams

SCOTT BURNETT

ISBN: 979-8845825933
10 9 8 7 6 5 4 3 2 1

GET YOUR BONUSES NOW!

To walk you through the journey of learning Microsoft Office 365 applications, in collaboration with Mike Collins and Linda Carter, I have created two guides on time management and productivity strategies that will help you get the most out of this book.

We believe that these strategies are vital not only in the process of learning new things, as in this case, but in all aspects of life. Indeed, they will help you achieve set goals with less effort and without wasting time.

- Free Bonus #1 (eBook) -
PRODUCTIVITY STRATEGIES FOR BEGINNERS
Discover all the secrets to exploding your productivity, consuming less time and achieving your goals effortlessly.

- Free Bonus #2 (eBook) -
TIME MANAGEMENT STRATEGIES FOR BEGINNERS
Discover all the secrets to organizing yourself and ending procrastination and hit your goals effortlessly

All these bonuses are **100% free**, with no strings attached.
You don't need to enter any details except your name and email address.

To download your bonuses scan the QR code below or go to

https://scottburnett.me/bonuses

TABLE OF CONTENTS

BOOK1: GETTING STARTED WITH OFFICE

Introduction

U   nderstanding how to use a tool or an app is the first step to benefitting from it. With the advent of more
     work, physically and digitally, technology has helped. It is still helping us get things done better and more
     efficiently, and this all-inclusive package from **Microsoft's** table has many benefits to offer you, so long
you know your way around it.

Microsoft Office 365 is a subscription service that includes a long list of tools that help you as an individual, team, or organization. The service has virtually a tool for everything you may need to do and aid you in doing it more effectively and efficiently. If you have been looking for a tool to help you carry out tasks **the right way,** with the **least waste of effort and time,** as well as an avenue to work smarter rather than harder; the tools embedded in the full subscription services can achieve this for you, as long as you are subscribed to the service. Get practical, target a goal and objective, a meet such goals with the help of the right tools on hand for the right job.

Your efficiency, effectiveness, and productivity can only improve with many great tools, like Teams, Planner, Forms, and many others.

This user guide will help you know how to get maximally the best from this subscription service to take your personal and work-life to the next level.

Chapter 1: **Office Packages**

eciding which plan to use is an interesting decision any individual or organization that has decided to use the Microsoft 365 solution will make. Not all Microsoft 365 are available in every plan, and your plan determines how much you get from Microsoft 365. And frankly, you do not necessarily need every feature of Microsoft 365, whether as an individual looking to use it for personal in-house usage or as a business.

Microsoft has also made this easier by grouping the plans into relevant sections and, more importantly, subsections to help you optimize your decision on what to use. Hence, a small business doesn't have to buy the same plan as a more significant business that may need more utilities from Microsoft 365, and this ensures everyone can choose their plan and remain happy.

There are four plans available in Microsoft 365, each, of course, having its sub-plans:

- Microsoft 365 for **Home.**
- Microsoft 365 for **Business.**
- Microsoft 365 for **Enterprise.**
- Microsoft 365 for **Education.**

Each plan has features and available applications, and this chapter will guide you on what plan to use.

***Before subscribing to any of the Microsoft 365 plans, you must log in to your Microsoft account. Remember, it is one account for everything; create your account and get checked in.

Microsoft 365 for Home

Want to purchase immediately? Visit https://www.microsoft.com/en-us/microsoft-365/buy/compare-all-microsoft-365-products and select the "**FOR HOME**" tab on the page.

There, you can select any of the four tabs and go ahead to purchase your subscription.

- Microsoft 365 **Family.**
- Microsoft 365 **Personal.**
- **Microsoft** Office Home and Student.

- **Microsoft** Office Home and Business.

Microsoft 365 for Business

Want to purchase immediately, visit https://www.microsoft.com/en-us/microsoft-365/business/compare-all-microsoft-365-business-products

There, you can select any of the four tabs and go ahead to purchase your subscription.

- **Microsoft 365** Business Basic.
- **Microsoft 365** Business Standard.
- **Microsoft 365** Business Premium.
- **Microsoft 365** Apps for Businesses.

Microsoft 365 for Enterprise

Want to purchase immediately, visit https://www.microsoft.com/en-us/microsoft-365/compare-microsoft-365-enterprise-plans

There, you can select any of the four tabs and go ahead to purchase your subscription.

- Microsoft 365 **E3.**
- Microsoft 365 **E5.**
- Microsoft 365 **F1.**
- Microsoft 365 **F3.**
- Office 365 **F3.**

Microsoft 365 for Education

All Education plans are strictly out of reach for **ineligible personnel**. The plans contain free productivity tools that can help you improve collaboration in the classroom and school, whether as a student or **a teacher**. To take advantage of these offers, you will need to prove that **your institution is an accredited academic institution**.

Want to purchase immediately, visit https://www.microsoft.com/en-us/microsoft-365/academic/compare-office-365-education-plans

There, you can select any of the four tabs and go ahead to purchase your subscription.

- **Microsoft 365** A1 (for students)
- **Microsoft 365** A1 (for teachers)
- **Microsoft 365** A3 (for students)
- **Microsoft 365** A3 (for teachers)
- **Microsoft 365** A5 (for students)
- **Microsoft 365** A5 (for teachers)

Chapter 2: **What is the Cloud?**

If you are into computers (even just a little), you will most likely have heard someone say the phrase "in the cloud" and you might or might not know what they're talking about. Then again, they might not know what they're talking about either! You can do many things "in the cloud," but not everything works the same way. There are several ways to get yourself up there, and it will depend on what you want to accomplish and your available options to do so.

The cloud is not a cloud (obviously) but rather a way of using the Internet to access hardware and services at locations managed by other people and companies. These cloud locations could be anywhere from down the street to halfway across the world and you often won't know where they're located.

Many cloud-based services are cover a variety of things. However, for the most part, they are used by larger organizations that want to outsource their hardware and its maintenance to other companies rather than manage it themselves. You can run your software in the cloud, have your servers located in the cloud, and even run your network in the cloud.

One of the primary services that companies and even home users utilize when it comes to the cloud is for storage purposes. There are many levels of cloud storage; some are consumer-based, while others are designed exclusively for large businesses. The focus of this book will be to get you familiar and comfortable with the smaller end user types of cloud storage that you can use at home and for your small business that is either free or comes at a low cost.

Chapter 3: **Purchasing Office Online**

Purchasing a Microsoft 365 membership entails selecting the Office edition you want and entering your payment information.

- Go to **Office.com** in a web browser.
- Go to your **Microsoft account** and sign in.

- The Office site opens when you sign in, where you may use the Office Online programs and manage your Office subscription.
- Click on **Buy Office**.

- If you wish to pay an annual membership, choose Buy now for the Office subscription you want. If you'd rather pay a monthly membership, choose or purchase for $9.99.
- Review the contents of your Cart and click **Checkout**.

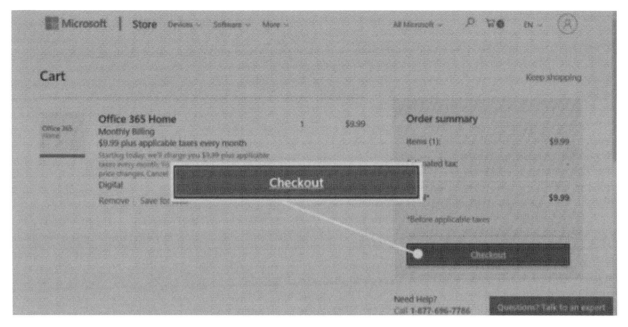

- Decide on a payment method. Choose from a credit or debit card, PayPal, or a bank account as your payment method.
- Fill up the payment information.
- Click the **Save button**.

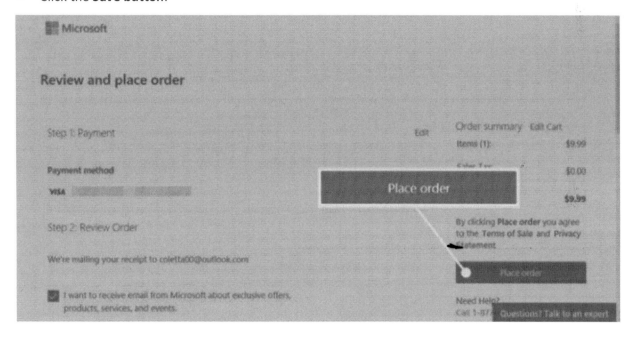

Decide on a placement order. (NB: Your purchase will be processed, and you will get an email receipt).

Chapter 4: **Downloading Office Suite**

nstall Office on your PC after purchasing a Microsoft 365 subscription. The process:

- Install Office on the machine where you want it to be installed.
- Sign in to your Microsoft account on the Microsoft 365 gateway page.
- **Select** Install Office.

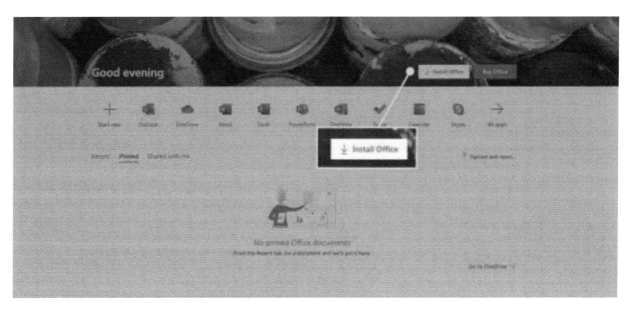

- Select **Install Office** from the Microsoft 365 Home web page.

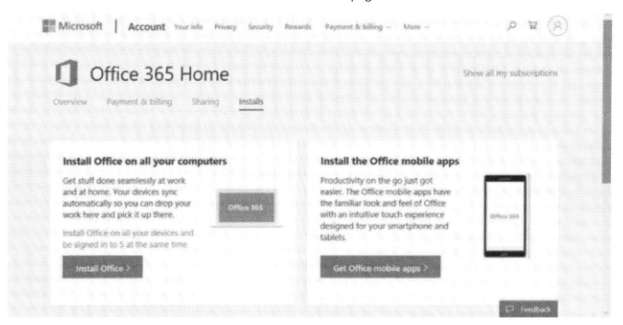

- Select Install from the Download and install Microsoft 365 Home page.

- A popup to Run or Save the downloaded file may appear, depending on your web browser. Select the Run option.
- Office prepares the environment before installing the Office applications.

- After the installation is complete, Office may ask for your email or phone information to provide you with a link to download the Office mobile applications.

Chapter 5: **Create a Microsoft Account**

Having a Microsoft account allows you to enjoy some benefits on Word. Some benefits involve storing data in the cloud, getting updated features directly from Microsoft, etc. To create an account with Microsoft, follow the steps given below;

- Go to the **Microsoft Office Website** from your browser **https://www.office.com**

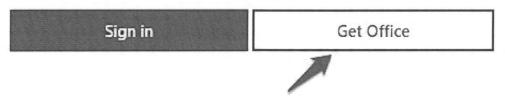

- When the page is open, click on **Get Office**
- On this page, there are two options to select: For **Home and Business.** Select any of the options and click on **Buy Now**

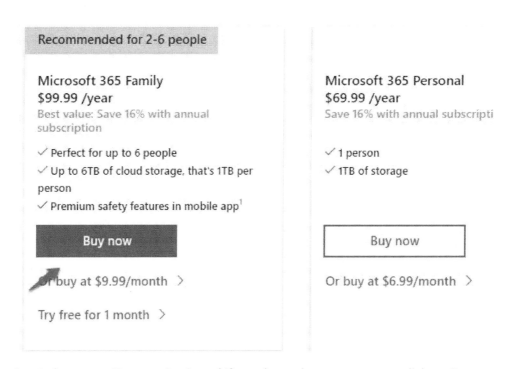

- A sign-in window pops. You can sign in and if you do not have an account, click on **Create one**

- Create an account by either entering an e-mail address or phone number by clicking on **Use a phone number instead** and enter the phone number. Then click **Next.**
- Enter your password in the Show password option and click **Next**.
- Fill in the biodata displayed on the page and click **Next.**

- Microsoft will request to send a verification code to your e-mail or phone number; click on **Send Verification Code**. When you receive the verification code, please enter it in the verification box and then click on **Verify**

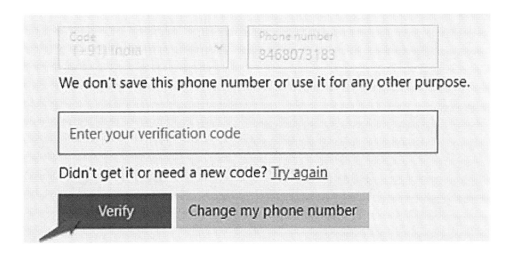

- On this page, enter your username and password and re-enter your password. Select the box asking if you want information, tip, and offer. Then click on **Sign in**

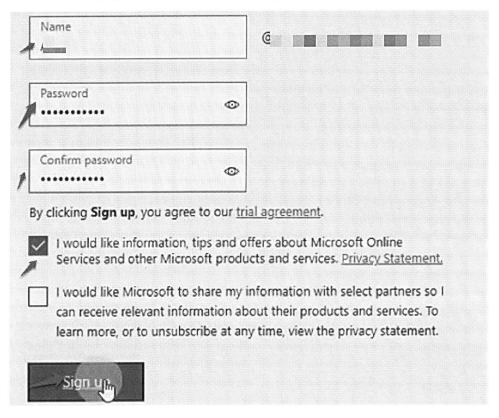

- Input the characters in the **reCAPTCHA**
- Select the options to pay by credit card or debit card, bank account, or PayPal. Then input the necessary information and click on **Save.**

- Select or deselect the box asking if you want promotional e-mails from Microsoft. Then click on **Subscribe.**
- Once the payment is successful, you will be directed to your Office dashboard, where you install Office by following the instructions.
- After you are done with these processes, click on **Next.**
- Finally, you can now access the programs in Office by clicking on the **Start menu**

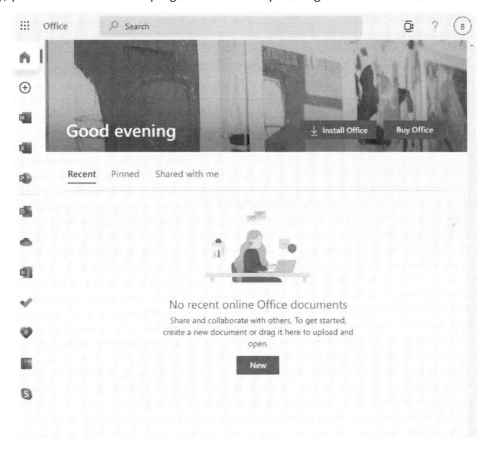

Chapter 6: Outlook Email On Your iOS and Android Devices

Understanding The Mobile Difference

The desktop version and the mobile app are substantially different from one another. One striking difference between the two is the mobile app's tab-based inbox, which divides incoming emails into two distinct groups to make viewing them on a mobile device easier. Using this function, the Focused tab will display just the most critical emails, while the **Other** tab will include the less important ones. As users navigate between tabs in the app, it can determine what information is most important to them.

The app also features a feature that allows users to instantly swipe their left finger to select what the app does with a particular email. This feature is included as part of the app's swipe functionality. It is entirely modifiable and users can assign the left swipe action to either delete or flag an email.

The Outlook apps for Android and iOS allow users to access various email services, including Gmail, iCloud, and Office 365, all from within the app. Additionally, it is simple to integrate with file-sharing services such as Dropbox, OneDrive, and Google Drive using this tool.

Accessing Mobile Email

Reading Email

Launch the Outlook app on your iOS or Android smartphone, and then hit the symbol that looks like your profile in the top-left corner of the screen. To access the Settings panel, hit the **gear** symbol at the very bottom of the menu. Choose **"Play My Emails"** from the drop-down menu under "Mail" in the "Settings" section. Select one email account from the list at the top of the page under **"Mail Accounts."**

Replying To Email

- You'll find a button labeled "Reply to All" at the bottom of your email in Outlook for iOS and Android.
- You may also use the arrows to reply to the message, forward it, or edit the recipients.

Composing Email

- Click the icon labeled **"Compose."**
- Message composition, the addition of attachments and images, and the transmission of your availability may all be done from this screen.
- After composing the message, you may send it by tapping the arrow in the upper right corner of the screen.

Archiving, Scheduling, And Deleting Email Messages

To archive email messages

To archive, a message, go to your inbox, tap and hold on to the message you wish to save, and then release the tap. Tap all the additional emails you wish to save in your archive after your first message has been chosen. To archive messages in Outlook, use the button at the very bottom of the program.

To schedule email messages,

- Long-pressing the message that you wish to postpone allows you to schedule it for a later time.
- To access the schedule, tap the button with the three dots on it.
- Pick the time that works best for you: later on today, tomorrow, or sometime in the next week, or choose a time.
- If you choose to "Select a Time, browse through the available dates and times until the time you want is chosen and highlighted.

Deleting Messages

- Launch the folder that contains the messages you want to remove from your inbox.

- To erase the first message, tap and hold until the Delete button appears.
- Tap the individual messages that you wish to get rid of.
- Tap the **"Select All"** button at the very top of the screen if you want to get rid of everything in this folder at once.

Managing A Group Of Messages

To access your account from the mail view, hit the three horizontal lines symbol in the app's upper left corner.

To extend a list of folders for a particular Microsoft 365 email account, tap the arrows that drop down to the right of the account and choose the account that has groups enabled.

To open Groups in the mail view, tap on the Groups icon.

Select the group with the shared mailbox you are interested in seeing.

Using Your Mobile Calendar

Navigating The Mobile Calendar

The Outlook program has a built-in calendar, which can be viewed by touching the calendar button in the screen's bottom right corner. To go to a different day or month on the calendar, pull down the drawer located at the top. You may switch between an agenda, day, three-day, or month view by clicking the icon in the upper right corner of the screen.

Creating A New Appointment

Tap each line of text on the form to see the configuration options for that particular aspect of the appointment you have in mind. This will allow you to specify the specifics of the appointment. By going through the form and adjusting each item to the value you choose for it, you may determine the date, time, and location, among other things.

Chapter 7: **Setting Up Outlook Desktop App**

lectronic communications keep us in touch with coworkers, customers, friends, and family. Outlook 2022 is a perfect choice for workers who rely on electronic communications, especially those who work in organizations that utilize Microsoft Exchange Server, SharePoint, and Skype for Business to handle collaboration. You can easily create, save, organize, manage, and retrieve messages, address books, calendars, and task lists from a single location. Moreover, Outlook makes this information accessible whenever and wherever you need it.

The pieces that determine Outlook's appearance and how you interact with it are referred to collectively as the user interface. Some parts of the user interface, such as the color palette, are purely aesthetic. Others are utilitarian, such as toolbars, menus, and buttons. You may customize the aesthetic and functional features of the user interface to fit your tastes and working style.

How To Open Outlook

How you launch Outlook 2022 depends on the operating system on your computer. For instance: Outlook can be launched in Windows 10 through the Start menu, the All Apps menu, the Start screen, and the taskbar search box.

In Windows 8, you can launch Outlook from the Apps screen or search results on the Start screen.

Outlook can be launched via the Start menu, the All Programs menu, or the Start menu search results in Windows 7. You may also have an Outlook shortcut on your desktop or Windows taskbar.

When you launch Outlook, it examines your computer's default application settings. Suppose Outlook is not the default email application. In that case, it shows a notification and the choice to make it the default so that any email generated outside of Outlook, such as from a Microsoft Word document or File Explorer, is created in Outlook using the main Outlook account.

To launch Outlook on a Windows 10 system:

1. **Select the** Start button, **followed by the** All applications option**.**

2. In the app list, select any index letter to see the alphabet index, then hit O to browse to the apps beginning with that letter.

3. *Scroll the list as needed, then pick Outlook 2022 to launch the application.* (NB: If Outlook 2022 is not shown, it may be located in a Microsoft Outlook folder in the M area.)

To launch Outlook on a Windows 8 system:

4. Display the Apps screen from the Start screen.

5. Click any index letter to view the alphabet index after sorting the Apps screen by name.

6. **Click O** in the alphabet index to see the list of applications beginning with that letter. Click Outlook 2022 to launch the application.

Manage Office and Outlook settings

You can access application settings via the Backstage view, notably the Office Account page and the Outlook Options dialog box. This subject describes the configuration options available on the Office Account page of the Backstage view.

The Office Account tab of the Backstage view provides information on your installation of Outlook (and other Office applications) and the resources to which you connect. This information consists of:

- Your Microsoft account and management connections.
- The window's current backdrop and theme.
- Storage locations and services (such as Facebook and LinkedIn) to which Office has been linked.

- Your subscription information and links to manage, if you have Office through an Office 365 subscription.
- The version number and update choices for the app.

Microsoft Account Options

If you use Office 365, Skype, OneDrive, Xbox Live, Outlook.com, or a Windows Phone, you already have a Microsoft account. (Many non-Microsoft products and websites use Microsoft account credentials.) Suppose you do not have a Microsoft account. In that case, you may register any existing email account as a Microsoft account, establish a free Outlook.com or Hotmail.com account and register it as a Microsoft account, or create an alias for an Outlook.com account and register it.

Numerous websites and applications validate transactions using Microsoft account credentials. It is thus advisable to register a personal account that you manage as your Microsoft account rather than a corporate account that your company controls. Thus, you will not risk losing access if you quit the organization.

You may rapidly customize the appearance of your Outlook app window by selecting a backdrop and theme from the Office suite. *(NB: These are Office-specific and have nothing to do with the Windows theme or desktop backdrop.)* The application window's title bar has a modest style backdrop. There are 14 backdrops to pick from, or you may choose for no background.

At the time of this writing, three Office themes are available:

- **Colorful:** Displays the app-specific color for the title bar and ribbon tabs, with light gray for the ribbon commands, status bar, and Backstage view.
- **Dark Gray:** Displays the title bar and ribbon tabs in a dark gray color, while the ribbon commands, status bar, and Backstage view are shown in a light gray color.
- **White:** Displays the title bar, ribbon tabs, and ribbon commands in white, while the app-specific color is used for the status bar.

From the Connected Services part of the page, you may link Office to your Facebook, Flickr, and YouTube accounts to view photos and videos, SharePoint sites and OneDrive storage locations, and LinkedIn and Twitter account to share information. You must already have an account to connect Office to one of these services.

Outlook does not provide access to storage sites unless you have established a connection with them. When entering a photo into an email message, you can insert a locally saved image or search online for an image. After connecting your Facebook, SharePoint, or OneDrive account, you may insert images from those sources.

Changes made on the Office Account page are applied to all Office applications installed on all machines linked with your account. For instance, changing the Office backdrop in Outlook on one computer affects Outlook on all other computers that are linked with the same Office account.

Some options on the Office Account page are accessible through the Backstage view's Outlook Options dialog box. This dialog box includes hundreds of choices for configuring Outlook's behavior. It is advisable to acquaint yourself with the dialog box's content to know what may be modified.

Chapter 8: **Setting up OneDrive on iOS**

Step 1: Go to OneDrive and download porter on your iOS smartphone. The URL is *https://www.microsoft.com/en-us/microsoft-365/onedrive/download.*

Step 2: Press Download. After that, the link will automatically take you to the app store (iOS App Store) to download and install the file.

iOS OneDrive:

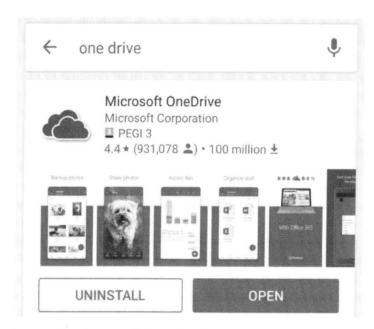

Also, you can go to the Google Play Store or iOS Application Store directly and search for Microsoft OneDrive. From there, install the application and follow its on-screen instructions to log in with your Microsoft account.

One advantage of using OneDrive on Windows 10 is that it comes pre-installed. This means that you do not need to download anything. You do not even need to log in to OneDrive if you have signed in to Windows with a Microsoft account—it does that automatically. Though, synchronizing OneDrive with distinct clouds like Dropbox and Google Drive has more steps. Nonetheless, here is how to organize OneDrive on your Windows Personal Computer.

Chapter 9: **Office Apps for Android**

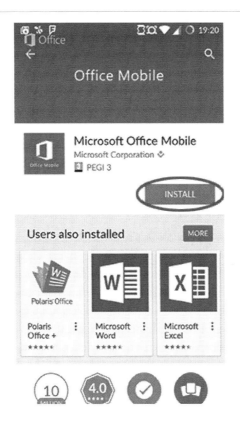

1. Go to Play Store.

2. Look for a Search app like Excel or Word (the step are equal).

3. Click the app icon to 'Install' and 'Accept'.

4. Once you finish the installation, open that application.

5. When asked, tap 'Allow' to access the contacts and files.

6. Login with that same login you applied for activating the Office 365 subscription.

Now, you are done.

If the android device has the rest of the applications of Office, it will get added automatically to OneDrive.

You can track everything you do by syncing across all your devices, and you can take notes at the point of need, with any device available, and find your notes anytime. Even if you are with another of your devices, you can plan like a pro effectively.

Talk about potent tools to aid your teamwork as well. Wherever you are – home, work, or school, you can improve your productivity with Microsoft 365, this user guide has set you on the right path to starting to benefit from it, and it can get only better with use.

Chapter 10: USING OFFICE ON THE WEB: WEB APPS

Microsoft Office 365 comes with first-class Office apps, more cloud storage, innovative and advanced security, and many other features. Microsoft Office 365 has almost everything you require to help organize your life.

Moving further, you can also protect what's essential on your Microsoft Office 365 just by Backing up and accessing pictures and files on all your devices, which comes with 1 TB of OneDrive cloud storage. Also, you can get an extra layer of security for the files that are more important to you with Personal Vault in OneDrive. You can as well access your files with the latest mobile app for Android and iOS, which joins Word, Excel, and PowerPoint into one single app.

If you happen to be a Microsoft 365 subscriber. You'll be able to access a rising catalog of premium Word, Excel, and PowerPoint templates, including high-impact pictures and 3D models. Microsoft Office 365 also has your back with readily available technical support through chat or phone, which will cost no extra charge.

Word

Microsoft Word, popularly identified as **'Word,'** is word processing software produced by Microsoft. Microsoft Word is a significant part of the Microsoft Office suite of products and is the most commonly used word processor worldwide.

According to records, it is even estimated that the number of Microsoft Word users worldwide is crossing about 1 billion. Microsoft Word was first introduced in 1983 but with a different name. Sometime in 2018, Microsoft Word celebrated its 25th birthday.

It is commonly used worldwide because of its straightforward nature and because it can be utilized in multiple operating systems, including Windows and Macintosh. Microsoft Word can be purchased as an individual product or part of Microsoft Office, including programs such as PowerPoint and Excel.

The first version of Microsoft Word (Word 1.0) was launched in October 1983, and it was developed by former Xerox programmers, identified as Richard Brodie and Charles Simonyi. These two prominent individuals were hired by Microsoft founders Paul Allen and Bill Gates.

Around 1981, Microsoft Word was referred to as Multi-Tool Word because it was made for PCs using the UNIX OS. Word also represented WYSIWYG, meaning "What you see is what you get." A different meaning to the above is that a document displayed on a screen will look exactly how it will be once it is printed.

Microsoft Word allows users to create, save, and print text documents. However, it was unsuccessful, because WordStar and WordPerfect word processing programs existed.

Fast forward to 1985, when Microsoft Word Version 2.0 was introduced and it also contained more features such as word count and spell-checked. In recent years, Microsoft has re-coded the program several times to work perfectly on different OS, including Macintosh and Disk Operating System.

In 1993, Microsoft introduced Word 6.0, which worked perfectly on Disk Operating Systems, Macintosh, and Windows. Microsoft Word 6.0 was the final version introduced to run on the Disk Operating System and the final version to be known by a version number because the next set of Word versions didn't come with numbers.

Since 1993, Microsoft has continued to release new versions, maintaining a minimum of one version every two years. The latest release of Microsoft Word was recorded in the late stage of 2018 and early 2019.

Microsoft Word and the entire Office suite are highly integrated and can run on Android, Windows, OS X, and iOS. The recent version of Word came with numerous new features determined to improve its functions and make sure it tallies with the ever-changing computing times.

Here are some of the new features found in Word:

a. **Learning Tools:** This new feature assists Word users in making their documents easy to understand and helps with reading. Furthermore, Word users can use it to alter column width for a better focus, page color so the page can be easily scanned with reduced eye strain, and reveal breaks between syllables to enhance word pronunciation and recognition. Finally, users can explore this tool to read their documents aloud.

b. **SVGs and Icons (Scalable Vector Graphics):** Microsoft Word introduces this feature that acts as a library of icons and 3D images, which can be placed into documents to make them very attractive and to make changes. The stated changes can be used for effects and colors.

c. **Digital Pen:** For Word users with a touch-enabled device, the new version of Microsoft Word (alongside other Office Products) allows you to draw with a mouse, digital pen, or your finger for writing notes and annotation without stress.

Translator: The new version of Word can now translate sentences and words into other languages. This new feature can be done using the Microsoft Translator tool, which can easily be accessed below the Review tab. The Microsoft Translator tool is also included in OneNote, PowerPoint, and Excel.

Excel

Microsoft Excel is one of Microsoft's most popular and commonly used software. It is not just used in business but also used in different areas like social media, sports, education, retail, politics, and many others. In 2019, over 70% of all computers installed one Excel version.

Excel supports multiple file formats like TXT, CSV, XLSX, and many others. It is one of the most user-friendly software tools to handle data. With the introduction of Microsoft 365, Excel is integral to that. Microsoft Excel is a part of Microsoft Office 365 subscription plans.

The essential features of Microsoft Excel are the same as in the standalone version.

The difference is that Excel is a part of an Office 365 subscription that includes the use of several other Microsoft products.

We have to admit that Excel, as a single tool, is a lot more than we have covered here.

The essential features of Excel make it the best database software.

- It can be used to manage information and create data that can be used for analysis and reporting.
- It has the features like conditional formatting, charts, data tables, calculation, pivot tables, and more.
- Data can be stored in various formats like Excel, PDF, SQL, XML, CSV, and many others.
- Excel allows users to create spreadsheets in several file formats, like CSV, XLS, TXT, and HTML.
- An Excel spreadsheet allows adding multiple sheets to a single document.
- Excel allows us to sort data on different criteria and can be sorted on various columns.

Excel enables one to create conditional formats, which enable you to format different portions of the spreadsheet depending on its values.

PowerPoint

Presentation files are the basic unit of a digital presentation. PowerPoint is Microsoft's desktop productivity application suite in Microsoft Office 365. You can use PowerPoint for several purposes, such as creating, editing, sharing, formatting, printing, and converting. We can use the applications as follows, PowerPoint for Office 365, Office PowerPoint, Online PowerPoint, Excel Office 365, PowerPoint in Office 365, and Microsoft PowerPoint Online for Office 365.

PowerPoint can be used for a wide variety of presentations and activities. For example, PowerPoint is used for creating charts, graphs, and images. We can use it to create an interactive web presentation. We can also use PowerPoint for creating educational and training materials. You can save presentation files in PPT format or PPTX format. PowerPoint presentation files can be used to display documents, graphs, or slides and can be embedded in websites, social media, or email, as well as exported as a PDF file.

- Format—You can add images, logos, text, and tables.
- Slides—You can add multiple slide backgrounds, text, objects, images, and hyperlinks.
- Images—You can add multiple images and create custom shapes.
- Charts—You can create line, bar, and pie charts.
- Animations—You can add various animations to the slideshow like fade in/out, text effects, motion graphics, and video effects.
- Audio—You can add audio files to your slides, make PowerPoint read a text out loud, and add voiceovers.
- SmartArt—You can add tables, charts, shapes, arrows, and shape-style graphs.
- Document—You can create new presentations and add and remove various objects from the slides, including images, shapes, text boxes, tables, and media.
- Animations—You can add animations to slide objects and create slide transitions to make the slides seem more dynamic.
- Templates—You can choose from hundreds of templates to give your presentations a professional look.
- Slideshows—You can add fades, motion graphics, and video effects to your slides.
- Image gallery—You can insert various image galleries from Bing, Flickr, and the web.
- Media gallery—You can insert movies, audio, and other media from your computer or the web.
- Notes—You can add notes to the slides for your presentations or lecture notes.
- Links—You can add links to your documents or web pages.
- Maps—You can insert maps from Bing or Google Maps.
- Surveys—You can create questionnaires or surveys.

Presenter View—You can choose from several pre-created templates to quickly present your content and create a dynamic and unique presentation.

Mail

Microsoft introduced Mails in their Office 365 application and we are using it with our current Office 365 subscription. It doesn't just add some extra functionalities to your email application but also takes a big part of the functionality of Microsoft Outlook to your mailbox and puts it in a mailbox folder.

Let's take a quick look at how Mails is implemented and how we use it in Office 365.

How Mails Is Used

In general terms, Mails comes with 4 folders: Inbox, Outbox, Drafts, and Sent items. We will show you how we are using Mails in the Sent items folder in this guide;

Let's start with the Inbox, Outbox, and Drafts folders.

If you are using Microsoft Outlook, your Inbox is where all the emails sorted for you will go. You can also find a couple of valuable actions such as mark as read, flag for spam, or move it into a folder, if necessary.

Likewise, the Outbox is where emails are stored for your replies.

Drafts are where you store draft emails that are yet to be sent. However, emails are moved from your Inbox to your Sent items folder if they get sent. Microsoft has implemented Mails in their Office 365, which enables you to see all the emails that have been sent to you, and received by you.

Calendar

In Microsoft Office 365 Calendar app, the Calendar web app that runs in your browser, there are three types of calendars: Calendars, Scheduling calendars, and Shared calendars.

•A Calendar stores the information of your personal Office 365 account. When you create a new Calendar item, you only need to type the calendar's name. You can store any type of information in the Calendar. You can also sync the Calendar with your phone so that you have the same information in both your phone and your calendar. When you use the Calendar on your phone, all your events, and appointments will also be displayed. You can also use your phone to create new calendar items. You can also share your Calendar with your colleagues, so they also have access to your Calendar. This way, they can create new calendar items and send reminders. All of your coworkers will have the same level of access to your calendar that you do. They can see your appointments on their respective calendars. Your phone or the browser on your computer will display all of the information. If you have a subscription to Office 365, you can read the appointments that other people have made in their Calendars.

- A Scheduling calendar is an appointment service. To create appointments on a Scheduling calendar, you need to fill in all the appointment details in your calendar. These details include the name, subject, and appointment start and end time. In addition to that, you will have to select a time slot. You will need to note the appointment and let the other people know about it. Additionally, you can check and manage your appointments using the mobile app.
- A Shared calendar is where you can invite others to join a Calendar. You can invite others through a link sent in an email or by giving them a link on your phone. When you share a calendar, you get a link to it, which looks like an invitation to join. If the recipient of the invitation clicks on it, they will see the calendar and they can also add their appointments to the calendar.
- A Personal calendar is where you can create your appointments. You can create events on your calendar using the Calendar app. Or you can create and add new events to a shared public calendar. This means that other people can join that shared calendar and see the events that have been created.

Calendar events are appointments that you create. These are either private, public, or shared. You can also choose to invite other people to the event. Once the event is created, you can share it with your friends, family, and colleagues. You can also decide to hide the event. If the event is not displayed, it means that it is hidden.

People

If you have used the contact list feature of Microsoft Outlook, you are using People. It is where information about your personal and business contacts is found. You can keep track of a lot of information with this tool. Use it to store your contact's phone numbers, email address, office address, birthday, job title, and even general notes about the person you want to remind yourself of. In addition, collaboration features are built-in to enable you to start a chat session with a contact quickly, send an email, or see recent emails you received from the person. Microsoft People is necessary to help you organize your contacts in a clean and easy-to-use interface.

Sway

Sway is a presentation app where users work on a web-based canvas. It is possible to add images, text, documents, videos, charts, and maps from many different sources to the presentation called a "sway." Sway may also be used for reports, newsletters, personal stories, tutorials, and so on.

Everyone with a Microsoft account can use Sway for free, but 365 subscribers can take advantage of considerably higher content limits per sway for headings, images, videos, and so on.

Sways automatically adapt to devices with different screen sizes, and it is easy to build nice-looking presentations with Sway. You add content and select how it should be presented, and the app suggests presentation design and layout from that input.

The Sway homepage at sway.office.com shows templates for new sways, sways created by you, and sways to get inspiration from.

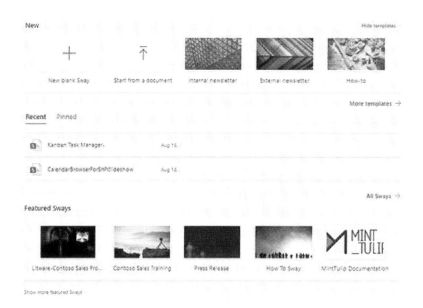

Sway and PowerPoint share a similar goal: to present information in a compelling, visual way, often as a help to a speaker. Technically they are, however, very different. From a feature standpoint, Sway makes it easier for users to create stunning visual effects, while PowerPoint gives you more control over the details. You don't have complete control when you use Sway, even if the options are many.

Another drawback is that sways are stored in Azure in Microsoft's data centers, not in OneDrive or SharePoint. Therefore, it is currently impossible to use a sway offline or save it "as."

There is a desktop app, but it requires an internet connection as it just synchronizes the user's web-based Sway. You must export your Sway content to a DOCX or PDF file if you want an offline copy.

BOOK 2: ONEDRIVE

Introduction

Microsoft OneDrive is simply a web-based storage and sharing platform. It is very similar to Microsoft SharePoint. Its advantage over its counterpart is that it provides a more personal experience for end-users to store private files or to collaborate with others both inside and outside the organization.

Whilst SharePoint is very much an organization-wide storage and collaboration solution, OneDrive provides a cut-down, more individual experience and is frequently likened to being the 'My Documents' replacement, while SharePoint characteristically replaces file servers.

Microsoft OneDrive is stored in the form of a cloud which can be accessed with any device that contains it. It enhances the easy storage of files and documents without much stress. Microsoft OneDrive assists you in keeping the proper arrangement of files and the ability to access your relevant documents, photos, and any other related files from a different device. It also does much work on how to share those documents or photos with friends, family, and co-operators. Microsoft OneDrive can be opened on your PC, website, and your mobile phone. It also assists in the proper updating of every file on your PC. Any documents that are being edited or added in OneDrive will be synced through the cloud to people or devices you have shared with previously.

Microsoft OneDrive has become a very interesting storage folder because of its easy accessibility. One of the most interesting things about OneDrive is the ability to open it with a mobile phone which makes it easy for everyone to use because not everybody can afford to get a PC. Even if you don't have the folder on your PC or the app on your mobile phone, you can access it through direct internet by typing *OneDrive.com*, and it also performs the same action as the one on your PC and mobile app.

Another thing that is very relevant here is to know how you can add the file to OneDrive. This is done when you have already installed the app; then, you find the OneDrive folder on your PC, and after that you drag and drop the file in the folder. In the case of a mobile phone, you can add files using the OneDrive app. You will turn on camera upload for you to save every photo and video taken, and it will facilitate quick and easy views of the files on other devices.

One important thing you will understand is how to share files and create documents on Microsoft OneDrive without stress. Sharing of files via OneDrive solves the problems of sending massive files through emails. When you share with OneDrive, they will receive the link to the folder or files. You should also bear in mind that everything you put on Microsoft OneDrive is only seen by you, except you share it with family and friends. With OneDrive, you can also create Word documents like OneNote notebooks, PowerPoint presentations, and Excel spreadsheets from any device via OneDrive websites. You just sign in and select "**New**" the word document you want to create will show up and then you click on it. There are many more things you will learn about Microsoft OneDrive as we proceed to the following chapters.

Editing Files

OneDrive is built in a way that there are channels through which you can access the platform. That is what makes it unique, and I love it. The three major ways you can access OneDrive are:

- Computer
- Phone and
- Web

Accessing OneDrive Through Computers

When you sign into OneDrive using your computer, the OneDrive folder is automatically created on your computer. What that means is that once you upload any file or document in that OneDrive folder, it is synced across all your devices. But know that the file or document is synced across your devices when your computer is connected to the internet.

To access OneDrive on your computer, click on the OneDrive icon pinned at the button right-hand corner of your computer desktop section. The photo below displays the tabs you will see on clicking on the OneDrive icon.

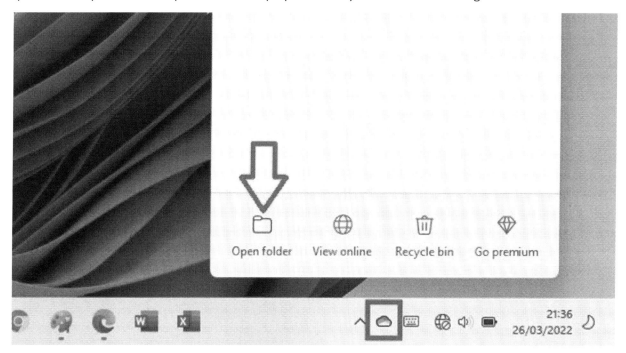

About To Access OneDrive Folder of a Computer

From the options that you will see when you click the OneDrive icon at the bottom-right of your computer screen, select the **Open folder** option, which is indicated in the above photo. This action will open the OneDrive folder on your computer. From there, you can start working on your OneDrive cloud storage platform. From here, I will walk you through how you can carry out some tasks on that folder.

Uploading Files

People think that OneDrive is only for storing files or documents, but it is not so. Microsoft OneDrive can also be used to upload files like **photos, music, videos, etc.** Under this sub-heading, we will explain in detail how to use your personal computer to upload files or documents in OneDrive without stress. Follow the procedure below to get it done.

1. First, locate the **file** you wish to upload on your computer. From the screenshot below, I indicated the file I wanted to upload.

| What Is OneDrive_ - | Getting started with OneDrive | 156679929_92135 1751949382_3884 | 70856937_54383 519701209_3795 |

2. Then click on the **file** you want to upload and drag it to the OneDrive's folder.

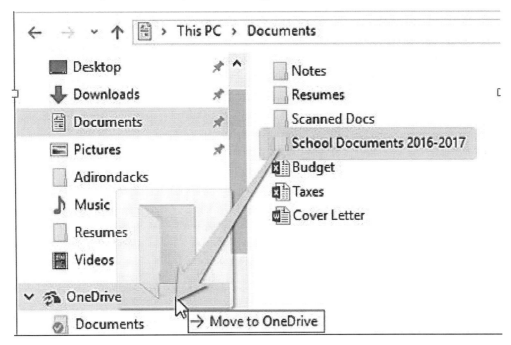

3. Next, you will see your document showing in the OneDrive.

How To Upload Files on The Web in OneDrive

In a situation where you do not have access to the OneDrive PC app, uploading through the web will be an alternative. With a **web uploader,** you can upload your files on the net without much struggle. But compared to the PC app, it is a bit slow and time-consuming and is also an easy procedure to upload your files or documents anywhere you find yourself. These are the steps to follow in file uploading on the web;

4. Move to **OneDrive.** Then you locate and choose the **upload** button.

5. You have to locate and choose the file you want to **upload**. You can upload numerous files as you wish. Just simply select and hold down the **Ctrl** key, then click on open.

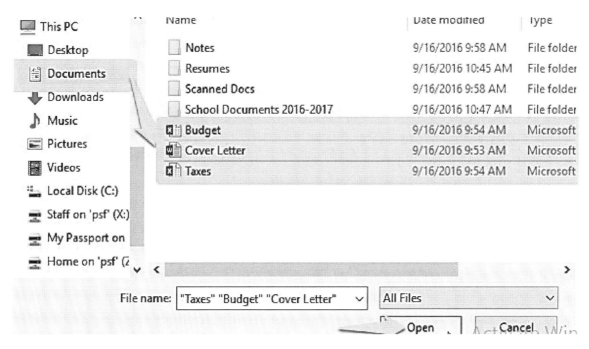

After a few processes, your file will be sent to your OneDrive.

Organizing Files

There are several activities that you can perform on a particular file or folder in your **Microsoft *OneDrive*** account with the aid of the **"Manage"** alternative. First of all, you have to choose a folder or file and after that action, you will click on the **"Manage"** alternative displayed at the top, and the obtainable alternative is shown to you at the down-drop menus which contain **"Rename," "Delete," "Move to," "Copy to," "Version History,"** and **"Properties"**. The alternative of seeing the folder or file is that you made a recent change before is made possible through the version history and also, the property section gives you detailed information concerning the item you have chosen. The details will be stated below and some of the icons will be highlighted in bold form.

How To Sort Out Your Files

If you move to the OneDrive key page, you will view every file and folder on the main page. You will then decide

the files you want to see just by choosing several alternatives in the **left triangulation panel**.

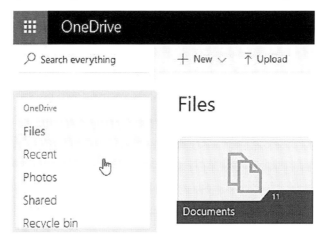

You can also alternate how your file should be displayed via clicking the **Outlook Alternative** icon at the top right

corner.

There are several methods you can use in viewing files on Microsoft OneDrive. Below are ways you can view files on OneDrive with illustrative examples.

6. **Photo Outlook**: This is one of the best ways to view your file or folder, especially when you have a particular folder of photos that you do go through intermittently. It gives you an overview of thumbnails of your photos climbed down in the grid.

7. **List Outlook:** this permits you to view your files with the names associated with them and other necessary information that you may be conversant with if you normally work with those folders and files on your personal computer.

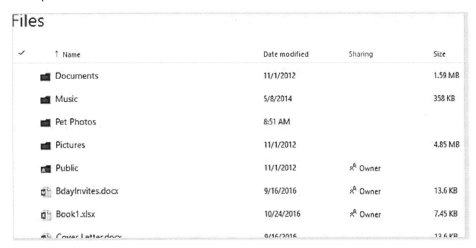

8. **Tiles Outlook:** the tiles outlook allows you to view your files and folders in a grid of icons. This type of view is an evasion view for your folders and files.

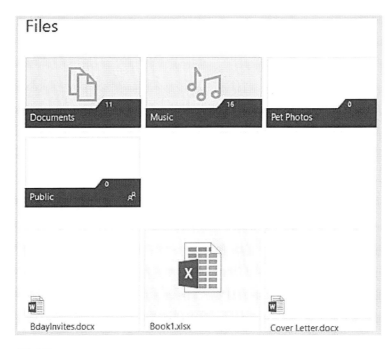

Working With Your Folders

Your folder can be used to organize your files. You can store your documents in a folder and you can also move a document from one folder to the other without stress. The aspect of moving documents between different folders is very suitable because the document can be shared just by moving the document to a **Shared Folder**. For instance, let's assume you are operating on a certain project with some set of individuals; you may decide to share your folder with them. After that, you will decide on the file you wish to share with the set of the individual in the shared folder.

How You Can Move a File to A Folder

1. Move the mouse over any file, then click on the **checked box** at the top-right flank. You can decide to choose **numerous files** simply by clicking extra checked boxes.

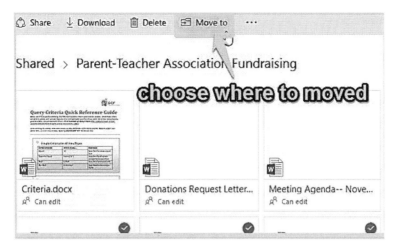

2. Tap on the **Move to** control in the menu at the top-right flank.

3. The **Move objects to** the panel will show on the right flank of the monitor. Choose the **folder** where you would like to transfer the file after you click on **Move**.

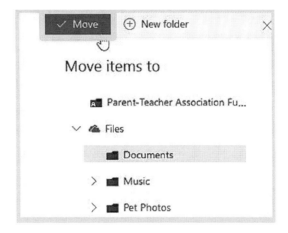

4. Your file will move as you instruct it. If you prefer your file to move to the **shared folder,** it will do so and will also be shared with a group and friends.

Other File Alternatives

If you want to get extra file managing alternatives, you will be required to **right-click** on that file. The screenshot below is an example of more options given to you.

Most of these alternatives include the following:

- **Version history**: Open and re-establish previously stored versions of the files.
- **Download**: this is a way of saving a copy of the file to your PC. The document which you downloaded before will not be upgraded when changes are being made to them in Microsoft OneDrive.
- **Rename**: in this option, you can rename your files.
- **Delete**: when you delete any file, it will be moved to the **Recycle Bin** automatically. For all the files to be finally deleted, you are required to **empty** the recycle bin.

Chapter 2: **Onedrive On Your Desktop**

Uploading Files

Uploading files on OneDrive is also a simple thing to do. To learn how to upload your files, simply follow these steps:

On the same page you searched for your files, simply click on "Upload at the top left corner of the OneDrive and then select "Files,'' as shown below

When you have clicked on "Files," it will open your documents on your desktop for you to choose the ones you want to upload.

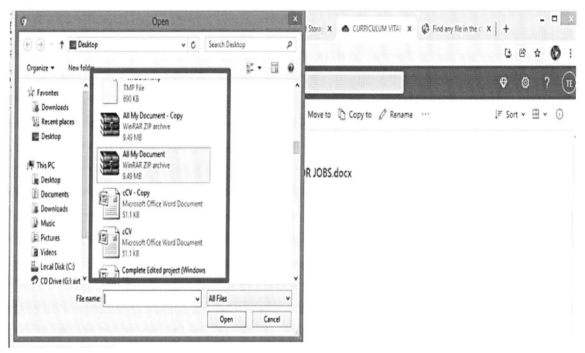

From the red-marked list, choose the document file you want to upload and where you want to upload Ccv from the list of marked red list, as shown below.

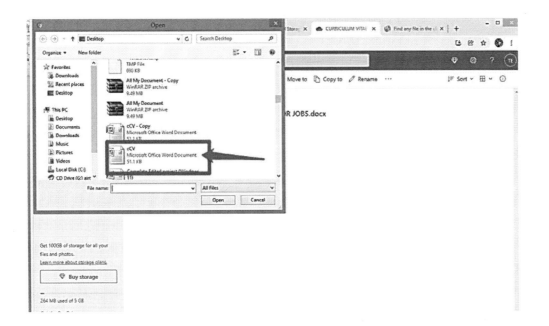

When you have done that, the next thing for you to do is to click "Open," and the file will be uploaded on your "OneDrive," as shown below.

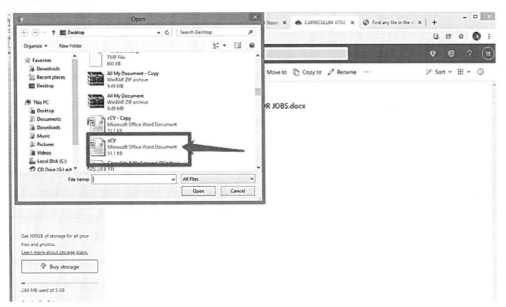

Searching for Files

If you check in your **OneDrive** locker on the web, it contains a **search everything box** located at the top right flank. Click on the box, then you enter the name of the file you are searching for, and available suggestions will be made for you to see whether that is what you are searching for. You can click on any of the suggested results if you found what you were searching for, or you click on the **see more results** to view the complete list.

OneDrive has some other advantages when searching for files and documents. OneDrive also searches on filenames and inside the document, like PDFs, Word files, and PowerPoint presentation files. At this point, you can also limit the suggested result that will be shown by searching through the files **type** and **date** drop-down menu at the top. This helps in reducing stress when searching for a particular file or document in Microsoft OneDrive. For example, if I want to see photos of the last two weeks, using the type and date drop-down menu will be of good help to you.

Another important thing is to save what you search for, so you can access it next time without much stress. The screenshot displayed below indicates a **saved search** menu where you've saved your documents. There is also a close search which will help you to end your search for any files or documents.

Accessing Your Files

To download files or folders from OneDrive into your iPad device. Follow the following steps:

1. Go to OneDrive on your iPad and log in**.**

2. Select the file or folder you want to download or save. Here you can select multiple files or folders if you so wish.

3. Then select or tap the **Save** button at the bottom of your window, and a pop-up window will appear. Then finally, click on the **Save** button at the upper right corner of your window and automatically, your file will download and save in your device's Download folder.

Upload Files to OneDrive

You may have some important files on your iPad that you want to upload to your OneDrive account; it is something simple to do. If, for instance, you are a businessman and you have a list of products you want to keep saved for you to have access to them on the go, it is possible to upload them on OneDrive.

To upload a file using your iPad application, you must make sure your iPad is connected to the internet using Wi-Fi or mobile data. And please make sure the connection is strong. After that, click the iPad application installed on your iPad for it to open.

As your OneDrive application opens, tap the **Files** tab if you are not placed there automatically. After that, tap the **+** sign at the top part of the app, just as indicated in the photo below.

The **+** sign you are to tap

As you tap the + sign, you will see a list of options, just select **Upload** among the options, and your iPad opens. Locate the file you want to upload to your OneDrive account and tap it. The file then gets uploaded to your OneDrive account.

Editing Files on iPad

To open the OneDrive app installed on your iPad, locate the app on your iPad home screen and click on it to open. On the other hand, if the app is grouped with the other Microsoft apps, tap on the folder it is grouped for the folder to open. And lastly, tap on the OneDrive icon for it to open.

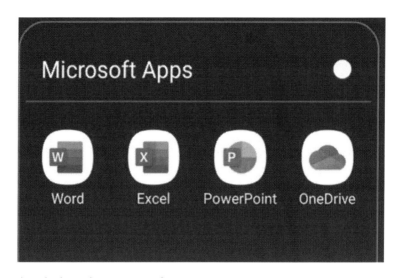

OneDrive app as grouped with the other Microsoft apps

When the app opens, the page you will see will look like what I have in the photo below.

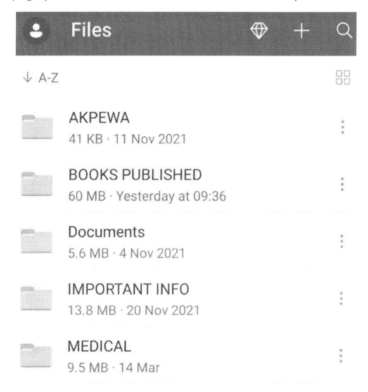

The OneDrive interface when opened on mobile

As you can see in the above photo, when the app opened, I landed on the **Files** tab of the app. This displays all the folders I created on my OneDrive. Also, the folders are arranged in alphabetical order.

Chapter 4: **Office Lens**

Office Lens is capable of doing a job that is far better than what the default camera on your phone can achieve. To make use of this feature inside the OneDrive app, choose the **camera icon** located at the very bottom of the screen. This activates your camera, and once it's open, you can use it to scan your phone for a picture or document.

You can also take photos of whiteboards, business cards, and regular photos, in addition to being able to take photos of documents. If you are modifying a document, choose "**Document**" from the options. You will see that the edges of the document are highlighted in a blue box, and if that successfully catches your document, you will be able to snap a picture of it.

You will click the "**Confirm**" button after it has now taken a snapshot of the document and determined where the edges are located. Your document is now ready for you to see, and it has undergone significant editing. You have some options below that allow you to add other photos to the scan, apply various filters to it, crop it, and then you have some more options if you want to rotate it or maybe add some text to it. If you are okay with the information that you have at this location, click the "**Done**" button.

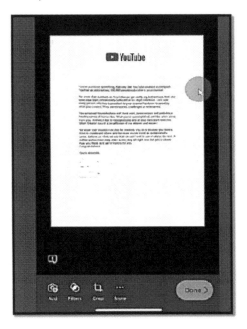

The next screen will provide you the opportunity to choose a destination for saving this file. You just place it inside the folder labeled "**Files**," and after you are all prepared, you will choose the check mark from the menu.

You can now see the document that you scanned in on your personal computer, and you can attest to the fact that this is a pretty nice document scan; the background looks really good, and it captured all of the detail and all you had to do to get it was taking a photo of it with your phone, and it is now available on your personal computer as well as anywhere else that you happen to be working.

BOOK 3: MICROSOFT WORD

Introduction

MS word 365 is the current version of MS Word. It is the new and advanced version of the word processor. It comes with various desirable features, which makes its release worthwhile and meaningful.

Word 365 comes with a 3D image compared with the previous version released before WORD 365 release, which is words 2013 and 2016. The mindset of the user is that word is only for processing word documents alone, but word 365 has changed that orientation with 3D images and graphic insertion. It is not just about inserting graphics and images; you will as well design it just as if you are using the graphic application. You can put the image into the shape to fill the shape, and you can as well insert text to the shape filled with the image and even set the alignment and direction of the text within the shape.

Aside from 3D images, there is an application called language translator, which was not available in the previous version. Word 365 settle and eliminate communication and language barrier with the app's translation which permits you to type any word, phrase, or sentence into another language. How to use a language translator with no stress has been fully explained in this user guide.

In addition to the word 365 feature, which is a side-to-side view. You can view two pages of the same document on a page by splitting the screen into two. Part of the different word 365 brings is the compound equation. You can select those equations and substitute them with the number and thereby break down every hurdle of the mathematics equation.

Furthermore, this user guide gives a summary of the various elements of the MS word 365 screens, including the backstage view option, adding page numbers to MS word documents, discovering and amending spelling mistakes, adding and customizing Headers and Footers, discovering and correcting grammar mistakes and lastly how to add ruler within the MS word.

MS word 365 offers you new and better ways of working with documents, such as side-by-side navigation, translator, and more new features. To overcome no obstacle that some call complicated obstacle, kindly pick up this user guide.

Chapter 1: **Starting Word**

Launching is a way of starting a program or an application. There are various ways of launching the Microsoft Word application, but we will be checking the two mostly used ways, which are explained in the subsequent section.

Starting Word With The Start Menu

To start Microsoft Word with the start menu, kindly:

- Click on the **window start menu** located at the bottom left or center of the desktop window.
- Scroll down to search for **Word**, then tap on it as soon as you see it. (It may be captioned as a word or word 365 depending on the version you are using).

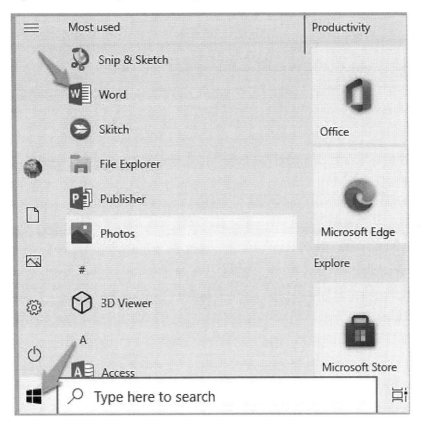

Starting Word From The Taskbar (The Fastest Means)

This is the fastest and even the easiest means of starting Microsoft Word. To make use of this method, you have to pin Microsoft Word to the taskbar first; once it is pinned to the taskbar, you will only need to single-click it on the taskbar for subsequent launching. To pin Microsoft Word to the taskbar, kindly:

- Click on the **start menu** and locate the program
- Right-click on it and select **More** from the drop-down list, then pick **"Pin to taskbar"** from the more drop-down list. Immediately the concerned program will be pinned to the taskbar.

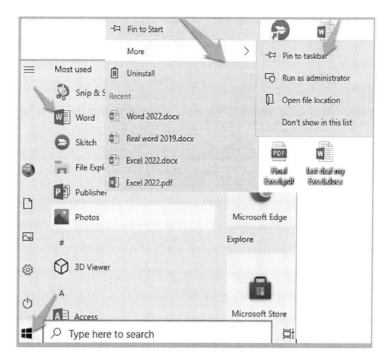

- Whenever you want to launch into the program, simply **single-click on its icon** on the taskbar.

Create A New Document

A document can be created either from the blank document or from the various available template that is available on MS word. After you are done creating the document, you can store such a document on your PC. To create the document from a blank document after you have launched into the program, kindly:

- Tap on the **blank document**, provided you have not been using the program before.

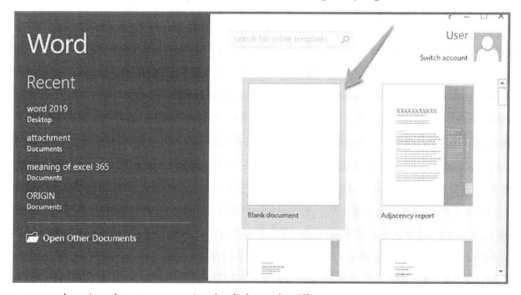

- If you are currently using the program, simply click on the **File menu**.
- Then tap on **New** from the file backstage**.**

Alternatively: after you have opened the Word main screen, press **Ctrl + N** on the keyboard for new document shortcuts.

To start from the template, simply click on **any template** of your choice from the available template, and it will be opened up.

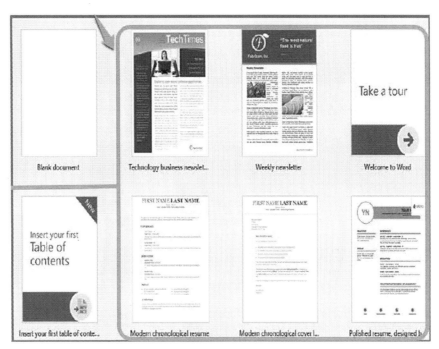

Observing The Microsoft Word Start Screen

Immediately after you launch word 2022, the first screen you will notice is known as the start screen. You can perform various activities with the start screen, as listed below:

- Select a document from the group of the **previous document** you have accessed in a recent time.
- Search for **any other document** inside your Word document.
- Click on the **Blank document** to create a new document.
- **Featured** is used to show various word online templates.
- **Personal** is a link to show each of the templates you customize by yourself.
- Type your desired template into **the search box** to run a check for you on the available template, e.g. (birthday format or Easter party).
- Select a template from available **offline templates.**

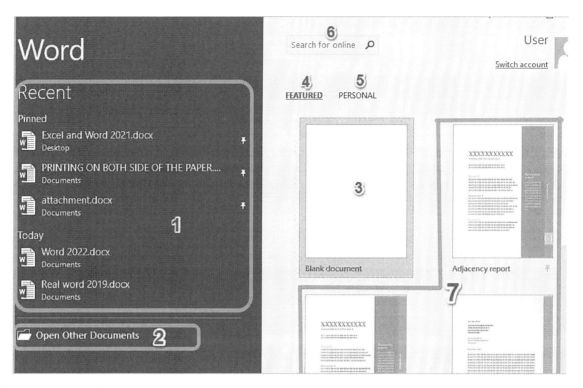

Observing MS Word Main Screen

The main screen shows the principal components of the word 2022 interface. Let us delve into those components:

- **The title bar:** the title bar will show the name you use to save your document. The default name is document 1 if you have not used any name to save your document at all.
- **Quick Access toolbar:** it contains a quick element that you can use to extract commands out of the available toolbar, such as On/Off, save, undo, redo, etc.
- **Tab:** a particular title or name given to each group of the ribbon.
- **Ribbon**: it shows a group of connected commands under each tab.
- **Command group:** this represents the gallery of related tools within tabs. For instance, within the Home tab, there are multiple commands such as Clipboard, Editing, Fonts, Paragraph, and so on.
- **Horizontal Ruler:** it is mainly used for measuring working areas horizontally.
- **Vertical Ruler**: it is used for measuring the working area vertically.
- **Cursor pointer:** it is where your typing entry will start from.
- **Scroll bar:** it is used to scroll up, down, left, or right within the given document.
- **Working area:** this is the largest area on the main screen. It is the area that will accommodate all your text entries.
- **Status bar**: it gives an exact description of your documents, such as the number of pages and words.
- **The view option**: the view option shows the current view option, such as Read mode, Print layout, and web layout.
- **Zoom slider:** it is used to adjust (increase or reduce) the size of the window screen.

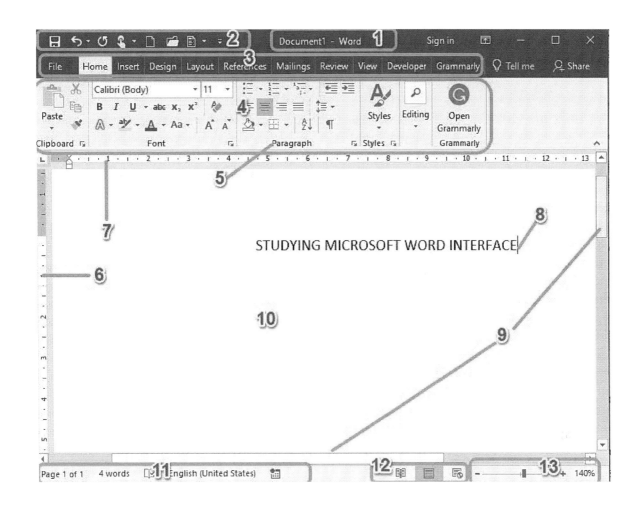

STUDYING MICROSOFT WORD INTERFACE

The Home Ribbon

In MS Word, the "Home" tab is the one that comes up when you open the program. It's usually broken down into groups: the Clipboard, Font, Style, and Editing. It lets you choose the color, font, emphasis, bullets, and where your text is. Besides that, there are also options to cut, copy, and paste in it. After selecting the home tab, you will get more options to work with.

The Insert Ribbon

This part can be used to input anything into your document. Examples of things you can insert are tables, words, shapes, hyperlinks, charts, signature lines, time, shapes, headers, footers, text boxes, links, boxes, equations, and so on.

The Design Ribbon

Here, you can choose from documents with centered titles, off-centered headings, left-justified text, and more. You can also choose from a variety of page borders, watermarks, and colors in the design tab.

The Page Layout Ribbon

You can use it to make your Microsoft Word documents look the way you want them to look. It has options to set margins, show line numbers, set paragraph indentation, apply themes, control page orientation and size, line breaks, and more.

The References Ribbon

This tab allows you to add references to a document and then make a bibliography at the end of the text so you can look back at it. It's common for the references to be stored in a master list, which is used to add references to other documents. It has options like a table of contents, footnotes, citations and bibliography, captions, index, table of authorities, smart look, etc.

The Review Ribbon

The Review Tab has commenting, language, translation, spell check, word count, and other tools for you to use. A good thing about it is that you can find and change comments very quickly. These options will display when you click on the review tab.

The Mailings Ribbon

One of the best things about Microsoft Word is that you can write a letter, report, etc. and send it to a lot of people at the same time, with each person's name and address in the letter.

The View Ribbon

In the View tab, you can switch between a single page and a double page. You can also change how the layout tools work. You can use it to make a print layout, outline, website, task pane, toolbar, and rulers, as well as to make a full-screen view, zoom in and out, and so on.

Fil Backstage

The "File" menu tab contains the menu options related to document file management. This is occasionally referred to as the backstage perspective. The "File" menu tab provides the menu options required for document editing. It's called backstage since it's not utilized for text entry or editing. It includes document status information and menu choices for viewing, printing, saving, and safeguarding the document. Additionally, it has configuration options.

You'll note that the "File" option is unique among Word's tabs. By selecting the "File" menu tab, the current document is completely replaced with the "File" menu items. By clicking on another tab, a new set of icons in the ribbon area becomes available for usage with the currently open document.

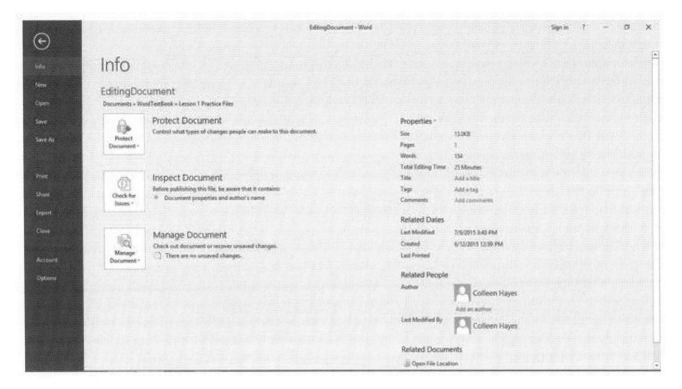

The left column of the "File" menu comprises key categories of document-related actions. The "Info" section of the "File" menu provides information about the current document and its contributors.

The "New" submenu of the "File" menu has options for generating new documents. This is the same view that was presented when Word was opened for the first time. You'll note that you have the option of creating a blank document or one that is based on a template. Templates are advantageous because they frequently contain data, formatting, and computations associated with popular word processing documents such as reports, letters, resumes, and flyers.

The "Open" option is used to provide a separate document for Word to open. You can open recently used documents or pick a document stored on OneDrive (a Microsoft cloud service) or locally on your computer.

Typically, you'll open files with the.doc or.docx extension. The.doc extension refers to documents stored in Microsoft Word 2007 or older versions. The.docx files are those saved in the Microsoft Word 2010/2013/2016/2019 format. Word is backward compatible, meaning it can open and edit both types of files.

Additionally, Word has a handy feature that will open.pdf files and convert them to the editable Word format. This converting ability is advantageous if you need to modify a pdf file. Occasionally, not all of the pdf file's contents, notably the picture layout and formatting, are converted successfully. As we shall see later, Word can also save documents in the pdf format.

The "Save" and "Save As" menu choices enable you to (1) save the current document, (2) save a copy of it with a different name or location, or (3) save a copy of it as a different file type. These settings may be advantageous as you acquire familiarity with some of Word's more complex functions. The illustration depicts a variety of various file formats that can be used to save your content. Take note that one of the save-as options includes a pdf version.

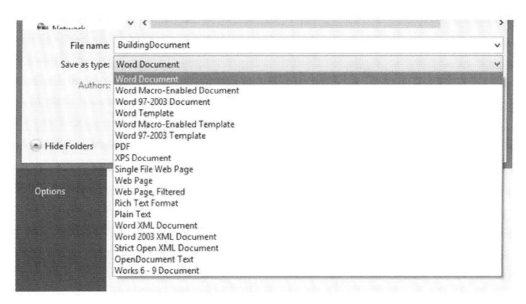

The "Print" menu section includes options for printing a document. These things include selecting the appropriate printer, controlling the printer's different features, and printing a document. Additionally, the "Print" tab gives a sample of how a document will appear when printed.

The "Share" menu option provides productivity tools that make it simple to share your work with coworkers. You should click on the other navigation items to access the submenu items' choices. The "Share" option is frequently advantageous when working in a team endeavor. The same outcomes may be obtained outside of word by sending email attachments or uploading your work to the cloud. However, the facilities included in Microsoft Word make it simple to share your work. The four submenu items are as follows:

- Share with Others—save to the cloud and send a link to a colleague.
- Send the document through email as a.doc or.pdf attachment, or share a link to a previously saved document.
- Present Online—upload it to a website where it may be seen using a browser.
- Post to Blog—publish it to your blog.

The "Export" tab enables you to convert your work to a different file type (such as .pdf) for evaluation by colleagues who prefer to use a different program. This option duplicates some of the functionality of the "Save As" file type.

The "Close" menu item effectively closes the currently open document. The "Options" menu item group enables you to adjust Word's design and functionality. Finally, you may manage your Microsoft accounts using the "Account" menu.

Applying Styles to Text and Paragraphs

- Highlight the text to be altered

Word's for Printing

A Word document is formatted to fit on a specific size page with the text automatically flowing from one page to the next. Excel supports printing, but its page breaks are not obvious, and because it's printing area can extend multiple pages horizontally as well as vertically the page breaks can be difficult to manage.

- Go to the "Home tab," which is your default displayed Word 365 interface

- On your right-hand side, second to the last, you will see the "Styles" ribbon

- Select one of the styles above; you can also click on the drop-down arrow to view other styles. Let's

assume we choose "Heading 1"

Word's for Printing

A Word document is formatted to fit on a specific size page with the text automatically flowing from one page to the next. Excel supports printing, but its page breaks are not obvious, and because it's printing area can extend multiple pages horizontally as well as vertically the page breaks can be difficult to manage.

- Your highlighted text will be converted to the selected style, which is "Heading 1"
- You can also do something similar to your paragraph by also highlighting it

Word's for Printing

A Word document is formatted to fit on a specific size page with the text automatically flowing from one page to the next. Excel supports printing, but its page breaks are not obvious, and because it's printing area can extend multiple pages horizontally as well as vertically the page breaks can be difficult to manage.

- Go to the "Home tab," which is your default displayed Word 365 screen

- On your right-hand side, locate the "Style" ribbon

- Now, let's select the second heading, which is "Heading 2"

Word's for Printing

A Word document is formatted to fit on a specific size page with the text automatically flowing from one page to the next. Excel supports printing, but its page breaks are not obvious, and because it's printing area can extend multiple pages horizontally as well as vertically the page breaks can be difficult to manage.

- Your paragraph text will change to "Heading 2" styling

Creating a New Style

- Go to the "Home tab"

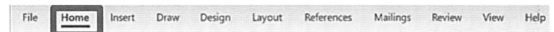

On your right-hand side, second to the last ribbon, you will see "Styles," select the dropdown arrow as illustrated below

You will be shown different options; among the options, choose "Create a Style"

- Another dialog box will pop-up titled "Name," name it according to your choice

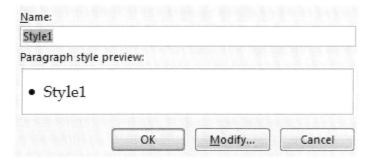

- Then, select "Modify" for more modifications to your newly created style

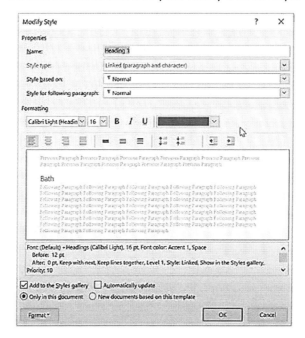

Once done, click "Ok," your newly created style will be added to the styles list

Renaming Styles

- Make sure your text that carries a style format is highlighted to recognize the specific style to be renamed

- Go to the "Home tab"

- On your right-hand side, you will see the "styles" ribbon

- Below the "styles" ribbon, click on the little arrow

- A dialog box will appear, indicating your selected or created style

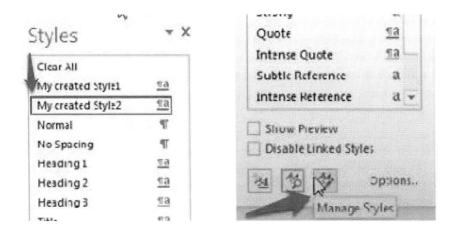

- Below the "Styles displayed box," select the last option "Manage Styles." Double-click on "Manage Styles"

- Another dialog box will appear; make sure your style is highlighted as indicated in the illustration below, then click on "Modify"

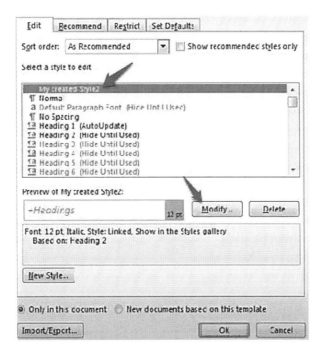

- You will be brought to the modification box named "Properties." This is where your selected style can be edited, renamed, and your font size, style, color, alignment, and the rest can be worked upon. Once done, hit "ok"

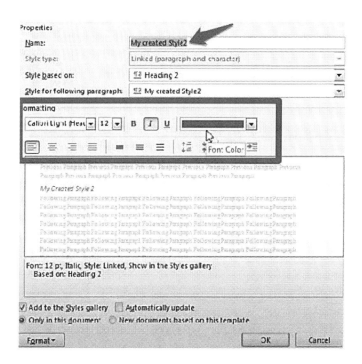

- Let's assume I renamed my style from "My created Style 2" to "My 2"

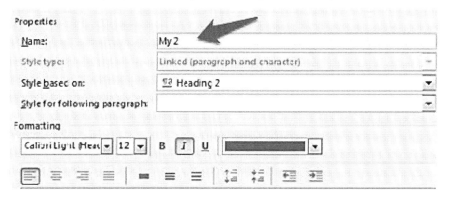

Once done, click "ok"

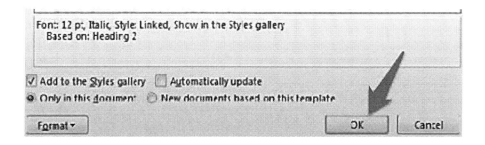

- Your previous displayed box titled "Manage styles" will also affect the new changes; click "ok" to see your styles ribbon having the same effect

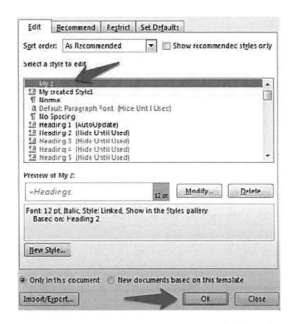

- Now, you will see the changes we made on renaming our style from "My created Style 2" to "My 2"

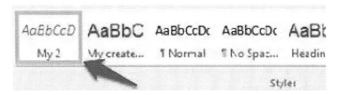

Editing Paragraph Styles

Modification is majorly in two ways: you either modify your existing style or your created style. I explained *"Creating a New Style"* and illustrated how to change it. Here, I will be demonstrating how to modify existing styles

- Go to the "Home tab"

- On your right-hand side, you will see the "Styles" ribbon. Assuming we want to modify "Heading 1", right-click on it, and a dialog box will appear with many options, select "Modify"

- Here is where your "Heading 1" modification which is one of the existing styles on your list. You can modify the font style, font size, boldness, color, and many more. For simplicity and illustration purpose, click on "color" and choose "red" color, then click "Ok."

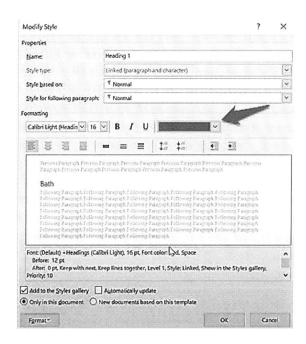

- Note the changes, "Heading 1," which is one of the existing styles, will have the effect of the color red, which we modified to

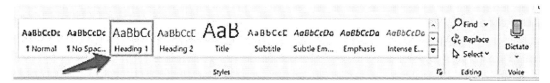

Bold, Italic & Underlined

To Bold Text & Adjust The Font Size By Increasing It

To bold text, select the portion you want to bold, then go to the home tab and select the **B** icon, which stands for bold. Your text will be in bold format; make sure it is still highlighted, then also go to font size as indicated below through the pink arrow, click on it or type the font size you want. You can use **Ctrl + B** as a shortcut to bold text.

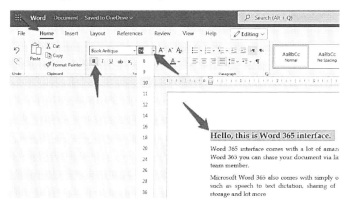

Underlining Your Text

Go to the home tab

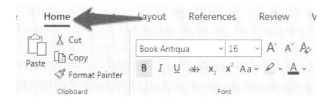

Make sure the text you want to underline is highlighted

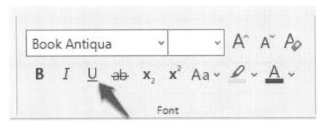

Select the underlined icon (U)

Your highlighted text will become underlined

Italicizing Your Text

Go to the "home tab" and select the text to be italicized by highlighting it with your mouse

Go to the "Font ribbon tab" beside your bold icon (**B**), click on **the italic icon (*I*)**

Then, your highlighted text will become italicized

Hello, this is Word 365 interface.

Word 365 interface comes with a lot of amazing features for Microsoft users with Word 365 you can share your document via link and track your progress with your team member.

Microsoft Word 365 also comes with simply outlook for user friendly environment such as speech to text dictation, sharing of document via link, OneDrive cloud storage and lot more

Superscript & Subscript

The **Subscript** button is used to write small letters just below the line of text. This tool is primarily used in Mathematics to differentiate between different variables. If you are conversant with Mathematics study and in any way have seen a variable like C_2, know that the "**2**" was made possible by the use of a subscript button/tool. In Word 365 environment, the subscript button is identified as x^2.

The **Superscript** icon is the next after the subscript. The superscript button is used to write small letters just above the line of text. I firmly believe that you went through primary and secondary schools. Do you remember that time when you were taught **Indices**? Do you remember those times your teacher asked the class to give an answer to question 2^4 (pronounced as 2 to the power of 4)? That number **4** hanging on top of **2** is made possible using the superscript tool. The superscript icon is represented as $\mathbf{x^2}$ in Word 365.

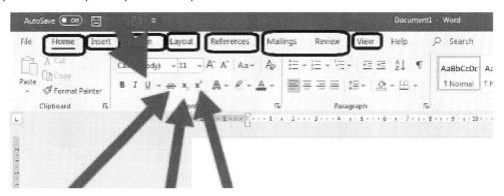

Let me assume that you have opened your Word 365 desktop application. I will then teach you how to apply these explained tools to get the expected result.

- To underline a few texts on Word 365, highlight the texts and then click the underline (U) button.
- To strikethrough words or letters, just highlight the word and then click the strikethrough button.
- If you want to apply subscript to any text or characters, first write the texts or characters (example C2), then highlight the text or number you want to subscript (in my given example of the two characters, I will highlight only "2"), and finally, click the subscript button. Once you do this, the letter will be below the main letter (for example, "2" will be below the "C" line).

To superscript any text contained in other texts, you have to highlight the text which you want to make superscript (for example, in text "K2," I have to highlight 2 because I want to make it superscript). After you have highlighted the letter/text which you want to make superscript, then click the **Superscript** icon. Once you do this, the text is made superscript.

Highlighting Text

A mouse can be used to select a block of text in major two perfect ways, either by dragging over the text or by clicking; we have to check the two ways for more understanding:

To make a text selection with the mouse dragging over, simply:

Locate where you want your selection to start from **and place your mouse cursor at that location.**

Immediately you place the cursor at the beginning of the spot and **drag the mouse over the text to the exact end** where you want to end the selection.

Excel is a spreadsheet application with the major purpose of organizing and carrying out the calculation on the data. It is a tool for recording, analyzing data and representing such data on a graph or chart.

Note: as you are dragging the mouse over the text, you will see the way the text is highlighting to the exact end where you release the mouse.

To make a text selection with the mouse clicking, I have never seen the fastest and most accurate means of selecting a block of text other than the mouse-clicking method; let us quickly check the mouse-clicking method:

Area Of The Text To Be Selected	Position And Action Of The Mouse
A single word	Double-click the mouse over any point within the word.
A line of the text	Go to the edge of the left margin of the line you want to select, and click the mouse cursor once on the edge.
A sentence	Place your mouse pointer to any spot within the sentence, hold down the Ctrl key, and left-click the mouse immediately. Such a sentence in the question will be highlighted.
A paragraph	Clicking any spot around a paragraph three times or click the left margin next to the paragraph twice to select the paragraph concerned.

Text Color

To change the look of your text, highlight your text.

If your Word 365 interface is not on the "home tab" as its default display, simply go to the "home tab" and click on it.

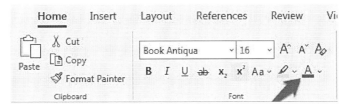

Below the "home tab," select "font color," which is identified by a capital letter A underlined with a red stroke as illustrated with an arrow sign below. Are we together? Right, let us continue.

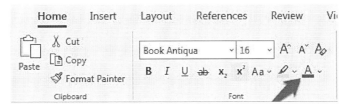

Remember that your text is still selected (highlighted). Once you click on "font color," your highlighted text will change to red color.

Hello, this is Word 365 interface.

Choosing More Color

You can also click the little arrow beside the "font color" to select your preferred choice. If not found, check below for "more colors."

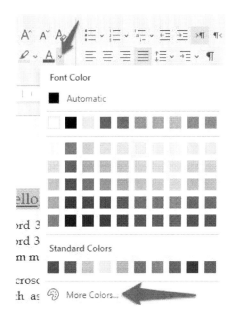

You can also decide to change the ***"font style"*** known as ***"font name"*** by selecting the ***"home tab"*** check on the little arrow beside your current font. Dropdown options will be displayed. You can select your preferred choice, but for similarity and understanding purpose, select ***"Calibri Light (Headings)."***

Your highlighted text will take effect immediately

Before

Hello, this is Word 365 interface.

After

Hello, this is Word 365 interface.

Text Justification

Paragraph alignment deals with the position of your text within a paragraph, whether it is to the left, right, or center, while the justification arranges your text neatly between the right and left margin and gives it a refined appearance, justification together with other alignments can be found in the Paragraph group under Home tab.

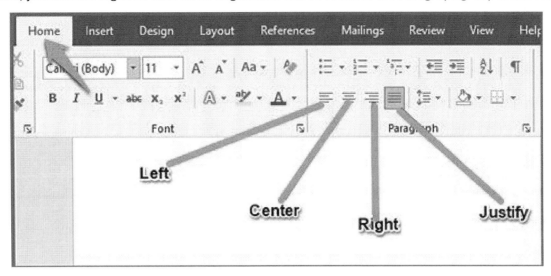

Left Alignment

Left alignment is used by the majority. According to research, out of 100 percent of the users, 70% will align their paragraph to the left, while the remaining 30% go for right and center alignment. To align the paragraph to the left side, kindly:

- Click the **left alignment command**. It is the first alignment on the paragraph group under the Home tab to align your paragraph to the left.

> Many people prefer PDF format of a document than the original word format of a document, though the universal acceptable format is that of the word format whether you are sharing a document on the web, saving it on the cloud or sending it to other via email, but some personality will specify PDF format for instance employer can specify your resume or CV to be in PDF format, to change word format to PDF, kindly study the guides below

- You may use shortcuts as well by pressing **(Ctrl + L).**

Center Alignment

Center alignment occupies the middle position or is centered between two edges, which is between the left and right alignment. This alignment is majorly used for Heading and subheading the pages. To center a text on the page, do well:

- Tap on the **center alignment command** and the second alignment on the paragraph group under the Home tab to center your text.

> Many people prefer PDF format of a document than the original word format of a document, though the universal acceptable format is that of the word format whether you are sharing a document on the web, saving it on the cloud or sending it to other via email, but some personality will specify PDF format for instance employer can specify your resume or CV to be in PDF format, to change word format to PDF, kindly study the guides below

- The shortcut for it is **(Ctrl + E).**

Right Alignment

Right alignment places the text on the right edge. The probability of seeing people aligning their work to the right is very slim. To right align a text on the page, take cognizance of the following:

- Tap on the **right alignment command**. It is the third alignment on the paragraph group under the Home tab.
- Right alignment shortcut is **(Ctrl + R).**

Justify Between The Left And Right Paragraph

This regulates the spacing by adding additional space between words and arranging them properly to occupy the entire line so that the alignment will be a balance between both left and right alignment. To justify a text on the page, kindly:

- Tap on the **justify command**. It is the last command inside the alignment section on the paragraph group under the Home tab.

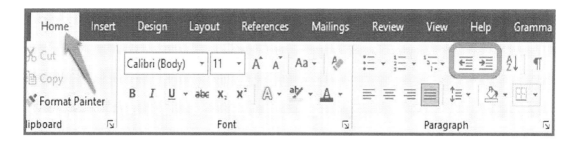

Many people prefer PDF format of a document than the original word format of a document, though the universal acceptable format is that of the word format whether you are sharing a document on the web, saving it on the cloud or sending it to other via email, but some personality will specify PDF format for instance employer can specify your resume or CV to be in PDF format, to change word format to PDF, kindly study the guides below

- The justified command shortcut is **(Ctrl + J).**

Note: this is the alignment used majorly in producing online textbooks and magazines.

Paragraph Indents

You may want to create a certain expression that will warrant you to indent the whole paragraph. Do you wish to indent an entire paragraph? Then do well to:

- Tap on the **Home tab** and maneuver to the paragraph group.

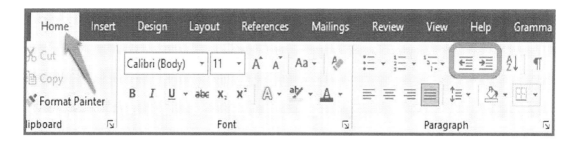

- Use **increase indent** to indent the paragraph. Increase Indentation will shift the paragraph to the front.

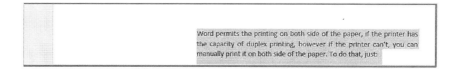

Word permits the printing on both side of the paper, if the printer has the capacity of duplex printing, however if the printer can't, you can manually print it on both side of the paper. To do that, just:

- **Decrease Indentation** will reverse or decrease the indented paragraph.

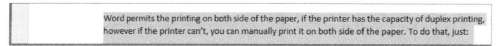

Word permits the printing on both side of the paper, if the printer has the capacity of duplex printing, however if the printer can't, you can manually print it on both side of the paper. To do that, just:

First Line Indent

When you indent the first line, the first line will shift forward from the margin while the rest line will remain unmoved, before people used to use the tab key to indent the first line. To indent the first line legally and in a modern way, kindly:

- Tap on the **Home tab or layout tab** and maneuver to the paragraph group.
- Click on the **paragraph dialog box launcher** to access the Paragraph dialog box.

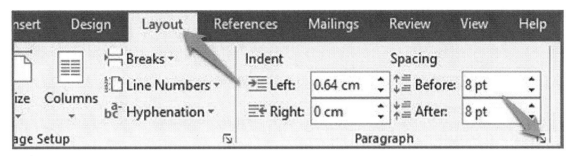

- **Within the dialog box, locate the** special button and tap on its down arrow, **and choose the** first line from the drop-down list.
- Use the **"By" button up and down** to set the indent space to 0.5 per normal indent space, which is the equivalent of a normal tab stop.

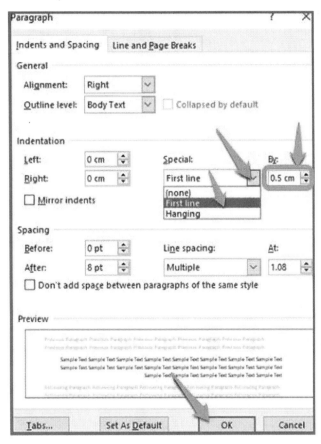

- Then tap **Ok.**

> Word permits the printing on both side of the paper, if the printer has the capacity of duplex printing, however if the printer can't, you can manually print it on both side of the paper. To do that, just:
>
> Once windows decide that your printer can't print on both, you will have to opt in for odd and even pages printing, and thus you will have to print both odd and even pages one after the other. To do that kindly:

Note: To clear the First line indent, follow the same processes as above. The only change is that of the special section. Instead of picking the first line, you would rather pick (none).

Hanging Indent

Hanging indentation, the opposite of the first-line indentation, is not always used to indent a document. You can find hanging indentations in indexes, bibliographies, and resumes. Hanging indentation makes other lines of the paragraph indented except the first line. To make a hanging indentation, do well:

- Click on the **paragraph launcher dialog box** from either the Layout or Home tab.
- **Tap on the** Special down arrow and choose Hanging, **then set the value with** the "By" box.

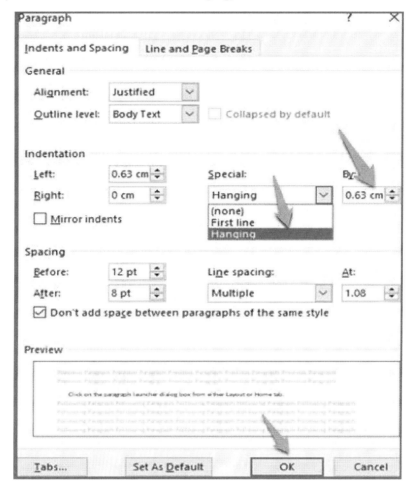

- Then tap **Ok.**

Note: the fastest way to create a hanging indent is to press (Ctrl + T), and you can reverse the hanging command by pressing (Ctrl + shift + T).

Paragraph Spacing

Adjusting The Space Between Paragraphs

- Go to the "Design tab"

- Look at your right-hand side and select "Paragraph Spacing"

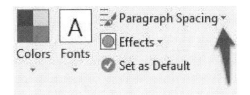

- A dialog box will appear displaying multiple options available for use

- Once you select your preferred choice, the effect will take place automatically on the entire document.

The Difference Between Line Spacing Under "Home Tab" & Paragraph Spacing Under "Design Tab"

- **Line and paragraph spacing under the *"home tab"*** adjust text manually, and it is done per paragraph, except you highlight the whole of your document.
- **Paragraph spacing under the *"design tab"*** adjusts text automatically. This affects the whole of your document.

Line Spacing

Adjusting The Space Between Lines

- Go to the "Home tab," which is Word 365 default displayed interface

- On your right-hand side, locate "Paragraph ribbon" you will see the "line and paragraph spacing" icon

- Once you click in, you will be shown multiple options for line spacing between text or if your preferred choice is not in the list, click on "Line Spacing Options" to manually decide your choice

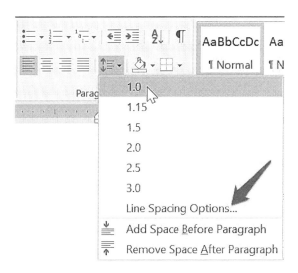

- If you click "Line Spacing Options" a dialog box will appear for you to decide your line spacing measurement. "Before" & "After" once set to your preferred choice, hit the "Ok" button below

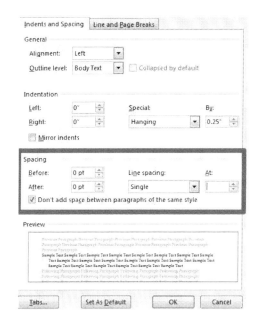

- It will automatically take effect on your opened document.

Tabs

The tab key is the shortened word for the word Tabulator key. The tab key is the cursor advancement to the next tab stop in the text, which represents the insertion of space characters with wide measurement compared to the spacebar. A tab stop is the limited space character to the next tab stop, and that is why you should set your tab stop appropriately when you use a tab key. Instead of striking a spacebar key twice or more. Your document will be arranged in order and accordingly. Just like the text and other characters, you can eliminate tab key characters with the use of the delete or spacebar key.

Viewing The Tab Character

You may view the tab character the way you use to view the text and other characters in the document. Tab character has an icon. Its icon is just like the shift icon but facing the right side. When you see a tab character, you can't do anything with it. You can only use it to adjust tab stop measurement.

To view tab character in a jiffy, quickly:

- Tap on the **show/hide command** in the Paragraph group under the Home tab.
- The **show/hide command** shows all special characters.

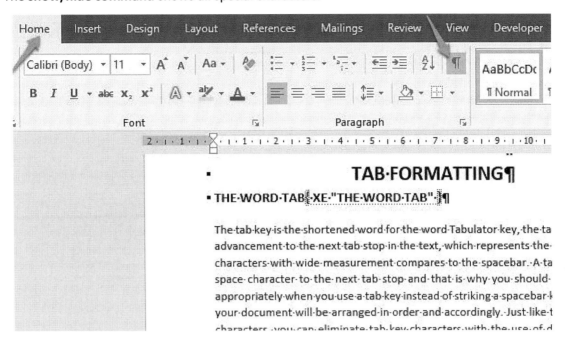

To view only the tab character in the text and ignore other characters, kindly:

- Tap on the **File and select the option** from the File backstage to access the Word Options dialog box.
- Pick **Display** from the left side of the Word Options dialog box.

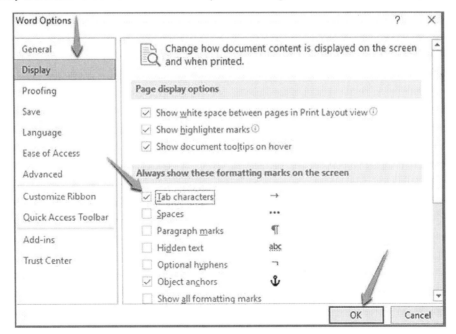

- Tick the **tab character option and tap on Ok**. As you click Ok, you will be referred back to your document, where you will be able to see the tab character icon.

· 1 · 1 · 2 · 3 · 4 · 5 · 6 · 7 · 8 · 9 · 10 · 11 · 12 · 13 · 14 · 15 ·

2.→ Click on the print range arrow drop-down below the settings heading and select Only print pages from the Range drop-down list.

3.→ Tap on print button to print odd pages, turn the paper and reinsert it into the printer.

4.→ Then now select Only print Even pages from the range drop-down list and tap on print butto print even pages also.

Setting And Adjusting The Tab Stops With The Ruler

You can't see tab stops in your document, but they affect any text you input after the striking of the tab key, which proves tab stops existence. To set and adjust the tab stop, you will have to make the tab stops visible by bringing out the ruler option. How? By:

- Tapping on the **View tab.**
- Locate the **show section and tick the ruler box**, provided it has not been ticked.

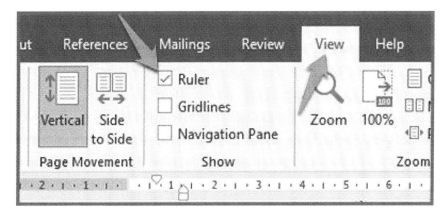

- Instantly, the ruler will come forth above the working area, and below the menu bar, it will show the Tab icon at the top of the vertical ruler and to the left of the horizontal ruler.

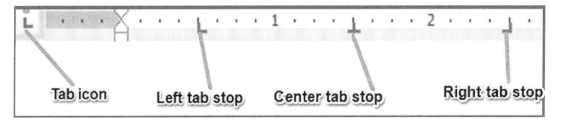

Note: you may not see those tab stops until you set a tab stop. The tab stop that you are using may be a default tab, and the default tab does not use to be visible, but the tab icon is always available at the top of the vertical ruler and the left side of the horizontal ruler, which is what you will use to set the tab stop within the ruler.

To set the tab stop in your document, you will have to observe the following processes:

- **Continue clicking the tab icon** till it shows you the required tab stop, then move to the ruler side.
- **Single-click the actual position** on the ruler where you want the selected tab stops to set in. for instance. You may click 2 or 5 or 6 in the ruler, which will be the position where whichever tab stops set will be stopping.

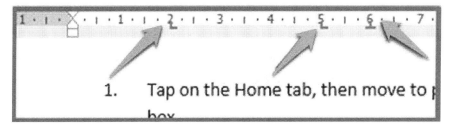

Note: anytime you set a tab stop, that tab stop will be visible on the ruler side, then you can drag it to adjust the settings of that particular tab stop. as you continue clicking the tab icon, you will see the two remaining tab stops, which are decimal and bar tabs. You can set as many tabs stops you want in a line.

Setting Tab Stops With Tabs Box Dialog Box.

To see all apparatus of tabs and all other tabs aside from left, center, and right tab such as decimal tab stops, you have to call for tabs dialog box. But remember, any time you want to set any tab stops when you are done with the setting, you should tap on **Set** then, after that you can tap Ok if you click on Ok million times without clicking on the set button, the tabs stop will not set. To summon the tabs dialog box and set a tabs stop, do well to:

- Tap on the **Home tab,** then move to paragraph group and click on **dialog box launche**r to open the paragraph dialog box.
- Click the **tabs button** inside the paragraph dialog box, and the tab dialog box will come forth.

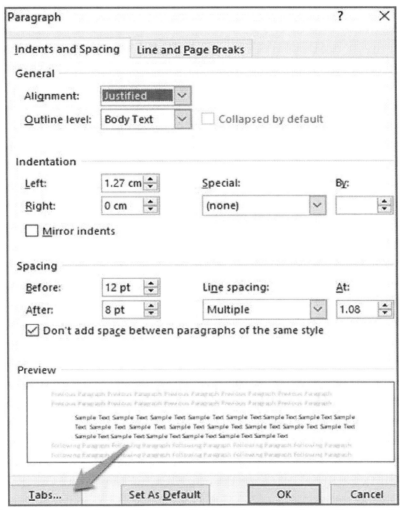

- Insert the **tab position** into the position box field, such as 2.5, depending on where you want your tab stops to set in.
- Select the **tabs stops type** you want in the alignment section.

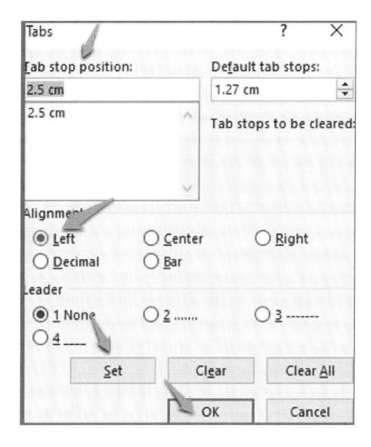

- Click on **Set,** and it will set immediately. You can use steps (2-5) above to set as many as possible tab stops, where the tab will be stopping on the line.
- After you have set all the tab stops you want in a line, then tap **Ok.**

Note: it is essential to click on set as you set each tab stop because, without that, tab stops will never be set.

Producing Two- A Tabbed List With Left Tab Stops

The left tab stop is majorly used in typing the text to move the cursor pointer to the front to another position of the left tab stop. Beyond that level, the left tab stop can as well be used to create a two-column tabbed list, even three tabbed lists. To create a list of two sides with a left tab stop, kindly study the below one on one guideline:

- Move to a new line, strike the **Tab key and insert the item** at most two to five words.
- Strike the **tab key a second time and insert the second** item also two to five words as well.

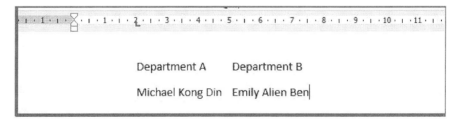

- Strike the **Enter key** to move to the next line and begin another line
- Repeat **steps (a-c)** to enter all the items for each of the lines in the list.

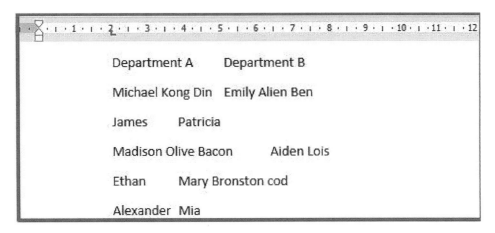

- **Highlight all the items** in the list that you want to arrange into the two-column and **move to the tab icon** at the top of the vertical rule and the left side of the horizontal ruler.

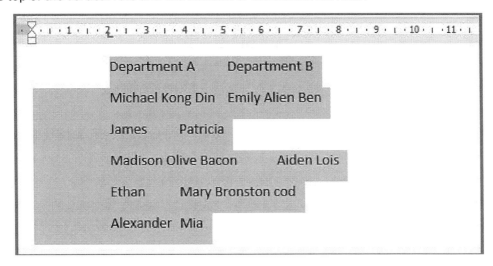

- **Continue clicking the tab icon** to set the tab icon to the left tab stop.

- Then move to the working area, and click the first position on the ruler measure, which will represent your first tab stop. For instance, 4 inch, you will see the reflection immediately.

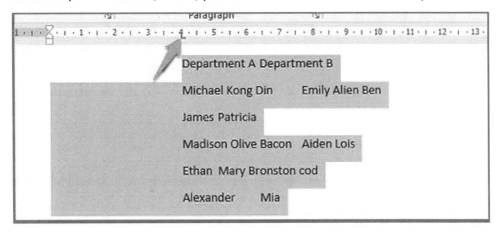

- Click on the second ruler's second position on the ruler measurement, which will represent your second tab stop. For instance, you may click 9inch depending on the width of the column. Behold! You have created a two-tabbed list.

- You can shift either or both tab stop to adjust the position of the tabbed stop if you wish. Shift it by double-clicking the tab stop and dragging it to the preferred location.

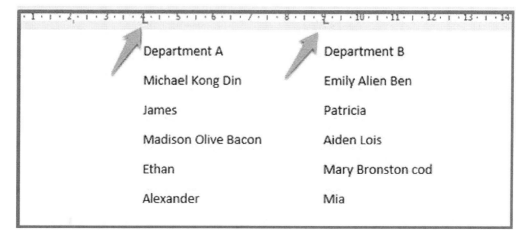

Note: you may as well use the left tab to prepare a three-tabbed list, but it depends on the details so that it will not be jam-packed.

Creating Tab Style With Leader Tabs

Leader tabs are not tabbed in an actual sense but are used to create a style for the tab's blank space. Instead of leaving a tab space blank, it is more attractive to add style. Leader style comes with 3 styles which are dot, dash, and underlines. How do I apply the leader tab to the tab blank space? This is the way, simply:

- Produce a tabbed list, just like the one we created above with a two-tabbed list.
- Select **all the items** in the tab list

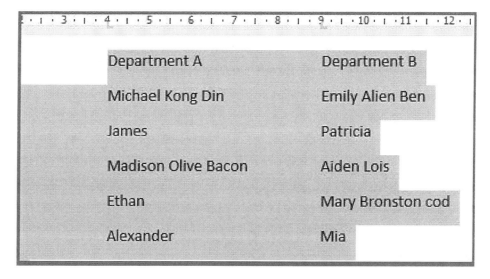

- Quickly send for tabs dialog box by simply **double-clicking on any tab stop** within the ruler area but if no tab stop is available, summon the tab stop dialog box from the paragraph dialog box by clicking on its launcher either from the Home or Layout launcher.

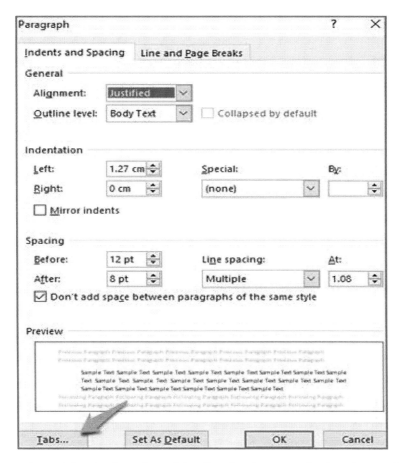

- Input the **exact tab position** in the tab position list. For instance, in the above tab list, the last tab stop, which is the blank space, is 9cm.
- Select your preferred **"leader style"** and tap on the **Set button.**

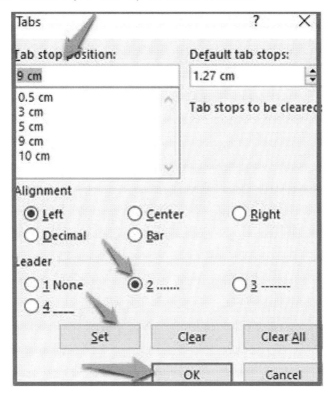

- Lastly, tap on **Ok**.

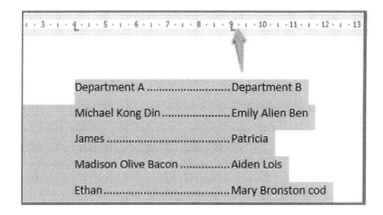

Clear A Tab Stop

You might set a tab stops wrongly, or you may not need it in your text anymore. To clear a tab stop, kindly:

- **Highlight the paragraph** that carries the tab stops you want to erase.
- Double-click on the tab stops **and** drag down **to clear any tab stops.**

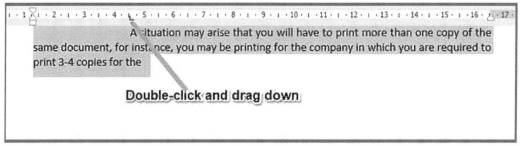

To clear multiple tab stops, perhaps the tab stops are not accurate and are affecting other tab stops. You may choose to clear all the tab stops. to clear all tab stops, kindly;

- Summon the tabs **dialog box.**
- Then **select any position** in the tap position list.
- Tap on the **Clear All button** and click Ok for verification.

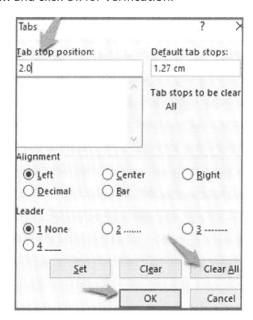

Note: when you tap on the Clear All button, all the tabs stop will be cleared.

Bullet Lists

Creating Bulleted Lists

- Highlight the portion of text that you want the bullet list to take effect on

- Go to the "Home tab," which is your display settings interface

- On your left-hand side in the "Paragraph ribbon," the first tool you will see is the "Bullets list"

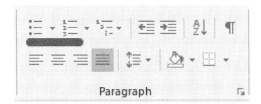

- In the "Bullet" list, select your preferred choice from your "bullet library" and click on it

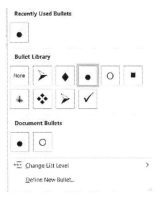

- It will automatically take effect on your highlighted text

List of fruits
- Orange
- Apple
- Blueberry
- Watermelon
- Guava
- Banana

- Or you can click on "bullet list" and select your preferred choice on a free space in the document, which also grants you access to listing your item automatically.

List of fruits

- Once you enter an item and you click on the "Enter key" from your keyboard, it will continue the bulleting automatically

List of fruits
➢ Orange

Numbered Lists

List of fruits
Orange
Apple
Blueberry
Watermelon
Guava
Banana

Highlight the portion of text that you want the numbering list to affect

Go to the "Home tab," which is your display settings interface

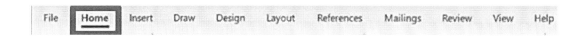

On your left-hand side, locate the "Paragraph ribbon," the second tool you will see beside the bullets icon is the "numbering list," click on it.

You will be given many options to pick from. You can pick the numbering of your choice.

Note: The numbering library consists of number listing, alphabet listing, and roman figure listing. It's not designed for numbers alone.

Immediately you select the number list (you can pick your preferred choice), and it will automatically take effect on your highlighted text.

List of fruits

1. Orange
2. Apple
3. Blueberry
4. Watermelon
5. Guava
6. Banana

Or you can check "number list" and select your preferred choice on a free space in your document, which also grants you access to listing your item automatically.

List of fruits

1.

Once you enter an item and you click your "Enter key" on your keyboard, it will automatically continue the numbering.

List of fruits

1. Orange
2.

Sorting Text

Sorting means an arrangement of a thing in a particular order. Sorting can sort an item or the text automatically for you. To sort the text, do well to:

- Put each item into a separate line and select them as a group.
- Tap on the **Home tab** and move to the paragraph section.

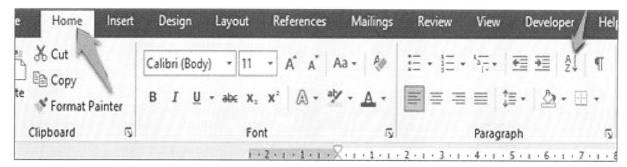

- Tap on **Sort commands** to open the Sort dialog box.

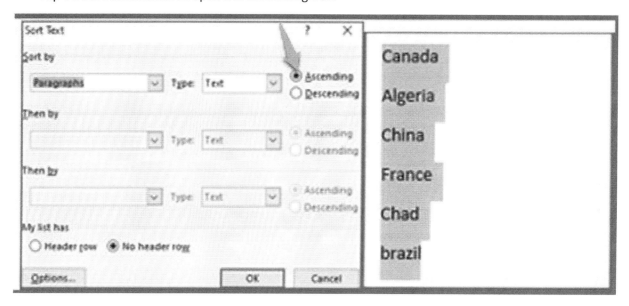

- Select **Ascending or descending,** depending on the order you prefer, and tap the Ok button

Cut, Copy & Paste

Once you select a range of text (block), the such block can be moved or copied. Copying means retaining the original and duplicating it to another location while moving means taking away the original block to another location. Let us quickly check what it involves to move or copy a block:

- Select the **block of text** you want to move or copy.

RELEVANCE OF EXCEL

The relevancies of Excel cannot be overemphasized which makes it a preferable spreadsheet application over other spreadsheet programs, which is the key reason why it always finds expression in both small and big offices. To say the facts we can't talk about all Excel relevancies but we will touch over essential ones.

- Touch the **Home tab.**
- Move to the clipboard group and choose **copy or cut** for copying and moving, respectively.

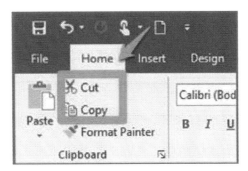

- Place the cursor pointer to the spot where you want to paste the block you have copied or cut above in (d).

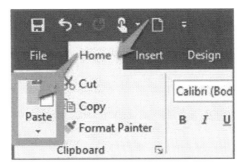

- Tap on the **paste command button** in the Clipboard group to paste the block you have copied or cut. In a jiffy, it will be pasted to the location where you place the cursor pointer.

The relevancies of Excel cannot be overemphasized which makes it a preferable spreadsheet application over other spreadsheet programs, which is the key reason why it always finds expression in both small and big offices. To say the facts we can't talk about all Excel relevancies but we will touch over essential ones.

The relevancies of Excel cannot be overemphasized which makes it a preferable spreadsheet application

Note: You can as well use the keyboard shortcut for cut and copy, which is (Ctrl + X) and (Ctrl + C), respectively. To paste an action with the cut and copy command, kindly press (Ctrl + V).

Tip: The texts you have cut or copied are on the clipboard, and therefore you can paste them as more as you want to the current or another document, even another program, until you cut or copy another command to the clipboard.

Using the Clipboard

The clipboard is the main storage of all the items you have cut and copied. Immediately you cut or copy the text, and it will be sent to the clipboard and will be there for some hours. The beauty of the clipboard is that any text you have cut or that you copy can be pasted again to your document at any location. To make exploitation from the clipboard, let us quickly delve into those steps:

- **Put the cursor pointer** to the place where you want to paste the cut or copy clipboard information.

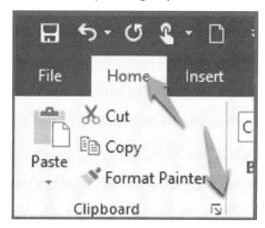

Tap the **Home tab** and move to the clipboard group to click the dialog box launcher.

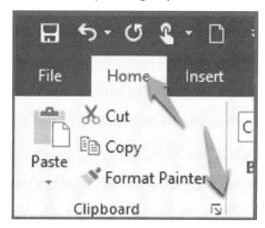

- Immediately you click **the clipboard dialog box launcher, the** clipboard task pane will come forth, then place the mouse pointer at any text or image you want to paste from the clipboard task pane, and instantly a menu drop-down at the right of the text or information.
- Tap on the **menu drop-down button and select the paste command.** In a jiffy, it will be pasted to the spot will you place the cursor pointer in (a) above.

Inserting Symbols

There are various "special characters and symbols" embedded in the insert tab. To access them, kindly:

- Tap on the **insert tab** and move to the symbols section at the right end.

Tap on the **symbols menu** to access some symbols and special characters.

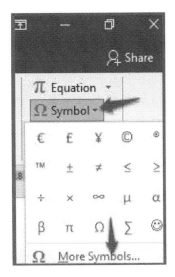

- Search through the field symbol to select special characters and symbols. If you can't find them here, simply tap on more symbols to go to the main field of symbols, where all symbols and characters dwell.

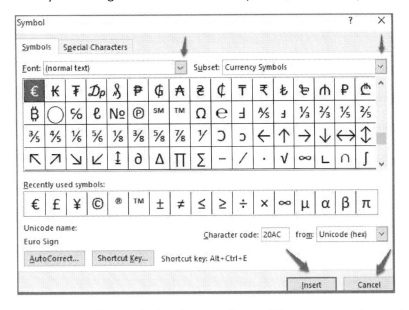

Note: to insert any symbols click on the symbol and tap on insert. When you are done using the symbols menu, tap on cancel.

Tips: tap on Font and subset to see other sections of symbols and special characters. Perhaps the symbols and characters you are finding are not among the listed.

Hidden Characters

Tap on the **Home tab** and maneuver to the paragraph section, then tap on the **show/hide command button** to make every hidden character visible.

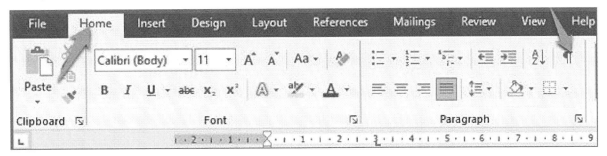

Equations

You can perform complex mathematical equations such as polynomial, binomial and other equations. To achieve this, simply:

- Tap on the **Insert tab** and move to the symbols section far right of the screen.

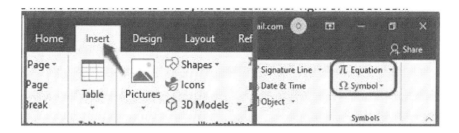

- Click on the **equation button** and select the **equation** you want to use from the list, the equation will come up from the spot where you place the cursor pointer.

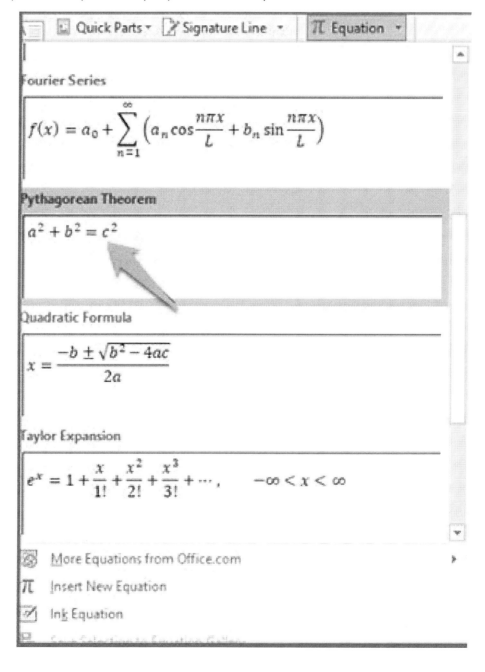

- Then change the equation format by using the numbers to replace the letter.

Note: word can give you millions of equation formulas but will not calculate for you.

How To Save A Document Directly To Your PC?

- Go to "File menu"

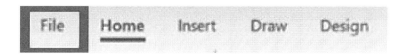

- Select "Save option"

A dialog box will appear, select the location you want to save, name your document on the "File name box" and click "Save".

Note: saving your document on your PC is only for licensed users, Microsoft Word online free version saves automatically online on OneDrive storage.

How To Save A Document Directly To Your OneDrive Cloud Storage?

- Go to "file menu"

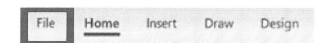

- You will see multiple options, select "Save as"

- A dialog box will appear, you will see the "OneDrive" option, once you click it, your document will be saved online. If you have many folders on your OneDrive storage, you will be asked to choose the destination you want your work to be saved in. Once done, hit "Save".

Saving as a Different Format

Many people prefer the PDF format of a document to the original word format of a document. However, the universal acceptable format is that of the word format whether you are sharing a document on the web, saving it on the cloud, or sending it to others via email, some people will specify PDF format. For instance, employer can specify that your resume or CV to be in PDF format, to change word format to PDF, kindly study the guides below:

- Update the current changes by saving your document once more either with Ctrl + S or other means.
- Tap on **Print** from the File tab backstage to send for the print screen.
- Tap on the **printer menu** to access the list of available printers.
- Select **Microsoft Print to PDF** and tap on the **Print button**. It will not print anything but you will be transited to the Save Print Output As dialog box.

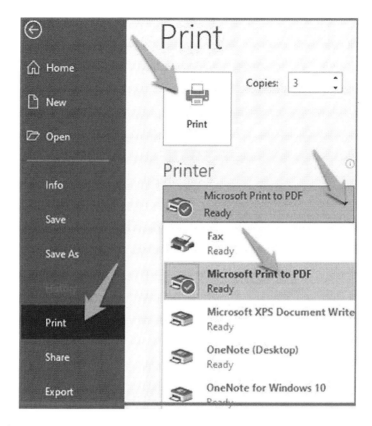

- **Select a** file location for the NEW PDF document **and insert a** file name.
- Tap on the **Save button** to create the PDF file.

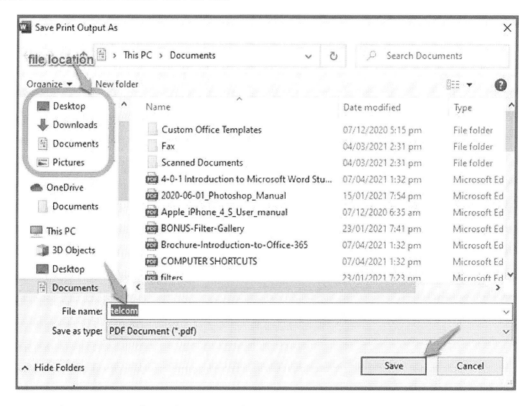

Note: when you print a document out from the printer, the original document remains untouched likewise when printing PDF format, it will not change anything from the original document that you converted into PDF. You can open and edit PDF files the same way you edit MS word documents.

Opening Saved Documents

You can open your document from the Word application or directly from your device.

To open an existing document from Word:

- Go to the backstage view by clicking on the **File** tab.
- Click the **Open** tab.
- **Open** pane appears.
- Select the location of your document.
- An **Open** dialog box appears.
- Select the folder or your document. You can scroll down the left side list of locations on your device to locate your document.
- Click **Open**.

Alternatively, if you recently opened your document or pinned it to Word, it will be available in the **Recent** or **Pinned** list in the backstage **Home** panel, and you can click on it to open it.

If you often use or work on your document, it will be better to pin it in Word.

To pin your document to the word:

- Locate the document in the recent list.
- Move your cursor over the document.
- Click the pin icon in front of the file.

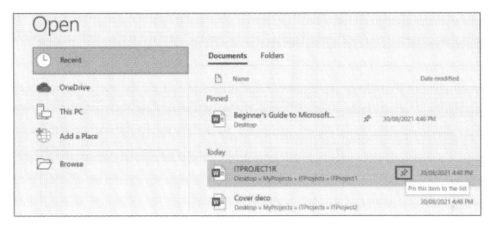

To open an existing document from your device:

- Ensure you have the Word application installed on your computer.
- Locate your Word document on your device.
- Double-click to open it if it has a Word icon, if not, right-click on the file.

Select **open with** from the menu that appears and select **Word**.

Sharing Documents

Your word document can be easily shared directly as an email body or as an attachment to an email address with the **Send to Mail Recipient** command in Word. **Send to Mail Recipient** command is not available in the Word user interface by default and needs to be added. You can preferably add it to the Quick Access Toolbar by customizing it.

To add 'Send to Mail Recipient' to Quick Access Toolbar (QAT):

- Right-click on the **QAT**.
- A dialog box appears.
- Select **Customize Quick Access Toolbar**.
- Word Options dialog box appears.
- From the **Choose commands from** the drop-down list, choose **Commands Not in the Ribbon**.
- Locate **Send to Mail Recipient** in the list. The list is arranged alphabetically for easy location.
- Click **Add>>** button.

- Word adds it to Customize Quick Access Toolbar.
- Click **OK,** and it appears in your Quick Access Toolbar.

To share your document as an email body:

- Ensure your computer is connected and sign in to your email account.
- Click on **Send to Mail Recipient** command in the Quick Access Toolbar.
- The mail Composing window appears under the ribbon with your document title already added.
- Add the recipient's email address and other information as desired. You can also change the title as desired.
- Ensure you have an internet connection.
- Click **Send a Copy**.

Word sends your document and closes the composing email window. To close the email window manually, click on the icon in the Quick Access Toolbar.

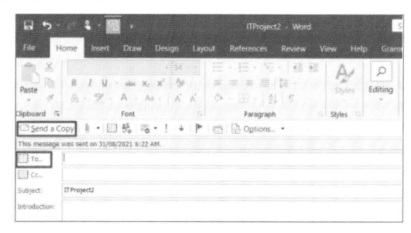

Chapter 5: **Printing Documents**

Printing a document is the result of creating and saving a document, printing is not just printing through a hard copy alone, it also involves distributing the information online so that every potential user can have access to it.

The print preview gives you an outlay to view how the document will be presented or the result you are likely to get and use that as a yardstick to decide if there will be any adjustments such as a blank page and another editing before printing. How do I preview a document? That should not be a problem, kindly:

- Click on the **File tab and choose Print** from the File backstage or press **Ctrl + P** to summon the Print screen box.
- **Use the** zoom controller to increase or decrease **the look of the document.**
- Switch throughout the pages in the document with the switch button at the bottom of the print screen, if you want to apply any editing click on the back arrow or Esc to return to the document and make the necessary adjustment.

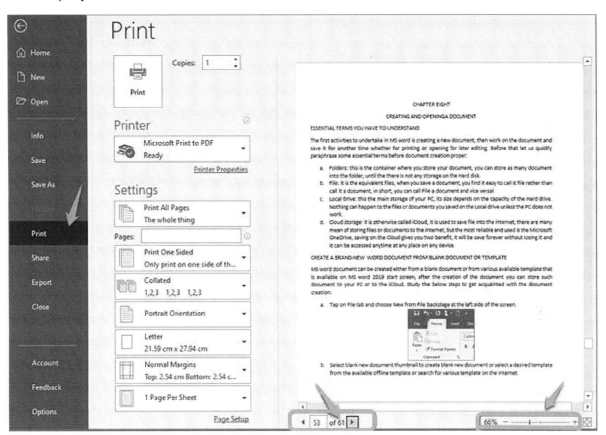

Printing The Whole Document

To print all the pages of your document, study the following steps:

- Save the document by pressing **Ctrl + S,** then "ON" the printer, and insert the papers.
- **Click the** File tab and select print or press Ctrl + P.
- Then tap on **the print button,** immediately print screen will dismiss and the document will be coming forth from the printer.

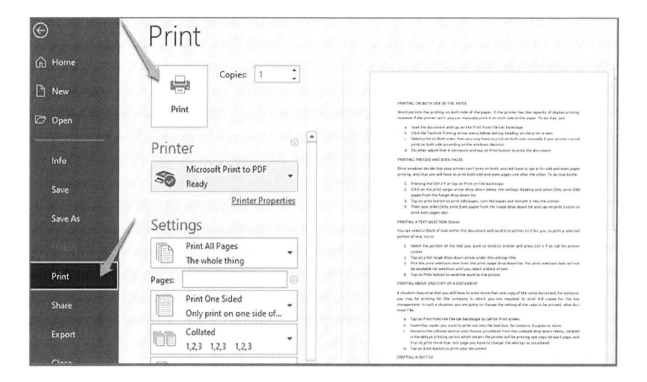

Note: if the printer does not begin printing immediately, do not press the print command again not to end up printing more than a necessary document, wait patiently. It depends on how fast each printer works.

Some documents are structured in such a way that they will specify the type of paper needed to print them, and thus endeavor to insert the suitable paper any time the document request such a thing.

Printing An Exact Page

There may be a demand to print an exact page, perhaps one of the pages printed got missing or any other reason, and thus you will be left with an option to print that very page alone. To print the exact page out of the whole document, look at these steps;

- **Maneuver to that exact page** and ensure that the cursor pointer is at that very page by checking the status bar to confirm if you are at that definite page, for instance, page 8.

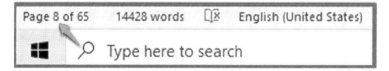

- Tap on **File and click on print** from backstage.
- Click on the **print range arrow drop-down** right below the settings heading.

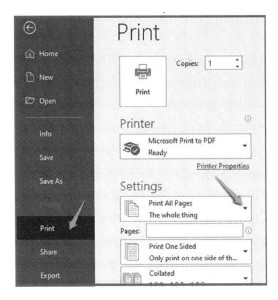 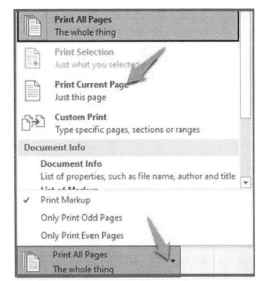

- Select Print current page from the print range drop-down menu.
- **Tap on the** print button.

Note: it will print the specified page per the whole formatting of the whole document.

Printing Range Of Pages

You can print choices of any pages, whatever range of any type, including even and odd pages. To print choices of pages kindly bring forth the print screen by:

- Pressing the **Ctrl + P or tap on Print** on the File backstage.
- Click on the **print range arrow drop-down** below the settings heading.
- Select the **custom page** from the print range drop-down to activate the range box.
- Below the print range is the range box, insert the **exact range** you want your printer to print out into the range box, such as 2-5 for printing page 2 through to page 5, or 6-7 and 8, and 10-14 for printing page 6 through to 7, and page 8 then page 10 through to 14, depending on the choice of pages you want to print.
- Tap on the **Print button** to send the range of documents to the printer.

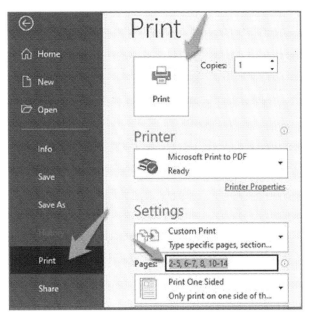

Printing On Both Sides Of The Paper

Word permits the printing on both sides of the paper if the printer has the capacity of Twofold printing, however, if the printer does not, you can manually print it on both sides of the paper. To print on both sides of the paper, just:

- Save the document and tap on the Print **from File tab backstage.**
- Click the **One-sided heading arrow menu** below the Setting heading on the print screen.

- Select **print on Both sides with flip pages on the long side**, you may choose flip pages on the short side if you want to bind the document, provided your printer can print twofold, but if it can't print on both sides, you will have to choose manual print on both sides but you will have to reload paper when next you want to Print on the second side.

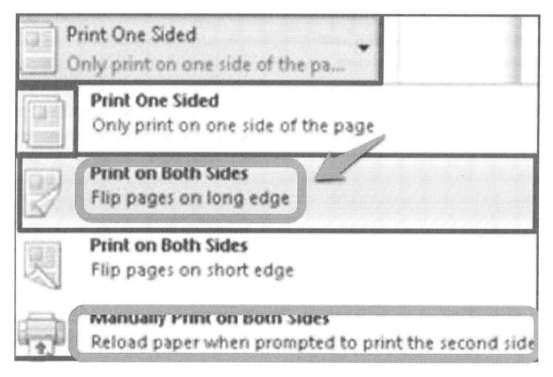

- Carry out other adjustments that are necessary and tap on the **Print button** to print the document.

Note: the decision of whether the printer can print on both sides is the sole right of the window, not the decision of the program you are running.

Printing The Odd And Even Pages

Once windows decide that your printer can't print on both sides, some users prefer to use the odd and even method rather than choosing manual printing, and thus you will have to print both odd and even pages one after the other. To do that kindly:

- Pressing the **Ctrl + P or tap on Print** on File backstage.
- Click on the **print range arrow drop-down** below the settings heading and select Only Odd print pages from the Range drop-down list.

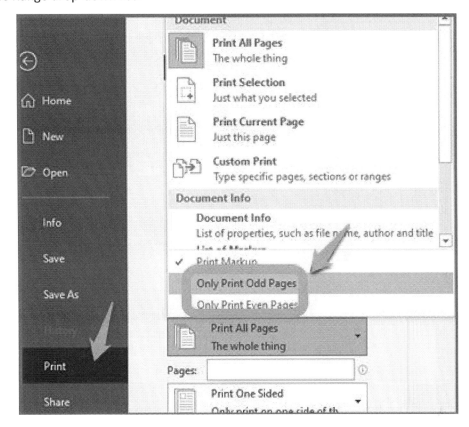

- Tap on the **print button to print odd pages,** turn the paper and reinsert it into the printer.
- Then now **select Only print Even pages** from the range drop-down list and tap on the print button to print even pages also.

Note: you will print the odd pages first then follow the same procedure to print the even pages as well.

Printing A Text Selection (Block)

You can select a block of text within the document and send it to the printer to print a selected portion of text, try to:

- Select the **portion of the text** you want to send to the printer and tap on **Print** from the File backstage to call for the printer screen.

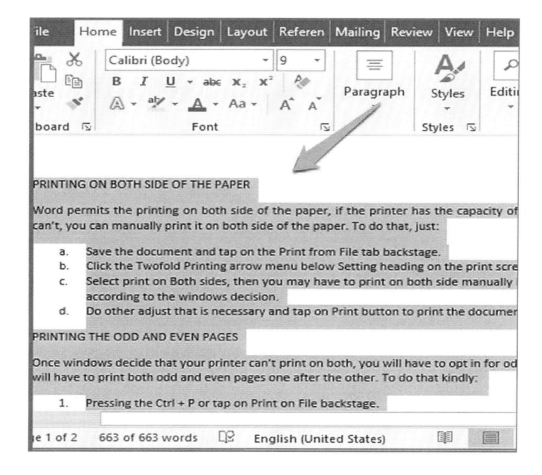

PRINTING ON BOTH SIDE OF THE PAPER

Word permits the printing on both side of the paper, if the printer has the capacity of can't, you can manually print it on both side of the paper. To do that, just:

a. Save the document and tap on the Print from File tab backstage.
b. Click the Twofold Printing arrow menu below Setting heading on the print scre
c. Select print on Both sides, then you may have to print on both side manually according to the windows decision.
d. Do other adjust that is necessary and tap on Print button to print the documer

PRINTING THE ODD AND EVEN PAGES

Once windows decide that your printer can't print on both, you will have to opt in for od will have to print both odd and even pages one after the other. To do that kindly:

1. Pressing the Ctrl + P or tap on Print on File backstage.

e 1 of 2   663 of 663 words   English (United States)

- Tap on the **print range drop-down arrow** under the settings title.
- Pick the **print selection item** from the print range drop-down list, the print selection item will not be available for selection until you select a block of text.
- Tap on the **Print button** to send the work to the printer.

Printing Above One Copy Of A Document

A situation may arise that you will have to print more than one copy of the same document, for instance, you may be printing for the company in which you are required to print 3-4 copies for the top management, in such a situation you are going to change the setting of the copy to be printed, what do I mean? By:

- Tap on **Print from the File tab backstage** to call for the Print screen
- Insert the **copies** you want to print out into the text box, for instance, 3 copies or more.

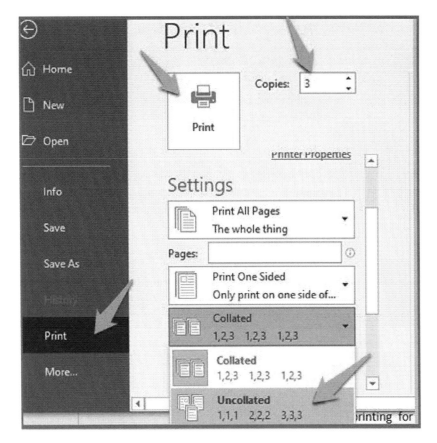

- Move to the **collated section** and choose **uncollated** from the collated drop-down menu, collated is the default printing option which means the printer will be printing one copy for each page, and thus to print more than one page, probably between 3- 5 pages, you will have to change the settings to uncollated.
- Tap on the **print button** to print your document.

Chapter 6: **Page Setup**

A page is a complete portion of a document that equals what you can print out as whole information. There is major formatting to be carried out on the page before it will be qualified to be called a proper page, such as page margin, orientation, and lots more.

Setting Your Page Size

Page size is the actual measurement that looks like a booklet, this is the room that will accommodate the text you inserted into the document. There are different sizes of paper, you can select any one depending on the type of document you are making, for instance, legal paper, A4 paper, and so on. To pick a certain page size or change the one you are using currently, kindly:

- Tap on the **layout tab** and maneuver to the page setup section.
- Tap on the **size button-down arrow** from the page setup section and select **your desired page size**.

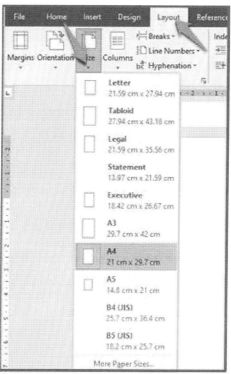

Note: the page size you selected will have a reflection by the time of printing, and you can't just choose paper anyhow unless your printer can print different paper aside from the one selected in printing a document. The paper you selected is a copy of how your whole document will appear.

Changing From One Page Orientation To Another

Page orientation has to do with whether the page is positioned landscape or portrait when the document is on landscape orientation, it means the page is horizontally based (it has more horizontal length than its vertical length), while the portrait-oriented is vertical based (its vertical length is more than its horizontal length). To change from one orientation to another, kindly:

- Tap on the **layout tab** and maneuver to the page setup section.
- Click on the **orientation down arrow** and select either **Portrait or landscape** on the menu drop-down depending on the one you are having or using before because page orientation has only two options and that is Portrait and landscape.

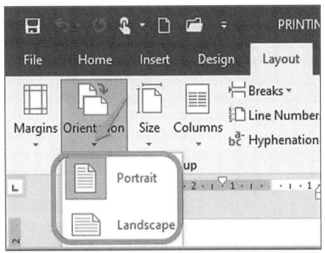

Note: Ensure you select the actual orientation for your document from the beginning, changing orientation from a text-filled document can be so frustrating by disorganizing the entire document and changing the paragraph formatting. However, you can have a separate orientation in a document by splitting the document into two sections with a page break depending on what you want to use the document to do.

Setting The Page Margin

Margin is the edge or border that encloses the text, it is the four borders of the page that is the top, bottom, right, and left edge of the page. if you set your margin accurately, you will see your text sitting on the Page properly. To select a page margin, do well to:

- Tap on the **layout tab** and maneuver to the page setup section.
- Click on the **margin down arrow** and select an **appropriate margin**. Margin is all about four options, given you the option to select the actual space your text space that will remain on four sides of the margin, the type of margin you select will determine the space you will be having at the four edges of the page.

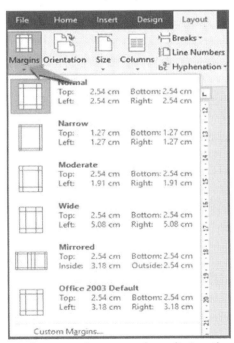

Note: you can select a different margin for your document by splitting the document into sections with a page break.

Command Page Setup Dialog Box For Page Setting

Page set up dialog box permits you to access all page setting in a single room and give you more access to further page setting. To access the page setup dialog box, examine the procedures to call it out:

- Tap on the **layout tab** and maneuver to the page setup section

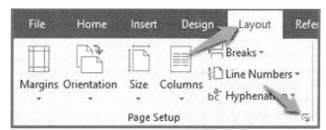

- Click on the **page setup dialog box launcher** to bring forth the page setup dialog box.
- Insert the margin values to the respective four sides (top, bottom, left, and right) in the provided field.
- Select if you want to apply the setting to the **whole document or from this point forward.**

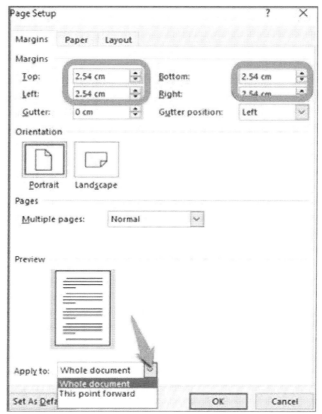

- Input all the settings you want and tap Ok for verification.

Note: click on either of the three-tab of the page setup box to adjust your settings (Margin, paper, and layout). The gutter option under the margin section deals with additional space for whatever edges you selected, for instance, project work usually has binding at the left side, you can use gutter to provide a house for the binding space without touching the text.

Adding Auto Page Number

MS word grants you the chance to insert page numbers into your document automatically, instead of numbering it one after the other page by page. You can use different formats for page numbering from the various number format from MS words, such as Arabic and Roman numerals. With much ado, let us dive into numbering pages automatically:

- Tap on the **insert tab** and navigate to Header and Footer section.

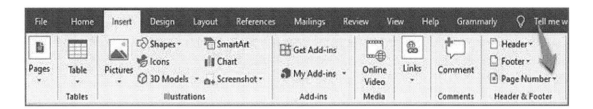

- **Tap on the Page number down arrow** and select the **actual position** (top or bottom) where you want to lay your page numbers.

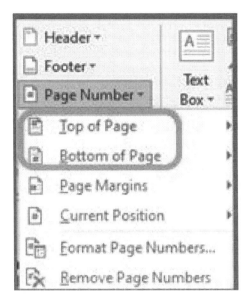

- Click on the **side arrow** of any of the options you made in (2) above to select the numbering style. You may scroll down if you have not yet gotten the preferable numbering style.

Note: instantly you select numbering style, Automatically MS word will number your document beginning with the first page as number 1, irrespective of the page number position you are in the document. Any adjustment you made in the document, the MS word we renumber for you, for instance, if you add or remove any page, word automatically renumbers the remaining pages for you.

Starting Page Numbering With Any Number

Anytime you are numbering a document, MS word starts from the first page with number one, However, you can dictate for MS word to start the first page by any number of your choice, for instance, you can start from number 60 depending on the situation. How will you do that? By:

- Tap on the **Insert tab** and maneuver to the Header and Footer section.
- Click on the **Page number down arrow** and **select Format page numbers** from the drop-down list to open the Page number format dialog box.

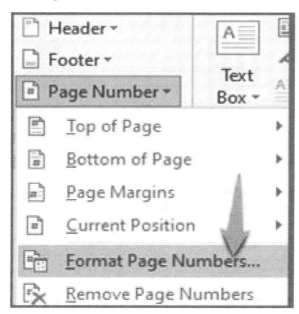

- **Tick on the "Start at" small circle** to select it and then insert the **exact number** where you want your document to start from.

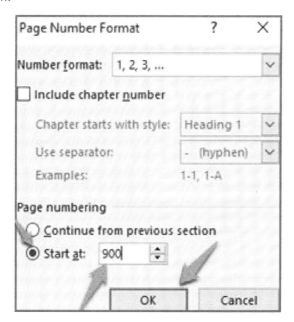

- Tap Ok for verification.

Note: if you type that your number should start with 900 at the start, the first page of the document will be 900, followed by 901 and the subsequent page will increase in that order.

Numbering With Another Format (Roman Numerals Or Alphabets)

Word number a figure with the normal number, you can dictate specific or change the numbering format for MS word, simply by:

- Tap on the **Insert tab** and maneuver to the Header and Footer section.
- Click on the **page number down arrow** and select **Format page number** from the drop-down list to open the Page number format dialog box.
- Tap on the **Number format menu** and select an appropriate style for your document in the dialog box.

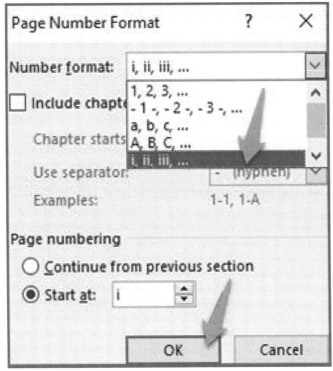

- Tap on **Ok** for verification.

Removing Page Numbers Of Any Kind

Perhaps you do not need a page number in your document or you have selected a wrong page number, quickly chase it out from your document with these little tricks:

- Tap on the **insert tab** and maneuver to the Header and Footer setting.
- Click on the **Page number down arrow** and select **Remove Page number** to send the page number out of the document.

Adding Text To A New Page

Text can be easily added to a new page at the end of the document, but what if the situation requires you to enter a text at the middle or the top of the document? You do not have to stress yourself about that, simply follow this little trick:

- Place the cursor pointer to the spot where one page ends and another one page to begin, suitably at the beginning of the first paragraph on the page.

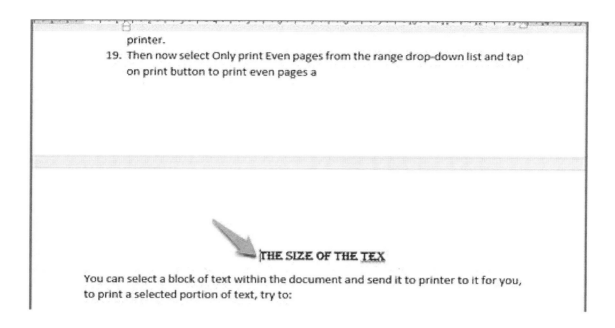

printer.

19. Then now select Only print Even pages from the range drop-down list and tap on print button to print even pages a

THE SIZE OF THE TEX

You can select a block of text within the document and send it to printer to it for you, to print a selected portion of text, try to:

- Tap on the **insert tab** and maneuver to the page section and tap on the **Break page.**

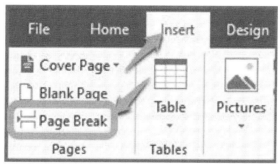

- Behold! A new page has come forth, whichever text you typed into the page will never affect the text of any page previously before it, if the text is more than a page another page will come forth without tampering with another section.

Note: a new page will come forth, the page above the cursor pointer will come above this new page while the page before the cursor pointer will come below the new page, this command is called a hard break, you can undo the hard page break with Ctrl + Z).

Adding A Blank Page

You can as well add a blank page within a document, but anytime the blank page is full it will shift the text in the previous page before its creation, and therefore adding a blank page is recommended for something that will not exceed a page such as a table or any image. To create a blank page within a document, do well to:

- Tap on the **Insert tab** and maneuver to the page group.
- Then tap on the **Blank page command button** to insert a new blank page.

Note: a new blank page will come forth, the page above of cursor pointer will come above the new blank page while the page before the cursor pointer will come below the new blank page, this command is called two hard breaks, you can also undo two hard pages with (Ctrl + Z).

Multiple Documents

Viewing files through more than one Window creates the possibility to work in another Window and not affect your original Window.

Steps on how to apply it:

From your current opened document, go to "View menu bar" by your right-hand side.

It is advisable to purchase a license Microsoft Office installation software because the one online is still very much under progressive development; not all features are on Word 365 web base.

Under the "view menu bar", click on "New Window" (which is known as document interface), your current document which is opened will be duplicated and named "document 1" by default, except you rename it. Another duplicated one will be named "document 2"

Document 1 - Saved to OneDrive ∨

Document 2 - Saved to OneDrive ∨

Any changes in one will automatically lead to the same changes in the other.

Putting Header on Pages

- Go to "Insert tab"

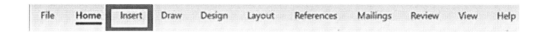

- At your right-hand side, look for "Header"

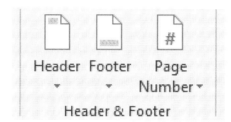

- A dialog box will appear, select your preferred alignment positioning

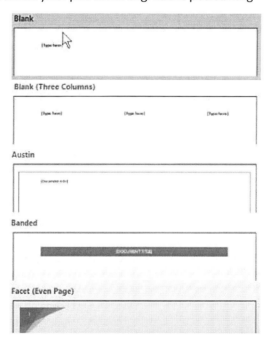

- Once done, you will be brought to your header editing edge to input your text

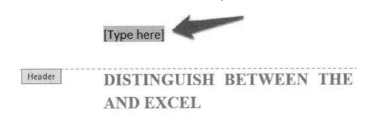

Word Handles Text Better

Note: You can also double-click on the top empty edge of your document to make use of the header format.

Removing Header from Pages

- Go to "Insert tab"

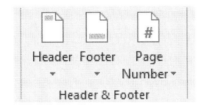

- At your right-hand side, locate "Header" and click on it

- A dialog box will appear below "Header" showing you header positioning, look down the list you will see "Remove Header". Once you click on it, your "Header" will be removed automatically

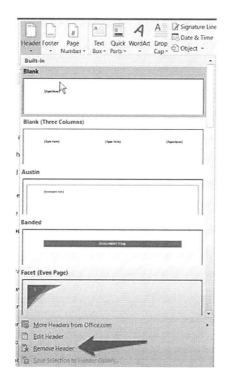

Putting Footer on Pages

- Go to "Insert tab"

- At your right-hand side, locate "Footer" and click on it

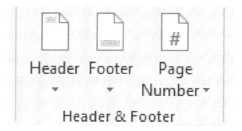

- A dialog box will appear, select your preferred alignment positioning

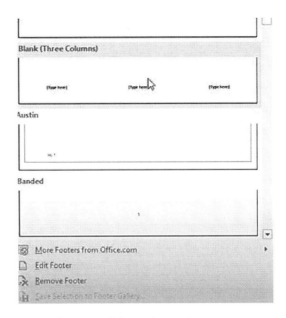

Once done, you will be brought to your footer editing edge to input your text

and rows to huge tables with hundr

supports tables it cannot handle large t

[Type here]

Note: You can also double-click below the page you want to insert the footer, you will be brought to an empty or footer format area where you can input your footer format.

Removing Footer from Pages

- Go to "Insert tab"

- At your right-hand side, locate "Header", click on it
- A dialog box will appear below "Footer" showing you footer positioning, look down the list, you will see "Remove Footer". Once you click on it, your "Footer" will be removed automatically

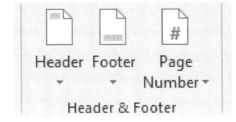

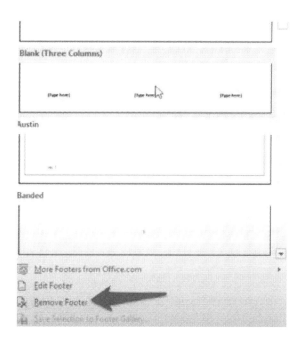

Page Numbering

Page Numbering is a way of making your content arranged serially for orderliness and reference purposes.

How to Insert Page Numbering

- Go to "Insert tab"

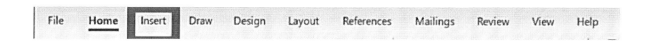

- At your right-hand side, you will see "Page Number" under "Header & Footer ribbon"

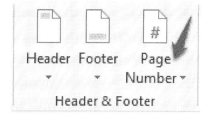

- Click on "Page Number", once you click on it, you will be given multiple options on where you want your page numbering to be positioned such as "Top of Page", "Bottom of Page", "Page Margins", "Current Position".

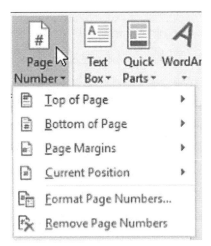

Or you can decide how you want your page numbering to look by clicking on "Format Page Numbers". A dialog box will appear for you to configure your Page Numberings such as "Number format", where you want to start effecting from, and lots more. Once you fill it, press "ok" to effect changes

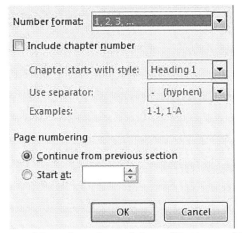

- Assuming you want the "Bottom of Page" option, click on "Bottom of Page" which is the normally used page numbering
- A dialog box will appear beside it, choose the middle numbering format

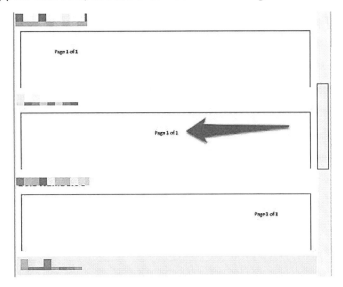

- By default, all your text will automatically be numbered serially

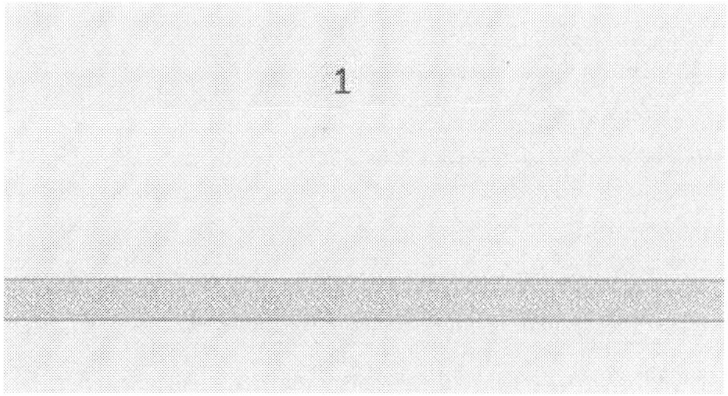

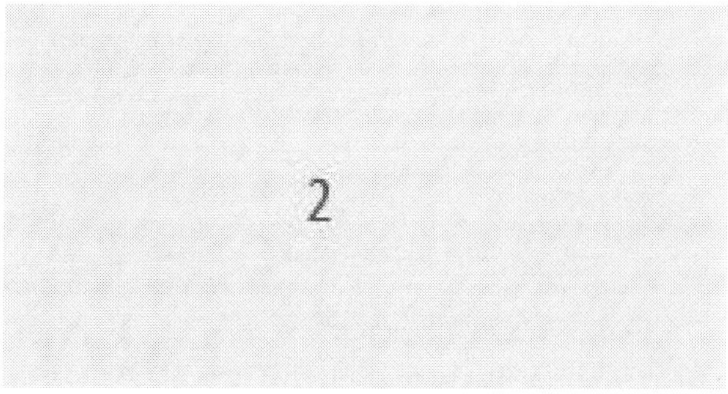

Remove Page Numbering

- Go to "Insert tab"

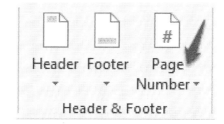

- At your right-hand side, you will see "Page Number" under "Header & Footer ribbon"

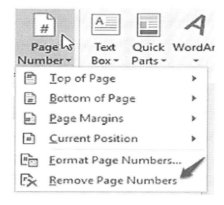

- Click on "Page Number", once you click on it, you will be given multiple options, look for "Remove Page Numbers", click on it, and every page numbering on your current opened document will be removed automatically

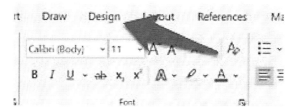

Page Borders

- Go to the "Design" tab

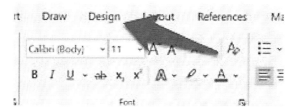

- Under "Design", at your right-hand side, you will see the "Page Background" ribbon, select "Page Borders"

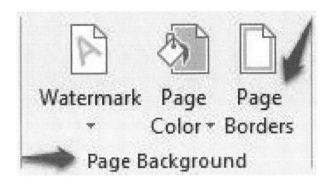

- Once you click on "Page Borders", a dialog box will pop up which is your "Page Border" configuration. On the left-hand side is the "Setting" option for various page border templates. By the side of the "Setting" option is the "Style" option where you can choose the kind of lines you prefer. Below "Style" is the "Color" option where you can determine which color fits into your page document border.

Below the "Color" option is the "Width" option which is the only component that controls the border thickness. Below the "Width" option is the "Art" option that reflects different kinds of art designs to be used for your framework, while at your right-hand side is the "Preview" option which gives you what your outcome configuration will look like before you click on the "Ok" option.

The "Apply to" option is where you determine where your effect should take place such as "Whole document", "This section", "This section first page only", and "This section all except the first page." Your choice determines your outcome, once done hit the "Ok" button to see your changes.

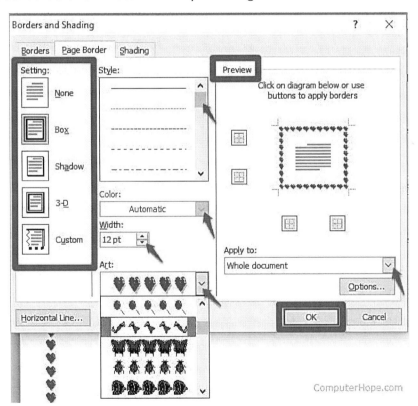

Page Breaks

Page break separates the content between pages. When the page break is inserted, the text starts at the beginning of the page.

To insert a page break in your document, follow the steps below

Click on where you want to insert the section break

Go to the **Layout** tab and click on the **Breaks** button

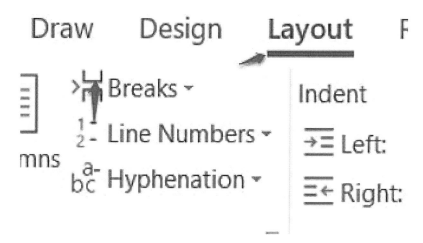

In the Break drop-down list, select any of the following options

- Page: This marks the point at which one page ends and the next page begins.
- Column: This specifies the text following the column break that will begin in the next column.
- Text Wrapping: This separates text around objects on web pages, such as captions from text from the body text.

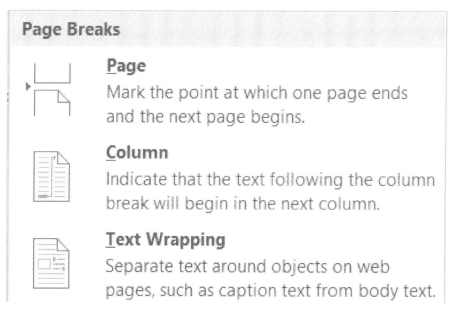

Deleting Page Break

To delete the page break inserted into your document, the first thing you need to do is ensure that the page break dotted line is visible in the document. If it is not, go to the **Home** tab, in the **Paragraph** group, and click on **Show or Hide**

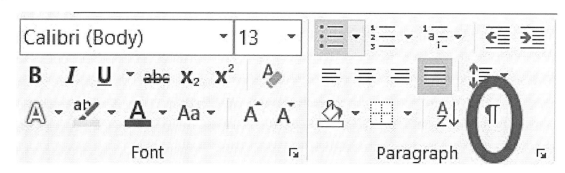

Change the view of your document to Draft view so that you can see where the section line is inserted. Click on the dotted line, and then press the Delete

I IUI I IU lab, ullun the uuvil allUW Uil the Diulato sullUI I
regional·language·from·the·drop-down·list.¶
Place·the·cursor·where·you·want·the·words·to·appear

----------------------------Page Break-------------------¶

dictate·to·Word,·PowerPoint,·or·Outlook:¶

—

Creating Columns

The rows or row columns or both may not be enough or more than required, it depends on the situation. To add rows or columns, do well to:

- Place the cursor pointer to the left or right of the rows or columns where you want the new row or column to stay.
- Then tap on the **table tool layout tab** and move to the rows and columns section.

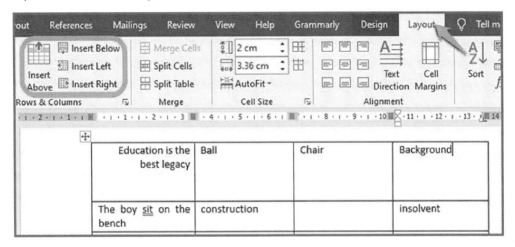

- Use the **insert button command** to add the respective row and column.

To remove the rows or columns, just:

- Select the row or column to be removed and move to the row and column section.
- Then tap on the **delete menu** and select the **proper delete option.**

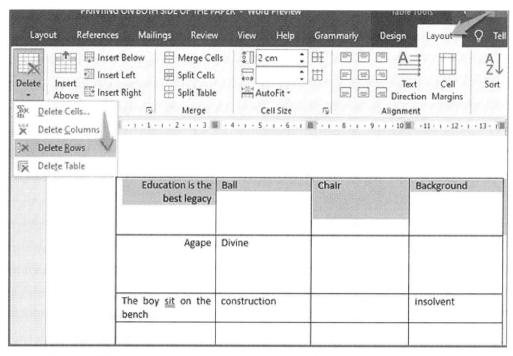

Note: To delete a cell, you will have one more option, you will decide the position of the neighbor cells before any cell will be removed.

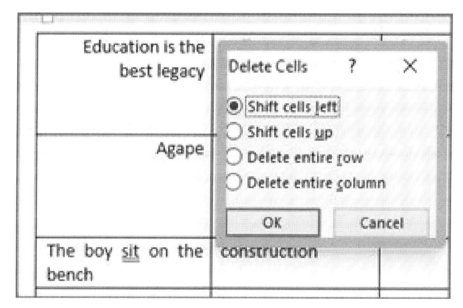

Adding Rows Or Columns With A Mouse

To add a new column, move the mouse pointer to the top edge at the very side where you want the new column to come forth and shift the cursor till you see the plus icon inside the circle, click it and a new column will come forth.

Education is the best legacy	Ball	Chair	Background	
Agape	Divine			
The boy sit on the bench	construction		insolvent	

To add a new row, move the mouse pointer to the left edge at the side where you want the new row to come forth and shift the cursor till you see the plus icon inside a circle, click it and a new row will come forth.

Adjusting Row And Column Size

The size of the row and column are adjusted so that the text can best fit into the cell, you should not adjust the row and column until the row is filled with the text. To adjust the row or column, simply:

- place your cursor on the line that will cause the row or column to be adjusted.
- then wait till the cursor change to a **double-headed sword.**
- **double click and drag** to adjust the size of the row and column.

Education is the best legacy	Ball	Chair	Background	
	click and drag			
Agape	Divine			
The boy sit on the bench	construction		insolvent	

Watermarks

A watermark can be an image or text that is implanted across or horizontally over the paper to beautify and pass out more information, though the watermark is usually dim so that it will not cover the actual text on the paper. Add a watermark to your document with this simple trick.

- Tap on the **Design tab** and maneuver to the Page background section.
- Tap on the **watermark down arrow** and select a **watermark template** from the available list of watermarks that you can put across your document, you can as well edit and insert your text into those watermark templates.

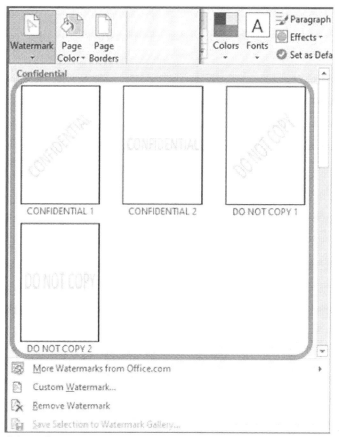

Note: customize a watermark by selecting Custom watermark from the watermark drop-down menu, create your watermark within the Custom watermark dialog box either with graphic or text.

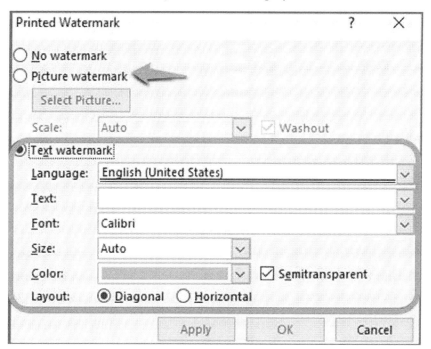

Remove the watermark by tapping the Remove watermark command from the watermark drop-down menu.

Cover Pages

A Cover Page is a front guide of every documentation, project, brochure, and other documents which gives a summarization of what your content entails.

How To Insert A Cover Page On Your Document

Go to "Insert tab"

At your left-hand side, you will see **_"Cover Page"_**

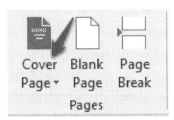

Click in to see multiple built-in "Cover Page" templates, select your preferred choice

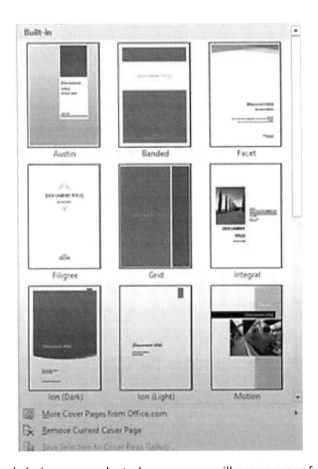

Once you select your preferred choice, your selected cover page will occupy your front page

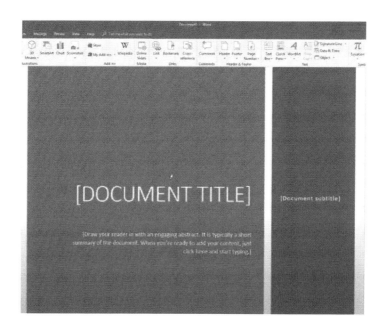

Then, you can start editing the title page, the writeup below your title, subtitle, and other aspects depending on the template you selected

Contents Pages

Microsoft Word includes a tool that lets you create a table of contents either automatically or manually using simple templates. You must write or prepare your document using the Word built-in headings in the Styles group to automatically insert a table of contents.

To Insert a Table of Contents:

- Ensure your document headings uses Word built-in headings styles
- Place your insertion point where you want the table of content to be.
- Go to the **References** ribbon.
- **Click** Table of Contents.
- A drop-down menu appears.
- Select an option:

The first two options automatically insert your table of contents with **all** your available headings.

The third option inserts the table of contents with placeholder texts and allows you to replace them with your own headings.

Select More Tables of Contents from Office.com **for more templates.**

Select the **Custom Table of Contents…** to customize your table. A dialog box appears, edit as desired, and press **OK**.

If you already have a table of content in your document, you can delete it by selecting **Remove Table of Contents.**

Updating Your Table Of Contents

Word does not update your table of content automatically if you make changes to your document. You will have to update it manually.

To update your Table of Content:

- Position your cursor in the table of content.
- Table borders appear with buttons at the top-left.
- Click the **Update Table** button.
- A dialog box appears.

- **Click the** Update entire table.
- Press **OK.**
- Word automatically updates your table.

Alternatively,

- Right-click on the table of content.
- A drop-down menu appears.
- Select **Update Field.** You can also select **Update Table** in the **Table of Contents** group in the **References** ribbon.
- A dialog box appears.
- **Click** Update the entire table.
- Click **OK.**

Note: Do not always forget to update your table after making significant changes that affect the headers or page numbers.

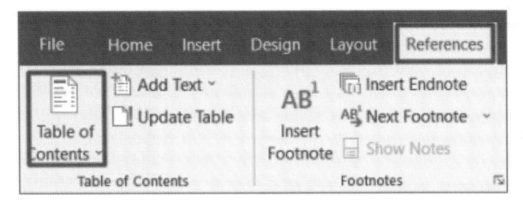

Indexes

With the **Index** group, you can add index in your document. Instead of doing this manually, the Index tab makes it fast and easy for you. With the **Mark Entry**, you mark the keywords you want to have in your index section, which is usually at the last pages of the document. To mark any keywords, just highlight the word, click the **Mark Entry** tool, and then click **Mark** button of the dialog box. And with **Insert Index** tool, you insert those keywords you have marked as entry.

Step by Step Guide on Inserting Index Automatically in Word

To insert index at the last page of your document, just follow this step-by-step guide:

- Highlight the words or phrases you want the have in your index
- Click **References** tab and then click **Mark Entry** tool to see a dialog box as shown below:

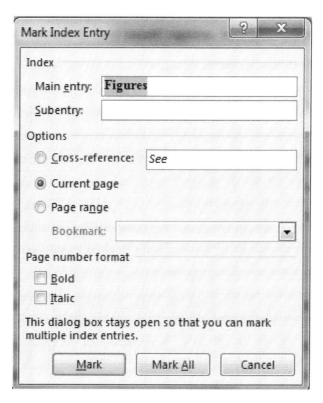

In the **Main entry,** the word inside is **Figure** because I highlighted the word before I clicked **Mark Entry** tool. Leave **Subentry** empty unless you have any to add there. Under **Options**, select **Current page** as shown in the image. Under **Page number format**, you can leave the boxes empty or tick any if you want the words or keywords to be written in bold or italic when they appear on the index page.

- Click **Mark** or **Mark All** button

When you click **Mark**, only where the word appears on the page at that moment will be recorded when you finally insert index page in your document. But if you click **Mark All,** where that word or keywords appear in the entire document will be recorded by Word 365 system.

- Click **Close** to close the dialog box

When you click the **Close** button, you will notice that all the paragraph marks and hidden symbols in your document will be shown. To return the document to its normal state, click the **Home** tab, and then click **Show/Hide Paragraph** tool which takes the shape "¶".

- Repeat step 1, 2, 3, 4 to add all the word, keywords, and phrases you want to have in the index page of the document
- Scroll down to one of the last pages of your document where you want to insert the index page and click at the spot.
- Click **References** tab and then click the **Insert Index** tool to show dialog box below:

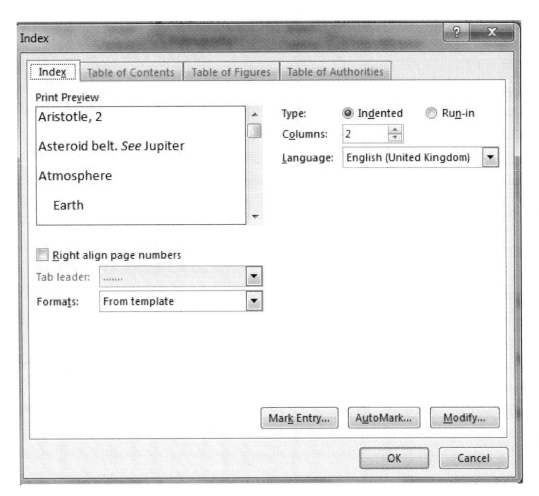

In the **Formats**, you can click the dropdown to choose the format you want. As you choose the format, you will see the sample of how the index will look like in the **Print Preview**.

- Click **Ok** button for the index to be inserted

Chapter 8: **Graphical Works in Microsoft Word**

Adding Images

A Picture is a static image used for different illustrations and purposes. Now, how do we insert pictures into our Word document?

- Go to "Insert" in your menu bar

- Under the "Insert" tab, locate the "Illustrations" ribbon. In the "Illustrations" ribbon, select "Pictures"

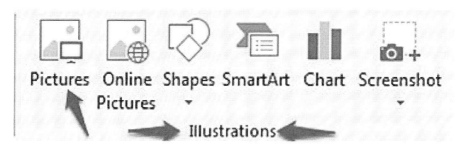

Once you click on "Pictures", a dialog box will pop up and direct you to your PC storage, locate the folder where your pictures are stored and click on your preferred image, then click "Insert"

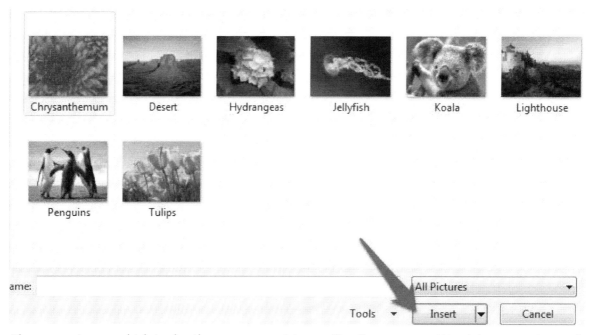

- Then, your image which is also the same as a picture will reflect on your Word document immediately. You can resize your image at the dots areas and rotate it if need be, using the curved arrow icon as illustrated below

Adding Clipart

Adding clip art and images to your document can be a great way to highlight important information or add a decorative accent to your existing text. You can import an image from your computer or browse the wide variety of Microsoft clip art to find the image you need. After inserting the image, you can format the text to fold the image.

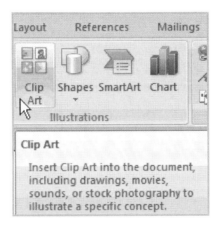

- Choose the Insert tab to find clip art.
- In the Illustrations group, select Clip Art.
- In the Search for: section, enter keywords associated with the image you want to upload.
- Click the drop-down arrow in the Results column.
- Select the media types you do not want to view.
- Select the media type to display
- If you also want to search for clip art on **Office.com**, place a check mark next to Include **Office.com** Content. Otherwise, it will only search for clip art on your computer.
- Click Go.

To import clip art:

- Check the results of a clip art search.
- Insert the insertion point into the document where you want to insert the clip art.

153

- Click the image in the Clip Art window. It will appear in the document.
- Select Clip Art

You can also click the drop-down arrow next to an image in the Clip Art window to see more options.

Wrap Text Around Images

Word allows you to join texts and images together to explain a document. This is made possible by wrapping text around your image.

To wrap text around an image, follow the steps below:

Select the image you wish to wrap text around

Click on the **Format** menu that appears at top of the Word's ribbon and selects **Wrap text.**

Select any of the following in the **Warp Text** drop-down list

- **Square:** Choose this option if your image is square, and you wish to wrap the text around the square border of your image.
- **Top and Bottom:** Select this option if you want your image to stay on its own line, but between text on the top and button.
- **Tight:** Select this option if you wish to wrap text around a round or irregular-shaped image.
- **Through:** This option helps to customize the areas that the text will wrap. This is best used if you want to join the text with your image, and you do not wish to follow the line of your border.
- **Behind Text:** This option allows you to use the image as a watermark behind the text.
- **In Front of Text:** Select this option if you wish to display the image over the text. You can change the color, or make the text illegible.

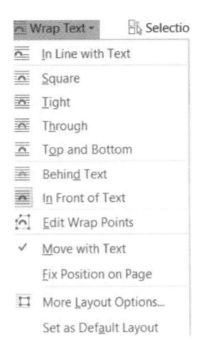

SmartArt

The **SmartArt** tool under **Insert** tab is used to communicate information virtually. It has graphical application. Through **SmartArt**, you will have access to many graphics integrated into Word 365 by Microsoft. SmartArt consists of many categories. The categories are **All, List, Process, Cycle, Hierarchy, Relationship, Matrix, Pyramid, Picture** and **Office.com**. Each of these categories contains graphics related to it. But **All** contains graphic designs that cut across the other categories.

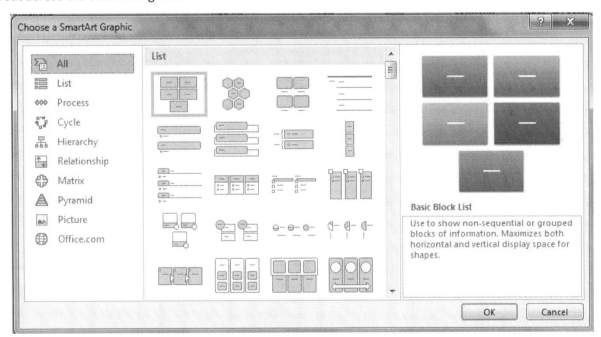

In this section, I will walk you through on how to use SmartArt tool.

Step by Step Guide on how to use SmartArt Tool

To apply SmartArt tool in Word 365, take the following steps:

- Click your Word 365 to open and then select **Blank document** to open the Word environment
- Click **Insert** tab and select **SmartArt** which is in **Illustrations** category
- Select any graphic representation from the graphics category

You can choose from any category depending on what you are preparing. Take for instance I want to have graphical representation of salespersons positions in the company I work, I will choose one illustration under **Pyramid** category.

- Click **Ok** button

Once you click the **Ok** button at the right-hand side of the graphics gallery, the graphics will be inserted into your Word 365 environment.

- Start designing your graphics to fit into what you want to build at the end.

Since in this illustration I am building with pyramid to show the ranks of salespersons in insurance, I have to start my design. There is provision where I am to type texts and they reflect in the main pyramid stage. If I want to add more pyramid steps, I will right-click in any of the stage and select to **Add shape** option. From there I can choose to add the shape before or after. You can also adjust the position of the design by press and drag with your cursor.

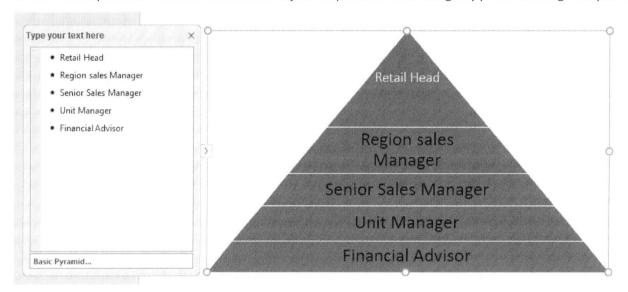

Click out of the section after design

Chapter 9: **Tables and Charts**

Adding Tables

Creating a table has been for different purposes such as for grading, calculating, listing of names, items, and so on. To create a table, simply follow this procedure

Go to the "Insert" tab

Below the "Insert tab", you will see "Table", click the little arrow under to get the dropdown table options

Once you click on the arrow, you get the dropdown rows and columns which is known as "Table Grid". Select the numbers of rows and columns you want, then, click on the last selection of row and column to display it on your Word document

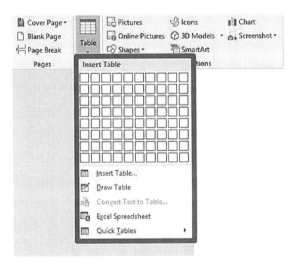

Assuming we pick five rows and two columns, at the last selection, right-click on your mouse to effect it on your Word document

Here is the result that you will have on your Word document

Quick Table

Quick tables are tables you can modify for your use. To begin, Put your cursor where you want to Insert the table. Click on the Insert tab on the Ribbon. Select table in the table group followed by quick table from the drop-down menu as shown in figure 3. Choose the table you want from the gallery. Then enter your content by typing over or deleting the table example text.

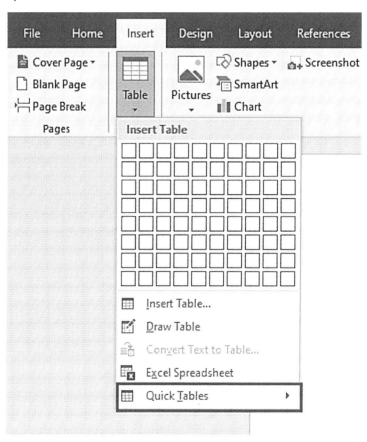

How Do I Enter Text into a Table

Once you have selected the number of rows (horizontal) and columns (vertical), then your table will be displayed in your Word document. Assuming it is three rows and five columns, place your mouse cursor on the table to type your text and number

Then, start typing your words inside

Number	Text	
1	One	
2	Two	
3	Three	
4	Four	

Table Styles

Go to "Insert"

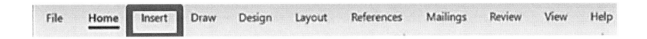

Below the "Insert tab" you will see "Table", click the little arrow to get the dropdown table options

Once you click on the arrow, you get the dropdown rows and columns which is known as "Table Grid". Select the numbers of rows and columns, then click on the last selection of row and column to display it on your Word document

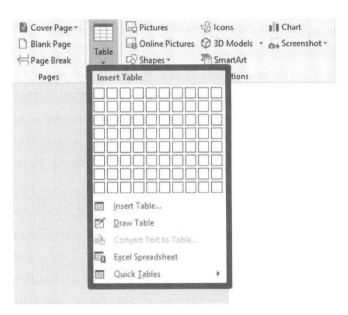

Once you have selected the number of rows (horizontal) and columns (vertical), then your table will be displayed in your Word document, let's assume it is four rows and three columns

Click inside one of the columns, once you do this, it becomes active to receive text

Immediately, the menu bar will show "Table Tools" which are the "Design" table tab and "Layout" table tab, click on "Design table tab"

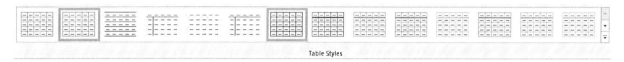

Under "Design", you will see "table" styles which consist of predefined table styles to use, click on any colorful style to see its effect on your table

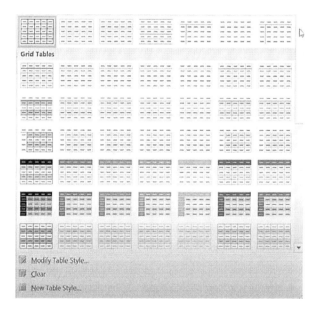

Table Styles

You can also click on the dropdown arrow on your right-hand side to view other table options

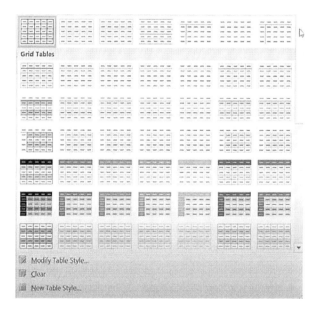

Once selected, your created table will be transformed into the predefined template

Note: "Table Tools" only show up whenever the table cell is active.

Formatting Tables

Borders are the lines that form table edges. With borders, you can decorate your table and design it to your preferred choice. How to decorate your table with borders and colors will be explained step by step below

- To save time because of the process of creating another table, we will be using our calendar table. Highlight your heading cell which is "January 2022" or you point your cursor into the "January 2022" row. Note you can use any cell, just for a well-ordered work, we will use the heading cell (January 2022)

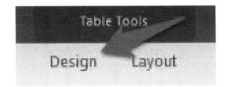

January 2022						
Sunday	Monday	Tuesday	Wednesday	Thursday	Friday	Saturday
						1
2	3	4	5	6	7	8
9	10	11	12	13	14	15
16	17	18	19	20	21	22
23	24	25	26	27	28	29
30	31					

Then, the table options will appear named "Table tools", under it is "Design" and "Layout", click on "Layout"

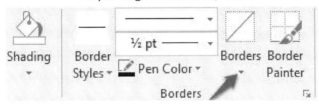

- At your right-hand side, locate "Borders"

Click on "Borders" to select a different line style format to replace the default borders. For example, we could choose a triple line border

We can also change the line weight to one and a half point ($1\frac{1}{2}$ pt)

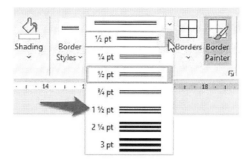

We can also change the border color by picking the orange color

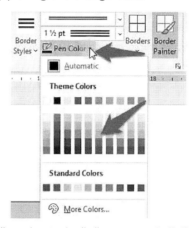

Once your color has been selected, the "Border Styles", "Line Weight", "Line Styles" and "Pen Color" will have the effect of your chosen color. Note that your "Border Painter" is selected automatically

Once your "Border Painter" is selected, your mouse cursor will change to pen cursor, simply place it on the line edge you want your triple line and color to affect. Note, if you place it wrongly, you will need to select "Border Painter" again

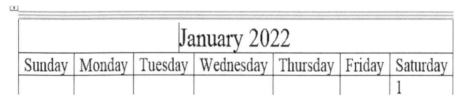

But there is also another way out without having to click and wrongly place line edges; simply click on "Borders"

Then, select what area you want your border to cover such as "Bottom Border", "Top Border", "Left Border", "Right Border" and so on. We will be clicking on "All Borders"

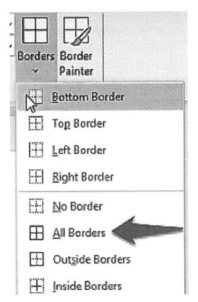

Once "All Borders" has been selected, your created calendar table will be formatted on your active cell which is "January 2022" where your mouse cursor is pointing.

			January 2022			
Sunday	Monday	Tuesday	Wednesday	Thursday	Friday	Saturday
						1
2	3	4	5	6	7	8

NOTE: If you want the remaining rows and columns to also be formatted, then, you need to highlight the entire table to perform such an operation.

You can also add shade color on the background of "January 2022" by changing the white background. To do this, click on "Shading"

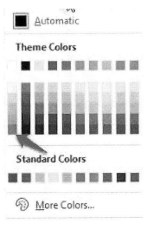

Select your preferred color. For illustration, I will pick the gray color to achieve a color blend.

Your outcome if you choose the same color with me, will be the illustration below

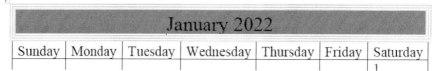

January 2022						
Sunday	Monday	Tuesday	Wednesday	Thursday	Friday	Saturday
						1

Exploring more on Borders

In continuation of ***"Decorating your table with borders and colors"***. It is important to note that there is also more to Border Style

Still on our created calendar table illustration

January 2022						
Sunday	Monday	Tuesday	Wednesday	Thursday	Friday	Saturday
						1

- Click on "Design" table tools

At your left-hand side, you will see a dropdown arrow, click on it

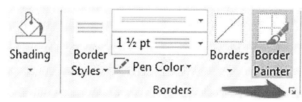

You will be brought here, where all our formatted styles are reviewed and edited. It consists of "Borders settings", "Page Border settings" and "Shading settings". If you remember, previously, we choose an orange color, that is why you are seeing orange color and one and half width. Click on the "Shading" option

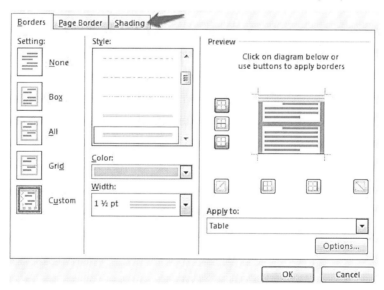

Once you click on "Shading", you will be brought to this page, where you can set your "Shading Patterns", "Style", "Color" and "Apply to". Under "Apply to", select "Table", then click "Ok" to see the effect

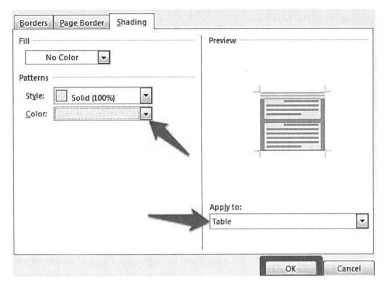

Here is what your result will be if you do exactly as I did

January 2022						
Sunday	Monday	Tuesday	Wednesday	Thursday	Friday	Saturday
						1
2	3	4	5	6	7	8
9	10	11	12	13	14	15
16	17	18	19	20	21	22
23	24	25	26	27	28	29
30	31					

Adding Row and Column

Once you select the number of rows and columns and you have inputted your texts, there is a possibility of needing an additional table to continue your content, simply place your cursor at the edge of your table as illustrated below.

Position	Type	Location
Computer Engineer	Full-time, two months	Clearwater
Software Developer	Full-time, open-ended	Tampa
UI Designer	Part-time, two months	St. Petersburg

Once you see the plus sign (+), click on it, another empty single row and column will be created

Position	Type	Location
Computer Engineer	Full-time, two months	Clearwater
Software Developer	Full-time, open-ended	Tampa
UI Designer	Part-time, two months	St. Petersburg

You can then fill up the empty rows and columns with your desired text

Position	Type	Location
Computer Engineer	Full-time, two months	Clearwater
Project Assistant	Full-time, three months	Coral Springs
Software Developer	Full-time, open-ended	Tampa
UI Designer	Part-time, two months	St. Petersburg

Resizing Rows o Columns

Place your cursor on any column, click on the layout tab and click on cell size group there is a height option, click to expand it and the height of the column increases, same with weight, etc.

To Get an equal height of each column, click on distribute rows and all rows will have equal height. Same with the column, click on distribute column to get an equal column.

To resize an entire table, click the resizing handle in the bottom right of the table. You may be required to move your pointer over the table to reveal the handle. Then drag the table to the size you want upon the **+** sign on the bottom side of the table.

Merge Cells

Beyond explanation, it is also important to understand the little element that the big element is made up of. "Cell" is the inputted part where your text and number are inserted into. So, why merge cells? Merging of cells is mostly needed for various reasons such as naming your table, constructing a calendar.

The month and year (for example, January 2022) need to occupy the first rows in a bold and large format to give a clear update on what the table is all about as seen in the image below

January 2022						
Sunday	Monday	Tuesday	Wednesday	Thursday	Friday	Saturday
						1
2	3	4	5	6	7	8
9	10	11	12	13	14	15
16	17	18	19	20	21	22
23	24	25	26	27	28	29
30	31					

Then, how do we merge cells?

Since I have shown you how to insert tables, Let's assume we want to create something similar to the calendar format above. For us to merge our table, if you count the rows, you will notice it is seven (7) in number, while the columns are eight (8) in number including the heading (January 2022). This is also an opportunity to create a calendar with Office Word document. After creating your table, input the text and number in its various location

January 2022						
Sunday	Monday	Tuesday	Wednesday	Thursday	Friday	Saturday
						1
2	3	4	5	6	7	8
9	10	11	12	13	14	15
16	17	18	19	20	21	22
23	24	25	26	27	28	29
30	31					

Then, place your cursor at the beginning of "January 2022"

January 2022						
Sunday	Monday	Tuesday	Wednesday	Thursday	Friday	Saturday
						1
2	3	4	5	6	7	8
9	10	11	12	13	14	15
16	17	18	19	20	21	22
23	24	25	26	27	28	29
30	31					

Once your cursor is blinking at the beginning of January 2022, simply hold down "Shift key" on your keyboard with the "forward Arrow" at the right-hand side of your keyboard. It will be highlighting your first row, once your highlighting gets to the last row, release your hand from the "Shift & "Arrow keys" on your keyboard, below is where the highlighting of your rows should stop

January 2022						
Sunday	Monday	Tuesday	Wednesday	Thursday	Friday	Saturday
						1
2	3	4	5	6	7	8
9	10	11	12	13	14	15
16	17	18	19	20	21	22
23	24	25	26	27	28	29
30	31					

After highlighting it, go to the "menu bar", click on "Layout"

Under "Layout" look at your left-hand side, you will see the "Merge" ribbon, click on "Merge cells"

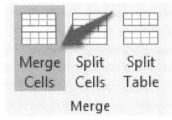

By default, your highlighted row will be merged as one, you will also notice the column lines that separate the entire table is no longer applicable to the "January 2022" row

January 2022						
Sunday	Monday	Tuesday	Wednesday	Thursday	Friday	Saturday
						1
2	3	4	5	6	7	8
9	10	11	12	13	14	15
16	17	18	19	20	21	22
23	24	25	26	27	28	29
30	31					

Align Cell Text

Simply go to "Insert tab"

Below "Insert", you will see "Table", click the little arrow to get the dropdown options

Once you click on "Table", you get the "Table Grid", select the numbers of rows and columns you want to work with, then click on the last selection of rows and column to display it on your Word document

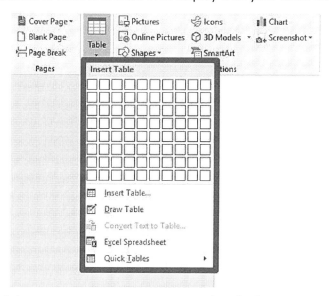

Once it appears on your Word document, you can type your text into it. For us to see how to align a table, I will use my previous table to illustrate how to align your table

Position	Type	Location
Computer Engineer	Full-time, two months	Clearwater
Project Assistant	Full-time, three months	Coral Springs
Software Developer	Full-time, open-ended	Tampa
UI Designer	Part-time, two months	St. Petersburg

Once you click any part of your table a little plus (+) sign will appear on your left-hand side, click on it

Position	Type	Location
Computer Engineer	Full-time, two months	Clearwater
Project Assistant	Full-time, three months	Coral Springs
Software Developer	Full-time, open-ended	Tampa
UI Designer	Part-time, two months	St. Petersburg

All your table will be automatically highlighted

Position	Type	Location
Computer Engineer	Full-time, two months	Clearwater
Project Assistant	Full-time, three months	Coral Springs
Software Developer	Full-time, open-ended	Tampa
UI Designer	Part-time, two months	St. Petersburg

Then, go to your "home" tab

By your right-hand side under the "Paragraph" ribbon, there are four types of alignment; left alignment, center alignment, right alignment, and justify alignment. For understanding, we will be using center alignment to see the effect, because by default your table is on left alignment; simply click the "**center alignment**" which is the second alignment icon from your left

Paragraph

You can press the shortcut, "Ctrl + E" on your keyboard, your table will be moved to the center point. Once you select center alignment as illustrated, here's what it will look like

For further information about any of these new jobs, or a complete listing of jobs that are available through the Career Center, please call Mary Walker-Huelsman at (727) 555-0030 or visit our website at www.fpcc.pro/careers.

Position	Type	Location
Computer Engineer	Full-time, two months	Clearwater
Project Assistant	Full-time, three months	Coral Springs
Software Developer	Full-time, open-ended	Tampa
UI Designer	Part-time, two months	St. Petersburg

To help prepare yourself before applying for these jobs, we recommend that you review the following articles on our website at www.fpcc.pro/careers.

Text Direction

Create a table of your choice as you were taught earlier, you can decide to replicate the one I'm using for illustration, two (2) rows, and three (3) columns. Make sure your cursor is blinking inside the one cell

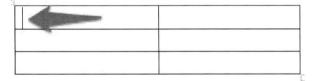

Next, look above and locate "Table tools". Under "Table Tools", click on "Layout"

Then, locate "Properties" and click on it

Properties

169

Once you click on "Properties", a dialog box will be opened titled "Table" properties, under "Table", locate "Text wrapping", by default it is on "None", simply select "Around" and then press "Ok"

Adding a Chart

How to Insert "Chart"

Select "Chart" in the "Illustrations" ribbon

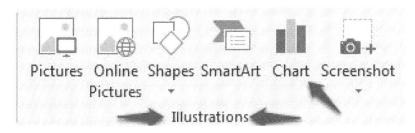

A dialog box will appear consisting of the "All Charts" features such as "Column", "Line", "Pie", "Bar", "Area", and other charts. It's majorly used to view the estimation of data after it has been concluded.

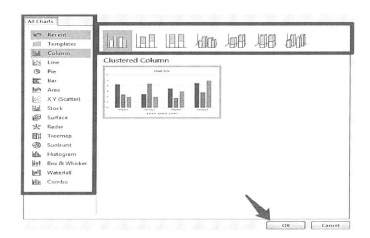

Chapter 10: **Templates**

Finding a Template

MS word document can be created either from a blank document or from the various available template that is available on the MS word 2022 start screen, after the creation of the document you can store such document on your PC or the iCloud. Study the below steps to get acquainted with the document creation:

- Tap on the **File tab** and choose **New from File backstage** on the left side of the screen.
- Select a **blank new document thumbnail** to create a blank new document or select the **desired template** from the available offline template or search for the various templates on the internet.

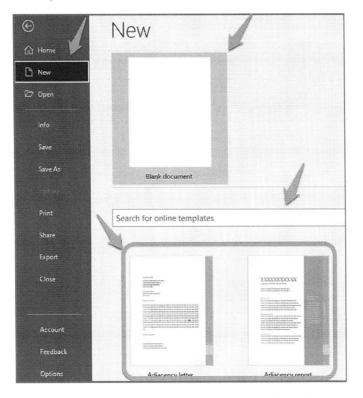

Note: you can create a document with a quick shortcut by pressing (Ctrl + N), word permit you to create as many documents as you want, each document can have several pages.

Making Your Own Template

Follow the steps below to create a new template;

- Click on the Ctrl + N button to create a new document.
- Locate the File tab and choose the Save As option.
- Click on the Browse option.
- Open the Save As option and choose Word Template.
- Insert a name that can be used to describe the template and click the Save button.

Create Document from Saved Template

MS word document can be created either from a blank document or from the various available template that is available on MS word 365 start screen, after the creation of the document you can store such document to your PC or the iCloud. Study the below steps to get acquainted with the document creation:

- Tap on the **File tab** and choose **New from File backstage** at the left side of the screen.

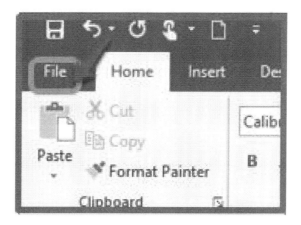

- Select a **blank new document thumbnail** to create a blank new document or select the **desired template** from the available offline template or search for the various templates on the internet.

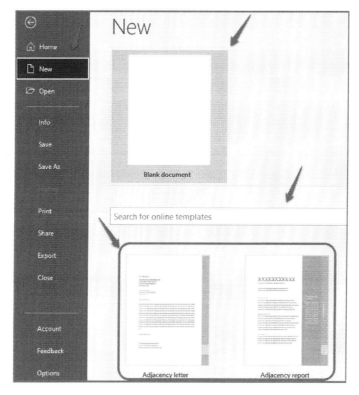

Note: you can create a document with a quick shortcut by pressing (Ctrl + N), word permit you to create as many documents as you want, each document can have several pages.

Chapter 11: **Mailing**

Printing on Envelopes

- Go to "Mailings"

- Under the "Mailings" tab, at your left-hand side, you will see "Envelopes", click on it

- Simply fill in all the required details such as "Delivery address", "Return address", "Add to document" if need be. Once everything has been verified, click on "Print"

Mail Merge

Mail Merge is a nice property that Microsoft integrated into her Word 365 software. With the mail merge tool, you can send mail to large number of people once. Just arrange their email addresses and the other details the way they are to be and send the mail once to them.

Take these steps to start and finish mail merge:

- In your current document, type the mail you want to send the way you want it to appear to the recipients.
- Click the **Mailings** tab followed by **Start Mail Merge** command
- From the options, select how you want the mail communicated to your recipients (preferably **Normal Word Document** since the mail is composed using that channel).

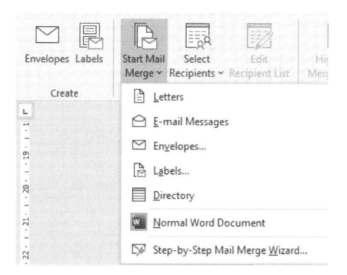

- Click Select Recipients command

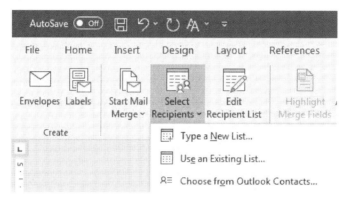

- As you are shown some channels where you can get the list of the people you want to send mail to, you can select any. If for example you have prepared their names, phone numbers, email addresses, home addresses and other details in an excel spreadsheet which is saved in a folder of your computer, just select **Use an Existing List** and upload the file from your computer. But here I assume you have not done that so select the option **Type a New List** which will display a dialog box that I show below:

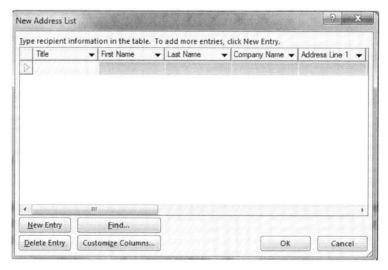

- In the dialog box, click under each heading and fill the required information. Fill the necessary information and when you are done click **Ok** button. Know that you must not fill all the information in the table, but first name, last name, company name, city, state, zip code, country, and address are very important for you to get the expected result. Also, when you are done with filling a recipient's detail, click **New Entry** button to start filling a new one. Do this until you fill the details of the number of recipients you want to have.

- Click the beginning of your document where in a normal letter standard the address of the recipient is positioned and click **Address Block** command and in the dialog box that will show up click **Ok** command.
- Click **Greeting Line** command, in the dialog box, Select any option in the Greeting line format and an option for the invalid recipient names.

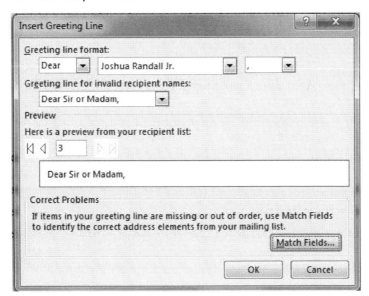

- Click **OK** button to save your selection.
- Click the **Insert Merge Field** command and choose the suitable option which is usually **Name**.
- Click **Preview Results** command to be shown how your mail merge will look like when sent or printed out.

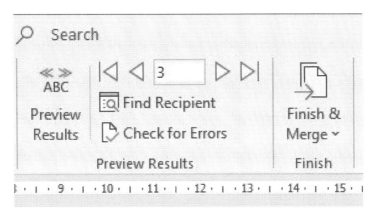

Click the arrow to see how each recipient's detail will appear as the mail is sent out.

- Click **Finish and Merge** and select **Print Documents** or **Send Email Messages** option and fill in the expected data.

Chapter 12: **Check your Spelling & Grammar**

Checking Spelling Errors

You can check for spelling errors in your documents by either correcting spelling errors one at a time or running a spelling check.

Correcting Spelling Errors One Step at a Time

You can correct your spelling errors without running the spell check method.

To do this:

- Locate the word that is underlined with a red line and then right-click on it
- Select the correct spelling from the **Spelling** shortcut menu
- After doing this, the word misspelled is replaced with the word you right-clicked on

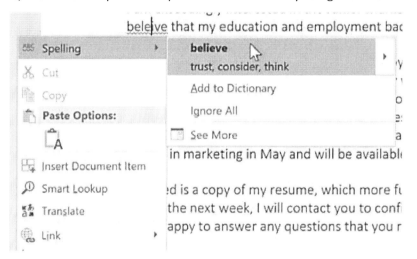

Running the Spell Check

Correcting spelling errors one by one can be a waste of time; therefore, you use the Spell check which is faster. To start your spell check, you can use any of the following methods

- Press **F7**
- Go to the **Status bar** and click on the **Proofing Error** button

- Go to the Review tab and click on **Spelling & Grammar**

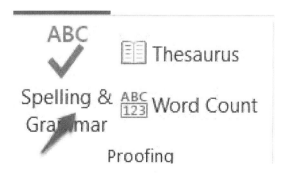

176

- The Editor task pane displays where you can view the number of spellings and grammar errors in your documents.
- Click on Spelling in the task pane to see the suggestions provided for a misspelling, and then click on the correct spelling.

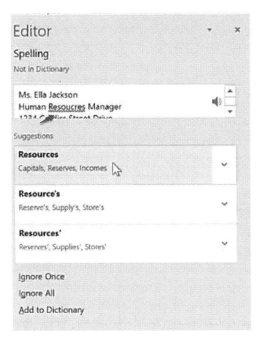

Preventing Text from Being Spell Checked

There are certain words in your documents that cannot be spell-checked especially words like address lists, lines of computer codes, and foreign languages such as French, Spanish, etc. To prevent text of this kind from being spell-checked, follow the steps below

- Select the text.
- On the **Review tab**, click on the **Language** button, and select **Set Proofing Language.**

- In the **Language** dialog box, click on the **Do not check spelling or grammar** check box

Correcting Grammatical Errors

Just like how spellings are corrected, the same techniques apply to correcting grammatical errors.

Correcting Grammatical Errors One Step at a Time

You can correct grammar errors by following the steps below

- Locate the word that is underlined with a blue line and right-click on it
- Correct the grammatical error from the **Grammar** shortcut menu
- After doing this, the grammatical error will be replaced with the word you right-clicked on.

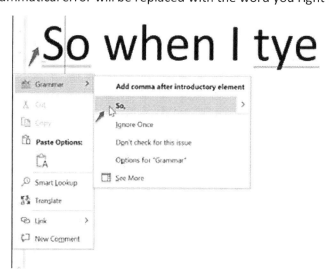

Correcting Grammatical Errors Using Editor Task Pane

You can use the Editor task pane to correct your grammatical errors. Primarily, you will need to open the Editor task pane. To open the Editor task pane, you any of the following methods

- Press **F7**
- Go to the **Status bar** and click on the **Proofing Error** button

- Go to the Review tab and click on **Spelling & Grammar**

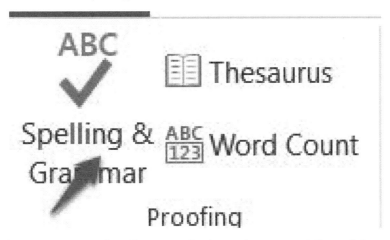

- When the **Editor** task pane opens, select **Grammar** in the task pane and then click on the option under **Suggestions.**

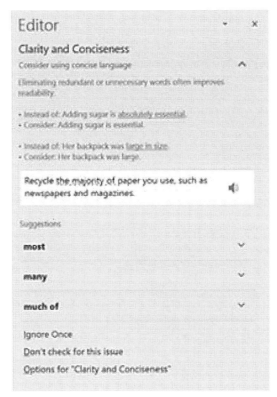

Ignoring Errors

It is no doubt that the spelling and grammar check is aimed at correcting errors, yet, it is not always correct. There are several instances where Word will see some words as errors when they are not. This happens a lot when the names and other proper nouns are not included in the dictionary, especially in foreign languages, or computer codes.

However, you can choose to ignore any word that is tagged to be an error by Word from the options provided by Word for both spelling and grammar checks.

For Spelling errors, you can choose any of the following options

- **Ignore:** This skips the misspelled word without changing it but stops on it if the same word appears again.
- **Ignore All:** This skips the misspelled word without changing it, and it also skips the same word if it appears again.
- **Add to Dictionary:** This adds the word to the dictionary so that it will not come up as an error. Ensure that the words are correctly spelled before adding them to the dictionary.

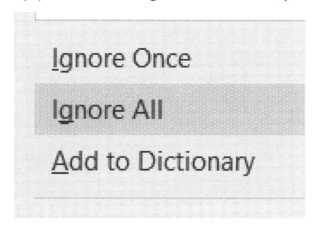

For Grammar errors, you get to choose just one option:

- **Ignore Once**: This skips the word or phrase without changing it.

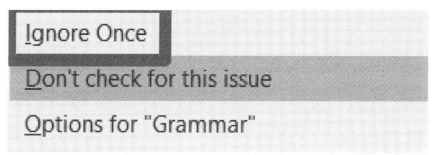

Customizing Spelling & Grammar Check

By default, there are some errors your proofing tools ignore without correcting, which you will want your proofing tools to correct.

To include all these in your spelling and grammar check, follow the steps given below

- Go to the **Backstage view** by clicking on the **File** menu.

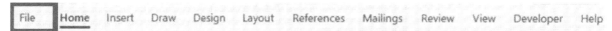

- Click on **Options** on the left pane.

- In the **Word Options** dialog box, click on **Proofing.**

- **On the left-hand side** when correcting spelling and grammar in Word**, click on** Settings.

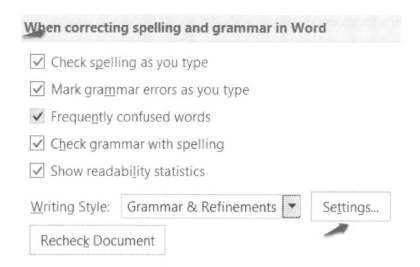

- In the **Grammar Settings** dialog box, select the options you wish to add to your spellings and grammar check, and then click on **Ok.**

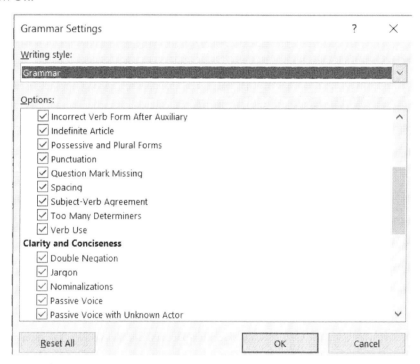

Hiding Spellings and Grammar Errors in a Document

In case you want to share your document with a person, and you do not want the person to see the red and blue lines. All you need to do is turn off the automatic spelling and grammar checks. Not only will the errors be hidden on your computer, but they also will not be displayed when viewed on another computer. To hide the spelling and grammar errors, follow the steps given below

- Go to the **Backstage view** by clicking on the **File** menu
- Click on **Options** on the left pane
- In the **Word Options** dialog box, click on **Proofing**

Go to Exceptions **and click on the checkboxes;** Hide spelling errors in this document only **and** Hide grammar in this document only.

Editing your Custom Dictionary

Word permits you to create a correctly spelled word that MS word has labeled as a misspelled word, as soon as you add them to a custom dictionary such texts will be recognized as correct spelling. U can add a word to the custom dictionary and remove any text. To do so, simply:

- Tap the **File tab and select the Option** from the file backstage to open the Word Options dialog box.
- Select **proofing** from the box and click the **custom dictionary.**

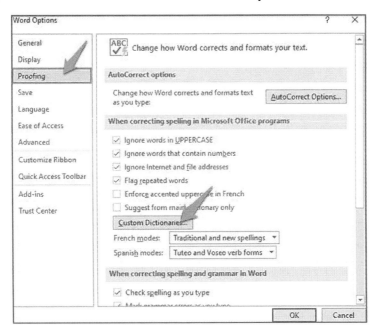

- The custom Dictionary dialog box will come forth, select the **"Custom. (Dic (Default)"** you may not have any other option apart from "Custom. Dic (Default)" unless you upgrade your PC.
- Then tap **Edit word list**, and a dialog box will be opened, which will provide you with a box where you can **add a new word to the Custom dictionary**, and also you will see the previous list of the word you have added, to erase any word from the list, kindly click on any word and choose **delete.**

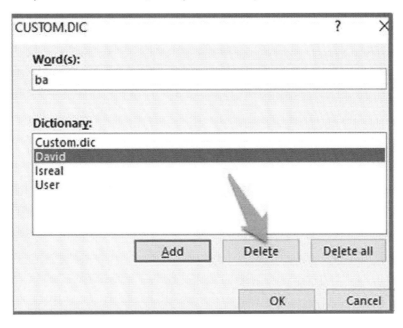

Thesaurus

The Thesaurus is a software tool in a Microsoft Word document that allows you to look for synonyms and antonyms of selected words.

There are three ways to open and use the Thesaurus:

- Press Shift + F7
- Right-click on any word, select **Synonyms** and then click on **Thesaurus**

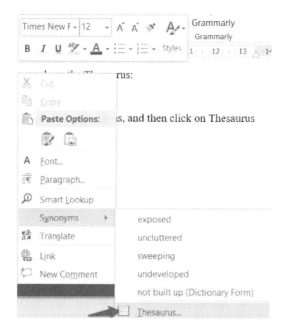

- Go to the **Review** tab, and click on the **Thesaurus** button

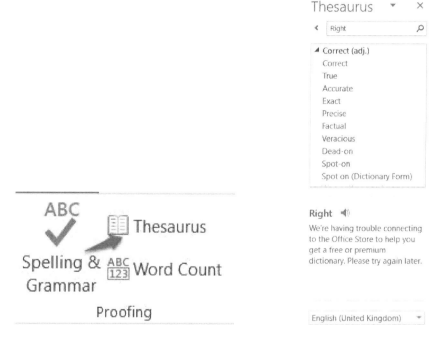

Rewrite Suggestions

Another newly added feature of Microsoft Word 365 is the "Rewrite Suggestions" which gives subscribers access to rephrase words. Let's see how it works

Assuming I typed the below sentence

Now, you highlight the area which you want to rephrase. Let's assume it is "always working" in the above illustration

I'm always working to continuously improve my videos.

Right-click on the selected text, a dialog box will appear, locate and click on "Rewrite Suggestions"

Once you click on "Rewrite Suggestions", another dialog box will appear at your right-hand side with a suggestion of my highlighted text instead of "always working to" you can say "constantly working to" or "working all the time to"; I will click on "constantly working to"

Then my highlighted text will be replaced with "constantly working to".

I'm constantly working to continuously improve my videos.

Search & Replace

This allows you to use the Navigation pane to search for specific words or phrases in a document. To use this command, follow the steps given below

- Go to the **Home** tab, click on **Find** and the **Navigation pane** appears.

- In the **Search document** box in the **Navigation pane**, enter the text you wish to find.
- Use the arrows under the search box to move to **Previous** or **Next** search results.
- When you are done, click on the **X** button to close the **Navigation pane**

Advanced Find Command

This command allows you to search your documents for more specific items, such as match cases, wildcards, whole words, etc.

To use the Advanced Find command, follow the steps given below

- Go to the **Home** tab, click on the **Find** button list arrow and select **Advanced Find**

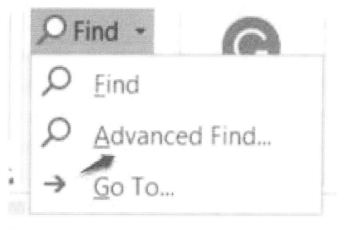

- In the **Find and Replace** dialog box opens, enter the word of the **Find** box.

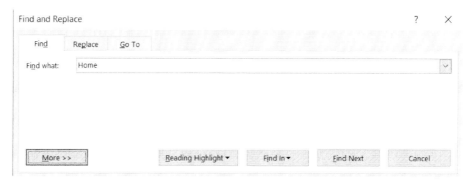

- Click on the **More** button; the More button allows you to set some options such as Match Case, Wildcards, Match prefix, etc. on how to search.

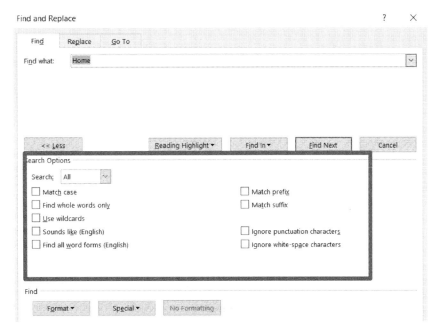

- Click on **Find Next** and Word searches from the current cursor location to the end of the document. If you click on **Find All**, Word searches the entire document.
- Then click on **Close** at the top of the dialog box.

The Replace Command

The Replace command allows you to find any word in your document and replace it with another. This can come in handy when you have misspelled a word in many places and wish to correct it. To use the Replace command, follow the steps given below

Go to the **Home** tab, click on **Replace**

In the **Find and Replace** dialog box, open the **Replace t**ab

Enter the word you need to find in the **Find what** text field

Enter the word you want to replace within the **Replace with** text field

Select any of the replacement options.

- **Replace**: This replaces individual instances of the text.

- **Replace All**: This replaces every instance of the text in the entire document.

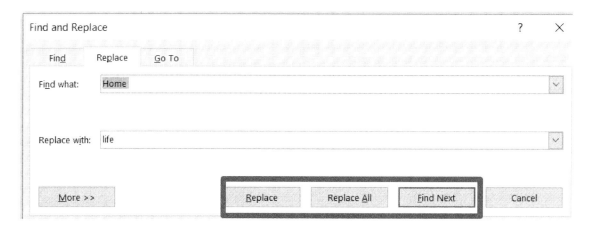

Click on **Ok**

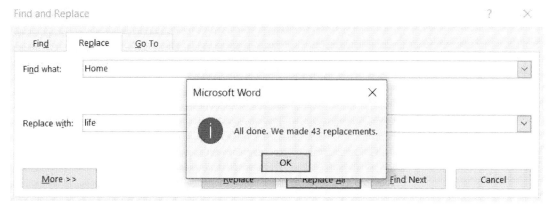

Then Press **Close** when you are done

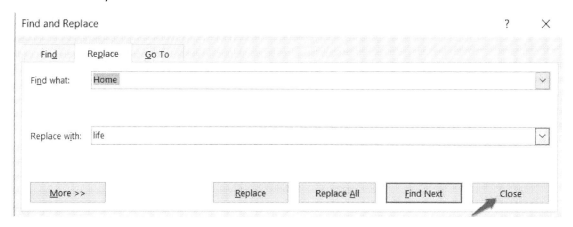

Chapter 13: Office Add-ins

Word 365 is a great computer application, which has a lot to write on. So, the learning is on how to complete other possible tasks which are possible through any tool available in **Insert** button of Word 365.

The Components of Add-ins Category

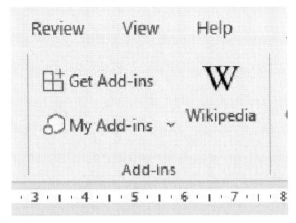

As shown in the picture above, the components of **Add-ins** category are **Get Add-ins**, **My Add-ins** and **Wikipedia**. As the component names sound, so is their roles. I will explain further.

Working with Add-ins Category

Just like any other tool used in Word 365, **Add-ins** tool is one of them. The **Add-ins** can be found when you click **Insert** menu. When you enable **Add-ins** in Word 365, it adds custom commands and new features to Office programs. This makes you to work more productively in the Word application. With Add-ins security settings feature, you can deny hackers access to your important Word files. Add-ins can be purchased from its developers online and they get installed in your Word 365. But before you install any add-ins in your Word 365, make sure you trust the source.

Get Add-ins

When you click **Get Add-ins,** a new word window shows some add-ins you can purchase or get for free from the Office store. The screenshot is shown below:

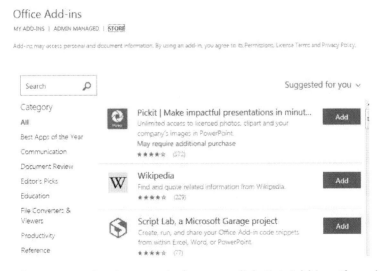

Make sure your computer is connected to internet before you click **Get Add-ins.** If you have any add-in in mind before clicking the **Get Add-ins** button, you can search for it using the search box on the top part of the interface. Click **Add** button, grant permission to install the add-in in your Word 365, and then start using it after the installation.

My Add-ins

Through **My Add-ins** button, you can see the add-ins you have already installed in your Word 365. By default, if you click that button, it will notify you that you have no add-ins installed in your Word app. But if you have installed any in your Word app and click on it, it will show you the available one. You can also delete already installed add-in which you do not want to have again through this tool.

BOOK 4: MICROSOFT EXCEL

Introduction

Excel Office 365 is a new update patching into an excel program. It uses a more powerful tool that allows you to create a document better and work with others conveniently. Excel 365 permits you to put together a lot of information from various people and sectors into a single worksheet, above all, you will be permitted to work with two or more persons on a similar worksheet at the same time which in turn improves efficiency and leads to a new vision for an organization as information is shared with all relevant personalities within the organization. In the same vein, it introduces an Excel pivot that can let you convert Excel into a driving force that can combine considerable volumes of data from numerous sources and construct a connection between them.

It is the free version of Excel that allows you to use a web browser by signing up for a Microsoft account with a new email or an existing email address with monthly or yearly payment to have access to Excel 365 features as well as the privilege to update to the latest version and effective security updates and bug fixes.

Above all, it securely stores all your document into the cloud with 1 TB of one cloud storage, nevertheless, you can access this cloud anywhere.

Do not get it twisted, Online Excel remains Microsoft Excel with a few differences from the traditional Excel. For instance, you run Excel on your computer by navigating to the start menu, search for Excel and click on it to open it, while Excel Online runs on the cloud and it can only be accessed with your web browser over the Internet by using Outlook.com or Gmail.com.

Once you acquaint yourself with the traditional Excel, you will find Online Excel interface very easy to work with because they are very similar in major aspects, though with little but significant differences, and thus there won't be a problem using Excel 365.

This is a well-designed user guide for all levels of users that is produced to grant you the prerequisite skills and knowledge you need to produce an accurate worksheet be it from a blank document or template with the necessary formulas for all data and text values input.

Chapter 1: **Starting Excel**

What's a Spreadsheet

An Excel spreadsheet document is referred to as a workbook. The workbook saves all of the information and helps you to filter and measure the results.

A Shared Workbook is a workbook that can be accessed and updated by several users on the same network.

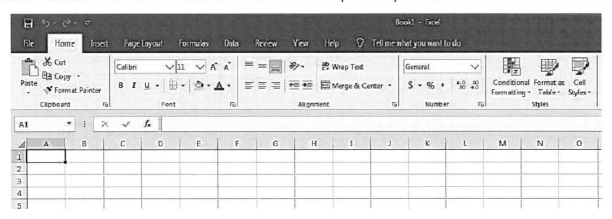

Worksheet

A worksheet is a text that is part of a workbook. Various sheets may be perched in a workbook, which is also known as a spreadsheet. Either of the worksheets you are currently working on is shown by tabs at the bottom of the page; it is also regarded as a dynamic sheet or current worksheet.

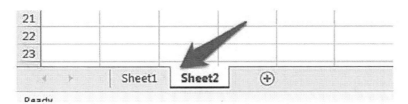

Starting Excel

Creating an Excel workbook from the scratch simply means starting up an Excel application and making the Excel working area ready for data input. The Excel working area can also be called the worksheet area. The workbook may comprise one or more worksheets. To create Excel workbook from the scratch or with a preset template, you have to open Excel 2022 program first by:

- Moving to the **left bottom of the window** and tap on the **start menu**.

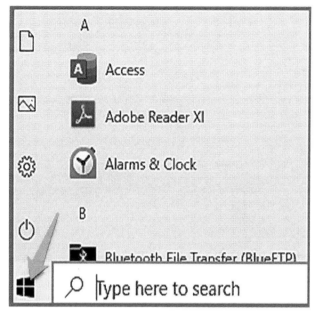

- Then **scroll down or up** within the application list to check for **Excel application** or you can type **Excel** on the keyboard to find the application.
- Immediately you find it click on **it (Excel)** to open the program.

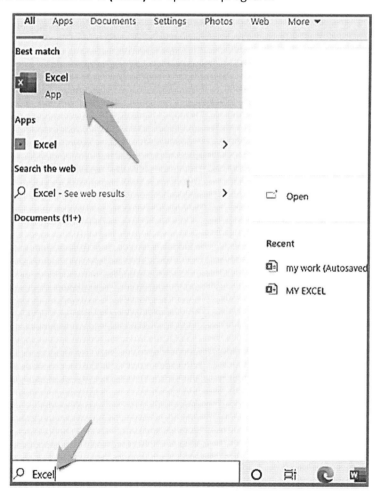

After you have opened the Excel application, you can then proceed to create a workbook by:

- Tapping the **New** from the Start screen of the Excel application and clicking on the **blank workbook.**

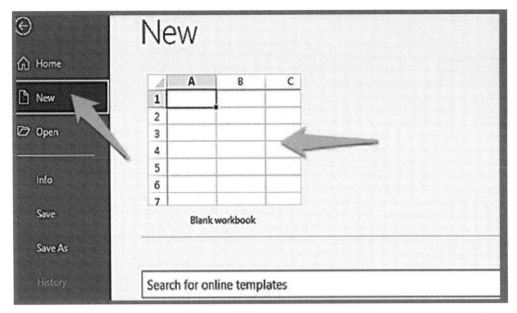

- the new Excel workbook will be created, you can then begin insertion of the data into the respective cell.

However, if you have decided to create Excel workbook from the preset template, you can achieve that from the Excel Start screen as well, simply:

- Scroll within the available **offline preset template** and double-click on the **template** of your choice.
- You can as well browse for **online templates** to have more access to the various dynamic and amazing templates by inputting the category name of the template you are searching for such as Sales template, Invoice template, and so on.

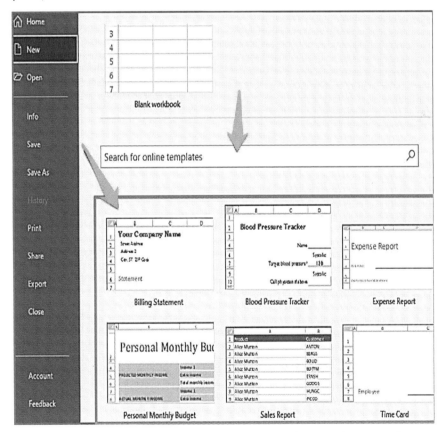

- You can then start to **edit the data cell** to the data you are having, because the template is preset, you will only edit and amend the preset on it by changing each text and number.

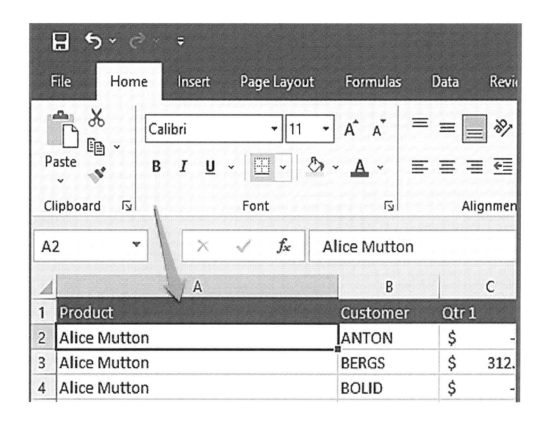

Chapter 2: **Enviroment**

Main Screen

The Excel window interface can be likened to an Excel environment with various components that make up the Excel window interface. Let us quickly check them one after the other:

- **Excel workbook:** this is the Excel document, that shows the title of the Excel work, the default name for any Excel workbook or document is **book 1, 2,** and so on, but the moment you save such workbook, the title changes to the name you use to save the document, the workbook contains one or more worksheet.
- **Excel worksheet:** this is the actual working area of Excel, the only area that accommodates your data input such as texts and numbers. It contains thousands of grid cells. The default name for a sheet is **sheet 1, 2,** and so on, you can change the default name.
- **Excel Ribbon**: just like every other ribbon, it contains major commands of the Excel application which are grouped into the row of tabs according to the function of each tab and each tab has many subgroupings under it, such as the Home tab, File tab, and many more.
- **Cell name box, Formula bar, and cell content**: **Cell name box** shows the address of the active cell, it is located at the top left of the worksheet below the ribbon while the **Formula bar** is located at the right side of the Cell name box and it has three buttons which are; **A cancel button** that removes your data entry in a cell, when you click on **the tick mark** it will insert the data into the cell, when you click on the **Insert function button** it will open up the Insert Function dialog box where all functions dwell **and Cell contents** which is located at the top right of the worksheet beside Cell name and formula bar, it simply displays the contents of the active cell for instance if the data you are inserting is too much that you can't see them all in the active cell, you may as well call it formula bar if you like.
- **Cell, row, and column:** cell is the **meeting point of row and column** which brings about billions of grid cells, rows of Excel occupy the vertical position while columns of Excel occupy the horizontal position.
- **Scroll bar:** it is used to **move up and down** inside the worksheet area, you can as well call it the navigator bar.
- **Worksheet shifting button:** it is designed to **move in between the worksheet,** when you tap on the front button it moves the worksheet to the front by one sheet and when you tap on the back button It moves the worksheet to the back by one sheet.
- **Add button:** when you tap on the plus button, it will add a new worksheet to the workbook, the more you click on it the more the worksheet you will be having.
- **Status bar:** as the name indicates, it includes **cell mode, page view, and Zoom slider,** the Cell mode is used to display the current mode of the worksheet, depending on what you are doing on the worksheet, for instance, you may be having either **Enter, Ready or Edit mode**, page view shows the structure of the page be it **normal page, page layout or break page preview,** Zoom slider button simply helps in regulating the view of the worksheet data by **shifting the slider to the right for increase view or to the left for decrease view**. Zoom does not increase the font of the data; it only changes the view of the data.

The Ribbon

The ribbon pane in Microsoft Excel is an array of accessible menus and icons that can be found on top of the Excel screen. It makes it easier to locate, comprehend and make use of simple functions to perform simple operations.

The Home Ribbon

This tab house commands that are most commonly implemented. Some of these commands include Copy, Paste, Sort, Filter, Format, etc.

The Insert Ribbon

Use the insert tab to include various images and objects in your worksheet. These objects can be charts, equations, tables, links, symbols, headers, footers, etc.

The Page Layout Ribbon

This menu helps you customize how your worksheet looks when onscreen and in hardcopy. It also allows you to configure settings such as themes, gridlines, margins, object alignment, etc.

The Formulas Ribbon

The formula tab makes it possible to input formulas, specify names and decide how calculations are to be carried out.

The Data Ribbon

This menu contains functions used for configuring worksheet data and also for the inclusion of data from external sources.

The Review Ribbon

This menu makes it possible to cross-check spellings, keep track of edits, include comments, and also safeguard worksheets and files.

The View Ribbon

This menu offers options for navigating around views in worksheets, locking panes, and also helps determine how multiple worksheets are displayed and arranged.

Fill Backstage

The file tab makes it easy to access a menu that shows necessary functions and options that can be used to manipulate files and workbooks.

Getting Started

Entering Data

- **Inserting Numbers**

Numbers can be entered manually in cells by placing your cursor on the desired cell. Autofill can also be used to automatically populate cells when dealing with sequential numbers or data. Just as for entering months of the year, the Autofill feature can also be used to populate rows or columns with sequential numbers.

- **Inserting Texts**

Placing your cursor on a cell and typing in alphabetical characters is the simplest way to insert texts in your data entry.

Also, using the **Insert** option present in the ribbon, click on **Text** and then choose the **Text box** option. Highlight the inserted text box and drag it to the desired position in your worksheet.

- **Employing the Enter Mode**

The enter mode in Excel makes a cell-active for you to enter data. Double-clicking on a cell activates the Enter mode.

Simple Text Formatting

The text formatting menu has so many useful tools for formatting, you can simply enter the text that you need, add some basic text formatting, and get the text formatted with ease.

Let's get started.

How to Bold Text

- You can bold a piece of text by going to the text, go to the formatting menu, and select "bold".
- Bold the text by simply clicking on the desired text.

How to Change Text Color

- Go to the formatting menu and select "text color".
- Change the color by simply clicking on the desired text.

The last text formatting method you'll see here is "font". To change the font, go to the menu at the top of the page and select "format cells". This is where you can do many of the things you can do when you format the cells.

Change font to a more readable font.

- Change font by going to the cell where you want to change the font and the formatting menu. Select "font".

How to Bold and Italicize Text

- In order to create bold and italicized text, there are three ways to do it: you can use the "bold" function, the "italic" function, and the "font" function.

Text Orientation

The default alignment of the text in the worksheet is to the left, while that of the number is to the right; both default alignments can be adjusted if the need arises. The data inside the cell can be adjusted to the left, right, or middle or from bottom to center, top, and vice versa. You may as well justify cell data. At the time you have to change the alignment of the subject heading so that its look within the cell will be outstanding and that of the worksheet at large.

To change the alignment of the text and number, kindly do the following:

1. **For horizontal alignment** (left to right or side to side alignment.).

- Select **the cells** that need alignment.
- Move to the **Home tab** then click on **the respective button** (left align, center align and middle align button).

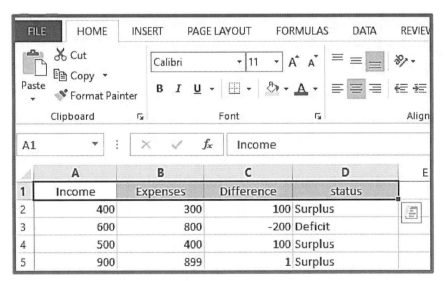

ALTERNATIVELY,

- Tap on the **Alignment** group button and pick the **Format Cell Alignment** option from the drop-down list.

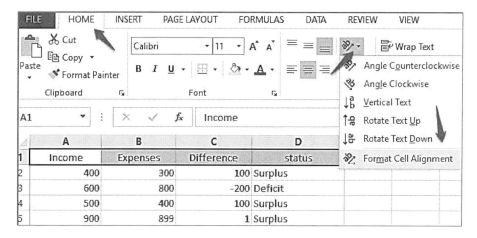

- Tap on the **Alignment** tab inside the format cell dialog box.
- Click on the **Horizontal section** and pick your desired alignment including justify that will fit your letter to the cell.

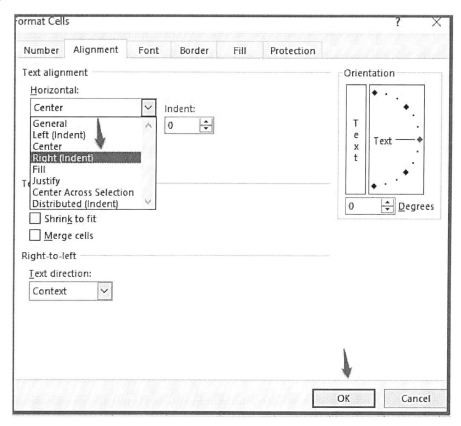

2. **For vertical alignment** (top to bottom or bottom to top):

- Select the **cells** that need alignment.
- Move to the **Home tab** then click on **respective alignment** (top align, middle align, and bottom align).

200

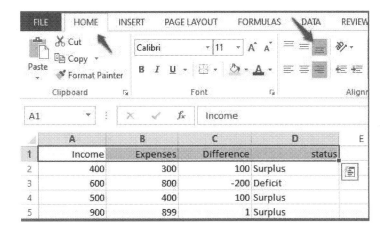

ALTERNATIVELY,

- Tap on the **alignment group button** and pick the **format cell** button from the drop-down list.

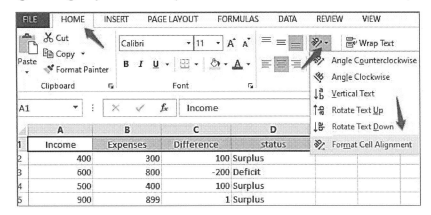

- Tap on the **Alignment** tab inside the format cell dialog box.
- Click on the **vertical section** and pick your desired **alignment** including justify that will fit your letter to the cell.

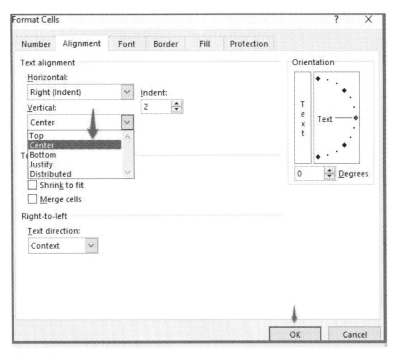

Resizing Rows and Columns

- Take your cursor to the edge of the column or row to be resized and ensure the cursor changes to the scaling arrow

- Drag the row or column to the desired size

The **Format** menu in the **Home** tab can also be used. Select this menu and choose a suitable option to adjust or AutoFit row and column size.

Inserting Rows o Columns

- Select the point where the new row or column is to be inserted
- Navigate to the **Insert** menu in the **Home** tab and select a suitable insert option

Erasing Columns and Rows in Worksheet

- Highlight the row or column to be deleted and make a right-click click
- Select the **Delete** option

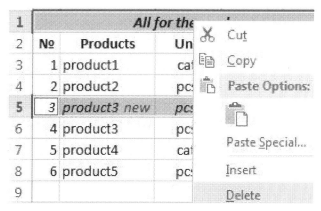

Alternatively, navigate to the **Delete** menu in the **Home** tab and choose a suitable delete option.

Sorting Data

To quickly sort, select your Sort Z to A / A to Z symbols within Sort & Filter set of the Data menu by clicking the arrow just under your Sort & Filtering symbol in the Editing set of the Home panel. Sort smallest to the largest & vice versa in Excel 2013.

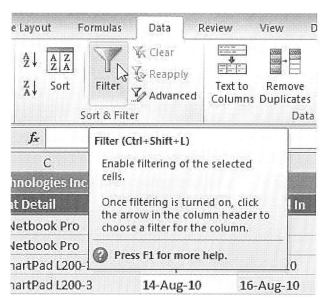

To do a more sophisticated sort, go over to the Home menu & select Custom Sort from the Editing group's arrow just below Filter & Sort & button. This opens the Sort dialogue box that appears when you click the Sort symbol within the Sort & Filter category of its Data ribbon.

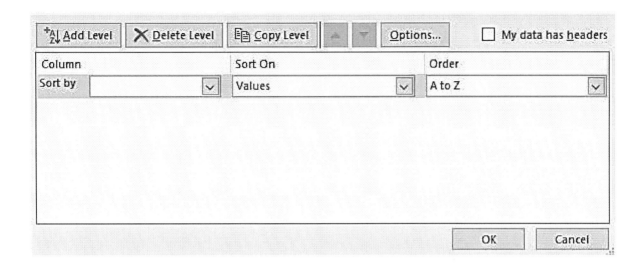

- Select the first column to sort from the Column drop-down menu. Tap the Add Level icon if you wish to sort several columns.
- Select how you want to sort under Sort On. In addition to data, Excel also sorts by cell and font color.
- Select Z to A (descending), A to Z (ascending) or Custom List under Order.
- To complete the sort, press OK.

Formatting Your Spreadsheet

Cell Alignment

This formatting operation allows you to decide how you want your data to appear and how they are arranged.

Alignment in Horizontal Direction

Three options exist for horizontal alignment of worksheet text or data:

- Left alignment
- Center alignment
- Right alignment

Alignment in Vertical Direction

Three options also exist for vertical alignment of worksheet text or data:

- Alignment to the top
- Alignment to the middle
- Bottom alignment

Text Format

Select any desired font from any of the tools previously highlighted. Font style and font sizes can both be formatted. You can also make your texts bold or italicize them during this formatting process.

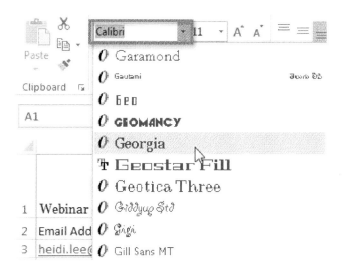

Text Wrap Formatting

This can simply be done by selecting the option to wrap texts in the Excel **Home** tab. This formatting option allows all text to be made visible in a cell.

Cell Borders

- Highlight the cells to which the borders or lines would be added

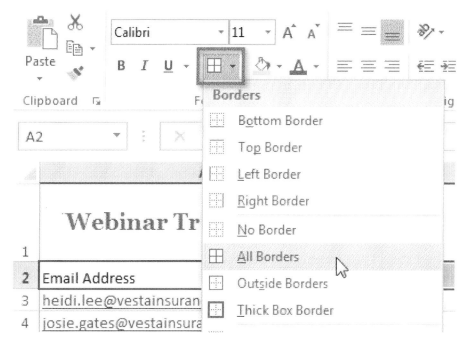

- Select the drop-down menu for borders and select a desired border option from the displayed list. You can add colors to borders by selecting the added border and then clicking on the icon for **Fill.**

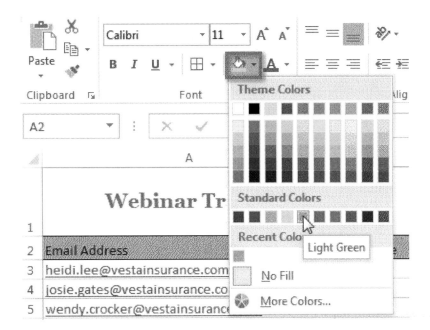

Opening a New Sheet

By selecting Excel Options from the Microsoft Office button, you can change the number of sheets that appear by default. When you're working, you can add new worksheets if required.

To Insert A New Worksheet

- Select the Insert Worksheet icon with a left click. A new sheet will be shown. Sheet4, Sheet5, or whatever the workbook's next consecutive sheet number will be the name.

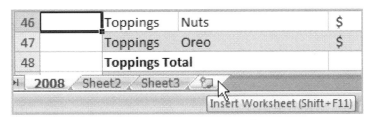

Or

- Instead, press Shift + F11 on your keyboard.

Deleting Worksheets

Any worksheet, including those with data, can be deleted from a workbook.

To delete one or more worksheets

- Select the sheet you decide to delete by clicking on it.
- Right-click the sheet, and the menu will appear.
- Choose Delete from the menu.

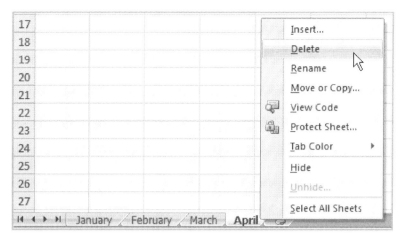

Grouping And Ungrouping Worksheets

A workbook is a multi-page Excel document with several worksheets. A group of worksheets can be created by combining several worksheets. When you group worksheets, you apply the same formulas and formatting to all the worksheets in the group. So, if you group worksheets, any modifications you bring to one will change the rest of the group.

To group contiguous worksheets

- Choose the first sheet you decide to group.
- On your keyboard, press and hold the Shift key.
- Then click the last sheet you decide to group.

- Release the Shift key.
- The sheets are now arranged into groups. The group consists of all sheets between the first and last sheets chosen. For the grouped sheets, the sheet tabs will be white.

- When you make any adjustments to one sheet, the changes will be displayed in all the grouped sheets.

To group noncontiguous sheets

- Choose the first sheet you decide to group.
- On your keyboard, press and hold the Ctrl key.
- Then click the next sheet you decide to group.
- Keep clicking the sheets you want to group.
- Release the Ctrl key.
- The sheets have now been grouped. For the grouped sheets, the sheet tabs will be white. Only the sheets you've chosen are included in the group.
- When you modify any one sheet, the changes will be displayed in all the grouped sheets.

To ungroup worksheets

206

- Select one of the sheets by right-clicking it.
- From the list, select Ungroup.

Copy Data Between Sheets

If you want to copy the contents from one worksheet to another, you can use Excel commands to copy the current worksheet.

Select Move or Transfer from the worksheet menu after right-clicking the worksheet you intend to copy.

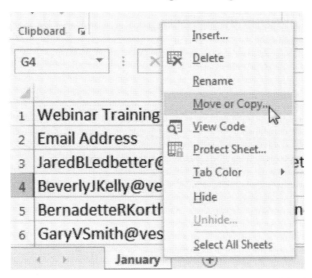

The dialog box "Move / Copy" will appear. In the Before sheet section, specify where your sheet should appear. In this case, you'll transfer the worksheet to the right of your current worksheet (move to the end).

Select Create a copy from the drop-down menu, then press OK.

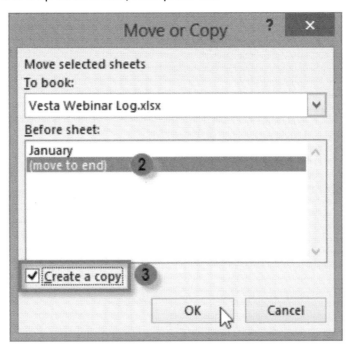

A copy of the worksheet will be created. It will have a similar name and version number to the actual worksheet. Since you copied a January worksheet in your case, the new worksheet is called January (2). The worksheet January (2) has been copied with all the material from the original January worksheet.

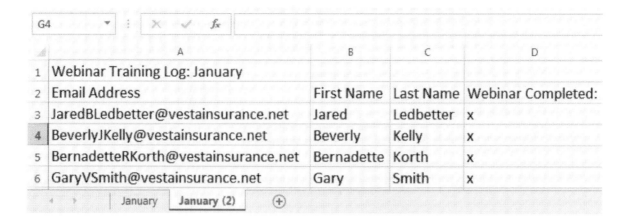

A worksheet can also be copied to a separate workbook. You can choose any accessible workbook from the workbook drop-down menu.

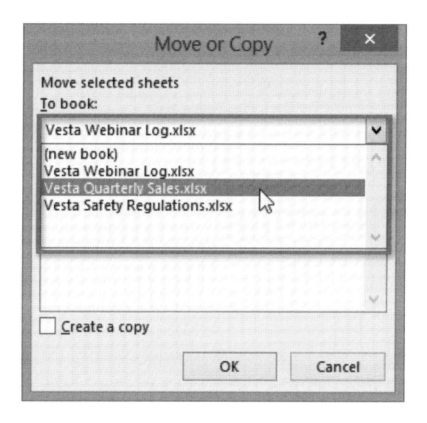

Freeze Panes

Rows, panes, and columns in Excel can be frozen to retain their view and content. Simply select the option for freezing panes in the **View** tab and select the desired option.

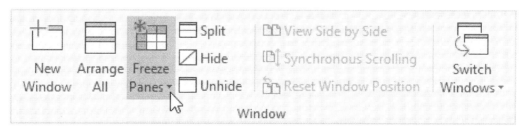

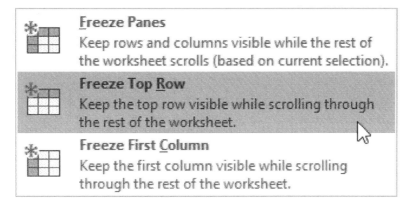

Importing Data

Data Importation from Different Sources in Workbook

- Go to Data and click Get Data from a Data tab.
- Then choose Workbook from the File menu.

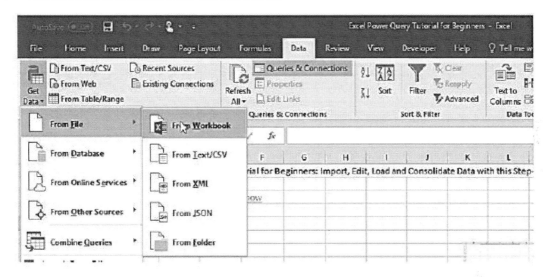

- Find the Workbook in the Import Data dialog box and double-click it.

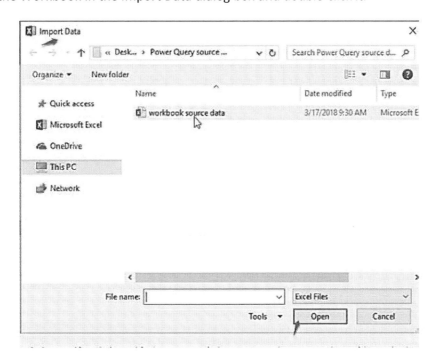

Data Import out of a CSV File

- Go over to Data and click Get Data from a Data tab.
- Then pick Text/CVS from the File menu.

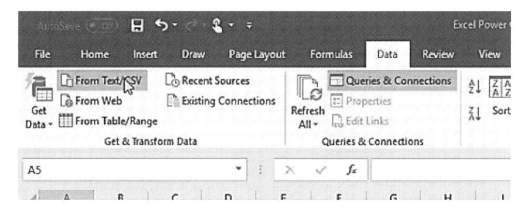

Data Import from Text File

- Go over to Data and click Get Data from the Data tab.
- Then pick Text/CVS from the File menu.

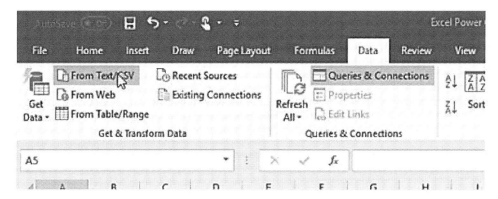

Conditional Formatting

Defining the Conditional Formatting to be Applied

- First, highlight the ranges of the cell to which the rule will be applied
- Select the menu for **Conditional Formatting** in the **Home** tab

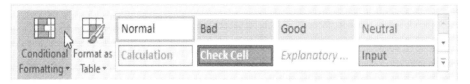

- Select any rule as suitable for your data

Implementing the Conditional Formatting Rule for Graphics

The Data Bars

- Highlight the cells where the formatting rule will be applied. Ensure not to highlight cells for summing operation.
- Navigate to the **Conditional Formatting** menu and select the option for **Data Bars**

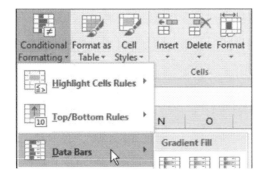

- Select the desired fill for your bar

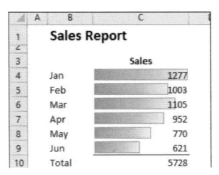

The Scales for Color

- Highlight the cells where the formatting rule will be applied
- Navigate to the **Conditional Formatting** menu and select the option for scales for color

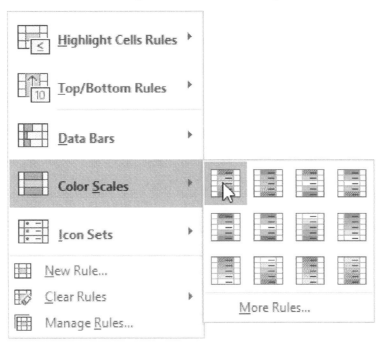

- Select the desired fill for your scale

The Sets of Icon

- Highlight the cells where the formatting rule will be applied
- Navigate to the **Conditional Formatting** menu and select the option for scales for color

- Select the desired icon for your data

Defining Formula Formatting Rules

Formulas can be defined for conditional formatting by selecting the **New Rule** option in the **Conditional Formatting** menu.

Relative and Absolute Cell References

- **Relative:** This method of referencing cells causes a change in the formatting with reference to the location of the row or column. It is defined without the dollar sign, e.g.: B1.

- **Absolute:** This method of referencing cells does not cause a change in the cell formatting with reference to the location of the row or column. It is defined with the dollar sign, e.g.: $B1.

Examples Of Formulas In Conditional Formatting

Formula to Select Weekends

- Highlight the cells where the formatting rule will be applied, usually a date data
- Navigate to the **New Rule** option in the **Conditional Formatting** menu

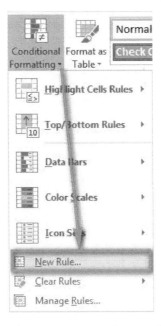

- In the resulting dialogue box, select the option to implement formulas for cell formatting
- Type in this formula with respect to the cell ranges highlighted:

=WEEKDAY(C3,2)>5

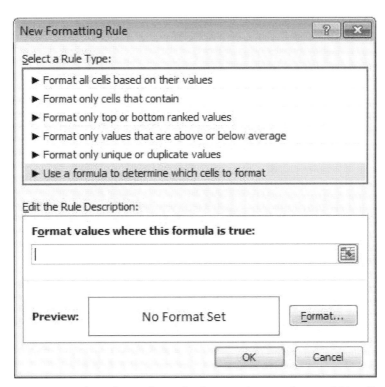

- Select the **Format** option and configure how the formatting results would be displayed

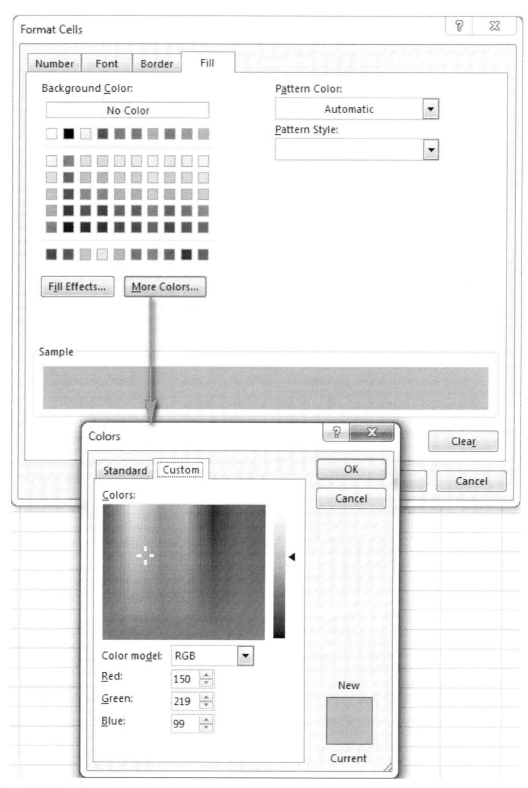

- Select **OK** when done

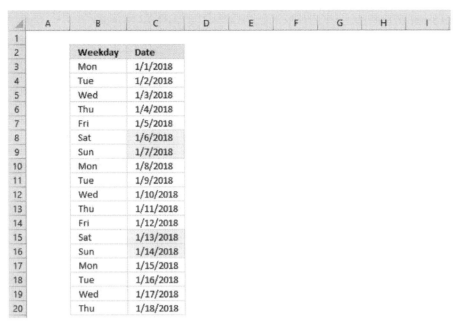

Selecting Rows Depending on Values

- Select the option to implement formulas for cell formatting in the **New Rule** dialogue box
- Type in this formula with respect to the cell ranges highlighted:

=$C2="Bob"

- Select the **Format** option and configure how the formatting results would be displayed
- Select OK when done

Management Of Rules For Conditional Formatting

Navigate to the option to manage your formatting rules in the **Configuration Formatting** menu. Select the rules to be managed and save accordingly.

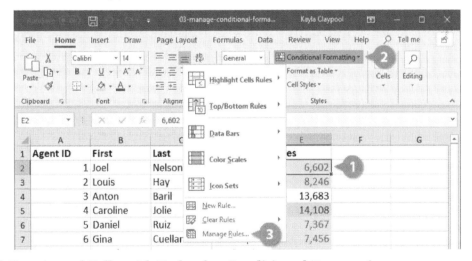

Pasting and Copying of Cells with Rules for Conditional Formatting

- Highlight and copy formatted cells, then select the option to paste the data in a special form

- Select the **Formats** option in the resulting dialogue box and select **OK**

Erasing Conditional Formatting Rules

Navigate to the formatting rules manager and select the rule to be deleted. You can also use the option for clearing rules in the **Conditional Formatting** menu.

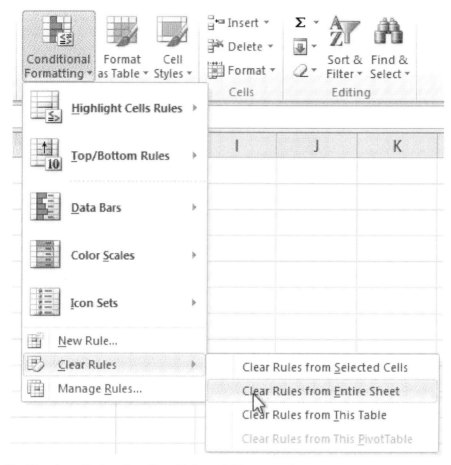

Identifying Cells Having Rules for Conditional Formatting

- Select any cell in your worksheet. You can also select a cell having a particular formatting rule to find that particular rule
- Navigate to the **Go To** option in the **Find** tab which can be found in the **Edit** menu
- Select **Special** and then choose the option for **Conditional formats**

Chapter 3: **Using Formulas**

Learning how to enter formulas into your worksheet is very important. So, you will be learning how to insert formulas in your worksheet using several methods, and they are highlighted below

Simple Insertion: The Simple Insertion method has to do with entering the formula into the cell or Formula Bar. The Formula bar can be seen above the column header. To use the Simple Insertion method,

- Go to the **Formula bar** or click on a cell
- Start typing an equal sign (=), followed by the name of the function, and then press **Enter.**

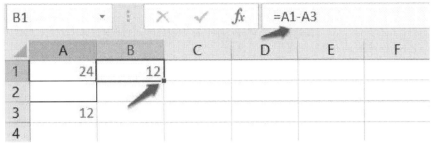

The Insert Function: One of the methods to enter a formula in Excel is the Insert Function command. The Insert Function consists of all functions found in Excel's worksheet. To locate the Insert Function

- Go to the **Formula tab** and click on **Insert Function** in the **Function Library**

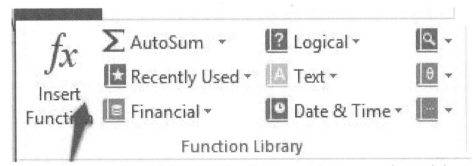

- In the **Insert Function** dialog box, click on any function you wish to use on the worksheet, and then click on **OK.**

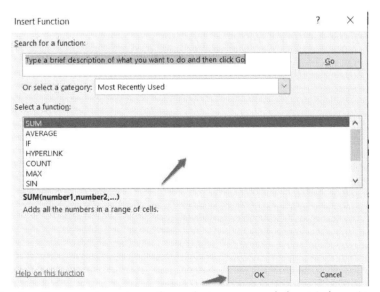

- **Group of Formula:** Another way to enter a formula in your worksheet is by using selecting any formula from the group of formulas in the Function Library group.

The group of formulas includes AutoSum, Recently Used, Financial, Logical, Text, Date & Time, Lookup & Reference, Math & Trig, and More Functions

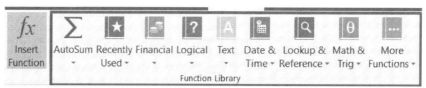

- **AutoSum Option:** This is used for quick and everyday tasks. To use the AutoSum Option, go to the **Formula** tab and click on **Recently Used** in the **Function Library**

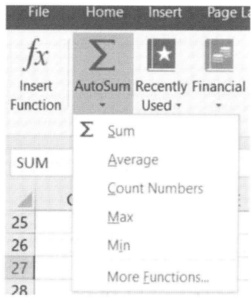

- **Recently Used Tab:** This tab comes in handy when you want to relieve the stress of re-tying your most recent formula. To locate this tab, go to the Formula tab and click on **Recently Used** in the **Function Library**.

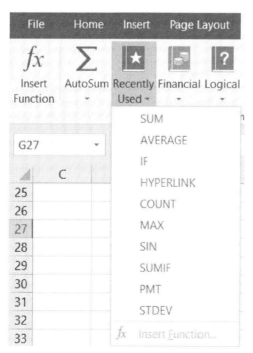

The Excel Formula Bar

The formula bar is located beside the **Name box** at the top of your worksheet, just at the base of the ribbon menu. It is used for entering or editing cell contents and formulas. The formula bar can be hidden and displayed as a user wishes. These steps should be followed to hide or display the formula bar:

- Navigate to the **View** menu
- Select the box labeled **Formula bar** to either hide or display the bar

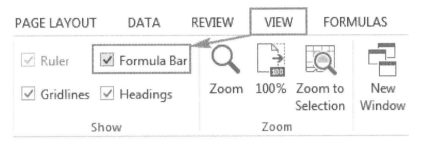

Increasing the Size of the Formula Bar

When dealing with advanced and extremely long formulas, it could be necessary to increase the size of the formula bar to aid the visualization of the typed formula.

To increase the size of the formula bar:

- Set your cursor on the lower edge of the bar for the adjustment cursor to be displayed

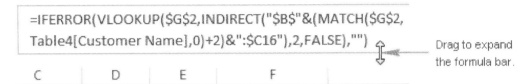

- Drag down your mouse to increase the size of the bar

These same steps can also be followed to reduce the bar's size; simply drag up your mouse instead.

Keyboard keys **Ctrl + Shift + U** can be used as a shortcut to both increase and decrease the size of the formula bar. The vertical and horizontal expansion buttons can be implemented as well.

The formula bar has the following parts:

- The input space

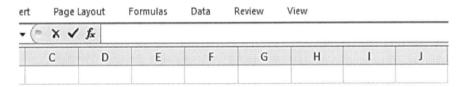

- Button for vertical expansion

- The **Cancel** and **Enter** button

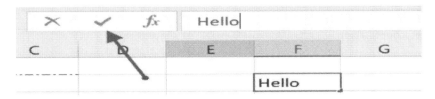

- Button for inserting functions

219

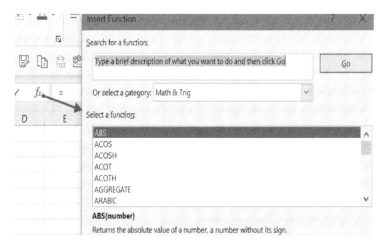

Getting Familiar With Excel Functions And Formulas

Basics of Formulas in Excel

Implementing Operators in Your Formulas

Adding operators in your Excel operations makes Excel aware of what you wish to be done. One or more operators can be added in an expression.

Operators in Excel are of the following category:

Operators for Arithmetic Operations

+ represents **Addition** operation.

Example: **=A9+B4**

- represents **Subtraction** operation

Example: **=A6–A21** or **–C17**

* represents **Multiplication** operation

Example: **=A21*B33**

/ represents **Division** operation

Example: **=B39/A20**

% represents **Percent** operation, i.e. division of numbers by 100.

Example: **=B34%**

^ represents **Exponentiation** operation

Example: **C16^7**

Operators for Comparison Operations

These operators are used when checking for a condition. These results are usually either TRUE or FALSE. The comparison operators include:

= represents "**Equal to**".

Example: **=A7=B31**

> represents "**Greater than**"

Example: =B36>A20

< represents "**Less than**"

Example: **=A2<D12**

>= **represents** "Greater than or equal to**".**

Example: **=B3>=A20**

<= **represents** "Less than or equal to**".**

Example: **=A12<=B23**

<> represents "**Not equal to**"

Example: **=A22<>B13**

Operator for Text Operations

The ampersand symbol (&) is used when combining two or more different texts in different cells to give one text or sentence.

Example: **=A32&" "&B31**. This operation is referred to as **Concatenation.**

Operator for Reference Operations

The **Colon** symbol (:) represents the **Range** operator for references cell ranges.

Example: =SUM(C14:D37)

The reference and range operators also include:

The **Comma** (,) symbol represents the **Union** operator. It brings numerous cell ranges into one.

Example: =SUM(A12,C4:D27,B13)

A **Space** represents an operator for **Intersection** that produces a cell reference in similarity with two references.

Example: =SUM(C13:C16 C13:E16)

Precedence of Operators in Excel Formulas

When your Excel formula or expression is built from multiple operators, Excel employs an order of precedence in dealing with such. Starting from the left direction, the precedence of operators in Excel is as follows:

- Negation
- Percent
- Exponentiation
- Division and Multiplication
- Subtraction and Addition
- Concatenation
- Comparison operations

Adding Functions To Formulas

Sample Formulas that Implement Functions

Formulas are expressions that carry out operations on the data in cells. They employ operators for their operations. Functions, however, are predefined expressions. They are used to carry out quick operations, letting you avoid the task of spelling out long formulas or repeating operators.

Common Excel Functions

- **SUM**

This gives the summation of the indicated cell range. E.g. **=SUM(E14:E28)**

- **MIN**

This gives the minimum number in the indicated cell range. E.g. **=MIN(E14:E28)**

- **MAX**

This gives the maximum number of the indicated cell range. E.g. **=MAX(E14:E28)**

- **AVERAGE**

This calculates and gives the average of the indicated cell range. E.g. **=AVERAGE(E14:E28)**

- **COUNT**

This gives the number of cells indicated in a cell range. E.g. **=COUNT(E14:E28)**

- **LEN**

This function calculates how many characters are present in a string. E.g. **=LEN(B27)**

- **SUMIF**

This function carries out an addition operation only if the stated condition is satisfied. E.g. **=SUMIF(D24:D28,">=900",C14:C28)**

- **AVERAGEIF**

This function carries out an averaging operation only if the stated condition is satisfied. E.g. **=AVERAGEIF(F24:F38,"No",E14:E18)**

- **DAYS**

This function gives the days' number present between dates. E.g. **=DAYS(D24,C24)**

- **NOW**

This function gives the present time and date of your device. E.g. **=NOW()**

String or Text Functions

- **LEFT**

This function gives the indicated characters present from the left of a text. E.g. **=LEFT("WISDOM",3)** gives **WIS**

- **RIGHT**

This function gives the indicated characters present from the right of a text. E.g. **=RIGHT("WISDOM",3)** gives **DOM**

- **MID**

This function gives the indicated characters present from the middle of a text. E.g. **=MIS("WISDOM",2,3)** gives **ISDO**

- **ISTEXT**

This function checks if the indicated value is a text and gives a result of either False or True. E.g. **=ISTEXT("WISDOM1")**

- **UPPER**

This function converts texts in lowercase to capital letters. E.g. **=UPPER(B12)**

Time and Date Functions

- **DATE**

This gives the particular number that represents the date in an entry. E.g. **=DATE(2022,9,12)**

- **MONTH**

This gives the particular number that represents the month in a date entry. E.g. **=MONTH("2022/9/12")**

- **YEAR**

This gives the particular number that represents the year in a date entry. E.g. **=YEAR("2022/9/12")**

- **MINUTE**

This gives the value representing minute in a time entry. E.g. **=MINUTE("9:31")**

Arguments in Functions

Arguments are used by functions for carrying out their operations. They are the values present in functions. Arguments in functions can also be singular: **UPPER(B12)**, or multiple: **SUM(C13:C16 C13:E16)**. The function **=SUM(E14, E15, E16)** has the following arguments:

E14, E15, E16

Some Excel functions do not require arguments, such as **TODAY()** and **NOW()**.

How To Insert Formulas In Worksheets

Inserting Formulas Manually

You can manually insert formulas in your worksheet by selecting the cell where you want the results to be shown, and then entering the formula. For example, to perform an addition operation on cells A21 and B21, with the result displayed in cell C21:

- Select cell **C21**
- Type in the formula **=A21+B21**
- Press the **Enter** key

Inserting Formulas by Pointing

You can also select the individual cells to create your formula.

- In cell **C21**, type the equality sign "="
- Select cell **A21**
- Type the summation symbol "+" in **C21**
- Select cell **B21**
- Press the **Enter** key

Inserting Name of Ranges in Formulas

- Highlight the cell where the name of the range would appear
- On the ribbon menu, select the **Formula** tab
- Navigate to the option to select what you can use in your formula and select the choice to paste desired names

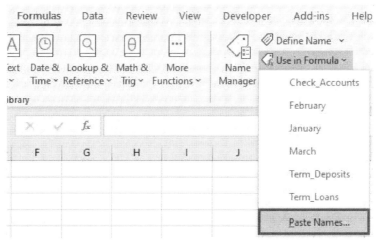

- Pick from the existing name of ranges and click the **OK** button

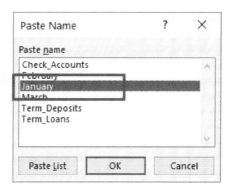

- Also, press the **Enter** key on your keyboard

Adding Functions to Formulas

- Navigate to the **Home** tab and select the drop-down icon on the AutoSum button
- You can also click to view additional available functions

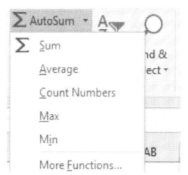

- Navigating to the **Formulas** tab and selecting the option to enter a function can be used. This action brings up the dialogue box for inserting formulas.

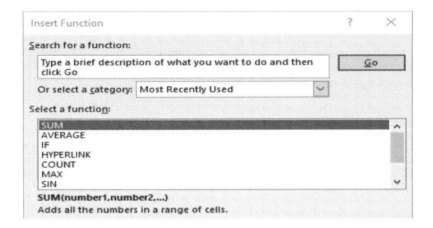

- Any option from the **Library of Functions** group can be used

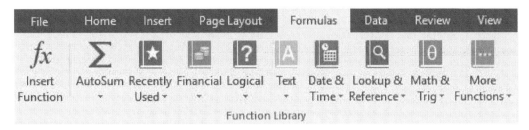

Pointers for Inserting Excel Functions

- Ensure the cell where you want the function result to appear is first highlighted
- Add brackets to your formulas or functions to indicate which should be first executed
- When writing complex and long functions, start the different sections of the function on a new line
- The handle for filling can be used to duplicate formulas and functions across multiple cells
- Keyboard keys **ALT + =** can be used to automatically sum up cell values:
- Highlight the cell where the result would be displayed
- Hold down the **Alt** key, type in **+,** and then **=**

Changing Formulas In Excel

- Select the cell where the formula was implemented
- Use the bar for formulas to then edit the formula

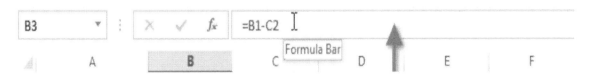

- You can also double-click on the cell itself to edit the formula

Referencing Cells In Formulas

Relative Cell Referencing

This type of cell referencing changes with the location of the cell. For instance, if you copy the formula **B2*D2** to another row, say row 14, the formula changes to **B14*B14**. The relative cell referencing for formulas can be copied and implemented using the drag and fill procedure.

Absolute Cell Referencing

Here, the cell reference remains constant, regardless of the location. They are indicated by adding the sign of dollar (**$**) in formulas. E.g. =**$B$3*$C$3*$E$1**

Mixed Cell Referencing

This cell referencing includes both the relative and absolute cell references. An example is **=(B3*C3)*$E$1** where the value in cell E1 remains constant. They can be used to reference cells where values such as discount, tax, etc. are entered.

Switching between Reference Types

The **F4** key on your keyboard can be used to alternate the types of cell references.

Referencing Cells in Other Worksheets

- Navigate to the cell to be referenced
- Take note of the worksheet name and the cell number
- Open the worksheet where the referencing is to be done
- Select the cell where the referencing result would be displayed
- Type in a formula in this format =**'Worksheet_Name'!Cell_Number**. E.g. = **'Wisdom'!D2**
- Press the **Enter** key

A change of name of the referenced worksheet results in an automatic update of the formula.

Referencing Cells in Other Workbooks

- Type in a formula in this format in the cell where the referencing result would appear

[Name_of_Workbook]Name_of_Worksheet!Cell_address

- **E.g** [Wisdom.xlsx]Writers!B2
- Press the **Enter** key

Implementing Formulas In Excel Tables

Summarizing Table Data

The **UNIQUE** and **SUMIF** functions are used to create a summary data table. The UNIQUE function works by indicating a range of cells from your dataset.

E.g =UNIQUE(A12:A21)

After this list is done, the SUMIF function is then introduced to fill the list created with the UNIQUE function. The **Spill Operator** is used with the SUMIF function to create an array that is dynamic.

E.g. =SUMIFS($C$12:$C$21,A$12:$A$21,E7#)

Implementing Formulas in Tables

- Select the table cell where the formula would be implemented
- Type in =**[**
- This brings up the list of available columns that can be included in your formulas

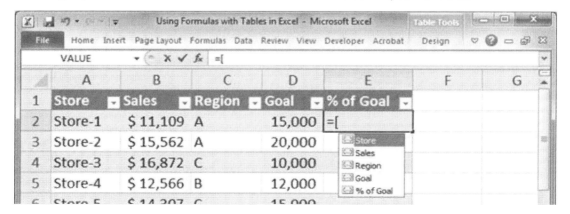

- Insert the @ symbol to indicate a reference to only the present row
- End the formula with] and press **Enter**

An example of a table formula is as follows: **=[@ Wisdom*@Writers]**

Using Functions

Count

The COUNT function This counts the number of cells that have a number value in them.

The COUNT function uses the following arguments

COUNT(value1, [value2], …)

With the range of cells provided below, use the COUNT function to find the number of cells with numerical values in them

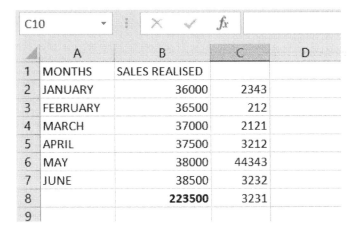

To find the cells with number values using the COUNT function, follow the steps provided below

- Select an empty cell **C8** and enter the function with the cell range in it; **= COUNT (A1:C8)**

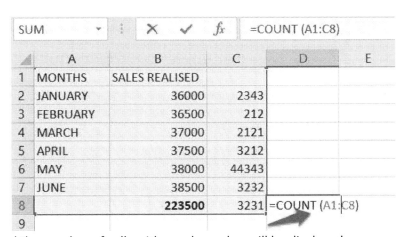

- Press **Enter** and the number of cells with number value will be displayed.

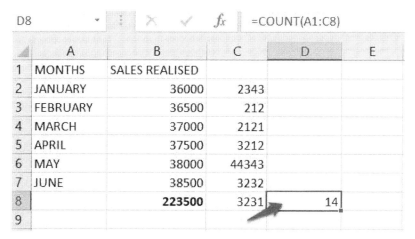

Counting All Data Types Using the COUNTA

The COUNTA function does not only count the number of cells with numbers in them, it counts the dates, time, strings, logical values, empty strings, or text.2

The COUNTA function uses the arguments below

COUNTA(value1, [value2], …)

Using the data given below, use the COUNTA function to find the number of cells containing data in them.

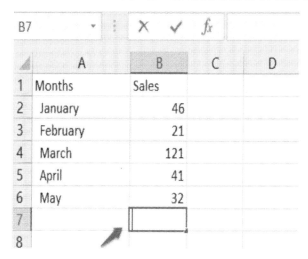

- Select an empty cell **D7** and enter the function with the cell range in it; = **COUNTA (A1:C6)**

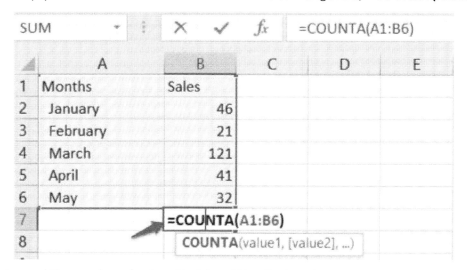

- Press **Enter** and the number of cells with data will be displayed.

228

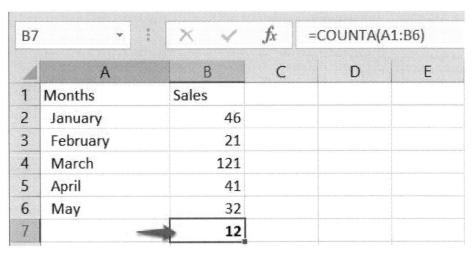

Counting Blank Spaces Using COUNTBLANK

The COUNTBLANK function returns the numbers of empty cells in a range of cells, and the COUNTBLANK function has just an argument

COUNTBLANK(range)

With the data below, find the number of empty cells with the range of cells using the COUNTBLANK function

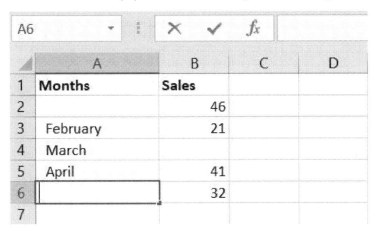

- Select an empty cell **D7** and enter the function with the cell range in it; = **COUNTBLANK (A1:C6)**

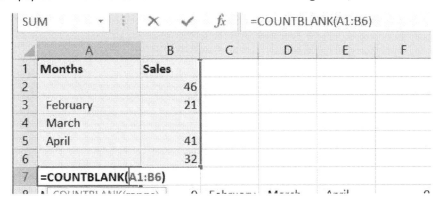

- Press **Enter** and the number of cells without data will be displayed.

CountIF

Formula: = COUNTIF (D5 ratio D12," is greater or equal than 21")

Conditional functions are used effectively in these two developed formulas. All cells that need specific criteria are included in SUMIF, and all cells that need measures are counted in COUNTIF. For example, suppose you may want to figure out how many containers of champagne you need for a client event by counting all cells that are larger than or equivalent to 21 (the minimum consumption age in the United States). As seen in the screenshot given below, COUNTIF may be used as an advanced approach.

Auto Sum

The AutoSum command incorporates the most common functions, such as AVERAGE, SUM, MIN, COUNT, and MAX, into your formula automatically. A function has been created using the SUM function to measure the total cost for a list of recently purchased goods in the example below.

- Choose the cell where the function will be placed.
- Click the arrow next to the AutoSum command in the Editing group on the Home page and select the desired function from the drop-down list. Select Sum for this case.

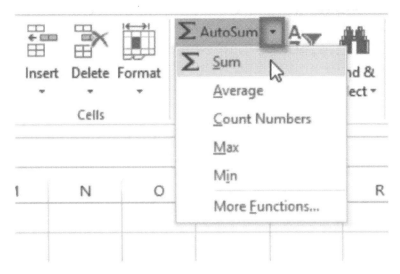

- The cell will display the chosen function. The AutoSum command will choose a cell range for the argument if it is located logically. You can also type the required cell range into the argument manually.

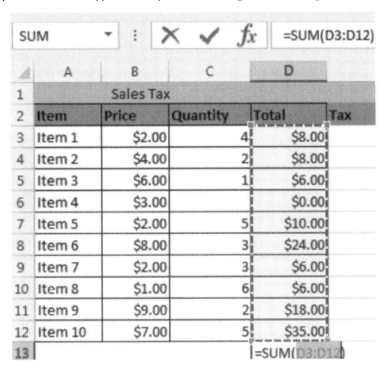

On the keyboard, press Enter.

Average

The **AVERAGE** function is used in determining the average point of a given data of a selected cell or a cell range. Let us take the below table as an instance by using the AVERAGE to estimate the average point score of the four students in three subjects. This is the structure of the AVERAGE function, =**AVERAGE(cell range).**

E4	▼	⋮	×	✓	*fx*	=AVERAGE(B4:D4)

⊿	A	B	C	D	E	F
2						
3		English	Maths	French	Average	
4	Alpha	80	50	60	63.33333	
5	Burney	70	50	40	53.33333	
6	Daves	40	80	90	70	
7	Hart	60	38	65	54.33333	

Excel exempts empty cells in the cell range during counting, but it regards zero (0) as part of the range and therefore computes for zero (0).

Max & Min

LARGE and SMALL is used to compare which value is largest and which one is smallest within a given range, let us take for instance, the total number of the bag sold in the market.

- 100: maximum bag sold in one month in the market (**MAX**).
- 8: the least bag sold in one month in the market **(MIN)**.
- 93: the second maximum bag sold in one month in the market (**LARGE**).
- 10: the second least bag sold in one month in the market **(SMALL)**.

D8	▼	⋮	×	✓	*fx*	=LARGE(B3:E6, 2)

⊿	A	B	C	D	E	F	G
1							
2	Market	February	March	April	May	Total	Rank
3	Lhasa	50	100	40	70	260	1
4	Slovalaa	10	60	88	80	238	3
5	Moorish	90	50	75	30	245	2
6	Qatar	8	30	93	20	151	4
7		MAX	MIN	LARGE	SMALL		
8		100	8	93	10		

While you are having LARGE and SMALL, you may still at times have to use MAX and MIN. Let us check the use of the four functions in a jiffy with the above worksheet as an example:

- **MIN:** it gives you the least number or value of the bags sold in the market throughout the whole four months with a given range of =**MIN(B3:E6).**
- **MAX:** it gives the largest number or the values of the bags sold in the market throughout the four months with a given range of: =MAX(B3:E6).
- **SMALL:** it gives you the nth position of the smallest value in the list. It will have two arguments, the first argument is the cell range and the second argument is the position of the nth lower value, which maybe 2nd or 3rd position, and the formula will be in a structure like this =**SMALL(B3:E6, 2) or =SMALL(B3:E6, 3)** depending on the nth position.
- **LARGE:** it will give you the nth position of the largest value in the list. It will have two arguments as well, which are the cell range and nth position either 2nd or 3rd and the formula will be structured like this: =**LARGE(B3:E6, 2) or =LARGE(B3:E6, 3).**

- **RANK:** it ranks the list of the data; the RANK function has three-arguments which are as follows:

	A	B	C	D	E	F	G
						=RANK(F5,F3:F6,0)	
1							
2	Market	February	March	April	May	Total	Rank
3	Lhasa	50	100	40	70	260	1
4	Slovalaa	10	60	88	80	238	3
5	Moorish	90	50	75	30	245	2
6	Qatar	8	30	93	20	151	4
7		MAX	MIN	LARGE	SMALL		
8		100	8	93	10		

Using cell G5, second-ranking

- The cell address with the value you are using for ranking. F5=245
- The cell range with which you will match the value in deciding the ranking, F3:F6
- The order of ranking, 0 for descending order, up to down, while 1 is for ascending order, down to up). 0

IF Function

The IF function is the most recognized used function for analytical comparison between a particular value and your expectation. True return means your expectation is right and if it is otherwise, then your expectation is wrong.

For instance, =IF(D1=8, "True", "False"), It means IF D1=8, then it's True, but if otherwise, return False.

	A	B	C	D	E	F
					=IF(D1=8,"true","False")	
1				8	true	

You can use the IF function to estimate text and values, it is called nest IFfunction, let us buttress more on the illustration below. IF(A4>B4," surplus" ", deficit").

	A	B	C	D	E	F	
					=IF(A4>B4, "Surplus","Deficit")		
1	Income	Expenses	Difference	status			
2	400	300	100	Surplus			
3	600	800	-200	Deficit			
4	500	400	100	Surplus			
5	900	899	1	Surplus			

The above illustration is saying IF(A4>B4, then return surplus, IF otherwise return deficit).

VLOOKUP

The VLOOKUP feature in Excel allows you to look up a specific piece of data in a table or data collection and retrieve the associated data/information. In plain English, the VLOOKUP feature tells Excel to 'look for this piece of information (e.g., bananas) in this data collection (a table) and tell me any corresponding information about it (e.g., banana price)."

The formula is:

=VLOOKUP (lookup value, table array, col index num, [range lookup])

To put it another way, the formula says, "Find this piece of information in the following field and send me some matching details from another column." The following arguments are passed to the VLOOKUP function:

- Lookup value (necessary argument)—Lookup value defines the value in the first column of a table that we want to look up.
- Table array (necessary argument)—The table array represents the data array to be scanned. The VLOOKUP feature looks in the array's left-most column.
- Col index num (necessary argument)—This is an integer that specifies the column number of the supplied table array from which a value should be returned.
- Range lookup (selectable argument)—This specifies what this feature can return if it cannot locate an exact match for the lookup value. The value of the statement may be TRUE or FALSE, which means:

TRUE—Estimated match, which means that the nearest match below the lookup value is used if an exact match cannot be sought.

FALSE—Exact match; if an exact match is not detected, an error would be returned.

Chapter 4: **Types of Data**

ext, value, and formula data are the three categories of data in Excel. This is the kind of information you put into cells. If Excel recognizes the submission as a formula, the formula would be calculated and the outcome shown in the cell. When the cell is involved, you could see the formula inside the Formula Bar.

If Excel senses that it isn't a calculation, it determines if it is text or meaning. The text inputs are oriented to the cell's left edge. Right-hand values are matched.

This information is essential to ensure that you are entering data correctly and that Excel 2021 recognizes your entries as the correct data sort.

Text Data

Text entries are all pieces of information that Excel can't define as a formula or a meaning. The majority of the text entries are labeled. Row and column labels are the titles of the rows and columns.

If Excel categorizes the data as text, the text would always be offset to the left side of the cell.

Values

Values are the fundamental components of all formulas you join. Values are figures that describe amounts as well as dates.

The cell's values are matched on the right edge.

Excel can say the values you apply as formula are values if it can't solve them.

Formulas

A formula in Excel is just an equation, which conducts a calculation. This may be as easy as 3 + 5 or as complicated as $(3+5)16 \div 3x$. You may do calculations in a solo cell, a series of cells (blocks), or even a set of cells through several worksheets. A chosen block or community of cells or blocks is referred to as a set of cells. Don't panic if this is all a little overwhelming right now. It will quickly become clear.

For the time being, note that every formula you enter into Excel must begin with an equality symbol: =. This can seem odd initially since an equality symbol typically appears after a mathematical equation, but it informs Excel that you would like to run a measurement right away. When the user wants to insert a formula to Excel, always begin using the equality sign, as seen below:

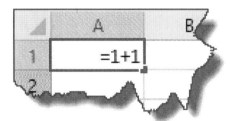

Press Enter or even the arrow key after you has inserted it into your cell to move to a different cell.

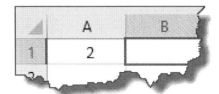

Excel completes the equation and shows the result in the appropriate cell.

Your formula will then appear in your Formula Bar if you click on the cell.

Cell Referencing

Excel references cells using an absolute or relative reference, or both. For instance,

- **= C4*D1**, is referred to a relative referencing because it refers to a certain location by one cell to the left or three cells up the row.

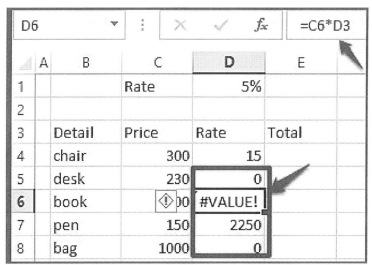

- And thus, if you decide to copy down the formula using Autofill, you will be getting an error notice, because each cell you copy will still be referring to one cell to the left and three cells up the row. In this case, it is either it will give you the wrong answer or give you an error because that D1 should apply to all formulas in that column. For instance, three cells above the row; in this case, it's a text (Rate), in the case of cell D6 =C6*D3, D3 is a text and it is because the formula is relative referencing.

- In such a scenario like this, we will make use of absolute referencing by making D1 fixed to this location for all the rows, do this simply by highlighting it and press **F4** to switch between relative and absolute cell referencing.

- Then, you can lock the column, row, and both; but in this scenario, we will keep cell D1 locked, then, if you copy it down now, it will copy the right formulas for each cell.

Note: Anytime you copy a formula, make sure you set the relative or absolute referencing appropriately in respect of how the formula will be applied to the data.

Chapter 5: **Charts**

Adding Charts

After entering your data, navigate to the **Insert** menu and select the option for **Charts.** Here, you can select any chart type that is suitable for your data by clicking on the option to view all available chart types.

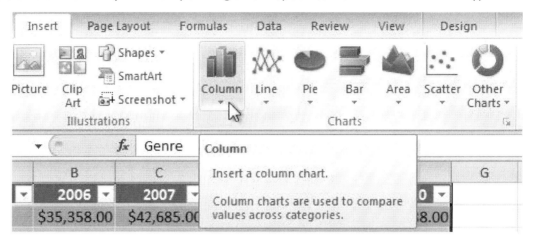

Interchanging Rows and Columns in Charts

Click on the chart and select the option to switch the row and column on the **Design** menu

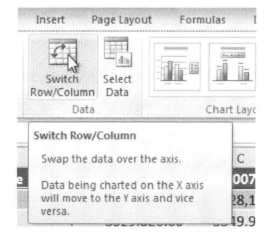

Inserting Chart Layouts

Select a chart layout from the chart group or click on the drop-down icon for **More** in the chart menu to access additional options for chart layouts.

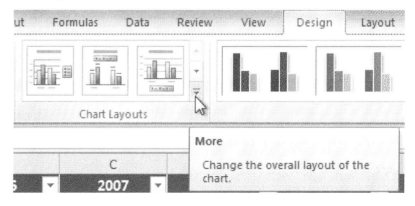

Changing Chart Styles

While in the **Design** menu, the group for **Chart Styles** can be selected from. Likewise, the drop-down icon to view more options can be selected.

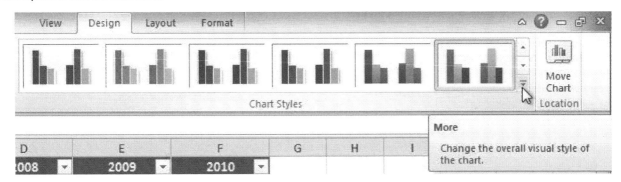

Including and Removing Chart Elements

- Select the chart and click on the **+** icon

Tick any box to include any chart element and untick a box to remove the element

Formatting Charts

Chart Elements

Introducing chart elements to your graph or chart will modify it by including context or simplifying data. While using the Add Chart Element dropdown menu in the upper left section (below the Home tab), you can choose a chart element.

To Display or Hide Axes

Click Axes. Excel will automatically pull the column and row headers from the defined cell range to present both horizontal and vertical axes on your chart. Below the axis,

there is a checkmark next to Primary Horizontal and Primary Vertical.

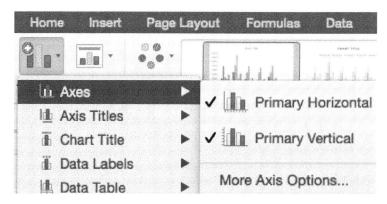

To make your chart's display axis disappear, uncheck these options. The year labels on the horizontal axis of your map will be removed if you choose Primary Horizontal.

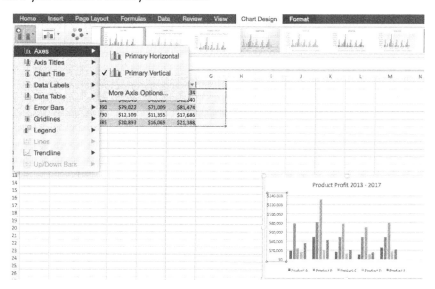

From the Axes dropdown menu, select More Axis Option to open a window with additional text and formatting options, such as adding labels, tick marks or numbers, or changing text size and color.

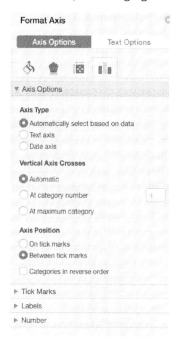

To Add Axis Titles:

Choose the Axis Titles from the dropdown menu of Add Chart Element. Since Axis Titles are not automatically added to charts in Excel, both Primary Horizontal and Primary Vertical will be unmarked.

240

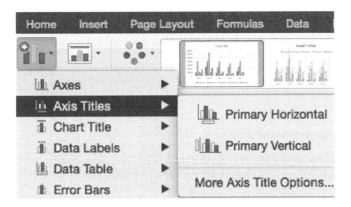

A text box will display on the chart when you select Primary Horizontal or Primary Vertical to create axis titles. In this example, we selected both. Type the titles to your axis. In this example, we give the titles "Profit" for vertical and "Year" for horizontal.

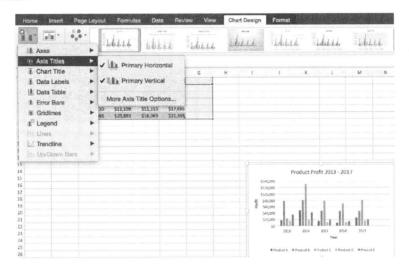

To Remove or Move Chart Title:

Select Chart Title from the Add Chart Element drop-down menu. Above Chart, None, Centered Overlay, and More Title Choices are the four options you'll see.

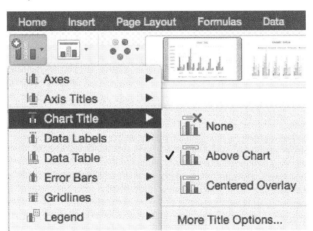

To place the title above the chart, click Above Chart. When you create a chart title, Excel will automatically set it above the chart.

To remove the chart title, click none.

To place the title inside the chart's gridlines, choose Centered Overlay. Use this option carefully; you don't want the title to hide your data or clutter up your graph.

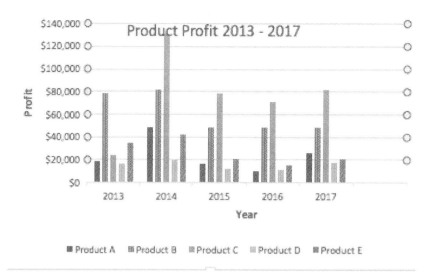

To Add Data Labels:

Select Data Labels from the Add Chart Element menu. For data labels, there are six options: Center, Inside End, None (default), Outside End, Inside Base, and More Data Label Title Options.

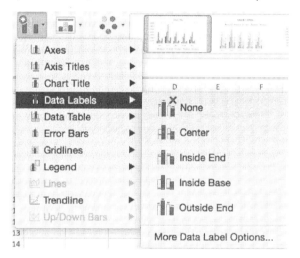

Each of the four choices will apply unique labels to each data point in your chart. Select your required option. If you have a small amount of precise data or a lot of empty space in your chart, this customization can be very useful. Adding data labels to a clustered column chart, on the other hand, will appear cluttered. For instance, if you choose Center data labels it will present like this:

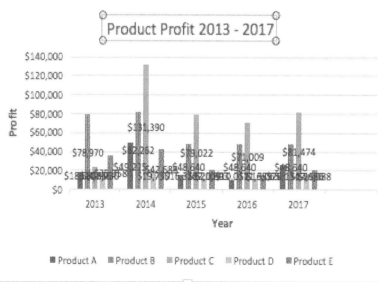

242

To Add a Data Table:

Select Data Table from the Add Chart Element menu. By selecting More Data Table Options, you can access three pre-formatted options with an extended menu.

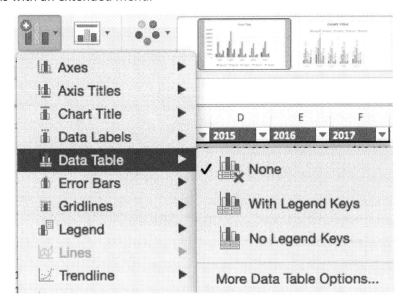

'Legend keys' show the data set by displaying the data table below the chart. The color-coded legend will also be added.

'None' is the default setting, where the data table is not recreated within the chart.

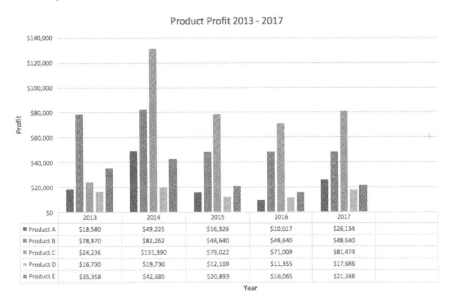

'No legend keys' also show the data table below the chart but without the legend.

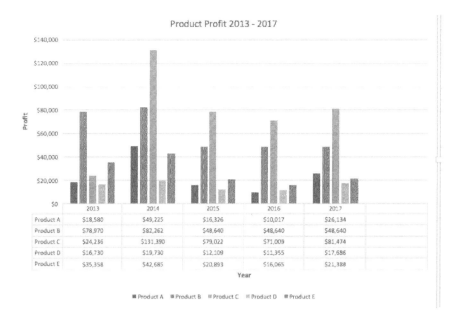

Product Profit 2013 - 2017

	2013	2014	2015	2016	2017
Product A	$18,580	$49,225	$16,326	$10,017	$26,134
Product B	$78,970	$82,262	$48,640	$48,640	$48,640
Product C	$24,236	$131,390	$79,022	$71,009	$81,474
Product D	$16,730	$19,730	$12,109	$11,355	$17,686
Product E	$35,358	$42,685	$20,893	$16,065	$21,388

■ Product A   ■ Product B   ■ Product C   ■ Product D   ■ Product E

Note: If you want to add a data table, you'll probably need to expand your chart to make space for it. To resize your chart, simply click the corner and drag it to the required size.

To Add Error Bars:

Select Error Bars from the Add Chart Element menu. There are four options in addition to More Error Bars Options: Standard Error, None (default), Standard Deviation, and 5% (Percentage). Adding error bars provides a visual representation of the possible error in the displayed data using specific standard equations for segregating error,.

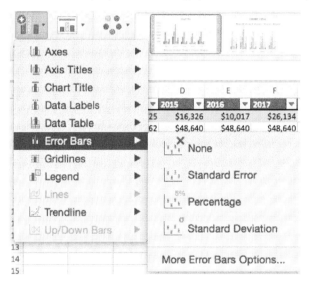

For instance, when we select Standard Error from the options, we obtain a chart similar to the one shown below.

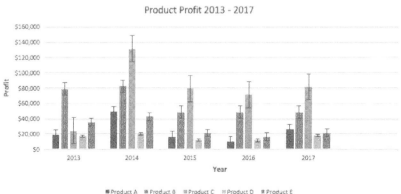

244

To Add Gridlines:

Select Gridlines from the Add Chart Element menu. There are four options in addition to More Grid Line Options:

Primary Major Vertical, Primary Major Horizontal, Primary Minor Vertical, and Primary Minor Horizontal. Excel will automatically add up Primary Major Horizontal gridlines for a column chart.

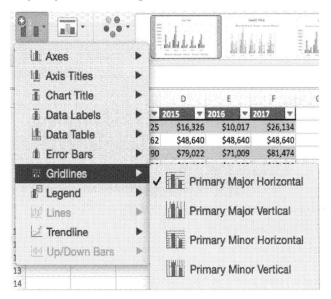

By clicking the options, you can choose different gridlines. For instance, when we select all four gridline options, our chart looks like this.

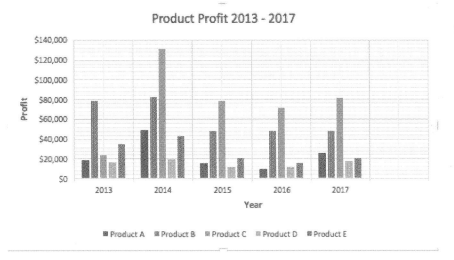

To Add a Legend:

Select Legend from the Add Chart Element drop-down menu. There are five legend placement options in addition to More Legend Options: Right, None, Top, Bottom, and Left.

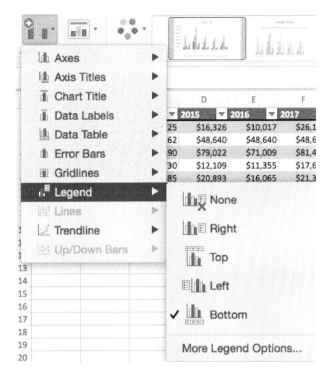

Legend placement will rely on the format and style of your chart. Select the option that best suits your needs. When we select the Right legend placement, our chart looks like.

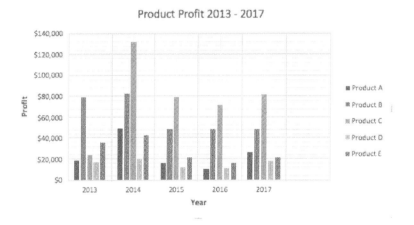

To Add Lines:

For clustered column charts, lines aren't available. But, in other chart forms where you compare two variables, you can add lines (e.g., reference, target, average, etc.,) to the chart by implementing the required option.

To Add a Trendline:

Select Trendline from the Add Chart Element drop-down menu. There are five options in addition to More Trendline Options: Exponential, None (default), Linear, Moving Average, and Linear Forecast. For your data set, select the required option. We'll use the Linear option in this example.

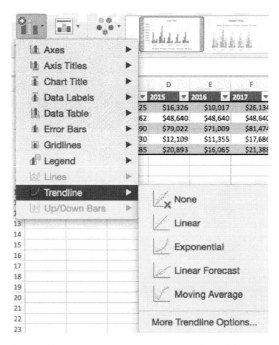

Excel will make a trendline for each product because we compare five different products over time. Click Product A and then click the blue OK button to create a linear trendline for it.

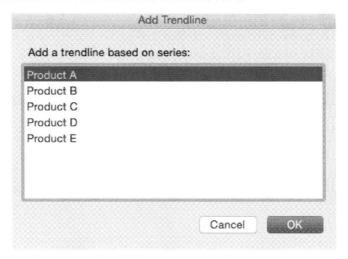

A dotted trendline will appear on the chart to display Product A's linear progression. Linear (Product A) has also been added to the legend in Excel.

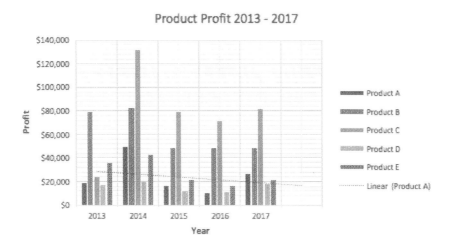

Double-click the trendline to show the trendline model on your chart. On the right side of your screen. A Format Trendline preview will appear on your screen's right side. At the bottom of the window, click the box next to Display equation on the chart. The equation is now visible on your chart.

Note: You can make as many separate trendlines as you like for each variable in your chart. Here's an example chart with trendlines for Products A and C.

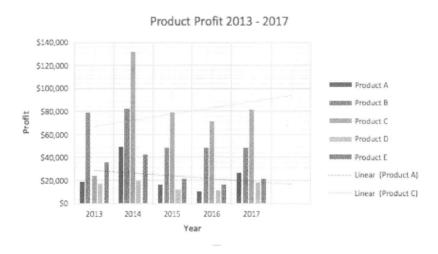

To Add Up/Down Bars:

In a column chart, Up/Down Bars are not available. But they can be used in a line chart to display increases and decreases between data points.

Customizing Charts

Change Chart Type

Select the option to change the chart type from the **Design** menu and select another chart.

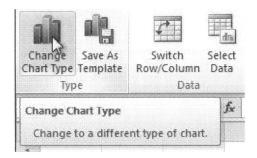

Move and Resize Charts

Resizing the Excel window can simply be done by taking your mouse cursor to the extreme top right of the window and then clicking on the Minimize icon (usually the middle icon). Clicking on this icon again maximizes the window.

An Excel Window can be moved about after being minimized by holding down and dragging the title bar of the window with the left button of your mouse.

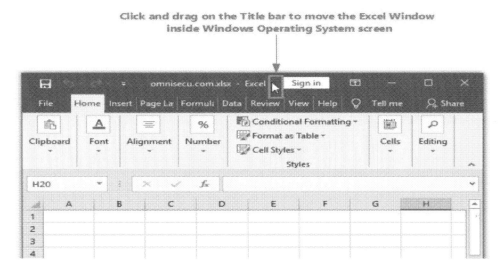

Data Analysis with Goal Seek

Goal seek command is simply a technique of data analysis that focuses more on the result by using the result to formulate an analysis that will help in getting the raw data which will give one the actual result one wants to achieve. Goal seek command is an order you give Excel to experiment result to get the raw data based on the result you desire to achieve coupled with necessary Excel argument.

Goal seek analysis input value in the place of raw data, for instance, you want to borrow money, you know how much to borrow and you have the ability to pay off the loan, and also know the period you will use to pay off the whole loan, but you do not know the exact rate of interest that you will pay in acquiring such loan, Goal seek command will help you in that area. Let us do the computation of interest rate to pay in acquiring a loan with the PMT function with the following guideline:

Enter the respective elements into the worksheet, for instance:

- B1= Loan amount, B2= period of the payment monthly, B3= Rate of interest, B4= month payment.

Enter the **respective value** for each element above in (1), for instance,

- Cell C1= $120000, that is the amount you prefer to borrow.

- Cell C2= 180, the number of times to pay off the loan if paid monthly.
- Cell C3= the interest rate we are about to calculate for the loan amount.
- Cell C4= the amount of payment every month, but you are not going to insert it here, it will be used in the Goal seek computation because it is the data result.

	A	B	C
1		Amount of loan	120000
2		Number of payment (Monthly)	180
3		Interest rate	
4		Payment	

Insert the formula into **Cell C4** by putting in **Cell 4=PMT(C3/12, C2, C1)**, this will give you the formula result for the monthly payment value. In this scenario, you wish to be paying $1200 each month, but you will not enter it, it will be using in Goal seek dialog box for interest rate computation. The formula breakdown:

- **C1** is the loan amount
- **C2** is the period it will take for paying off the loan.
- **C3** is the Interest rate that "Goal seek" seeks to find, and the 12 is 12 months, PMT calculates on yearly basis, and thus you have to divide it by 12 to convert it to a monthly basis. But, because cell B3 does not have anything inside, Excel will assume it to be Zero (0).

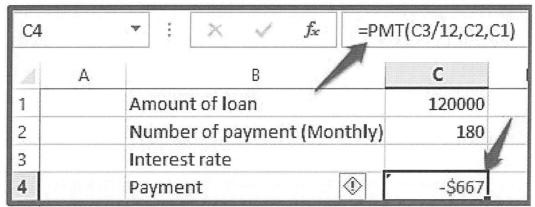

Move to the **Data** tab and tap on **What-if Analysis** and then choose the "**Goal Seek**" button from the What-if Analysis drop-down list.

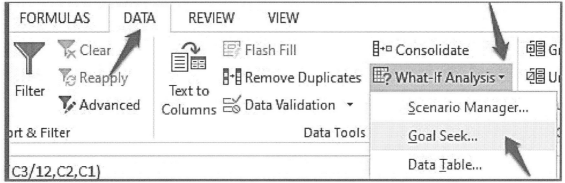

Once the "Goal Seeks" dialog box opens, insert the **cell reference** that comprises the formula you are looking at, in this case, it is C4.

Then type the formula result into the "**To Value box**", this is representing -1200 because it is the outflow.

Insert the **cell address** that comprises the value you want to change inside the **"Changing cell box"**; in this case, it is cell C3.

250

Tap **Ok** and Goal seek will run the check for you and provide you with the result.

Then format the cells to display the actual face value by navigating to the **Home** tab, then, click on the **"Number"** group, then move to currency to format it.

Chapter 6: **Pivot Tables**

Creating Pivot Tables

To create a pivot table, follow the steps given below:

- Select the cells you wish to create a pivot table for
- Go to the **Insert** tab, then click on **PivotTable** in the **Table** group
- In the **Create PivotTable** dialog box, set the following

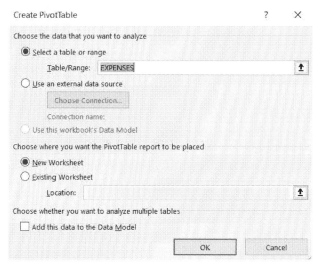

- **Click on** Select a table or range **under** Choose the data you want to analyze
- Verify the cell range under the **Table/Range**
- **Select** New worksheet **or** Existing worksheet **under** Choose where you want the PivotTable report to be placed
- Then click on **Ok**
- In the **PivotTable Field** task pane, drag the field names into the four areas displayed below (Filters, Columns, Rows. And Values)

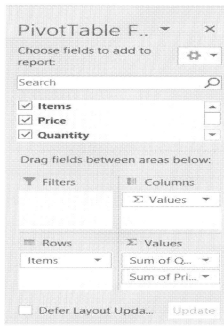

- After doing this, the data with the pivot table is displayed like the image shown below

Row Labels	Sum of Quantity	Sum of Price
Bread	10	2.89
Chicken	15	2.99
fruits	30	2.29
Turkey	10	3.99
Vegetable	20	2.29
Grand Total	**85**	**14.45**

Using Slicers

The slicer command provides options that allow you to filter your data in the table or pivot table. To add a slicer to your table, follow the steps below

- Click anywhere in the table
- Go to the **Insert** tab, then click on **Slicer** in the **Filter** group

- In the **Insert Slicers** dialog box, choose the checkboxes for the field you wish to display, and then click on **OK**

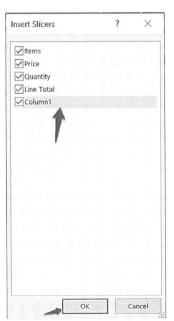

- Here in the table, a slicer will be created for the fields selected

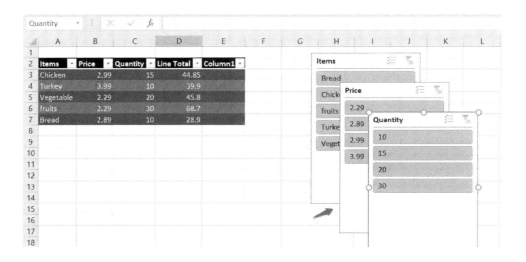

Sorting Pivot Table Data

Sorting out data in your table helps you to determine how the data will appear in your table. To sort out data in your table, follow the steps provided below

- Click on the arrow next to the column heading
- In the window that pops up, select any method of sorting out your data and then click on **Ok**

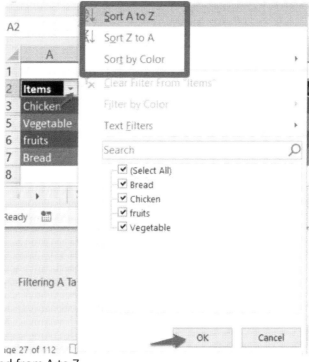

In the table below, data is sorted from A to Z

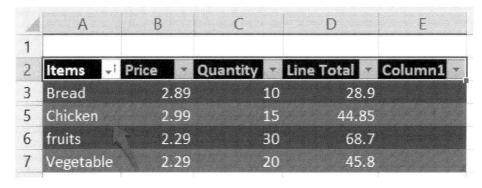

Pivot Charts

To create a pivot chart, follow the steps given below:

- Select the cells you wish to create a pivot chart for
- Go to the **Insert** tab, click on **PivotChart** in the **Chart** group, and then select **PivotChart** in the drop-down menu
- In the **Create PivotChart** dialog box, set the following

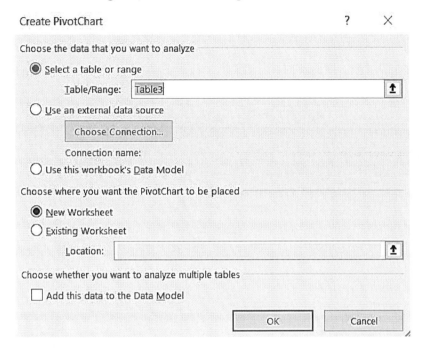

- **Click on** Select a table or range **under** Choose the data you want to analyze
- Verify the cell range under the **Table/Range**
- **Select** New worksheet **or** Existing worksheet **under** Choose where you want the PivotTable report to be placed
- Then click on **Ok**
- In the **PivotChart Field** task pane, drag the field names into the four areas displayed below (Filters, Columns, Rows. And Values)

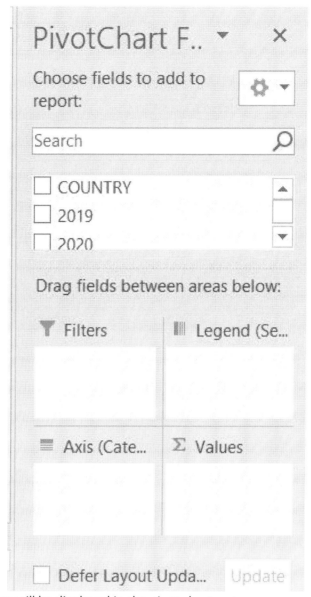

- After doing this, the data will be displayed in the pivot chart

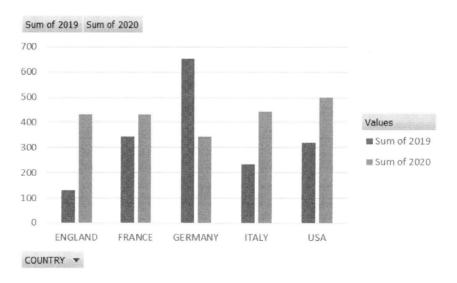

Chapter 7:

Validation Rules

Data validation is a special feature made by Excel that permits users to control what they enter into the cell. Data validation can help you to enter data in a preferred specified format, restrict the kind of data to be entered into the cell, and can be used to create a drop-down as well.

Let us now check types of data validation rule:

Allowing whole numbers and **decimal only:** to restrict the type of data that will enter into the cell such as whole numbers and decimal, you have to:

- Pick **the cell** you want to restrict its data.
- Move to the **Data tab** and select **data validation** to bring forth the data validation dialogue box.

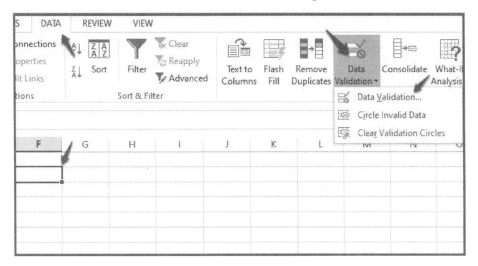

- Pick the **Data type** under "Allow" such as whole numbers and decimal.

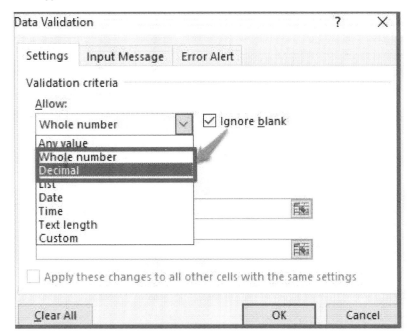

- Then establish the measures by choosing under **"Data"** perhaps it is between, equal to, and so on.

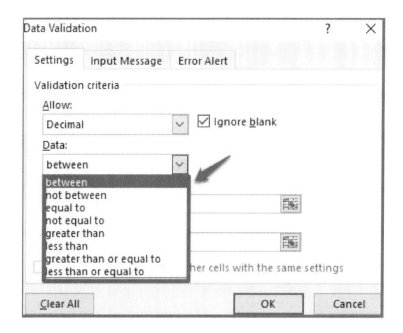

- Supply further information that is required for restriction guidelines such as "Minimum" and "Maximum". For instance, a filling station attendant with a customer number between 5500 to 10000 will set the minimum as 5500 and maximum as 10000. After that, tap on **Ok.**

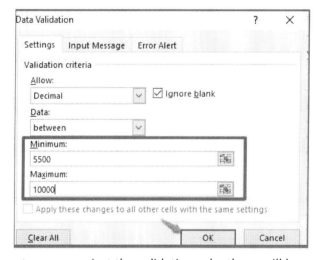

Note: immediately your data entry goes against the validation rule, there will be a prompt warning that the data doesn't match validation restrictions defined for the cell.

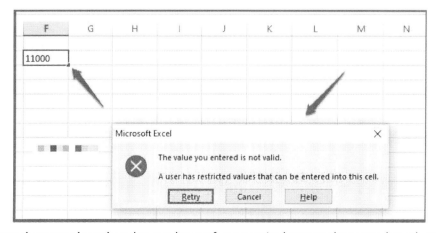

Setting rules for text character length: rules can be set for a particular text character length to limit the length of the text that can occupy the cell. To do that:

258

- Select the cell or cells that will receive the restriction guideline.
- Move to the **Data tab** and click on **Data Validation** to open the data validation dialogue box.

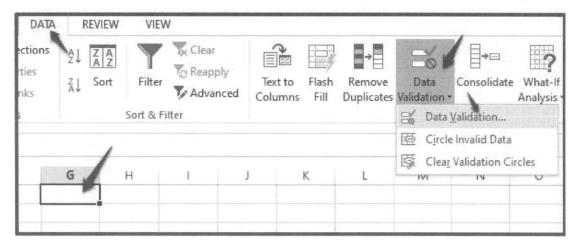

- Pick **"Text length"** under "Allow".
- Establish befitting measure under the **"Data"** option.

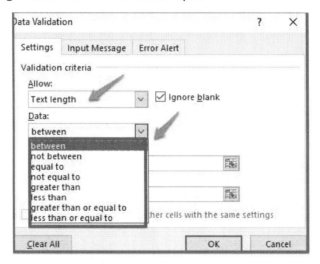

- Supply further information which will stand as a restriction guide. For example, you might want the applicant's username to be within a range of 7 to 15 length in character. Input 7 in the minimum box space and 15 in the maximum box space.

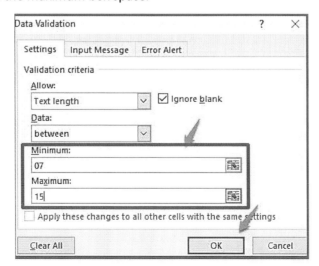

Validating dates and times: you may set a data validation rule to both the date and time to restrict specific entry into the cell. To achieve that, kindly:

- Choose the cell or cells that will receive the validation rule.
- Move to the **Data tab** and click on the **Data Validation** to open the Validation dialogue box.

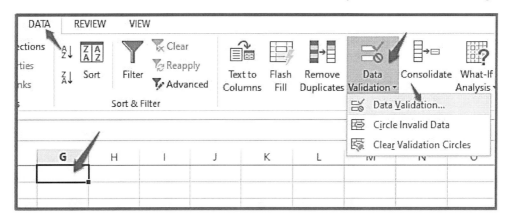

- Pick the **"Date"** or **"Time"** option under **"Allow"** depending on the restriction item you want to incorporate first.

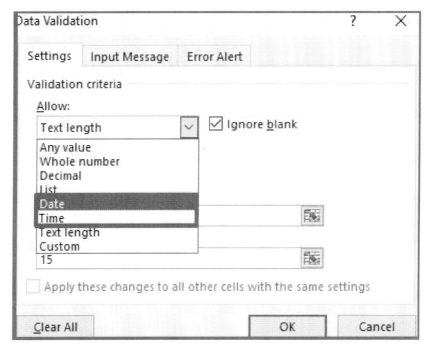

- Pick the accurate measure that suits your preference under "Data" options.

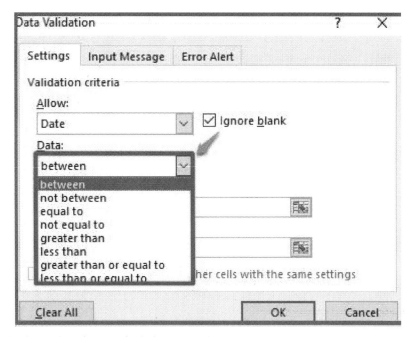

- Supply further details needed for guideline restriction. For instance, you can choose to set employees' leave periods within the limit of a specific week in a month (10th of June to 17 June). Set the **start date** as June 10 and the **end date** as June 17.

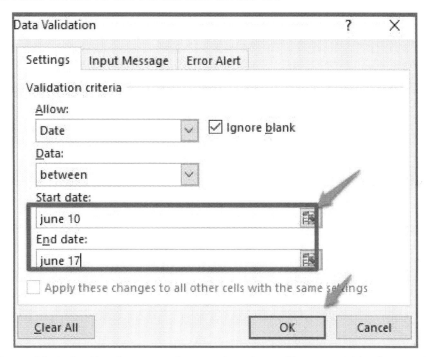

Note: Data validation guide helps Excel users to frame what they will enter within the restriction limit in such a way that it will not go beyond standard settings to avoid an error that may occur through data entry.

Chapter 8: **Displaying Messages**

W hile working on Excel especially in inserting formulas into your worksheet, mistakes are bound to occur from time to time. When these mistakes are not rectified, most times, you end up getting stuck in the middle of the calculation. To avoid this calamity, Excel provides several methods to rectify these errors. But before we go, let's quickly go through Excel Formula Errors Messages.

Excel Formula Error Messages

The following are the Excel formula Error Messages, meanings, and their causes.

#DIV/0!

Excel displays this error value when you are asking Excel to divide a formula by zero or an empty cell. Mathematically, if you try dividing a number by zero. It will not work, and this is also applicable in Excel. To rectify this error, change the value of the cell to a value that is not equal to 0 or add a value to the blank cell.

#NAME?

This error value appears when Excel does not recognize the name of the formula used as a valid object. This error occurs when one types the incorrect range name, refers to a deleted range name, or forgets to place the quotation marks around a text string in a formula. To resolve this error, thoroughly check the spelling of the formula you are trying to run, or you can use the Formula Builder to have Excel build the function for you.

#N/A

This error value appears when the numbers being referred to in the formula cannot be found. This can occur when you mistakenly deleted a number or row that is used in the formula, or when you refer to a sheet that has been removed or not saved.

To rectify this error, thoroughly check all the formulas be used and make sure to identify all the sheets or rows that may have been deleted or referenced incorrectly

#NUM!

This error value is displayed when the formula in your worksheet contains numeric values that are different from the arguments used.

To rectify this error, thoroughly check to see if you have inputted any formatted currency, dates, or special symbol. After this, you can now remove the formatting from the formula and keep the numbers.

#NULL!

This error value is displayed when you specified an intersection of two areas that do not intersect, or when the incorrect range operator is used. For instance, when you use a space instead of a comma between ranges in the function arguments, Excel will display the formula as #NULL! value error.

To rectify this error, ensure to check if the correct syntax is used in the formula. You can also follow the tips below to avoid

- Use a colon to separate the first cell from the last cell when referring to a continuous range of cells in a formula.
- Use a comma when referring to two cells that don't intersect

#REF!

This error value is displayed when you referring to a cell or a range of cells that doesn't exist. This occurs when you delete, a cell, column, or row, and then build a formula around the deleted cell, column, or row.

To rectify this error, check to see if there is no formula referring to any cell you have deleted. Before deleting cells, carefully where the formulas are referred to in those cells.

#VALUE!

This error value is displayed when Excel find spaces, characters, or text formula in a place where it is expecting a number.

To rectify this error, carefully check your formula to use numbers where it is needed. Ensure to also check out for blank checks, missing formulas that are linked to cells, or any special characters that are being used.

Using the Error Checker Button

One of the ways to check errors in your formula is to use the error checker. Using the Error checker keeps you informed on whatever error is faced or encountered.

To use the error checker, follow the steps given below to correct the error in the table provided

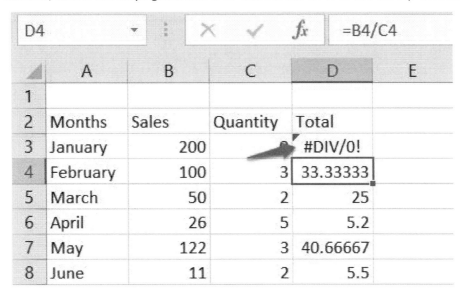

- Go to the **Formula Bar** and click on the **Error Checking** button in the **Formula Auditing** group

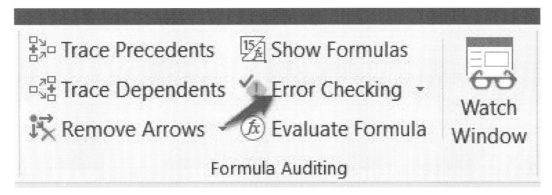

- In the **Error Checking** dialog box, the error in the formula is clearly stated, and then click on **Edit** in **Formula Bar** to repair the formula error.
- When you are done with the repairing of the formula error, click on the **Resume** button

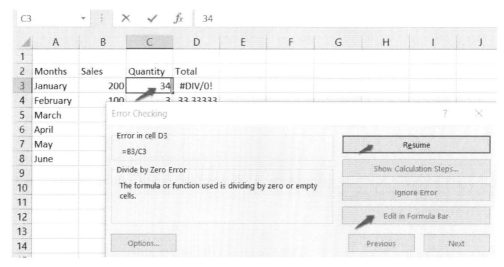

- After this is done, the error is removed as shown in the table below

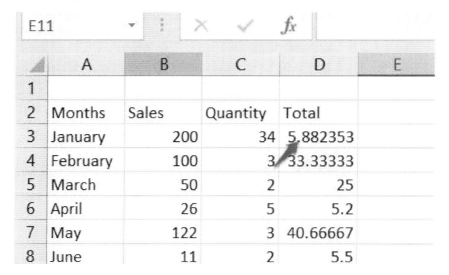

Chapter 9: **Create a Drop-Down List**

A drop-down list is a great way to offer the user a choice from a pre-defined set of options. It can be utilized to have someone complete a form or to make virtual Excel dashboards.

Drop-down lists seem to be very popular on websites and smartphones, and they are very user-friendly.

In this chapter, you will learn to how to make a drop-down list using Excel (it only takes few seconds), as well as all the useful tasks you can do with it.

How to Create a Drop-Down List in Excel

In this section, you will learn the exact steps to create an Excel drop-down list:

- Using data in cells.
- Entering data manually.
- Using the OFFSET formula.

Using Data in the Cells

Assume you have the following set of items:

To make an Excel drop-down list, follow these steps:

Choose one cell where you'd like the drop-down menu to appear.

Go to the tab Data ⯈ Data Tools ⯈ Data Validation.

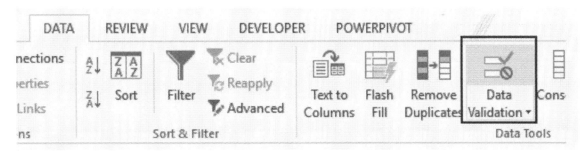

Select the List as Validation requirements in the Data Validation dialog box Settings column.

The source area will appear as soon as you select List.

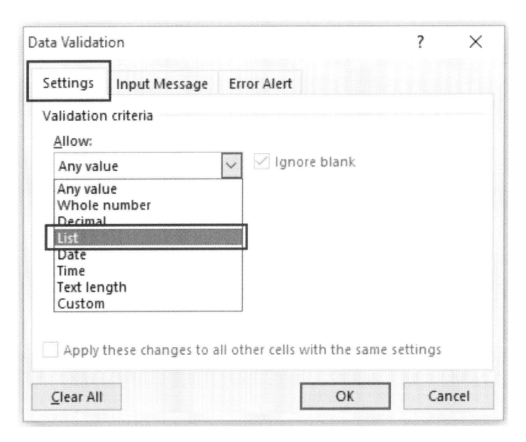

Enter =$A$2: $A$6 in the source field, or simply go to the Source field and select the cells with the mouse before clicking OK. In cell C2, this will create a drop-down menu.

Check the box for the In-cell drop-down feature (which is marked by default). The cell doesn't display the drop-down if this choice is unchecked, but you can manually insert the numbers in a list.

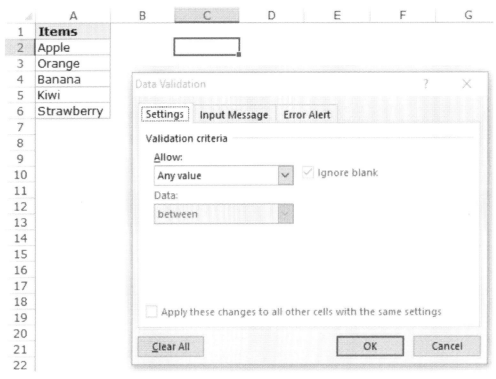

Note: If you wish to make drop-down lists in several cells at once, select all the cells you want to use and repeat the steps above. Ensure the cell comparisons are absolute (for example, $A$2) rather than conditional (A2, A$2, and $A2).

Entering your Data Manually

Cell references are included in the Source field in the illustration above. You can also manually insert objects in the root field to include them.

Let's assume you want to see two choices in a cell's drop-down menu: Yes and No. Here's how to put this directly into a data validation root area:

Choose the cell where you'd like the drop-down menu to appear (cell C2 in the following example).

Data Validation can be found under Data - Data Tools - Data Validation.

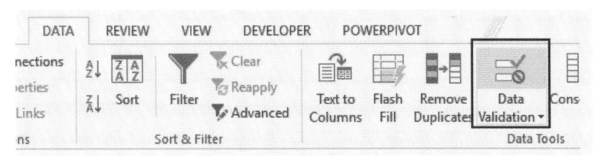

Choose List as Validation requirements within the Data Validation dialog box Settings column.

The source area will appear as soon as you select List.

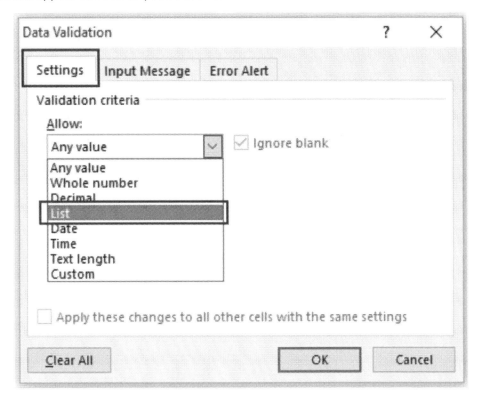

Enter Yes or No in your source field.

Check the box for the In-cell drop-down option.

Click the OK button.

In the chosen cell, the drop-down list will appear. The drop-down menu lists all the items mentioned in the source field, divided by commas, on separate lines.

The drop-down list displays all the items entered in the source field, divided by commas, in different sections.

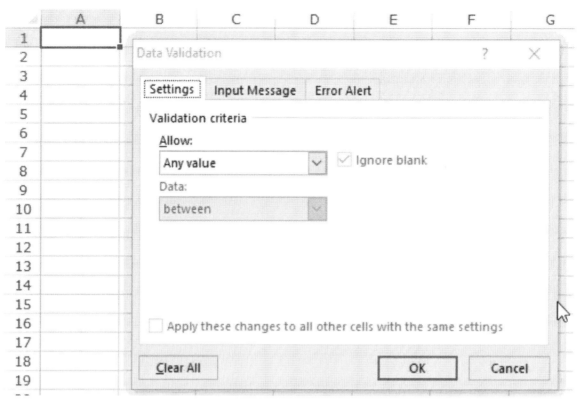

Note: To generate drop-down lists in several cells at once, select all the cells you would like to create lists in and repeat the steps above.

Using Excel Formulas

To generate an Excel drop-down list, select the cells and manually enter the details; you can use the formula in the source field.

In Excel, you can make a drop-down list using a method that returns a list of all values.

For example, assume you have the following data collection:

To make an Excel drop-down list with the OFFSET feature, follow these steps:

Choose the cell where you'd like the drop-down menu to appear (cell C2 in the following example).

Go to Data ▯Data Tools ▯ Data Validation.

Choose List as Validation requirements within the Data Validation dialog box Settings tab.

The source area will appear as soon as you choose List.

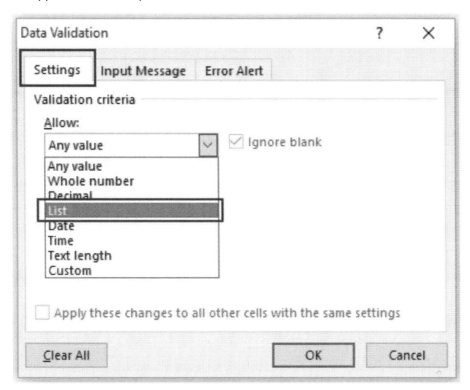

Enter the following formula in the source field: =OFFSET ($A$2,0,0,5)

Check the box for the In-cell drop-down option.

Click the OK button.

This will generate a drop-down menu of all the fruit names (as illustrated below).

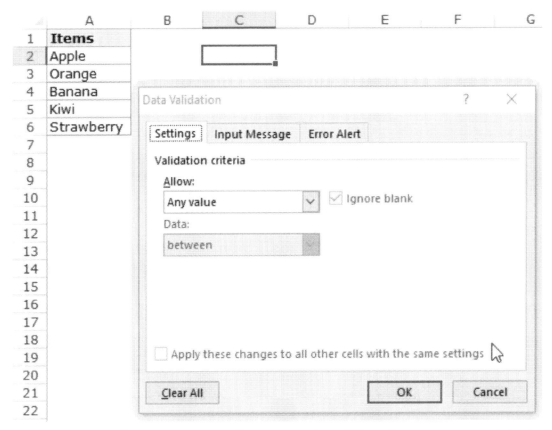

Note: To make a drop-down list across several cells at once, select all the cells you want to include the list in and repeat the steps above. Ensure the cell comparisons are absolute (for example, $A$2) rather than conditional (for example, A$2, A2, or $A2).

How do the above formulas work?

To build a drop-down list in the example above, you used the OFFSET feature. This gives you an outline of the items in the area.

It gives you a selection of objects from A2 to A6.

The OFFSET feature has the following syntax: = OFFSET = OFFSET (reference, cols, rows, [width], [height])

It has five arguments and, in this case, defined A2 as the index (the starting point of your list). You do not want to balance each reference cell, so Rows/Cols are set to 0. Since there are five items in the list, the height is set to 5.

When you use the formula now, an array is returned with a list of 5 fruits in cells A2: A6. You'll see that if you type the formula into a cell, select it, and click F9, it returns a list of the fruit names.

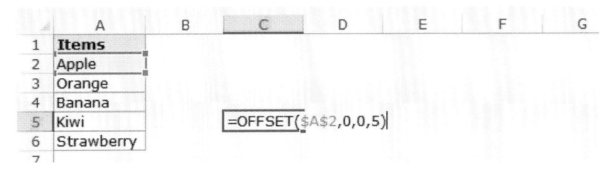

Chapter 10: **Locking Cells**

Protecting one's worksheet means preventing it from any form of editing and formatting from unauthorized users. What are you preventing? They are your cell contents, rows, and columns of your worksheet, addition or removing of any row and column and so on.

Let us examine how to protect one's worksheet from an unauthorized editor:

- Select the **worksheet** to be protected.
- Move to the **Review** tab and tap on the **Protect sheet** button**,** and you will be provided with a sheet protector dialog box.

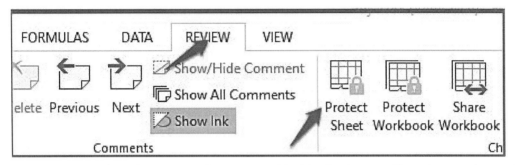

- Input a **password** in the password space provided in the Protect Sheet box so that only those you authorize by giving them the password to unprotect it will have access to it.

- In the Protect Sheet box, go to **"Allow All Users of This Worksheet To:"** list, click what you want other users to do like **format cell** if you want them to format it. You only have to deselect **the "Selected locked cell"** to prevent anyone from adjusting anything on the worksheet because initially, by default, all the worksheet cells have been locked, and by deselecting the **"Selected locked Cell"**, you excellently prevent any cell from been edited.

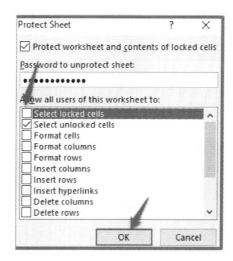

- Tap **Ok** to effect the changes. Perhaps you entered the password in (c) above, you will have to enter it once requested for again, then you can tap **OK**.

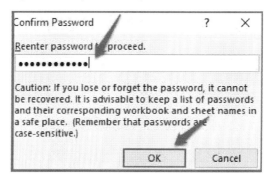

Note: you can unprotect the sheet you have previously protected by following these simple steps:

- Move to the **Review** tab and click on **Unprotect Sheet**.

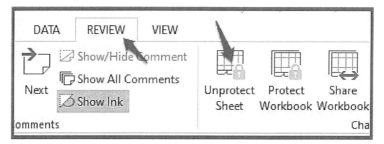

- Input the **password** you have previously attached to it when you were protecting it.
- Then tap **Ok**

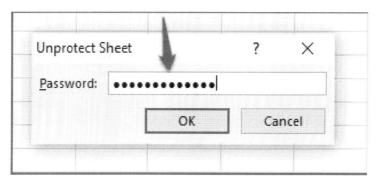

Chapter 11: **New, Saved, and Opened Document**

Page Options

In excel, Page orientation applies to how the production of the page is written. If you alter that orientation, it will immediately switch to the current paper orientation on page breaks. To check the orientation of that page:

- Go to the Style tab of the website and then to the orientation portion.
- When you tap on the orientation tab, you can see the drop-down of two portrait and landscape choices, which are already selected and highlighted.
- See the illustration below where the image is already picked, which implies that the direction of your existing document is now a portrait.

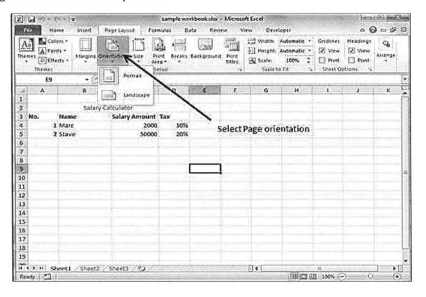

Margins

- Press the Microsoft Excel Page Layout tab.

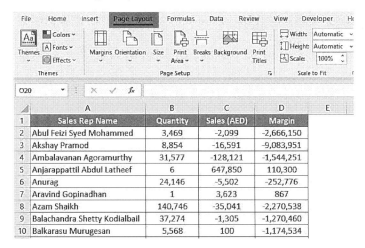

- Press on the "Margins" tab under "Page Layout," and you will see various margin choices. Ideally, there are four of them—Final Custom Settings, Standard, Broad, and Small margins. You should pick anyone according to your needs.

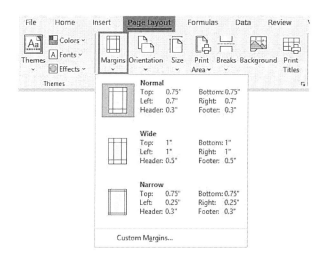

- Press on "Narrow" margins. They are narrow down margins; they also provide more capacity to obtain the columns.

Headers And Footers

- First, go to the Insert > Text Group, then press the Header & the Footer icon. The worksheet would be changed into the Page Layout Format.

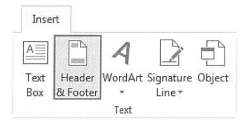

- Here you can type text, add an image, apply a preset header and special elements to each of the 3 header boxes, which are at the top of the screen. The central box is chosen by default:

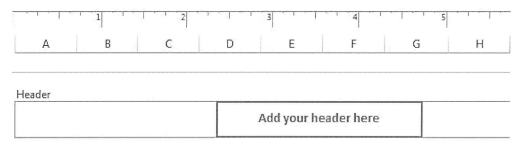

- In case you want the header to show at the top left and the top right side of the page, press the left or press the right box and type any detail there.
- When completed, click wherever on the said worksheet to exit the header field. Click Esc to leave the header box despite retaining the changes.
- As you wish to print out your worksheet, then the Header would be displayed on each sheet.

To Insert the Footer

- From the Insert tab, press the Header and Footer button inside Text Group.
- In the Design tab, select Go to Footer; otherwise, navigate down toward the footer box at the end of the said page

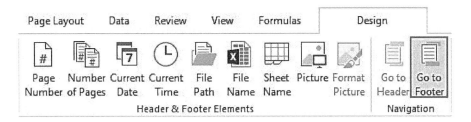

- Press the left, middle, and right-footer box, depends on the position you choose, and then type any text and insert the data you want. To insert a default footer, then please follow these measures to create a custom Microsoft Excel footer. Now see these instructions.
- When it's completed, click wherever on the specific worksheet to leave the footer field.
- E.g., add page numbers under the worksheet, select one of the footer areas, and then click on the Template tab inside the Header and Footer group.

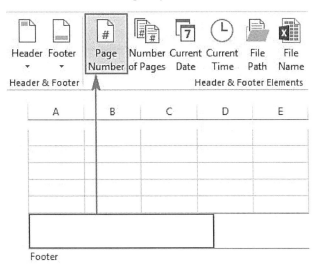

Customize the Header and Footer

- To easily change the font type or font color of the header as well as footer, pick the text along with the appropriate formatting setting in the pop-up box.

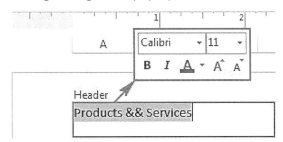

- Instead, pick the text header and the footer you wish to modify. First, go to Home, Font group, and choose the format choices required.

Print Options

Simply navigate to the **Print** option in the **File** menu or use key **Ctrl + P.** When in the print window, make necessary selections and configurations.

Print Row and Column Headers

Tick the box for **headings** in the Excel **Page Setup** dialogue box.

Print Gridlines

Tick the box for **Gridlines** in the Excel **Page Setup** dialogue box.

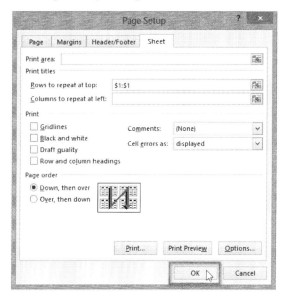

Print Selection

Removing some cells from printing can be done in any of the following two ways:

- Hide these cells
- Format these cells to blend with your worksheet background, e.g., if you have a white background for your worksheet, select a white font for the content of these cells

Print Titles

Select the tab to print titles and select the rows and columns to be repeated.

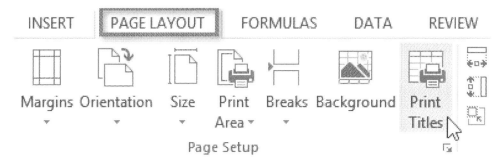

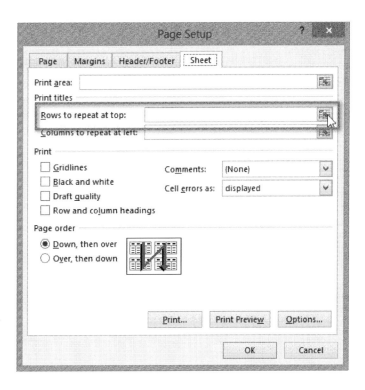

Opening a Saved Workbook

Opening New Workbooks

- Use the **File** menu and select **New.** Keyboard key **Ctrl + N** can also be used for opening new workbooks.

Opening A Saved Workbook

- Use the **File** menu and select **Open.** This opens a window where you can select saved workbooks from your File Manager. Keyboard keys **Ctrl + O** also open this window.

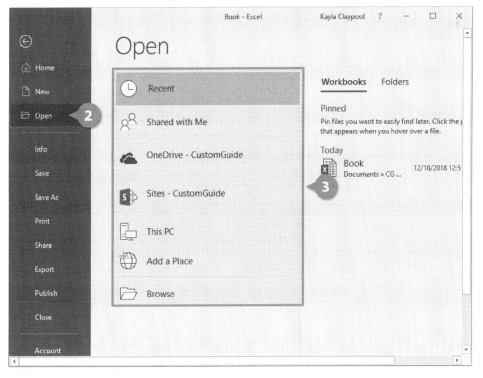

Saving Workbooks

- Use keyboard keys **Ctrl + S** to save your workbook.

- Type in a suitable name for the workbook to facilitate easy access in the pop-up dialogue box.
- Select the Save button.

You can also navigate to **File** and then select the **Save** or **Save As option.**

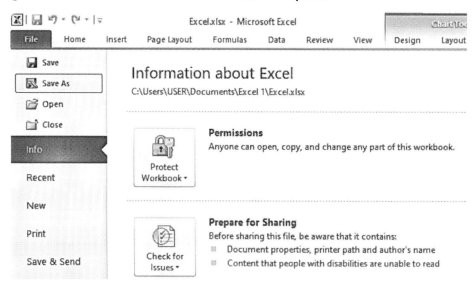

Save as a Different Format

Saving Your Workbook as a PDF File

- Select the **Save As** option in the **File** menu

In the box indicating the format in which the workbook will be saved, select the drop-down menu and choose the option for a PDF format.

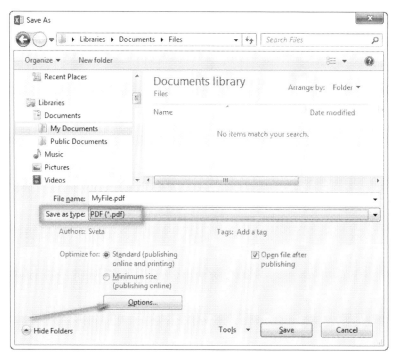

BOOK 5: MICROSOFT POWERPOINT

Introduction

Microsoft PowerPoint is a program that is used mostly for presentations. It was created by the duo of Robert Gaskins and Denis Austin at a software company known as Forethought Incorporations. This software was released on April 20th, 1987, and was initially made for Macintosh computers alone.

Three months after the creation of this software, it was acquired by Microsoft for a fee in the region of about $14 million. This was Microsoft's first very important acquisition, and they set up a new business unit specifically for PowerPoint in Silicon Valley. This was where Forethought had been located.

Afterward, PowerPoint became a part of Microsoft Office. At first, it was offered for the Macintosh alone in 1989 and 1990, along with several other Microsoft apps. Starting with PowerPoint 4.0, which was created in 1994, PowerPoint was integrated into Microsoft Office development and incorporated shared common parts and a unified user interface.

PowerPoint's market share was significantly lower initially, before it was introduced as a version for Microsoft Windows. It then grew very fast with the growth of Windows and Office. Since the late 1990s, PowerPoint's market share of presentation software worldwide has been estimated at 95 percent. Originally, PowerPoint was made to provide visuals for group presentations, mostly within business organizations. Still, this has changed over the years as it has now been widely used in many other communication situations, including business and beyond.

The impact of this widespread global use of PowerPoint has been felt like a powerful change throughout society, with very strong reactions that include advice on it being used less, used better, or used differently.

The first PowerPoint version, created in 1987, was used to produce overhead transparencies. In 1988 and 1990, the second and third were also used to produce color on about 35mm slides. The fourth version, produced in 1992, brought the video output of virtual slideshows to digital projects, which could completely replace the physical transparencies and slides over the years. Since then, about a dozen important versions have infused many additional features and modes of operation. They have also made PowerPoint available beyond the Apple Macintosh and Microsoft Windows, including IOS, Android, and Web access.

Chapter 1: **Getting Started**

MS PowerPoint Main Window

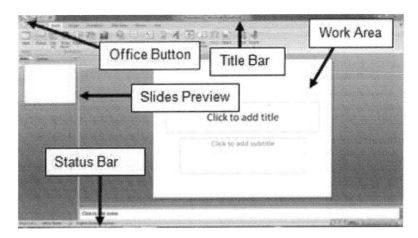

In this main window, you will see tabs such as Home, Insert, Design, Animations, Slide Show, Review and View. You can see the slide pane on the left, work area in the centre, status bar at the far bottom and the title bar on the top of the main window. Like any other MS Office program, the title bar of MS PowerPoint contains control buttons, Office Button and the Quick Access Toolbar.

Launching MS PowerPoint

There are many ways to launch any program in Windows OS. You can double-click the shortcut icon of MS PowerPoint on the desktop to run it, or left-click it if it is pinned to the Start Menu or Taskbar. Left-click the Start Button and check the Start Menu for MS PowerPoint icon. Not seen? Then click "**All Programs,**" link => **Microsoft Office** => **Microsoft Office PowerPoint**. I hope you can see it now. If not, then MS Office or PowerPoint might not have been installed on your computer.

Create a Shortcut

If you often use PowerPoint, it will be better to pin it to the start or taskbar of your computer.

To pin PowerPoint to start or taskbar:

- Right-click on the PowerPoint icon or click the arrow down as shown
- Choose **Pin to Start** or **Pin to taskbar** as desired.

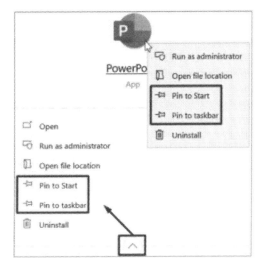

Follow the same steps above to unpin the application.

The Ribbon

The Ribbon Tabs are a group of commonly used commands to perform an essential task. The following are the tabs in Excel:

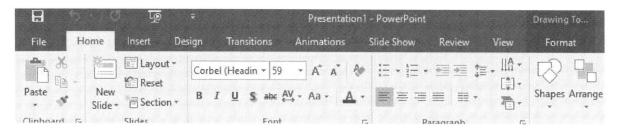

The Home Ribbon

This tab contains features such as Cut, Paste, Font, Paragraph, and other features necessary to add and organize slides in the presentation.

The Insert Ribbon

The Insert tab allows you to add objects such as pictures, shapes, charts, links, text boxes, videos, etc. to your slides.

The Design Ribbon

The Design tab allows you to add a theme or color scheme to your slide or format the slide background.

The Transitions Ribbon

This tab allows you to set up how your slides change from one to the other.

The Animations Ribbon

This tab allows you to maneuver the movement of things or objects in your tab. With this tab, you can use several animations in the gallery found in the Animation group.

The Slide Show Ribbon

This tab allows you to set up or arrange your presentation for others to see.

File Backstage

The backstage view can be accessed from the File tab at the ribbon's extreme left. Though it looks like a tab, when the file tab is clicked open, the header brings up a menu on the left-hand side of the backstage view. It is worth noting that there are no other menu options in the PowerPoint 2022 window interface.

The backstage view provides easy access to frequently used features for managing PowerPoint presentation files. As well as organizing files, this view enables users to save and create new files, search for hidden metadata or personal information, print slides, and set file options.

When the backstage view is opened up, about fourteen options can be found on the left-hand side of the pane. Any third-party PowerPoint add-in can also add extra options. Each of these fourteen options opens an individual tab.

When PowerPoint is launched, and there are no presentations, the home tab will be visible within the backstage view. The home tab will still be visible if the backstage view is already accessed with a presentation open. The fourteen tabs that can be seen include Home, New, Open, Info, Save, Save as, History, Print, Share, Export, Close, Account, Feedback, and Options.

To return to the backstage view from the normal view, simply select the back arrow button that can be found at the top of the left interface.

To open **the Backstage View**

- Click on the **File tab**

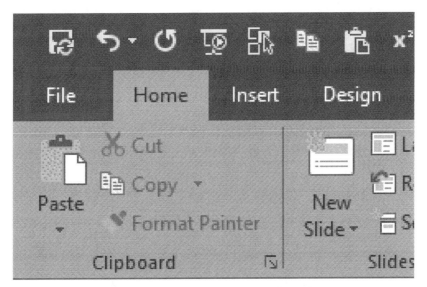

- When the Backstage view is displayed, you can select any of the fourteen options you wish to use

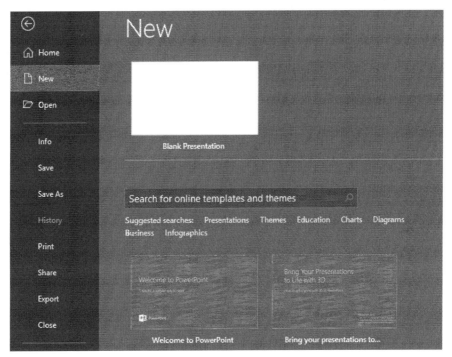

- To go back to the **Normal** view from the **Backstage** view, click on the **Back** arrow button at the top of the interface.

Chapter 2: **Creating a New Presentation**

When you open PowerPoint, it will take you to the start screen first

Next, an interface with various options such as a blank presentation or a presentation with themes will be displayed. It's best to choose a blank presentation to begin from the scratch

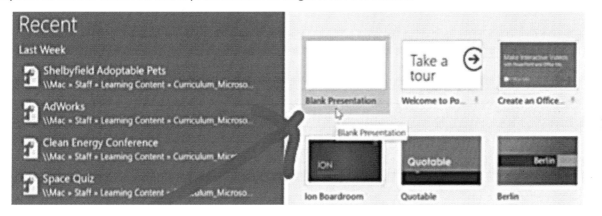

Here is what a blank presentation looks like

Designing a Slide

Microsoft PowerPoint templates give the widest range of choices regarding designs, making them perfect for modern and stylish presentations and pitches. PowerPoint themes, however, give room for many presentation topics, allowing you the freedom to select the best presentation templates designed for any project.

Microsoft provides different PowerPoint templates for free and premium PowerPoint for subscribers of Microsoft 365. Each template for PowerPoint enables the use of stylized charts and graphs while ensuring that a professional tone is kept. Whatever you choose to do, be it hosting a healthcare seminar, teaching a high school course, having to design a fashion magazine and lots more, any choice made will be supported by PowerPoint.

Even though Microsoft's PowerPoint presentation templates are designed professionally and require very little customization, they can also be heavily tweaked. A presentation can be customized easily if a more hands-on approach is needed. Each PowerPoint template can also be customized to meet specific needs.

Changing a Theme

To change a theme, simply open your presentation in PowerPoint. On the Design tab, in the Themes group, choose the theme that best suits your needs from the list. A preview option can be seen if you hover over any of them. When you're satisfied and ready to continue, just click **the theme**. It will be applied to the whole presentation.

Unless the previous theme is a PowerPoint default theme, which will appear under the list of default themes, when a new theme is applied to PowerPoint since it typically affects all slides, the previous theme will be completely removed.

How to Apply a New Theme to Selected Slides Alone

Simply open the presentation in PowerPoint and locate the design tab. Choose the **slide of the theme** that needs to be changed. If different slides are to be selected, simply hold the Ctrl/Cmd button and click on the slides simultaneously.

Select the theme you want to apply. You can preview a theme by hovering the mouse over the list of themes before selecting one. Note that should the overall theme of a presentation change much later, these slides will also be affected.

Importing a Theme

To bring in a theme from another source, start by opening the presentation in PowerPoint. On the Design tab, in the Themes group, select the **drop-down arrow**. Click on the **Browse for Themes** and a new window will be opened where the presentation containing the imported theme will be selected. Do note that the selected theme will be applied to all the slides, and any previously used theme will be removed.

Editing The Colors Of Themes

Based on the selected theme, it can have different colors or palette presets that enable a user to select and change the color of the items in the presentation. The colors of the themes can be edited by opening the presentation in PowerPoint, navigating to the design tab option and clicking on the variants group if the theme has variations.

The color palette can be changed by selecting the variant drop-down arrow, choosing colors, and selecting any preset. The customize color option can be used if a specific palette should be applied to the presentation. A new window will appear with the colors that will work best for the presentation. To the right of the window, you will see a preview.

Select the **variants drop-down arrow** and **background styles** to change the background color. You can choose any presets or select Format Background to create a background that can be solid colors, gradients, images, or even patterns.

If you choose to do this via the Format Background options, you will see a panel on the right side of the screen. To apply a customized background, simply select **apply to all**. All the background pictures will be taken off if the background is changed with the Format Background option,.

Adding Images

You can get **pictures** from your system if you want to. To get pictures from your system, click on the **picture** and select **this device**. This will take you to the locations where you have your pictures. Select an image of your choice and click **insert**.

Just like your table, you have **a picture format**.

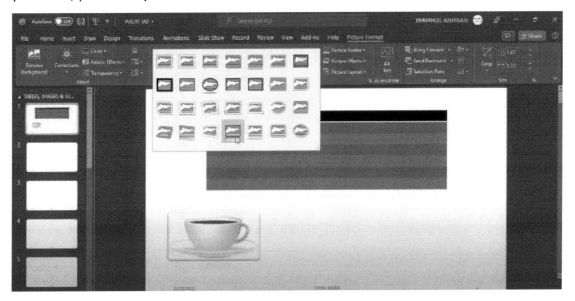

Here you may select any **picture style** you wish. You also have **a picture border, picture effect,** and **picture layout**. If you wish to, you can remove the background from your picture by clicking on **remove background**. When you click on remove background you have **mark areas to keep.**

This simply means you should mark the areas you will love to keep on your image background. Select the image and click the areas you wish to keep and it will remove the paint or color covering that area. If you are done, select **keep changes**.

You have **color** that helps you replace the color of your image or picture. You have **artistic effects** and **transparency effects** as well. It all depends on what you are designing, your creative ability, and what you are doing for your presentation.

Apart from getting pictures or images from your system, you can get pictures online or you may get pictures through stock images. Click on the **picture** and select **stock images**.

Your system must be connected online to use the **stock image** feature. You have many images under stock images you can make use of. You can browse the pictures given for your choice or type into the search box what type of stock images you are looking for.

If you type computer into the search box and press **enter**, it will show you pictures of computers you can use.

Still, on the **stock images**, you can get icons, cutout people, stickers, video illustrations, and cartoon people or type directly in the search option what you need.

You may also get pictures online. Select the **picture** and click on **online pictures**.

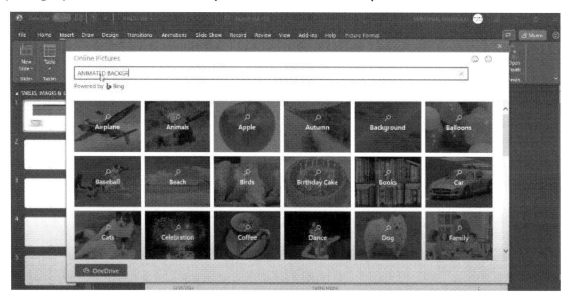

You can pick any option in the **online pictures** and browse for what you wish or go directly to the search box and search for what you need.

For instance, if you type **animated background** into your search box and click on **Enter**, it will give you animated background images that are online.

You don't have access to stock images if you use a lower version of Microsoft PowerPoint. You may download pictures to your computer to import them to your slides from your system. Go to your browser and type **pixabay.com** in your search box.

On **pixabay.com**, you have photos, illustrations, vectors, videos, music, and sound effects. You should type what you want into the search box and the area you want it from.

For example, type **computer** under photos, and you will find high-quality images you may use for your presentation. Click on an image of your choice and select download for free. You can bring it to your presentation after downloading it. Then use it for your presentation design.

Resizing Images

When a picture is added to a slide, there might be a need to adjust the size or move the picture to a different location entirely. To adjust the size of an image, simply follow the steps below.

- Choose the picture that needs to be adjusted. PowerPoint will automatically display handles on the picture that has been chosen.
- Drag the mouse arrow just over the handle. The mouse arrow will then point in two directions.
- Hold down the left button of the mouse then move the mouse. PowerPoint will then adjust the size of the chosen picture.
- Set free the mouse's left button when you feel satisfied with the new size of the picture.

To move an image, follow the steps below.

- Drag the mouse pointer right over the edge of the image that should be moved. The mouse will change to a four-way pointing arrow.
- Hold down the left button of the mouse then move the mouse. This way, PowerPoint will move the image.
- Set free the left button of the mouse when satisfied with the new position of the image.

When an image is added to a slide, it might need to be deleted. To delete the image, follow the following steps below:

- Choose the image that should be deleted. PowerPoint will show the handles around the chosen image.
- Click on **the delete button**. PowerPoint will then delete the chosen image.

Image Arrangement

Ordering an object is important when two or more objects will have to overlap. Objects are placed on top of one another according to the order in which you inserted them into your presentation, creating different **levels**. Ordering the objects means changing their levels as desired.

To change an object's level:

Select the object you want to change its level.

Click the object **Format** tab.

Click the **Send Backward** or **Bring Forward** drop-down in the **Arrange** group.

A drop-down menu appears.

Select an option to reorder your object automatically.

- **Send Backward and Bring Forward** send your object one level backward and forward, respectively.
- **Send to Back and Bring to Front sends your object behind and in front of all objects, respectively.**
- **Send Behind Text and Bring in Front of Text make the text and image feasible, respectively.**

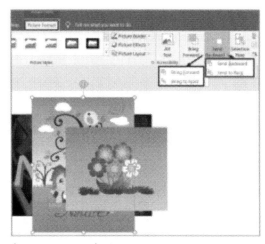

Alternatively, to have more control over your ordering,

Select the **Selection Pane** command in the **Arrange** group.

The selection navigation pane appears on the right side of your window with the list of all the objects starting from the first object at the top to the last at the back.

Select, Drag, and Drop any object to the desired level.

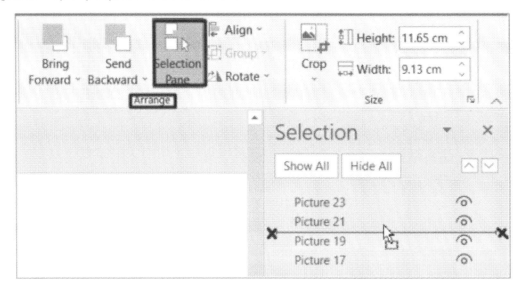

Adding Objects

There would be no point in PowerPoint slides without objects. Text, images, and charts ensure that the presentation has meaning and content to ensure that blank slides are meaningful to the audience. The use of objects in a presentation should be kept to a minimum when adding objects. Slides should not be crowded with too many objects so that the slide's main point is lost.

Most objects embedded in slides are text objects, enabling users to type text into the slide. Every slide has its layout, which has one or more placeholders. A placeholder is an area on a slide that is kept for text, a graph, clip art, or some other type of object. For example, a slide that uses the title layout has two placeholders for text objects: one is for the title and the other is used for the subtitle. The slide layout task pane chooses the layout when a new slide is created. This can be changed much later, and more objects can be added to the slide. Objects can also be moved, deleted, or resized to suit one's taste and meet specified needs.

Many types of objects can be added to a presentation, including clip art, graphs, shapes, etc. Content layouts enable you to create slides using a variety of tools that are displayed on the drawing toolbar that is located at the bottom of the screen. You can also add additional objects to a slide using the icons displayed in the slide's center . All objects have rectangular sections on their sides. The rectangular area might not be filled visually depending on the object's contents. Regardless, the outline of the object is visible when selected.

In addition to overlapping objects, they can also be grouped. Although they shouldn't usually overlap, sometimes their overlap creates a distracting effect. Some clipart can also have text overlaid on it.

Selecting Objects

Before any edit can be made on the slide, an object that contains what needs to be edited has to be selected first. As an example, a user can begin typing away to make an edit on the screen. Instead, the object that contains the text that needs to be edited has to be selected first. Furthermore, other objects must also be selected before their contents can be edited. It is worth noting that the normal view must be activated first before individual objects can be selected on the slide.

With the slide sorter view, the whole slides can be selected but not the individual elements they have on them.

Rules To Keep In Mind When Selecting Objects

To choose text objects so their text can be edited, have the point of insertion moved over the text that needs to be edited, then click the **OK button.** You can double-tap the text by using a mouse or touchpad. The text insertion point and a rectangular box will be visible around the object. A user can follow the text insertion point as they type.

The functions of other kinds of objects are slightly different. As soon as the object is selected, the rectangular box will appear around it to alert users that the object has been hooked. You must then drag the object around the screen or alter its size after it has been hooked. You cannot edit its content after it has been hooked.

The Ctrl Key: Much more than just one object can be selected by clicking on the **first object** and then holding down the CTRL key while selecting additional objects.

Click and Drag: This option is another unique way to select an object or more than just one object. Simply make use of the insertion point to drag a rectangle all around the object that needs to be selected. Point to a specific location above and to the left-hand side of the object that needs to be selected, then drag the mouse downward to the right-hand side until the rectangle surrounds the object. When the button was released, all the objects within the rectangle would have been selected.

Pressing the Tab key is another amazing option to select objects. Click the **Tab button** once to choose the first object on the slide. Press the Tab button again to choose the next object. Continue to press the Tab button until all the objects that need to be selected have been selected. Pressing the Tab button to choose objects comes in handy when it isn't so easy to point to the objects that need to be selected. This can be a problem and it can happen if the object that needs to be selected is under another object, or if the object is empty or invisible. The user is unsure of the location.

Resizing Or Moving Objects.

A box will appear around selected objects when they are selected. Closer inspection of the box reveals it has love handles on both edges, one in each corner. They are used for adjusting the size of an object. You can also move objects on the slide by taking the edge of the box between the handles.

The object will have every tendency to position itself with close objects if it is moved or its size is changed. The alignment lines will appear when the object is aligned with other objects on the slide. The object will adjust to the alignment shown if the mouse button is free when the alignment mark appears. Additionally, many objects will also have a rotating handle over them, represented as a circular arrow. The object can be rotated effortlessly by grabbing the handle and moving it around in a circle.

To change the size of an object, choose the object to be selected and then grab one of its love handles simply by clicking. Ensure you hold down the mouse button and then move the mouse to change the object's size.

The different handles on an object give different ways to change the object's size.

- The handles at the corners ensure that the object's height and width can be changed.
- The handles at the top and the lower edges make it possible to have just the height of the object changed.

- The handles on the right and left edges can change only the breadth of the object.

If the Ctrl key is held down while one of the love handles is dragged, the object will remain centered at its current position on the slide with its size adjusted. Furthermore, try holding down the shift key while moving an object using the corner love handles. The combination of both helps maintain the object's proportion when resizing it.

Adjusting the size of a text object's text does not mean the size of the text within the object will change; it will only change the size of the frame in which the text is contained. The change in a text object's width equals the change in margins in a word processor. This helps to make the lines of the text wider or narrower. If the text within a text object has to be changed, the font size must also be changed.

You can move an object by selecting just anywhere in the outline box except on a love handle, then dragging it to its new location. Users are not required to click precisely on the outline box for shapes and other graphic objects to move them- they can click and drag anywhere within the object to move it. For text-containing objects, it is necessary to click the outline box to move the object.

Shapes and Icons

PowerPoint 365 is designed with tools that allow you to insert shapes and icons into slides. With these tools in the Insert tab, you can place any shape of your choice in slides. Also, you can place an icon in slides with the icon command.

To insert shapes in a slide, do the following:

- Click inside the slide where you want to insert the shape.
- Click **Insert** tab.
- Under Illustrations category, click **Shapes** tool.

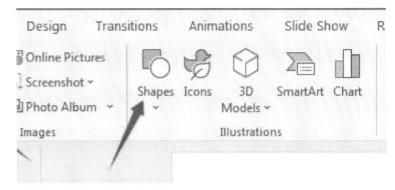

- Click any shape you want to place in the slide, and it gets placed inside the slide.
- Drag and resize the inserted shape until it suits what you want.

Also, to insert any icon in a slide, take these steps:

- Click inside your slide where you want to insert the icon.
- Click **Insert** tab of your PowerPoint.
- Under **Illustrations** category, click **Icons** command.
- Select or search for the icon you want to insert in the slide and click it.
- Drag and resize the icon to the way you want it.

SmartArt

SmartArt is a way to change ordinary text into something more appealing to the user and audience. It helps to draw attention to important information or makes it much easier to read and comprehend. This can also be called a diagramming tool in PowerPoint and allows creating a visual display of information.

SmartArt graphics can be created to match the look and feel of the presentation. It can also make process flow, cycle diagrams, pyramids, and organizational charts.

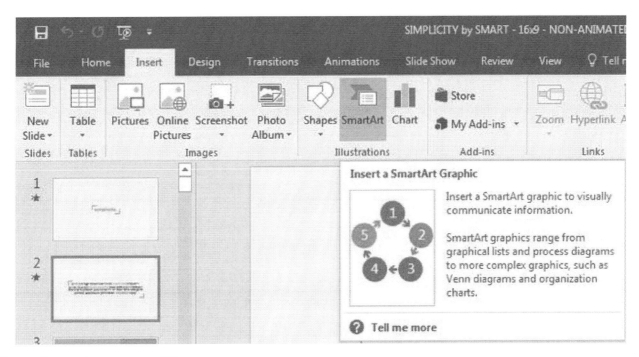

Creating a SmartArt Diagram

The easiest way to make a SmartArt diagram is to make a new slide and enter the bullet list just like the list will be displayed as normal text and then convert the text to SmartArt. Follow the steps below:

- Create a new slide with a title and a content layout.
- Type in the bullet list. Use one or two bullets, but ensure to keep the list as short as possible.
- Right-click anywhere in the list and choose the convert to SmartArt option. Choose the SmartArt type that should be used. If the SmartArt type preferred is not displayed in the menu, choose more SmartArt graphics to show the choose a SmartArt graphic dialog box.
- Click on the **OK** button and the diagram will have been created. The diagram can also be modified at any time.

PowerPoint provides eight different types of SmartArt diagrams.

These diagram types are mentioned below.

- **List:** This shows just a simple list. Some list diagrams display information with no specific organization; others help to show information in such a way that depicts a step-by-step progression, like the steps in a task.
- **Process:** This shows a process in which steps flow step-by-step.
- **Cycle:** This shows a process that occurs in a continuing cycle.
- **Hierarchy:** this helps to show the structure of the relationship, like in the organization chart.
- **Relationship:** this helps show the items that are related to each other. This includes different types of radial and Venn diagrams.
- **Matrix:** this helps to display four items arranged in a quadrant manner.
- **Pyramid:** This shows how elements are built upon one another to form a structure.
- A picture helps show information in various formats that add picture objects into the chart design.

Tweaking A SmartArt Diagram

After you create a SmartArt graphic, you may need to modify your PowerPoint presentation. Some examples of modifications include adding or removing shapes, altering their order of appearance, and altering graphic types and layouts.

- On the first slide, select the frame of the SmartArt graphic to choose the whole graphic.
- Choose the SmartArt tools design tab and select the more button in the layouts group.

- Choose the **more layouts button** and then choose a SmartArt graphic dialog box that will be displayed.
- **Select the** process category**.**
- Click on **the continuous block process layou**t. Not all graphics appear nice when a change to a different graphic type is made.
- When you click on the OK button, a new graphic type will be added.
- Locate the SmartArt Tools Design tab and select the right to the left button. This will change the graphic direction. If the right to the left button is selected again, the graphic will return to its original position.
- Select the **text pane button**. If the text pane does not show instantly, a text pane should be shown on the left-hand side of the graphic.
- In the text pane, change the word "production" to "manufacturing."
- Click the **close button** on the text pane that is close to it.
- On the graphic, choose the quality inspection shape and then select **the delete key** to taking it away.
- Finally, save the presentation.

Working With Organizational Charts

For business or other reasons, creating an organizational chart using SmartArt in Microsoft PowerPoint is very easy.

Move over to the **insert tab** option and then select SmartArt. In the option that indicates choosing a SmartArt graphic, choose the hierarchy category on the left-hand side. On the right-hand side, choose an organizational chart layout like an organization chart. When all of these have been completed, click on the OK button.

Next, choose a box in the SmartArt graphic and then type in some text. Type in the text that should be in place of the placeholder text. Choose an additional box in each SmartArt graphic and then type text in those boxes as well.

As an alternative, there is also an option to type in the text in a given text pane rather than typing directly into any of the boxes. If the "Type your Text Here" pane is not being displayed, select the control located on the edges of the SmartArt graphic. To have a box inserted, choose the box that is already in place and located closest to where the new box should be added. On the design tab, select the "Add shape" option. Type the new text directly into the new box through the text pane.

Deleting A SmartArt Graphic Or A Shape In A SmartArt Graphic

A shape can be removed from the text pane of a SmartArt graphic or from within the SmartArt graphic itself.

Overview Of Deleting Shapes

If a line of level 1 is deleted while there is still an existing line of level 2, the first line of level 2 text will then be moved to level 1 (i.e., the top shape). It is nearly impossible to delete a shape if it is part of a much larger shape. For instance, in the Bending Picture Accent list layout in the list type, it is not possible to delete just the small round shape from any of the three displayed larger shapes. All of the associated shapes must first be selected together. Note that associated shapes are the shapes that come together to make a much larger shape.

It is also impossible to delete background shapes like the arrow shapes or, better still, the divisor bar located in the counterbalance arrows layout.

To delete a shape from a SmartArt graphic, click on the border of the shape that should be deleted and press the delete button. After this must have been done, **it is important to note the following:**

- To delete a shape, it is best to click on its border. If the shape that should be deleted has text embedded in it and the inside of the shape is selected other than its border, there is every possibility that some of the text will be deleted when the delete button is pressed.
- If you make an attempt to delta a shape that is combined with other shapes to make a much larger shape, i.e. an associated shape, the shape won't be deleted in its real sense, only the text that is contained in the shape will be deleted.
- If a top-level shape or its text has been custom created already, any adjustment added to that very shape might be lost when a much lower-level shape is then promoted.

- If a connecting shape is chosen, like a line or an arrow that connects or links shapes one to another, just the text in that shape will also be deleted, as it is impossible to delete the shape in its entirety.
- In the layout of some SmartArt graphics, like the Matrix layout, the number of shapes in the SmartArt graphics is usually fixed, and as such, the shapes cannot be deleted.

Deleting Clipart Or Pictures From A SmartArt Graphic

If certain pictures or clipart have been added to the SmartArt graphic, they can be taken off by having the fill settings for the very shape that has the picture or clipart changed.

- Right-click on the border of the SmartArt graphic shape that a picture or clip art should be taken off of. If the picture or the clip art is added as a background to the whole SmartArt graphic, right-click on the border of the SmartArt graphic.
- Locate the shortcut menu and click on the **format shape or the format object option**.
- Get on the fill tab option and click on the no fill, solid fill, or gradient fill option based on what the picture or clip art is being replaced with, then select the **fill options that are preferred**.

After all these have been done, click on the **close button**.

Chapter 3: **Slides**

Adding a New Slide

When a blank presentation is created in PowerPoint, a default slide that has a title slide layout appears. Simply click into **placeholders** in the title slide and type the preferred text that needs to appear as the title and subtitle of the presentation. Inserting a new slide into the presentation and specifying the exact placeholder that should be displayed on the slide is how another slide can be added to the presentation. The slide layout selected for the slide inserted determines where the placeholders are displayed. After the slide has been inserted, you can change the placeholder layout that will be applied to the slide. To fix a new slide in PowerPoint, which will include a title and content slide, the layout, select the **Home tab in the Ribbon**. Right after that, select the **new slide button** in the slides button group. A new slide will then be added. You can always repeat this process to continuously add new slides.

In the alternative, to fix a new slide with a much different slide layout, select the **Home tab** in the Ribbon. Then select the **drop-down aspect of the New Slide button** in the slide button group. The drop-down menu that will be displayed will show the other slide layouts that are provided. Choose the name of the preferred slide layout in the drop-down menu to fix a new slide with the chosen layout.

Slide Master

The slide master is the topmost slide that is found in the slide master view. It is the very first slide in the slide pane in the slide master's view. It is usually a little bigger than the master slides.

Formatting: The changes made to the slide master will always affect all the other slides in the presentation. When a particular theme is chosen for presentation, what is really being done is assigning a theme to the slide master.

296

Due to the fact that formatting the commands that have been given to the slide master apply all through the presentation, the theme design, and the colors are also applied to all the slides. If there is a need for a logo to appear, simply place the logo directly on the slide master.

Modifying The Slide Master

The slide master has a default placeholder that is basically for the title slide, footer, date, subheadings, and more. Any formatting changes that will be made should be in the plain area. It is also possible to choose from PowerPoints themes in order to design the slide master. To select the elements in the slide master, it is also possible to select the master layout and then uncheck the placeholders that are not needed.

Modifying The Handout Master

To make some adjustments to the handout master,

- Click on **view the presentation views** and then handout master, or simply hold down the shift key while tapping on the slide sorter view button. The handout master will then be displayed, and it usually includes a handout Master tab on the ribbon.
- Play around with it. The handout master shows the arrangement of handouts for slides of different pages. It can include handouts for slides printed on two, three, four, six, or even nine pages, and also the manner of arrangement for printing the outlines. Using the slides per page control on the handout master tab, it is possible to transition from one handout layer to another. The downside is that the slides and outline placeholders that appear in the handout master cannot be moved, resized, or deleted. It is possible to add or modify elements that should appear on each page of the handout, such as the name and phone number, as well as a page number.
- Select the **close master view button** that is located on the handout master tab on the ribbon. PowerPoint will then go back to normal view.
- To confirm the changes, print a copy of the handout. Handout Master elements cannot be seen until they are printed, so it's okay to print at least a page to check if the changes were effective.

Note that when the handout pages are printed, the slides are adjusted based on the slide master. The way the slide master is displayed cannot be changed from the handout master.

Modifying The Note Master

Notes pages have a reduced image of the slide, and any note that is typed goes along with the slide. When printed, note pages are adjusted to suit the Notes Master. To make changes to the Note Master, follow the steps below:

Click on **view**, then **presentation view**, and then **Notes Master**. The Notes Master will then be displayed.

- The notes master has two main placeholders: one for the notes and the other for the slide. These objects can easily be moved or adjusted, and the format of text can also be changed in the notes placeholder. Elements that should be displayed on each handout page can also be changed or adjusted. It is also essential to note the convenient placement of the footer, date, header and page number.
- Select the **close master view button** and PowerPoint will go back to its normal view. So as to verify if changes have been made, print notes.

Using Masters

Master slides are very special and powerful slides. Typically, they deliver the same commands slightly adjusted for different slides. This depends on how well-formatted the slide master is and whether the changes affect all slides in the presentation or just a few.

Layouts

Start by choosing a slide layout and then adding the title and content so as to create a new slide. In the slide master view, PowerPoint offers a single layout for each type of slide layout in the presentation. By choosing and formatting the layout in the slide master view all over again, all the slides in the presentation that were created with the very same slide layout can be reformatted. For example, to have the fonts, alignments, and other formats on all the slides changed, choose the title layout in the slide master and then change the master styles on the title layout.

Each layout has control over its own little fiefdom in the presentation. A fiefdom also includes slides that are created with the very same slide layout.

Master Styles

Each master slide, i.e., the master slide and layout, provides the opportunity to choose and make changes to the master styles. The master style controls how the text will be formatted on slides. By changing the master style on a master slide, the look of the slides all through the presentation can also be changed. For example, when the master style font changes, the fonts in all the slide titles in the presentation will also change.

Slide master layouts and PowerPoint slides are designed according to the "trickle-down" principle. As soon as a master style is formatted on the slide master, the formats trickle directly down to the layouts, followed by the slides. The master style that is formatted on the layout trickles down to the slides that were created using the same layout. This chain-of-command relationship is created to work right from the top down, with the master slide and layout giving orders to the slides below. Slides receive orders from layouts, and layouts, in turn, receive orders from the Slide Master, in order to maintain consistency of design.

Overriding The Master Text Style

Other than making adjustments to fonts in the slides one after the other, it is possible to change the default fonts for the whole presentation. The font pairing (header font and body font) is a very important design decision when it comes to PowerPoint.

- Choose the **view,** then slide master.
- Navigate to the slide master tab and then choose the fonts drop-down menu. Click on the preferred font that should be used for all the slides in the presentation. It is not compulsory to select from the predefined font pairs on the menu; select the "customize fonts" option located at the lower part of the menu to choose the preferred font.
- Select the **Close Master View** option to have the master view closed. The text throughout the presentation will then be automatically updated to the new font.

Creating Another Slide Master

- On the View tab, select the slide master.
- Do one of the following in the slide master: In the edit master group, choose the insert slide master option. When a new slide master is inserted following this procedure, the new slide master will then be displayed under any previously existing slide master without any theme color or theme effect. Custom themes can, however, be applied with the use of any option in the background group.

On the slide master tab, within the edit theme group, choose themes, and then choose a new theme. If the presentation has just one slide master, choosing a new theme with the use of this procedure will change the theme of the other slide master with the new theme being put in place.

Adding Notes

Understanding Notes

Printing out PowerPoint presentation notes is basically printing slides with notes for yourself. They are mainly intended to help the user recall some of the slideshow's finer details in a very fast and accessible manner. Notes appear on the presenter's screen during the presentation, but not on the main screen so that anyone viewing the slideshow will not be able to see them. The slide show and notes should be printed together.

Adding Notes To A Slide

The Notes pane at the bottom of the normal view can be used to add speaker notes to PowerPoint decks. Presenters can see speaker notes during a slide show and they can also be printed. When PowerPoint slides are created, notes can be added, edited, and formatted.

Speakers' notes should include the following:

- Key talking points
- Key reminders to tell an anecdote or a story
- Optional or supplementary information
- Key references or sources
- Links to documents related to websites or websites
- Reminders to begin a video or an animation
- Prompts to start-up or gestures to another speaker or someone in the audience
- Reminders as regards taking lunch or a break
- Reminders for the audience to follow up or a call to action

If there is a need to check out the notes much later during the presentation, there will be a need to keep them short since there is quite a limited amount of space to check them in the presenter's view. Notes can also be formatted, and they can also be shared as a standalone document or as an alternative to the traditional PowerPoint handouts.

Adding An Extra Note Page For A Slide

The Notes pane is a box that is displayed below each slide. An empty Notes pane will pop up with text that says, "Click to add notes." Type the speaker's note in there. If the notes pane is not made visible or if it has been minimized to the barest minimum, click on notes on the taskbar located across the lower part of the PowerPoint window.

A vertical scroll bar will be displayed on the side of the notes pane if notes exceed the allotted length of the notes pane. The notes pane can also be enlarged by pointing the mouse directly at the top line of the pane and then moving upwards after the pointer changes into a double-headed arrow.

Displaying Notes On A Separate Monitor

Presentations can be made with the use of two monitors. The presenter view, when used, is a great way to view your presentation with speaker notes on a particular monitor, e.g., your laptop, while the audience sees the notes-free presentation on another monitor, probably a larger screen that has been projected to. To execute this procedure and split the view between the projectors in this manner, a connection must be made to the second screen.

 On the slideshow tab, in the monitors' group, choose the use presenter view option. This should leave the window display settings open.

In the display settings dialog box right on the monitor tab, choose the monitor icon that would be used to show the speaker's note, then choose the "this is my main monitor" check box. Once this box has been selected as unavailable, the monitor will automatically be designated as the main monitor.

Choose the monitor icon for the second monitor. This is the one that will be viewed by the audience. Then choose the "extend my Windows desktop onto this monitor" check box.

Changing the Slide Order

The Slide sorter view offers users a view of their slides in thumbnail form.

With this view, it is very easy for sequences of slides to be sorted and organized in preparation for printing the slides. The slide sorter view can be reached from the taskbar below the slides window or the view tab option located on the ribbon.

It is possible to rearrange slides in the slide sorter view before printing them, either due to a change of opinion about how the arrangement should look or to correct an error before the slide is printed.

Below is the very simple way slides can be rearranged in a slide sorter view.

- Change to Slide's Sorter view and all of the presentation slides will be displayed as thumbnails. Click and move the Slide in the desired location once you have located the slides you need to arrange. All slides in the presentation will be renumbered after the slide moves to its new location. After you have arranged everything that needs to be arranged, simply return to the normal view to continue editing the presentation.

Chapter 4: **Tables and Charts**

Insert a Table

The feature of creating tables in PowerPoint is similar to that found in Excel. Even though it doesn't have all the features that Excel has, its tables can also be used for basic functions like creating small sets of data within a slide. In addition, PowerPoint uses a spreadsheet format just like that of Excel to make the data an intuitive part of the slideshows. Although Excel is able to display a lot of data in its own interface, PowerPoint tables are typically very small and can only hold a few records that would fit on just one or two slides.

Standard templates are used for the layout of objects on a new slide. A blank template is one such object, where you can add what you want to the slide. The black template area displays six icon buttons. On the first row you see the insert table button. Simply because it displays an image that resembles that of an Excel spreadsheet, it is very easy to identify. There is an icon for each object that can be inserted. On the right side of the table, for example, is an icon depicting a graph sheet. Upon selecting this icon, the slide will display a graph. In the case of merely inserting a table, click the icon with the table image.

Tables are usually made up of rows and columns. Rows depict the horizontal sections of the table and also contain data for just one record. Columns are basically the fields that makeup one item in a record. If more records are required, use Excel, or take just a few records, use them in the slide show, and have all the other records in the Excel spreadsheet.

Note that the table will be the very same color as that of the presentation theme. The first row is always slightly darker so as to give an indication that it is the first row in the header row. In spreadsheet software such as Excel, the very first row is most often used as the header cell. The header cell shows the column names. These column names are also made to state the type of data that will be displayed in each of the fields.

If you select the **table** command you can produce tables in PowerPoint.

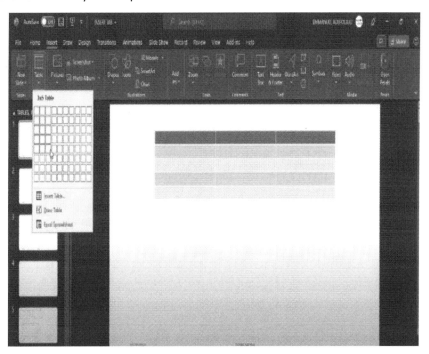

Simply select **Table** to include a table to your screen or you can select **Insert table** then select the number of **columns and rows** you wish for in your table. **Columns** are vertical aspects of your table while **Rows** are the horizontal aspect of your table.

For example, click on **Insert table** and select five columns and rows each for your table and click on Ok. You can start typing on your table after that.

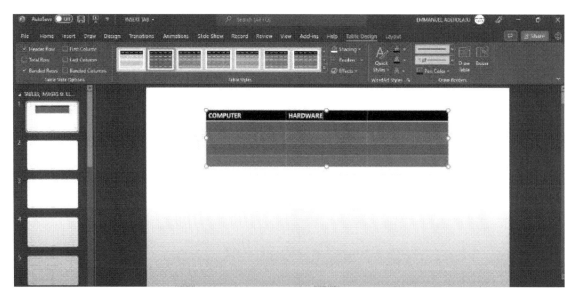

Table Design

You can transform the styles of your table. Click on **table styles** and choose a style of your choice. If you wish for a light, medium, or dark style for your presentation simply click it. You may adjust the **shading**, the **borders**, and the **effects** on your table under the **table design**.

Table Layout

In the **table layout** under the **rows and columns** command group, **insert above, insert below, insert left, and insert right** allows you to insert additional columns and rows above, below, left, or right of your table. Right-clicking also gives you the option of inserting additional columns and rows in your table.

You can **merge cells**. If you highlight two cells and select merge cells it will merge the two cells to one. You can as well split them back. Click on **split cells** to split your merged cells.

Under **table design** and **table layout,** you have many formatting tools that you can work with on your table.

Formatting Tables

After a table has been created, its look can be tweaked to suit the taste of the user. Once a table has been created, the design tab will be created, and this has lots of menu options where colors and styles can be changed.

The first section, labeled "Table Style Options," defines the header rows and columns. By default, the header row check box is always selected, which then shows a darker color in the first row so as to show that it is the header row. This color can also be added to the first column to give the rows a header section too.

There is another light and dark color in banded rows, making it easier to tell each row apart. In a table with a list of numbers, the Total Row option will place a darker color in the lower portion. Columns can be done in a similar manner. By doing so, a more distinct table can be created.

The style color for the table is determined in the table styles section. Depending on the theme, PowerPoint 2022 selects a color style, but you can change the coloration with any of the available styles. A flat color, a darker color, and a lighter color are some of the color combinations available for placing headers and banded rows.

Creating A Table In A Content Placeholder

The placeholder on a slide is used to represent the containers on the slide, which are shown with a dotted external border.

Placeholders can hold text, pictures, tables, charts, SmartArt graphics, and media clips. Placeholders will help to ensure that the design across an entire presentation is consistent and that the design across the whole presentation is the same to ensure that positioning and formatting can be made the same.

- Open the Home tab located on the Ribbon and then select the New Slide button in the Slides Group to add a slide with a title and content layout.
- Click on **the table icon** in the middle of the content placeholder. This will bring up the insert table dialog box.

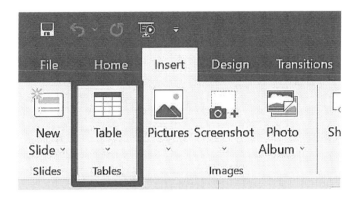

- Place the number of columns and rows.

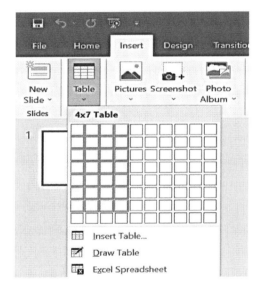

- Type in the needed information into the table cells. This can be done by clicking anywhere on the table and then starting typing. There is also an option to move from cell to cell by clicking on the tab key or the arrow keys.

Drawing A Table

The draw table command gives users the option to draw tables that are quite complicated on screen with the use of a very simple set of drawing tools, as the insert option won't fit. This command is necessary for creating tables that are not just a simple grid of rows and columns, but complex conglomerations in which some of the cells span more than one row, and others span more than a column.

To draw a table:

- Locate the Insert tab on the ribbon and then select **the table button** in the tables group and select **the drawing table** from the menu that is displayed. PowerPoint will then change the cursor to a pencil.
- Draw the entire shape of the table by moving the mouse to create a rectangular boundary for the table. When the mouse is set free, a table with a single cell will be created.
- Click on the **"draw table"** button that is located in the table tools design tab. The mouse pointer will change into a much smaller pencil when this button is selected.
- Cut the table into smaller cells by moving the lines across the table. For instance, divide the table into two rows, focus the cursor somewhere around the left edge of the table, and then select and move a line across the table towards the right edge. When the button on the mouse is released, the table will split

into two rows. Keep moving the line to cut the table into smaller cells. For each slice, focus the cursor at the edge where the new cell should start and select, then move to the other edge.

- If the size of the line or the style that has been drawn needs to be changed for a particular part, make use of the pen style and pen weight drop down controls in the draw borders group on the table tools design tab. The style of an already drawn line can be changed by tracing over the same line with another style.
- If, for instance, a mistake is made while drawing the table cells, select the eraser (the icon that has the eraser image displayed) button in the draw borders group and then erase the line segment drawn in error.

Working With The Layout Tab

This tab contains all the options that can be used to set up the layout of the document pages to your liking. There is a possibility of setting margins, applying themes, as well as controlling page orientation and size. The document can be divided into sections, lines can be broken, line numbers can be displayed, and the paragraph indentation and lines can also be fixed.

To change the layout, arrange the slide content with the different PowerPoint slide layouts as will suit your taste or to help improve the clarity and readability of the content in the slide.

- Choose the slide that the layout should be changed to.
- Choose the Home option, followed by the Layout option.
- Choose the layout that is preferred.

In the layout, there are placeholders for text, pictures, videos, charts, and shapes. There's plenty more. The layouts also have formatting for objects such as theme colors, effects and fonts.

Table Themes

Adding Style To A Table

By using the design tab menu under the table tools menu, you can format the table styles in PowerPoint. This menu controls all the styles used in the table, including the cell format, border color, shadow effect, and table background. By using this menu option, you can easily customize a table by using the quick style options, but if you need to use the advanced styles, you can choose from the other available options. If a quick style is preferred, any modern style can be easily applied to a chosen table.

However, if more style options are needed, draw the border section that has the pen color. Note that line properties can be very useful also. To have the border in a PowerPoint table changed, choose the pen color first, and then choose the cells where they should be added, moving over to the borders option. After all of this has been done, select the border style to be used.

Add a Chart

Charts can be created in PowerPoint. To add a chart to PowerPoint, simply follow the steps below.

- Click on **the insert button**, then select **chart**, and choose the **preferred chart** option by double-clicking on it.
- Change the placeholder data in the worksheet that is displayed with the information at your disposal.
- When a chart is inserted, some little buttons will be displayed next to its upper right-hand corner. Make use of the chart elements button to display, hide or make adjustments to things such as axis titles or data labels. You can also choose to make use of the chart styles button to swiftly make adjustments to the color or style of the chart.
- After all of this has been done, close the chart or worksheet.

Copying And Pasting A Chart Or Data From Excel

There are times when there might be a need to copy a chart from an Excel spreadsheet to a PowerPoint presentation so as to show the summarized data to the viewers or display the visualizations in the dashboards and reports.

To copy a chart from Excel to PowerPoint, simply make use of the copy and paste option from the clipboard. Move to the Excel spreadsheet and choose the range that should be copied. Click on "home" and then select "copy" and then navigate to PowerPoint and click on the "paste option." In PowerPoint, the simple paste option or the paste special option can be used. This is based on whether the chart will be pasted with a special format or pasted as an image. It is also possible to make use of keyboard shortcuts such as **CTRL + C** and **CTRL-P** to copy and paste the chart where necessary.

- If there is a need to insert a range of charts or data from Excel into PowerPoint, name the range in the excel spreadsheet and add the excel spreadsheet object to the PowerPoint presentation.
- Navigate to PowerPoint and select the "paste special option" from the home menu. After this has been done, add a Microsoft Excel worksheet.
- Ensure the paste link is chosen and then add the Microsoft Excel worksheet object.

After all this has been done, the table will then be added.

Formatting Charts

Chart Elements

With PowerPoint, you can add superfluous or adventitious elements such as titles, labels, legends, etc. to your chart. To add these elements to your chart, one of the easiest ways applying chart layout to your chart.

You can also add these elements to your chart one after the other. To do this, make a selection on the chart and click on the **Chart Elements** button.

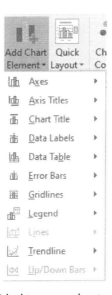

The followings are the elements that can be added to your charts

- **Axes**: These are lines found on the edge of a chart. The axes can be categorized into two; the x-axis at the bottom of the chart and the y-axis at the left edge of the chart.
- **Axis Titles**: These elements explain the meaning of each axis on the chart. The Primary Horizontal Axis Title and the Primary Vertical Axis Title are the two types of axis tiles commonly used in almost all charts.
- **Chart Titles**: This is what talks about the content of the chart and it is most time located at the top, Also, it can be dragged to any place on the chart.
- **Data Labels**: With this option, you can add labels to the data points on the chart.
- **Data Table**: This table displays the data used to construct the chart in the presentation.
- **Error Bars**: This helps to add a graphical element that displays the values of all the points.
- **Gridlines**: These are light lines displayed behind the chart to trace the location of any dot, bar, or line plotted by the chart.
- **Legends**: This helps to categorize the data series found in the chart.
- **Trendline**: This enables you to add line elements that display the trend of the data points, using different methods to calculate the trend.

Edit Chart Data

If a PowerPoint presentation has a chart, the chart data can be adjusted directly in PowerPoint; it doesn't matter if the chart is infused or linked to the presentation. The data can be updated or refreshed in a linked chart without the need to go to the program in which the chart was created.

- Right on the slide, choose the chart that is preferred. The chart tools contextual tab will be displayed at the very top of the PowerPoint window. If the chart tools tab or the design tab is not displayed, ensure the chart is chosen and selected. It is worth noting that the design tab under the chart tools is just not the same as the default design tab in PowerPoint. The chart tools tab will be displayed only when a chart has been chosen and the design layout or format tab under it brings up different commands about the chosen chart.
- Under the chart tools, choose the edit data option on the Design tab in the data group.
- Choose one of the following options next:

To make adjustments in PowerPoint, choose the Edit data option. This will open up a window from the spreadsheet.

To make adjustments to the data directly in Excel, choose the "edit data in Excel" option.

Make the necessary adjustments, which will be shown in the chart in PowerPoint.

Chart Styles

To change the style of the chart, do the following:

- Choose the chart that should be adjusted and the design tab will show
- From the design tab, choose the **more drop-down arrow** in the chart styles group.
- Choose the preferred style from the menu that is displayed.
- The chart will then be displayed as chosen.

The chart formatting shortcut buttons can also be changed to swiftly add chart elements, change the chart style, and filter the chart data.

Correcting Sharpness, Brightness, Contrast And Color

- Choose the preferred picture.
- Click on **picture tools**, then click on **format**, and then choose **Select Corrections**.
- Move over to the options menu to have the picture previewed and then choose the preferred one from the options displayed.

Removing Image Backgrounds

Microsoft PowerPoint offers a bit of picture magic in its ability to remove a background from a picture. To accomplish this part of the photo editing magic, follow the steps below:

- Choose the picture whose background needs to be taken off.
- Locate the picture tools option and then click on the format tab and the remove background button icon, which can be found in the adjust group option.

When this is done, PowerPoint will try to check which part of the picture is the subject of the picture and which portion is the background. PowerPoint will then develop a bounding rectangle with what it perceives as the subject in the picture. It will then check the colors in the picture to ascertain what it thinks are the background portions of the picture. The background will then be shown in purple.

After which the Background Removal tab will show on the Ribbon and when selected the background goes off

- If need be, change the bounding rectangle size so as to enclose the subject well enough.
- If need be, make use of the Mark Areas to keep and mark areas to take off buttons, and also change the location of the background of the picture. For instance, if an area that is a part of the subject is displayed as a background, choose the Mark Areas option to keep the button. Then choose the option of either clicking on the area that should be added or clicking and moving a line across a very large portion of the area to be added. PowerPoint will attempt to know the part of the picture that has been marked and add that area to the picture's subject.

Remember that the part to be included doesn't need to be circled, nor is there a need to be very accurate. PowerPoint will try its best to decipher the parts of the image to add based on the mark. Furthermore, if PowerPoint has by mistake taken a portion of the background as a subject, select the Mark Areas to take off the button and then click or draw a line around the area that should be taken off. If PowerPoint also misinterprets the mark, press the Ctrl + z button to undo the action or select the delete mark button icon and then choose the mark that should be deleted.

- Repeat the 4th step until the picture's background has successfully been removed.
- Select the "keep changes" button icon. The slide will go back to normal with the picture's background removed.

Slide Transitions

Using The Transition Tabs

A slide transition is simply how a particular slide is taken away from the screen and the next slide is shown during a presentation. PowerPoint provides lots of entertaining and different slide transition schemes. The secret is not to use too many different schemes in just one presentation. Be choosy and remember how the scheme should be before adding them to the slides. Test the schemes by opening the slide show and checking out their effectiveness. Ensure it's quality rather than just quantity.

To apply transitions to a presentation, select the **slide sorter view**, which can be found at the lower part of the screen. Thumbnails of all the slides in the presentation will then be displayed. Select the transition tab. The transition tab has the transitions for this slide group. From this group, select a special effect that should be applied between the previous slide and the next slide when the transition is ongoing.

Creating A Slide Transition

A slide transition can be defined as the visible effect of moving a slide from one to the next when a presentation is ongoing. It is worthy of note that in a transition effect, the speed can be controlled, sound can be added, and the look can also be tweaked to meet the user's needs.

To add transitions to slides, simply do the following:

- Choose the slide that needs a transition to be added.

- Click on **the transition tab** and then select a transition.
- Choose a transition to see the preview.

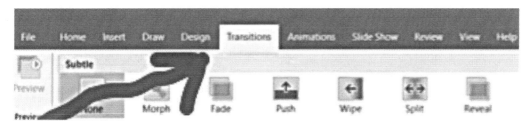

- Choose the **effect options** to select the direction and nature of the transition.
- Choose **a preview** to check what the transition looks like.

Click on the "apply to all" button to add a transition to the presentation. Select transitions and choose none to have a transition removed.

Morph Transitions

Morph transition is used for a smooth animation when moving objects from slides to slides during a presentation. It is an amazing PowerPoint feature that can make your communication easy and classic. For Morph transition to work perfectly, you must have at least two identical slides, i.e., the slides must have at least one object in common. You can duplicate the slides or copy the objects from slide to slide to achieve this.

To animate with Morph transition:

- Prepare a slide with all the elements you want.
- Right-click on the slide Thumbnail pane on the left. A drop-down list appears.
- Select **Duplicate** to reproduce the slide. Duplicate the slides as often as you need a smooth movement of objects between slides.
- Reposition the objects in the duplicated slides as desired.
- Select all the slides you duplicated except the first slide.
- Go to the **Transitions** tab.
- Select **Morph** in the **Transition to This Slide** gallery.
- Select the **Effect Options** to choose how the transition should work.
- Click the Slide Show to preview the effect.

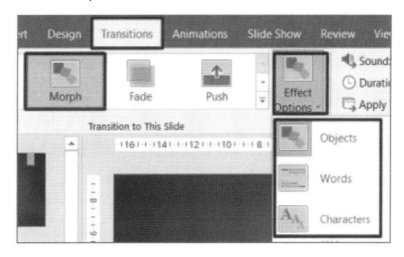

Notes:

- **Morph** transition creates an appearance of movement of objects in different locations from one slide to the other; therefore, you do not need to add animation to the object you want to morph. Animation effect overrides morph transition.
- Objects like text, shapes, pictures, SmartArt graphics, and WordArt **Morphs.** However, Charts do not morph but disappear from an initial position to reappear in the new position from slide to slide.

Tips:

You can morph one object to a different object in another slide by renaming the two objects with the same name and with !! in front of the names.

To rename an object:

- Select the object.
- Go to the object contextual **Format** tab (or **Home** tab, and click the **Select** button in the **Editing** group).
- Click the **Selection Pane.**
- Double click on the object name in the selection pane to activate the edit mode.
- Rename the object starting with **!!**
- Go to the second slide with the second object and rename the object with the same name as the previous one.
- Apply **Morph** transition to the second slide.
- Go to the Slide mode and preview how the first shape morphs smoothly into the second shape.

Animations

Animation Effect Options

You can choose from different effect options for some of the animation effects. The effect options available depend on the type of effect you choose. For example, the default **Fly In** effect option allows the object to fly in from the bottom. You can change this setting from the top.

To change the animation effect options:

- Select the object you have added an animation.
- Go to the **Animation** tab in the **Animation** group.
- Click on the **Effect Options**. A drop-down list appears.
- Select your preferred animation effect.

For more animation effect options, click on the dialog box launcher in the **Animation** group.

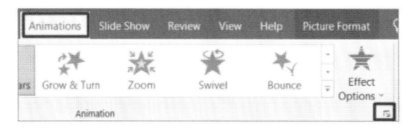

Animations Preview

Anytime you apply an animation to your slide, you can see the effect live on your slide by default. You can always replay the preview with the **Preview** command in the Animations tab. Click the Preview drop-down button and uncheck the AutoPreview command to turn off the auto preview.

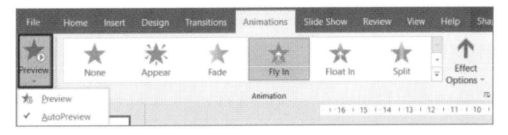

Tips:

- You can always tell the object that has an animation with a small number that appears at their left-top side, one for each effect. The number indicates the effect position on mouse click in the slide.
- The slide's thumbnail with an animated object(s) will also have a star icon.
- You can preview a slide animation and transition by clicking the star beside the slide left side thumbnail.

Adding Multiple Animations To An Object

You can apply only one of the animation effects in the **Animation** group to an object. Any additional effect you choose from the main menu will override the initial effect.

To add multiple animation effects to an object:

- Select the object.
- Go to the **Animations** tab.
- In the **Advanced Animation** group, click **Add Animation** Button.
- The Animation gallery appears exactly like the one in the **Animation** group.
- Add as many effects as you desire. Repeat the above steps to add multiple effects.

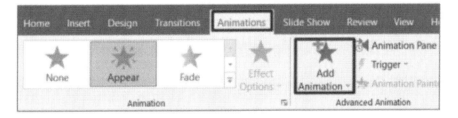

Animation Painter

When you want to apply animation effect(s) to an object just as you have applied to one, instead of going through the stress of applying the effects repeatedly, PowerPoint has a special command called **Animation Painter**. **Animation Painter** copies the animation effect(s) of one and applies it to the other.

To use an Animation Painter:

- Select the object that has your desired animation.
- Go to the **Animations** tab and in the **Advanced Animation** group.
- Click the **Animation Painter**.
- Your cursor turns to a paintbrush.

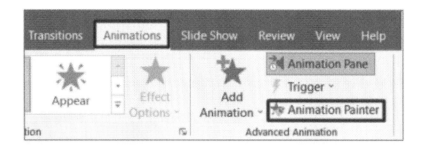

- Move the cursor to your slide and select the object you want to add the animation.

PowerPoint automatically adds the animation to the object like the one you copied.

Animation Painter turns itself off after each use. To keep it active for continuous use,

- double-click on it.
- Press the Esc key or click on the icon when you are done.

Animation Pane

You can do your slide animations' complete and advanced settings in the animation pane. You can order, set duration, set delay, repeat, trigger, and do so many settings in the pane. Opening the animation pane for easy settings will be advisable if you have many animations to keep track of. Given below is a screenshot of an animation pane and all its elements:

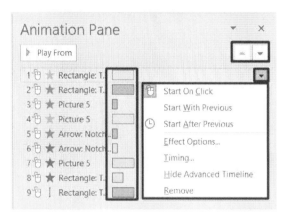

The animation pane consists of all the animation effects on the selected slide.

- The list consists of numbers arranged in the order of effects occurrence on mouse click,
- The effect category color symbols,
- The names of the objects that have the effects,
- The advanced timelines of the effects (i.e., the effects durations)
- A drop-down arrow in front of any selected effect for advanced settings
- Two arrow up and arrow down buttons to move the selected effects up or down.
- **Play From** button to preview the animation, from the selected effect to the last effect.

Tips:

- Hold down the **Shift** key to select multiple animation effects for settings and click on the effects one after the other.
- An effect that occurs automatically (i.e., not by mouse click) does not carry a number.
- Use the drop-down arrow to access more options and to fine-tune the effects.

Animation Start Options And Trigger

Animation Start Options

By default, animations are set to start when you click your mouse. You can change this setting and make some animation effects start automatically after or with the previous one.

To start animation effect automatically:

- Select the object that has the animation and click on the effect number you want to start automatically.
- Go to the **Animation** tab.
- Click the Start drop-down button in the **Timing** group.
- Select **With Previous** to start the effect at the same time as the previous effect or
- Select **After Previous** to automatically start the effect after the occurrence of the previous effect.

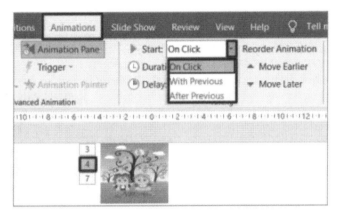

Alternatively,

- Open the Animation Pane in the Animation tab.
- Select the animation effects you want.
- Click the drop-down button in front of the effect.
- Select the desired option from the drop-down menu.

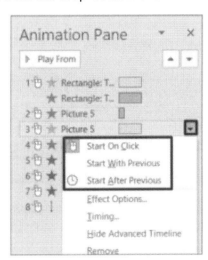

The first animation effect, set to start after the previous, automatically begins after the slide appears or after the transition effect of the slide, if any.

Trigger From The Same Or Another Object

Apart from starting the animation of an object on mouse click, you can also trigger the animation effect by clicking on the object with the effect or another object.

To trigger animation by clicking an object:

- Go to the Animation tab.
- Select the object and click the animation effect number you desire to trigger when you click an object.
- Click the Trigger button in the Advanced Animation group. A drop menu appears.
- Select the On Click of command. The list of all the objects on the slide appears, including the object that bears the animation effect.
- Select an object you wish to click to trigger your selected effect.

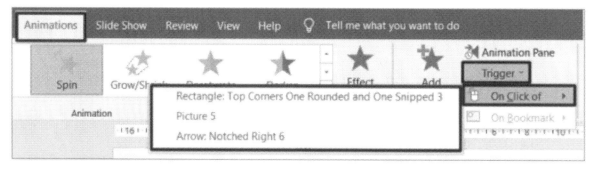

Ordering Animation

Suppose, you apply more than one animation on a slide. In that case, the animation will be arranged in the order you inserted them. The first animation you apply will be numbered one, the second one will be two, and so on. You can rearrange the animation order after you have applied them.

To reorder the animations on a slide:

- Select the object you want to reorder its animation and click on the number you want to change.
- Go to the **Animation** tab, in the **Timing** group,
- Click on either **Move Earlier** or **Move Later** buttons as desired, which order the animation with a level earlier or later. You can click the buttons several times until you get your desired number.

Alternatively, to have more control over your ordering,

- Select the **Animation Pane** command in the **Advanced Animation** group.

The animation navigation pane appears at the right side of your window with the list of all the animation effects on the slide, starting from the first effect at the top to the last at the bottom.

- Select, Drag and Drop any effect to the desired level or use the arrow key up or down after selecting the effect

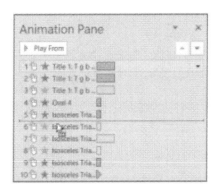

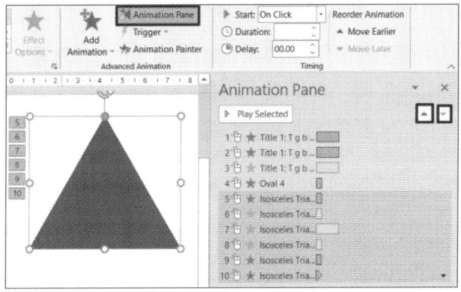

Setting Animation Duration And Delay

PowerPoint animation effects start immediately after it is triggered and play for the default duration. You can choose to delay the effect for some seconds after it has been triggered or play the effect slower or faster than the default settings.

To adjust the animation duration;

- Go to the **Animation** tab.
- Select the animation effect number you want to adjust its duration on the object.
- Set your desired duration in the **Duration** textbox in the **Timing** group.
  Or
- Go to the **Animation Pane,** click, and drag the right-side of the effect's **Advanced timeline** to the desired position. As you drag the timeline, use the box that shows you the **Start** and **End** time of the effect to set your desired position.

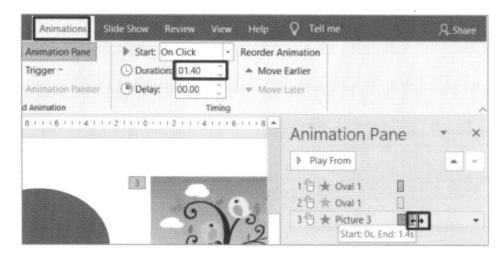

To add delay to the animation effect:

- Go to the **Animation** tab.
- Select the animation effect number you want to adjust its duration on the object.
- Set your desired delay in the **Delay** textbox in the **Timing** group.
  Or
- Go to the **Animation Pane,** click, and drag the whole effect's **Advanced timeline** to the desired position. As you drag the timeline, use the box that shows you the **Start** and **End** time of the effect to set your desired position.

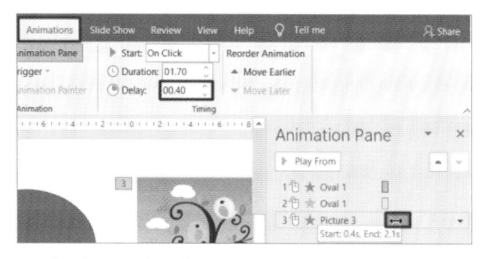

Note: The animation effect duration will be affected if you click and drag the left side of the Advanced Timeline.

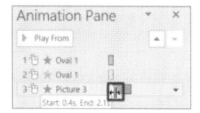

Make Text Appear One By One During A Presentation

PowerPoint animation can reveal your text paragraph by paragraph during a presentation. It can be a helpful feature as it can display your points as you want to discuss them by clicking.

To reveal your text paragraph by paragraph:

- Select the text box that contains the point you want to display one by one.
- Go to the **Animations** tab.
- Click the **Animation** group dialog box launcher.

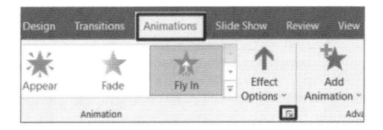

- Click the **Text Animation** tab in the **Effects Options** dialog box that appears.
- Click the **Group text** drop-down button.
- Select an option from the drop-down list as desired.

By **1st Level Paragraph** will bring a paragraph with its sublevels at once.

By **2nd Level Paragraph** will bring a paragraph first and all its sublevels next.

By **3rd Level Paragraph** will bring a paragraph first, its first sublevel next, and all other sublevels next. Etc.

- Press **OK** when done.

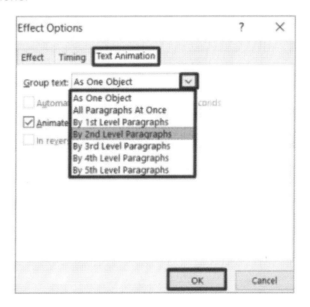

Repeat Animation

At times and for a particular reason, you may want your animation effect to repeat several times or continuously until you take action.

To set your animation effect to repeat:

- Go to the **Animation** tab.
- Click the **Animation Pane** in the **Timing** group.
- Select and click the drop-down button of the effect you want to repeat in the animation pane.
- Select **Timing…** from the drop-down menu. The effect dialog box appears.
- Click the **Repeat** drop-down menu and select an option as desired.
- Press **OK.**

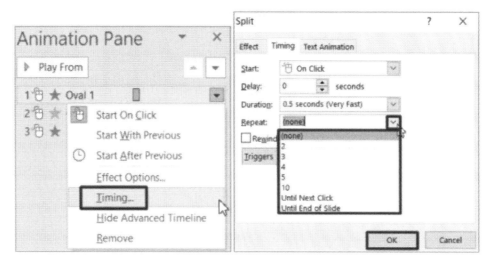

Remove Animations

To remove animation from an object:

- Select the object you want to remove its animation effect
- Go to the **Animation** tab.
- Set the animation to **None.**

Or

- Select Animation Pane.
- Select and click the drop-down button of the effect.
- Select Remove in the drop-down list.

Chapter 6: **Adding Video**

It doesn't matter if all you are doing is selling an idea, a product, or even a strategy; an audience's attention will be drawn faster with creative videos. It is very important to remember that a PowerPoint presentation is as good as the video inserted into it. This can be done within minutes if you need to make a very engaging, stylish, and informative video. Just follow the steps below to get this done promptly.

Inserting A Video From The PC

- Select the preferred slide, move to the menu, and click on the inset icon.
- In the top right hand corner, click on video, then choose the video on my PC option.
- Search for the preferred video and select the insert button.
- Make changes to the video format tool tab settings to ensure the video plays just how you want it to. If the video takes center stage immediately after it is selected, ensure the slide has been set to Play Full Screen and Start Automatically.
- Take a preview of the presentation to ensure the video plays just the way you prefer it, and that will be all.

Insert A Video From YouTube

To insert a video from YouTube, choose the insert video option and the online video option. Insert the web address for any video from YouTube, Vimeo, etc. Note that an internet connection will be needed for this to work during the presentation.

- Open the YouTube website, search for the preferred video, and click on the share button that can be found below the video frame to choose the embed option.
- Copy the embed code. Ensure that the code is the right one so the whole process goes smoothly. Do not copy the URL on the first "share" pop-up displayed on the screen. After selecting the "embed" icon, wait a little for the pop-up screen named "embed video". After this, select the **copy button** in the bottom right-hand corner. The correct code should begin with "iframe width."
- Navigate to PowerPoint and choose the slide to which the video should be added.
- **Select the** insert button.
- Click on **video** and choose the video from the website.
- **Choose the** video and select the playback option.
- Select the start menu to choose the way the video should be played.
- Ensure you are online when the play button is selected. Remember once again that an internet connection is needed for this.

Setting Video Options

The playback option in PowerPoint can control how and when a video should be displayed in the presentation. The video can be played in full screen mode; alternatively, it can be resized to preferred dimensions as specified. The volume can also be adjusted, the video played again and again (loop) and the controls of the media can also be shown.

Play a video in the click sequence, either automatically or when clicked.

- Return to the normal view and select the video frame on the slide.
- Right under the video tools, on the playback tab in the video options group, in the start list displayed, choose one of the options below;

The video plays automatically when the slide show is displayed.

When clicked, the video will only play when it is clicked upon.

In the click sequence, the video plays in sequence with the rest of the actions that must have been programmed on the slide, like animation effects. This option does not need a click. The video can be triggered to start with any mechanism that brings about the start of the next action on the slide, like pressing the right arrow key.

Play A Full Video Screen

A video can be played to fill up the entire slide when a presentation is being delivered. Based on the resolution of the main video file, it might appear distorted when enlarged. Ensure to always preview the video before adding it to the presentation. This way, if the video is shown as distorted or blurry, adjustments can be made to the undo button (Ctrl + Z) to change the full-screen option.

Suppose, the video is set to be shown as full screen and it is also set to start automatically. In that case, the video frame can be moved off the slide into the grey area. This way, it will not be shown on the slide or briefly just before the video goes full screen.

- Locate the normal view, choose the preferred video frame on the display that should play full screen.
- Right underneath the video tools, on the playback tab, in the video options group, choose the "play full screen" checkbox.

Resize A Video

If there is no need for a video to be played full screen, there is an option to resize the video to the preferred dimension.

- Right in the normal view, choose the video that should be adjusted.
- Do one of the following:

To adjust the formatting option, click on any corner sizing handle until a two-headed arrow is displayed, then move the arrow until it fits the frame.

To keep the middle of the video right in the same place, press down on the Ctrl button while moving. By default, this should keep the video's proportions (have the aspect ratios locked) as it moves.

Most videos have a resolution of 680 x 480 and a 4:3 aspect ratio. The default aspect ratio for PowerPoint 2022 presentations is 16:9. If the aspect ratios of the presentations and the video are not the same, the video will appear distorted when it is played.

- To be specific about the height-width proportions of the video,

Right under the video tools option, on the format tab in the size group, select the dialog box launcher.

Select size and then, right under the scale, choose the lock aspect ratio check box.

Under the size and rotate options, fill in the sizes in the height and width boxes or under scale in the scale height and scale width boxes that are displayed, and fill in the preferred percentage of size, in tandem with the video's original size.

Trimming Your Video

To trim an audio file, follow the steps below:

- Click on the video you wish to trim, go to the **Playback** tab and click on the **Trim Video** command in the **Editing** group.

- In the **Trim Video** dialog box, drag the **green handle** to set the start time & the **red handle** to set the end time
- Use the **Play** button to preview the trimmed video file and then click on the **Ok** button when you are done

Preview The Video

- In the normal view, choose the video frame.
- Select the play button. Find the play option in the preview group that can be found both on the format and playback tabs under the video tools.

Set The Volume Of The Video

- Right underneath the video tools, on the playback tab in the video options group, select the video option and select one of the following: low, medium, high, or mute.

Make A Video Loop

Make use of the loop feature to play a video in a repeated manner and continuously when a presentation is ongoing. Right under the video tools, on the playback tab in the video options group, click on the loop icon until a stop option is displayed in the checkbox.

After watching a video, you can rewind it.

To rewind the video after it has been played during a presentation, go right under the video tools option on the playback tab in the video options group, then choose the rewind option after playing in the checkbox.

Compressing Media

Compressing images in a Microsoft PowerPoint presentation can help reduce the presentation's overall file size while also saving disk space on the device it is saved on.

Open the PowerPoint presentation that has the images that should be compressed and then click on a photo. After this is done, it will automatically be in the picture format tab. After this, click on the "Compress picture" icon in the adjust group. The compressed pictures window will then be displayed. When in the compressed picture options group, there will be an option to choose if the compression should apply to the selected picture only or not. If this option is unchecked, PowerPoint will compress all the images found in the presentation. This option overrides any other option that has been set on the images.

Chapter 7: **Adding Sound**

A dding audio clips to PowerPoint presentations can be so much fun. Some might be wondering where sound should be added to a presentation. There might be a couple of reasons why an audio clip should be added, from adding a voice-over to just inserting a little background music to make the presentation more fun and less boring.

PowerPoint can insert audio clips from various files. The files include Mp3, WMA, or WAV files. These files are automatically infused into the presentation. Also, note that it is very good practice to put the audio files in the same folder in which the presentation has been saved before inserting them into the presentation.

Follow the steps below to insert audio clips into PowerPoint.

- Move over to the slide where an audio clip should be added. From the Insert tab of the ribbon, select the down arrow found below the audio button to drag up the drop-down menu. Right within this menu, select the Audio on My PC option.

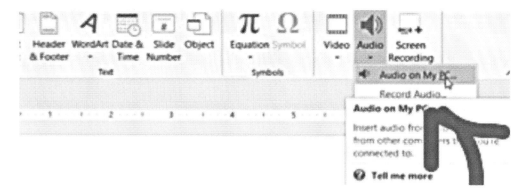

- After that has been selected, it will bring up the Insert Audio dialog box. Move to the saved audio clip folder and select the "any audio file option."
- Then, click on the **"insert" button**. Getting this done helps add the audio clip to the active slide and includes it as part of the presentation. This, of course, can blow up the size of the PowerPoint presentation file. If the file size is a problem, you can simply link the file to the presentation rather than include it.

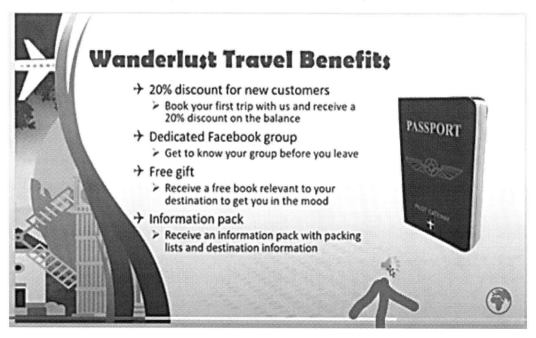

- If linking the audio clip is preferred over including it in the presentation, click on the down arrow next to the insert button. Getting this done will bring up a menu that has two different options: the Insert option, which is the default option that includes sound right within the presentation, and the Link File option, which does not add the audio file to the presentation, only links it. If this is the preferred option, always copy the audio clip to the same folder as the presentation before the file is added to the slide. If, by any chance, the presentation needs to be moved to another computer, the entire folder can be copied rather than just the presentation file.

- Immediately an audio file has either been linked or inserted, PowerPoint will have an audio file placed at the middle of the slide.
- It is worth noting that the player controls bar will be displayed when the mouse is moved over the audio icon in the normal view. A very similar bar will also be displayed in the slide show view. The play button on the player controls can be used to play the audio file. If the preferred option is for the sound to play automatically in the slide show view without having to click on the play button, click on the audio icon first so that the playback contextual tab will be made active on the ribbon. This tab provides various options to control the playback of the audio that has been chosen. Find the start option. Selecting this option will bring up a drop-down list. From this list, select the Automatically option. This step ensures that the audio clip will play automatically when the slide with the clip shows up in the slide show mode.

Always note that the default option is the click sequence. If this option is chosen, the sound will be played only when the space bar has been tapped or the cursor is selected in slide show mode to move to the next event. Furthermore, a third option can be displayed when clicked on in the drop-down list. This option shows the player control, and the play button must be selected before the audio file will play.

- When all of this has been done, save the presentation.

Investigating Sound Files

A presentation should be tested for sound before being saved and presented to an audience. This could result in hiccups during the presentation if the sound is not properly linked or inserted. You can avoid this drama by selecting the "from the beginning" option from the slide show tab and testing the sound. Always remember that the computer must have a sound card or sturdy speakers to hear sounds.

Setting Audio Options

Looping The Sound

There are instances when the sound length doesn't cover the whole presentation, but it can be looped so that it plays repeatedly. This feature is mostly used when the sound effect is quite cool and subtle, like the sound of waves crashing, and you deem it fit to continue playing as long as the slide is still in view. Just click the loop button to loop an audio clip until the stop checkbox is found in the audio options group.

Hide The Sound Icon.

The icon that shows an audio clip will be displayed on the slide while the side show is ongoing. Suppose, the sound has been set to play automatically. In that case, there is every possibility that the icon being displayed won't be needed. The audio options group has a checkbox with the heading "hide" when it is not being played. It just hides the icon when the sound is not playing; the icon will be shown when the sound is being played.

Fade In And Out.

The fade in and out options help to fade the audio clip in and out slowly. By default, these controls are always set at 0. This way, the audio clips begin and stop at the highest volume. By changing one or both of these controls to a value like 3 or 4 seconds, the sound in or out can be gently faded for a cooler effect.

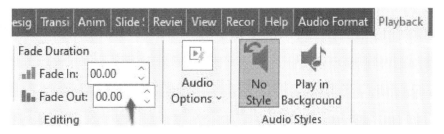

Audio Clip and Trim

Selecting the trim audio buttons helps bring up the trim audio dialog box. This dialog box helps to choose only the parts of the audio clips that should be played in the presentation by providing an option to choose the start and end times of the audio clip. The start and end times can be selected by dragging the green pointer indicating start and the red pointer indicating stop over the audio file waveform (the stop or endpoint can often be determined by looking at the waveform displayed in the Trim Audio dialog box).The time for the start and stop can also be entered in seconds in the start and end time boxes. Ideally, the start and end trim points should be chosen when the audio file is naturally silent to avoid the audio file ending abruptly.

Chapter 8: **Managing Slides**

Recording Presentations

Y ou can record your presentation and voice with this command for a self-running slide show. Selecting the command takes you to the slide show view, which records your presentation as you present.

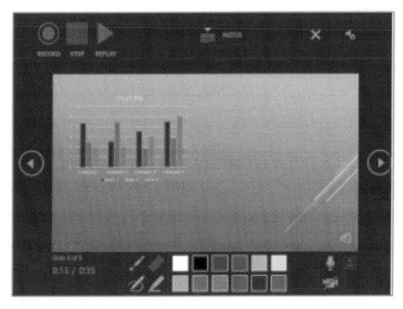

Click the red Record icon at the top-left side of the slide. Start presenting after the countdown number. You can pause, stop, and replay your record with the other buttons at the top-left side of the slide. Also available on the slide screen are drawing tools you can use during recording and some other options for settings before you start recording. Use the arrow keys on both sides to change the slide. Press the **Esc** key and save or share your presentation as a video or PowerPoint file as desired. Your presentation automatically starts playing when anyone opens it and selects play.

Export your Presentation

Immediately you are done recording with narration, timing, pen drawing, highlighter, and other things you want to include in the presentation, then you may proceed to convert your presentation to video by:

Tap on the **File** tab and select **Export** from **the File backstage**.

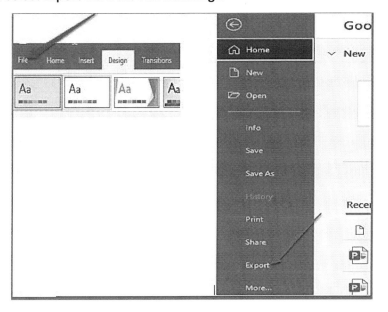

Select **Create a video** to access Create a Video dialog box.

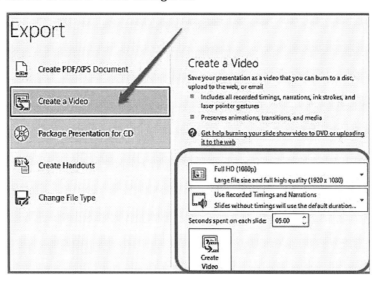

Click on the **first down menu** and select the **video quality(video resolution)** the higher the resolution the bigger the video size.

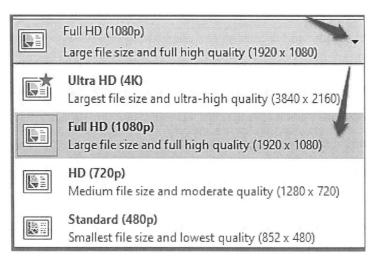

Click on the **second down menu** and tell PowerPoint whether the presentation has **timing and narration or not**, check below to know how to deal with the two options:

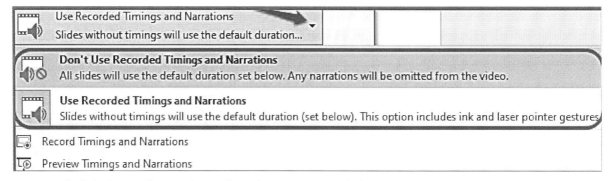

Don't use Recorded timing and narrations: if you have not recorded timed narration, you will select this option, it means all the slides will spend 5 minutes each by default, though you can change this setting by entering different times into "Second to spend on each slide" box, the new time you enter is the period that each slide will spend.

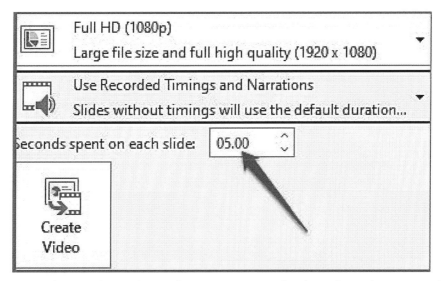

Use Recorded timings and narrations: this is the option you will select if you have recorded and timed the narration, to record time narration and view the time each slide will spend, kindly check (**Scheduling The Time That Slides Will Stay On The Screen**).

- Click on the **second down menu** again and select **Preview Timing and Narration** to glance through your video presentation to view how it plays.

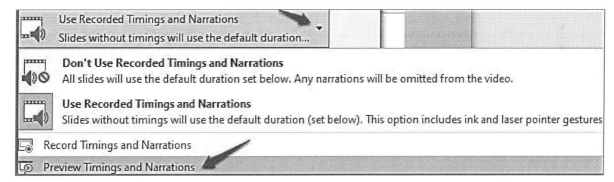

- Then you can tap on the **Create Video** command to access the Save as dialog box.

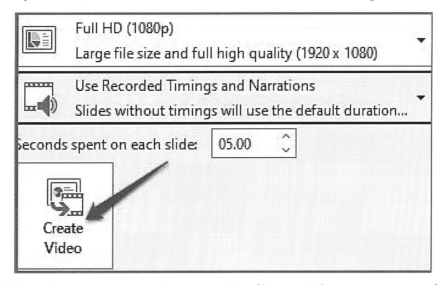

- **Specify the folder** where you want to place your video file, insert the **name** you want for the video and strike the **save button**.

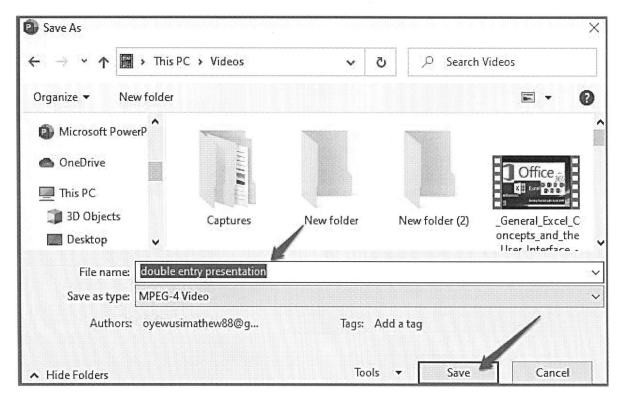

Note: you will see the progression of the video processing on the status bar at the bottom of the screen. The time taken to process a video depends on the size of the presentation you are converting.

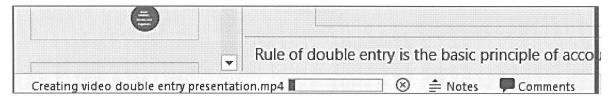

Chapter 9: **Photo Albums**

The Photo Album allows you to insert or import pictures into your presentation. The Photo Album allows you to select, adjust, rearrange, and apply text to your images.

Creating a Photo Album

Creating a Photo Album is easier than you think. To create a Photo Album, follow the steps given below:

- Go to the **Insert** tab and click on **New Photo** Album in the **Image** group

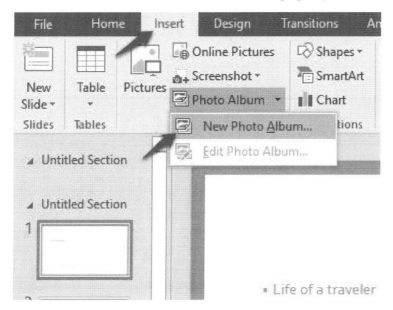

- In the **Photo Album** dialog box, go to **Insert picture from** and click on **File/Disk**

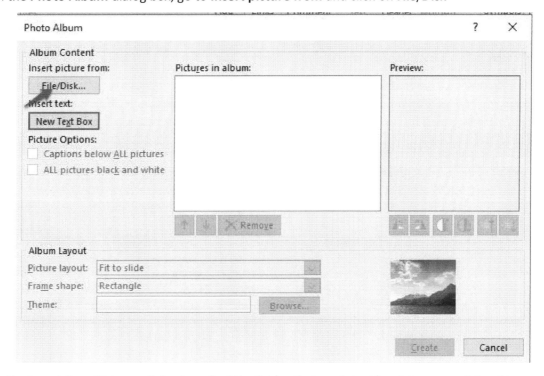

- In the **Insert** New Pictures dialog box, find the folder that contains the pictures you intend to use and click on Insert.

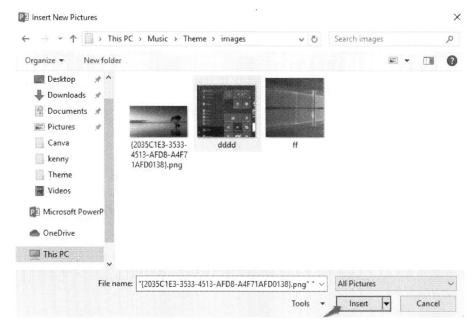

- You can select other options for moving, changing the layout of pictures, etc. and then click on **Create**

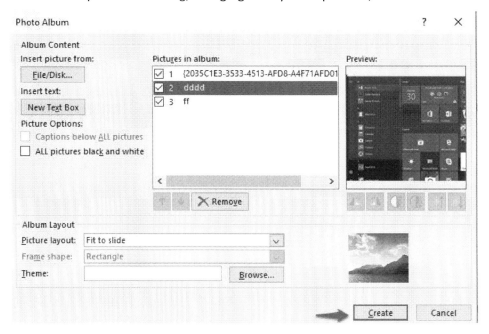

- Here, a new presentation is created for the photo album

330

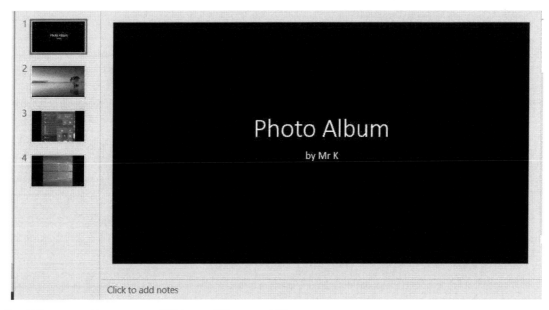

Changing the Picture Layout of Your Photo Album

To change the picture layout in your photo album, follow the steps given below

- Go to the **Insert** tab, click on the arrow beside **New Photo** Album, and then click on **Edit Photo Album** in the **Image** group
- In the **Photo Album** dialog box, go to the **Album Layout**, select any of the layouts of your choice in the **Picture layout** list, and then click on **Update**

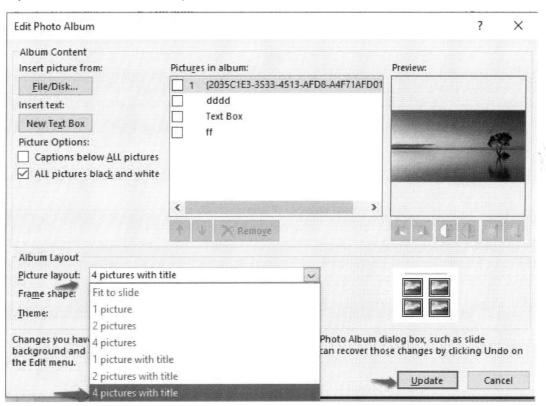

- Here, the frame is applied to the pictures in the presentation

331

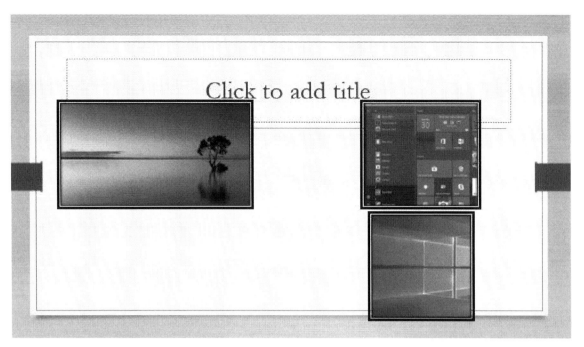

Adding Textbox to your Photo Album

Textbox allows you to add text to your Photo Album. To add a text box to your photo album, follow the steps below;

- Go to the **Insert** tab, click on the arrow beside **New Photo** Album, and then click on **Edit Photo Album** in the **Image** group
- In the **Photo Album** dialog box, go to **Insert text,** select **New Text Box**, and click on **Update**

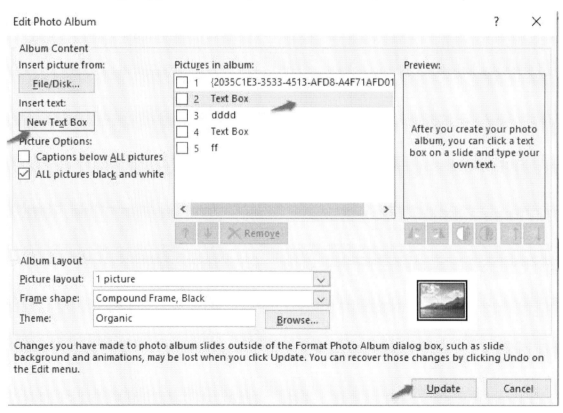

- The Textbox is displayed as a new slide where you can type whatever text you have in mind.

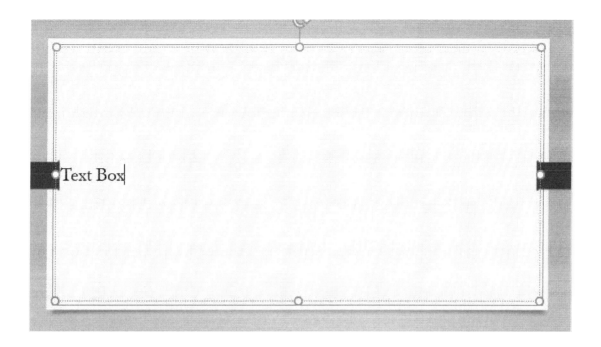

Selecting Theme for Your Photo Album

To apply a theme to your photo album, follow the steps given below

- Go to the **Insert** tab, click on the arrow beside **New Photo** Album, and then click on **Edit Photo Album** in the **Image** group
- In the **Photo Album** dialog box, go to the **Album Layout**, navigate to **Theme,** and then click on Browse

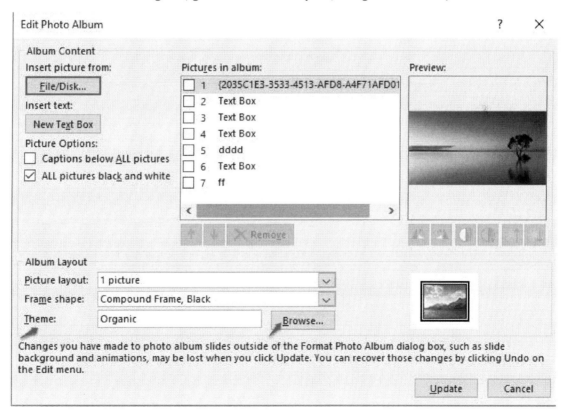

- In the **Choose Theme** dialog box, select the theme you want, and click on **Select**

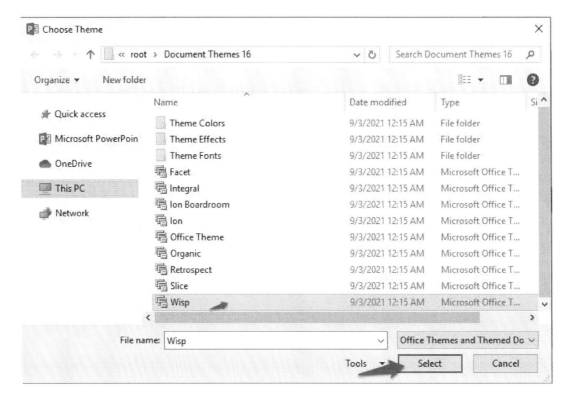

- Click on **Update** in the Photo Album dialog and the theme will be displayed in Photo Album

Changing the Pictures in the Photo Album to Black and White

To change the pictures in the Photo Album to black and white, follow the steps given below

- Go to the **Insert** tab, click on the arrow beside **New Photo** Album, and then click on **Edit Photo Album** in the **Image** group
- In the **Photo Album** dialog box, select **All pictures black and white** check box under **Picture Options** and then click on **Update.**

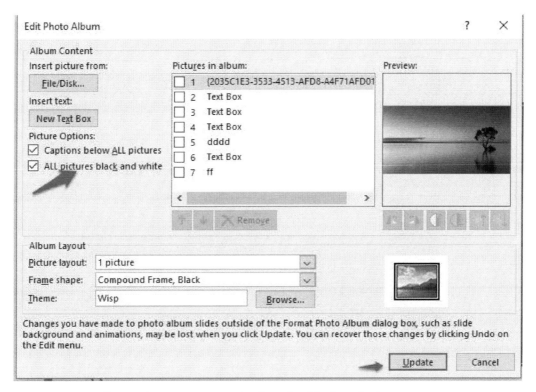

- Here in the Photo Album, the pictures are displayed in black and white

Removing Picture from a Photo Album

To remove a picture from the photo album, follow the steps below

- Go to the **Insert** tab, click on the arrow beside **New Photo** Album, and then click on **Edit Photo Album** in the **Image** group
- Select the picture you want to remove in the **Picture in the album** box and then click on **Remove.**

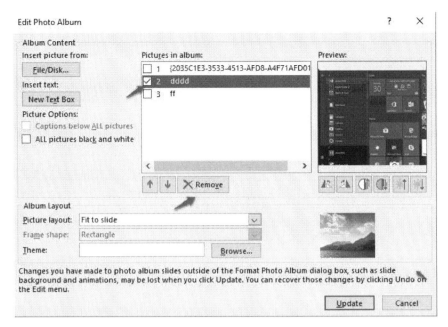

Other Important Features in the Photo Album Dialog Box

There are some important features in the Photo Album that can change the appearance of your pictures. These features are as follows

- Rotating picture clockwise
- Rotating picture counter-clockwise
- Increasing the contrast of a picture
- Decreasing the contrast of a picture
- Increasing the brightness of a brightness
- Decreasing the brightness of a picture

The features above are displayed in the **Preview** option in the **Photo Album** dialog box

Chapter 10: Microsoft PowerPoint Pen Support

You can add additional information to your slides during a presentation with the pen or highlighter. You can underline words or make a mark or any important word you wish to emphasize during a presentation.

To draw or highlight on a slide during a presentation, follow the steps below:

- Click on the **Pen** button located at the lower-left corner of the presentation screen, and then select any color from the menu that pops up
- Go back and click **Pen** or **Highlighter** and drag the mouse to draw or highlight on the slide
- When you are done using the pen or highlighter, press the **Esc** button

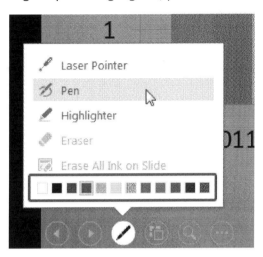

NOTE: You can do the following during a presentation

- To temporarily hide or show markings on your slides, right-click on the screen interface and click on **Screen** to select **Show/Hide Ink Markup.**

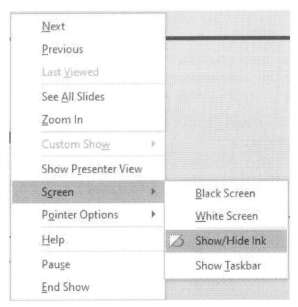

- To permanently erase markings, right-click on the screen interface and click on **Pointer Options** to select **Eraser.** When the Eraser appears, hover it on the markings to permanently delete
- To permanently erase markings all at once, right-click on the screen interface and click on **Pointer Options** to select **Eraser All on Slides.**

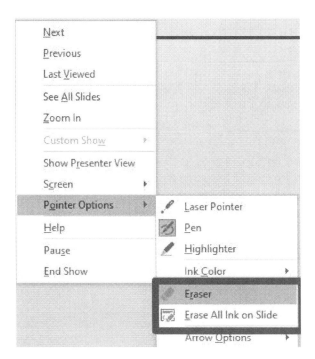

You can also do the following after a presentation

- To erase the markings, go to the **Review** tab, click on Hide Ink and select **Delete All Ink on Slide** or **Delete All Ink in Presentation.**
- To hide the markings, go to the **Review** tab, click **Hide Ink** and select **Hide Ink** in the options to hide

Chapter 11: **Setting Up Presentation**

A fter preparing your presentation, PowerPoint has a lot of options for you to set up your slide show in preparation for presenting your presentation. For example, you might want your slide show to play on its own continuously until you press the **Esc** key, maybe for advertisement or some other reasons.

To set up your presentation:

- Go to the **Slide Show** tab.

- Click the **Set Up Slide Show** command in the **Set Up** group. A dialog box appears.
- Make all your settings as desired and
- Press **OK**.

Present Online

In this section, I will explain how you can show your created slides online. To present your slides online, take these steps:

- Click the **Slide Show** tab.
- From the commands that will be shown to you, select **Present Online**.

- Select **Office Presentation Service**.
- Select the **Enable remote viewers to download the presentation**.
- Tick box if you want to allow your audience to download a copy of your created presentation file.

- Click **Connect** button for you to get connected.

Also, if you want to send your meeting invitation to attendees, you can select **Copy Link**.

- When you select **Copy Link**, you will copy a link you can share with people to access your presentation file.
- When you want to start your presentation, click **Start Presentation**.
- When you are done with the entire presentation process, click the **ESC** key of your computer's keyboard followed by **End Online Presentation**.
- To finally confirm you are exiting the online presentation, click **End Online Presentation** button.

Opening a Saved Presentation

You can open your presentation from the PowerPoint application or directly from your device.

To open an existing presentation from PowerPoint:

- Go to the backstage view by clicking on the **File** tab.
- Click the **Open** tab.
- **Open** pane appears.
- Select the location of your presentation.
- An **Open** dialog box appears.
- Select the folder or your presentation. You can scroll down the left side list of locations on your device to locate your presentation.
- Click **Open**.

Alternatively, suppose you recently opened your presentation or pinned it to PowerPoint. In that case, it will be available in the **Recent** or **Pinned** list in the backstage **Home** panel, and you can click on it to open it.

If you often use or work on your presentation, it will be better to pin it in the PowerPoint.

To pin your presentation to PowerPoint:

- Locate the Presentation in the recent list.
- Move your cursor over the presentation.
- Click the pin icon in front of the file.

To open an existing presentation from your device:

- Ensure you have a PowerPoint application installed on your computer.
- Locate your PowerPoint presentation on your device.
- Double-click on it, and it opens.

Saving your Presentation

To ensure all the hard work doing the content will not be lost in the future, it is of utmost importance to safeguard presentations. There is also an option to print the presentation if the hard copy is needed to be shared in a meeting, for example.

To save a presentation, **select a file,**

and then click **on the save as option** then choose PC to save to the computer in use and then type a preferred name for the presentation in the file name box and then click **on the save button.**

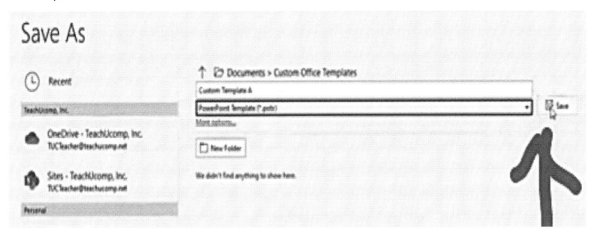

It's best to have the content saved while still working on it. This can give a guarantee that the files are well saved. Simply click on the **Ctrl + S button** often to have this done.

Save as a Different Format

Creating A PDF File

PowerPoint provides the option of saving presentations as PDF files. Saving your PowerPoint document as a PDF file is a very fast way to produce a PowerPoint file that is ready for reviewing, printing, and also emailing. The PDF will have all the formatting that has been applied retained, whether or not the recipient has the styles, fonts, or themes installed on the computer. Similarly, PDF files are a secure way to transfer presentations to anyone because they cannot be edited or tweaked. To create a PDF file, open the PowerPoint presentation, choose the file option, and select the Save As option. Find the file format downwards and choose the PDF option, then click on the Save button to have the PDF file created.

Always note that animations and sounds are not always activated in a PDF document. PDF files can only be edited with the use of special software.

Packaging Your Presentation On A CD

When a PowerPoint presentation is created, the plan is to present it in person from a place different from your office or where it was created. This would require the presentation to be copied on a storage device such as a USB drive or having it burned on a CD. **Note** that there is no need for a CD for each presentation; different presentations can be on a CD.

To package files on CD, follow the steps below:

- Locate the file menu in the ribbon
- Choose export from the options menu.
- Select the package for the CD option and then select the package for the CD command (this will open up the options dialog box).
- The space to enter the name of the CD will pop up. Enter a preferred name for the presentation.
- Keep in mind that the active presentation file has already been added to the list.
- To include more PowerPoint files, click on the "Add" button. This will open a new window where other slides can be selected. Double click on the preferred presentation and then repeat the same process to add other slides.
- Finally, click on the copy to CD option to start the burning process.

Note that PowerPoint will add a special program in the package known as the PowerPoint Viewer, which can show the presentation on a computer that does not have PowerPoint installed on it.

Making A Presentation Available On Microsoft Stream

To export a video option from a PowerPoint presentation. Select a file, then choose the export button, and then choose the "Create a video option." As an alternative, locate the recording tab on the ribbon and select the export to video option.

You can select either the HD (720p) 1280 x 720, medium file size, or the Standard (480p) 852 x 480, the smallest file size. Then, after creating the MP4 file, upload it to the stream.

It should be noted that recorded PowerPoint files are frequently very large, and as such, they will take some time to upload to the stream.

Chapter 12: Print Your Slides

The Quick Way To Print

In PowerPoint, slides, speaker notes, and handouts can be created and printed to serve the audience in case they get lost while the presentation is ongoing.

To print, simply choose **the file to be printed** and then select the **print option**, or use Ctrl + P for the very fast print option.

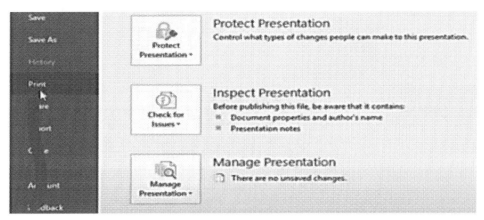

For the printer, choose the printer that should be used to print the document. Navigate to the settings option and then select the desired options;

Slides: From the drop-down menu, choose either to print all slides, selected slides, or just the current slide. Alternatively, in the slide box, type in the slide number or numbers that should be printed and separate the numbers with a comma.

Print Layout: Choose to either print the slides, speaker notes, an outline, or handout. The outline prints just the text embedded in the slides without the images. The notes of a presentation display the slide and similar speaker notes that can be found below it. If handouts are preferred to be printed, they can be printed on several slides on one page, making use of different layouts, some with space for taking notes.

Collated or uncollated: Select whether the sheets should be collated or uncollated.

color: Choose if you prefer the document pointed, grayscale, or pure black and white.

Edit Header and Footer: Choose to adjust the header and footer before printing.

Finally, choose the number of copies that should be printed, then click on **the print button**.

Printing From The Backstage View

To print from the backstage view, click on **the file menu**. This will leave the backstage view open. Choose the **print option** in the sidebar to show the options available. As an alternative, select the **Ctrl+P** shortcut on the keyboard.

Options that can be found within the Print tab option of the backstage view include:

Print

Click on the **print button** much later, after all, other options have been chosen.

Copies

Choose the specific number of copies that should be printed.

Printer

Choose the particular printer from the drop-down menu list that is preferred to print the document. This can either be a physical or even a virtual printer that makes PDF files.

Print what

Select from the **drop-down menu list** to check out more options. Choose whether **to print all the slides, sections, or just a selection of slides**. It is also possible to enter the current slide or a custom range of slides. If a custom range of slides is chosen to be printed, there will be an option to type in each slide number as well as the slide range. There is also an option to print hidden slides. If the hidden slide option is grayed out, this means there are no hidden slides in the presentation currently open.

Print Layouts

Click this option to show a drop-down list. There is an option to print regular slides or slides that are on the pages of the notes. Another option is to print just the text outline of the presentation. Furthermore, there is also an option to print different handout layouts that also include slide thumbnails.

- **Frame Slides:** This adds a black frame around the slides. This feature can be very useful when printing white or light-colored slides on white paper.
- **Scale to Fit Paper:** This feature helps to adjust the size of the printed slides to match the given size of the paper.
- **High Quality:** This feature helps to produce much better quality output. It is worthy of note that when there are too many slides, this feature can increase the amount of time spent printing.
- **Print Comments and Ink Markup:** this feature is made available if the presentation has any comments or ink annotations.

Collated

This option opens up a drop-down list. Collated permits the user to print in sequence even if many copies are to be printed. If, for example, four copies of a ten-slide presentation are to be printed, making use of the collate option will print all of the ten slides first and then print extra copies of the ten slides as well. If the uncollated option is chosen, four copies of the first slide will be printed, and then four copies of the second slide will also be printed.

Color

This is a default option that makes all documents printed in color form, provided the printer selected has the capacity to print in color.

Print More Than One Copy

PowerPoint provides users with the option of printing more than one copy of either a page or the whole document. All that needs to be done is to enter the numbers of each copy that should be printed into the box that pops up after the user has selected the print option.

For example, if a user enters four, the printer will print four different copies of that particular page.

Changing Printers

If there is access to more than one printer, a user can choose to change a printer for any of the following reasons:

If the printer connected to the laptop or computer initially is not colored and the printer has to print a colored document, the user can change the printer by connecting another printer to the laptop or computer. When the print option is selected from the PowerPoint, the user will also choose the preferred laptop (the new one that has just been connected) and then print out the document.

Faded Ink: A user can also choose to use a different printer if the ink of the printer currently in use has dried. The documents printed from a printer with drained ink are often not always clear, hence the need to change printers.

Printing Part Of A Document

There are times when just a portion of a presentation is needed in hard copy. All the user needs to do is to go to the very page that is needed and then use the shortcut command (CTRL + P). This will immediately send that very page to the printer and print out the document, leaving out other parts of the presentation.

Using Print Preview

The print preview is a feature that enables users to view the pages that are about to be printed, giving users the opportunity to see these pages the exact way they will look when they have been printed.

By having a preview of what the layout will look like when it's printed without actually printing it just yet, users can check for possible errors and ensure these errors are fixed before they continue with the printing option.

This feature is often used by every user and is useful for making sure that the layout is exactly the way the user expects it to be and is void of any form of error.

Microsoft PowerPoint also has this feature, and it helps users check the pages of each slide well before they are printed.

Chapter 13: **Online Collaboration**

Working together with a team to complete a project, there might be a need to pass files back and forth, making use of email addresses or file sharing, and then it becomes pretty hard to stay in sync on the particular project.

The solution to all of this is to make use of PowerPoint in order to stay in sync and work together as a team. Microsoft has included this feature in PowerPoint to help people solve the problem of teamwork so that different users can work at the same time.

When collaborating, the first thing that will be done is to have the PowerPoint presentation saved on OneDrive; this way it will be stored in the cloud for collaboration. To save the file to OneDrive, locate the save as option and choose OneDrive. This will have the presentation saved to the cloud, so others can work together with you.

To invite those that will work with you, locate the share button close to the upper right-hand side and tap it to invite others or team members to the presentation.

A new window where others can be added will then be displayed in the PowerPoint presentation. Enter an email address to invite anyone to collaborate on the presentation. Also, you can make a choice on how the people that are invited to collaborate with you will work by selecting between the "can edit" and "can view" options. This way, the control they have over the files can be monitored.

Working with OneDrive

Most of the features in Microsoft Office are tailored toward saving and sharing files online. OneDrive is Microsoft's online storage space that can be used to save, edit, and share presentations and other files. OneDrive can be accessed from a computer, smartphone, or any other device that has access to the internet. To get started with using OneDrive, all that is needed is a Microsoft account. If you don't have one, do sign up for one.

Features of OneDrive

- **Access to files anywhere:** When files are saved on OneDrive, they can be accessed from any computer, tablet, or just about any device that has access to the internet. New presentations can also be created from OneDrive.
- **Backing up files:** Having files saved to OneDrive guarantees an extra level of protection. If, for instance, the computer in use develops a fault, OneDrive will still keep the files safe and they can still be accessed by any other computer.
- **Share files:** It is quite easy for files to be saved on OneDrive with friends and those you work together with. There is also an option to choose their roles, if they can only read the files or if they also have access to edit the files. This option is quite amazing for the sole purpose of collaboration, as lots of people will be able to edit the presentation at the same time, which is also known as co-authoring.

Sharing A OneDrive Presentation

When a PowerPoint presentation is saved to OneDrive, your team can collaborate on the presentation at the same time. For this to happen, everyone needs to work with PowerPoint 2010 or a more recent version.

To Share A Presentation

- Open the PowerPoint presentation and choose the share option in the top right-hand corner of the ribbon when all is set to collaborate with your team. If the presentation has not been saved on OneDrive yet, there will be a prompt that will allow that to be done.
- Locate the send link box and enter the email address of those that will be working on the presentation with you so you can share it with them. If the person's contact info is already stored on your device, all you have to do is enter the person's name. A drop-down list will be displayed and this will help determine if the invitees can edit the file or can only read the file.
- Finally, when all of this has been done, click on the share button. If the file has already been saved to the cloud (OneDrive), an email invitation will be sent to the invitees.

Whenever anyone is viewing or editing the presentation, the person's thumbnail picture will be displayed in the top right-hand corner of the ribbon. PowerPoint will display a prompt when anyone enters or leaves the presentation.

Alternatively, in the share pane section, the name of anyone viewing or editing the document at that point in time will also be displayed. There will also be an indicator on the thumbnail of the slide and on the current slide that will show the exact place where the person is working on the presentation. You can move the mouse over the indicator or select it to find out who is editing the presentation.

For accessibility sake, PowerPoint also provides the option for the automatic display of the editor's name to be turned on. To turn it on, select file, then options, then click on advanced, choose display, then click on the option to "Show presence flags for selected items."

After all of this has been done, save the file.

Working with Teams

If you are making use of Microsoft Teams to meet with other people that are working together with you but remotely, there are about 7 different options you can use to share PowerPoint slides with them.

- **Share the whole screen or desktop.**

This is the most common method that most people use because it is the closest to what is done in a meeting room when the participants are seated around the table. In teams, select the sharing option known as "Desktop." This will enable the audience to see everything that is shown on the desktop, and if the PowerPoint is not in full-screen mode, they will only see the wallpaper and any other application that is open with just the confidential information being displayed. They will also be able to see the small team window, except it has been minimized.

Once the slide show is started in PowerPoint, all the features will work, including animations and transitions. A presentation remote can equally be used to move through slides, or there is also an option to use the arrow keys. Since the slide takes up the whole screen, the teams' controls won't be visible; this means chats and questions from the audience might be missed. If Alt + Tab is used to switch to the Teams window in order to see the chat discussion, the audience will be able to see this also because they can see everything on the screen.

- **Share the slide show window.**

Due to the fact that Teams provides the option of sharing any window that is open on the computer, another option is to share the window that has the slideshow in it.

Before sharing is started in teams, start the slideshow in PowerPoint first. This will show the slides on the whole screen. Make use of Alt + Tab to move back to the Teams window. Locate the teams' sharing options and choose the window that shows the slideshow (make sure the slideshow is chosen and not the regular PowerPoint window).

Once again, since PowerPoint will be used in full, all features should work, and this is close to presenting in a meeting room before an audience. Since it's just a window that is shared, the audience will not see anything else on the screen. Due to the fact that the slides take up the entire screen, the teams window with chats won't be displayed. However, there is an option to switch to the Teams window with the use of the Alt + Tab buttons so as to check the chat conversation without the audience being able to see what is being done.

- **Share the editing window with a clean look.**

The first two options basically won't provide the option to see other documents or notes that may be on the screen due to the fact that the slides cover the whole screen. If there is no need for animation or transition features and it's okay for the audience to see just the edit view of the PowerPoint, there is an option to make use of a view that reduces the PowerPoint interface. This way, the slide will be the main focus.

In the normal editing view, have the slide thumbnails minimized by moving the vertical divider over to the left until the text showing that thumbnails are now available is displayed. Move the horizontal divider at the lower part of the slide downwards to Options notes that can be found underneath the slides. Click on the collapse indicator and this will collapse the ribbon in the bottom right-hand corner of any ribbon.

Finally, have the slide in the editing window maximized, and PowerPoint will have a much cleaner look than the normal editing view.

Move to the team sharing option and choose the window for this presentation. When moving through the slides, the animations and transitions won't be seen since the slideshow mode is not in use. Any media insert will not run automatically and must be played manually. Make use of the arrow keys or the page down and page up buttons to move through the slides.

- **Run the slideshow in a window and share that window.**

PowerPoint now allows you to run a slide in the window it is located in without taking up the whole screen. Many presenters are not aware of this option. This option is referred to as the "browsed by an individual mode" or the "reading view." To make use of this mode, locate the slideshow on the ribbon and select the setup right-hand slide show button. In the dialog box that is displayed in the show type section towards the left-hand corner, change the option by selecting the radio button for "Browsed by an individual." Choose the OK button to make sure the changes are saved and then leave the dialog box.

The slides will always run in this PowerPoint window instead of the full screen if you are in slideshow mode. The default value of "presented by a speaker" can, however, be changed after a meeting has concluded.

In the team sharing options, select the window for this PowerPoint presentation. Begin the slideshow mode in PowerPoint. This will show the slide show with some other added controls at the upper and lower parts of the window and, if possible, black bars on the upper/lower part of the left/right based on the size of the window and concerning the size of the slides. This can be a slightly different look for the viewers if they are used to seeing the full-screen version of the slideshow mode.

Because this is a slideshow mode, all animations and transitions work as expected. The only difference, apart from the full-screen show mode, is that the laser pointer, inking, and some other features will not be available. Since the sharing window is all that is in use, the audience will not see any other documents that may be open on the screen. To see the full teams window, you can select the small teams' window located on the lower right-hand side of the screen, and the audience will not have to see this either. This ensures that you remain in touch with every chat discussion while the presentation is ongoing. Since this option is sharing just one window, it uses less bandwidth than if it were sharing a full screen, and this will help users on lower-speed connections have a much better experience with little or no lag or distortions of any form. This option might offer the very best combination of PowerPoint features and presenter control options.

- **Using the PowerPoint sharing option in Teams**

Microsoft has created both Teams and PowerPoint, creating a presentation method that is simply unparalleled among other meeting tools. You can load a PowerPoint file from the SharePoint library or the computer by using the PowerPoint sharing option. The slideshow will be displayed via PowerPoint on the web inside the teams. This option provides some advantages, which include the use of less bandwidth as compared to screen sharing and does not require that PowerPoint be installed on the computer or the use of PowerPoint on the web features, the availability of co-presenting options, and also less usage of battery life as compared to screen sharing.

Though all of these advantages are lovely, the greatest disadvantage is the fact that this method makes use of PowerPoint on the web, which does not offer support for all features of PowerPoint yet.

Due to the fact that this method is infused into Teams, the slideshow occurs in the Teams window, and the Teams control bar at the top of the slideshow can be seen while the presentation is ongoing. You also have access to all the team options in the window. Since the slideshow is in the Teams window, the rest of the screen is also available for other documents that could be referred to.

- **Use the presenter view to show the audience the slides while you see the presenter view**

If the preferred option is to make use of the presenter view to see the notes while the audience sees just the slides.

- **Along with the PowerPoint slides, show a video.**

Microsoft Teams allows you to make presentations with video beside the PowerPoint slides so that facial expressions can be seen easily with the slides. In this case, the whole screen would be shared, with slides and video organized on the desktop. You can control the size of both the slides and the video in this way. Aside from making use of built-in features within PowerPoint and the operating system, this does not necessarily require any software to be installed.

Using Comments

Comments are used mainly to give feedback to colleagues after a presentation. This can help the person involved know what to do as regards the presentation, or it can also be in the form of an appraisal.

Chapter 14: **Using The View Tab**

There are many tasks you can complete through the **View** tab of PowerPoint presentation. View tab contains commands which center on how you can view your presentation file.

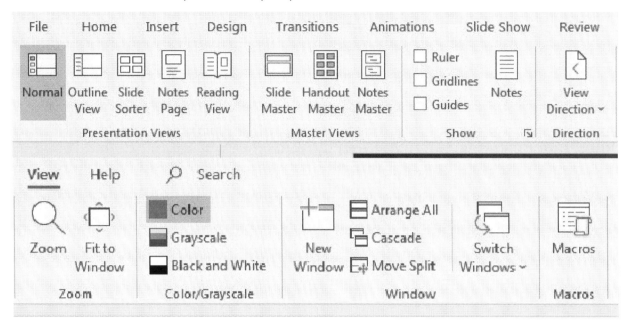

By default, presentation file is in **Normal** view. From the figure, the command that follows the Normal view is **Outline View**. Outline View allows you to edit and jump between your slides in the Outline pane. When you click Outline View command in the View tab, all your slides are lined up on your screen and you can edit them one after the other.

Click **View** tab followed by **Slide Sorter** to arrange your slides in slide sorter mode. When you have your slides in this mode, they are arranged horizontally just as seen below:

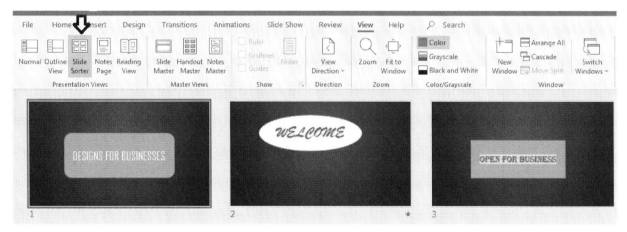

Notes Page command in the **View** tab puts your slides in a state that encourages you to add notes to each of your slides and shows notes added to any slide you created. If you want to add notes to the slides that do not have notes already in them, just click the part that says **Click to add text** and then type your notes. Click out after typing your notes and it is saved.

Reading View is another command in the View tab. As the name implies, this mode makes you play your slides in the PowerPoint window. If there is animation and transition added to the slides, you will be shown all without switching to full screen.

BOOK 6: MICROSOFT ACCESS

Introduction

Microsoft Access is a database management system (DBMS) used to store and manage data. This is a member of the Microsoft 365 suite of applications made for business and enterprise users.

Microsoft Access is also an Information Management Tool that allows you to store information for referencing, reporting, and analyzing.

Like Microsoft Excel, Access allows the users to view and edit data. One feature that makes Access better than Excel is that it can take in more data at a stretch.

Microsoft Access provides the users, the features of a database, and the programming proficiencies to create an easy-to-navigate screen (Forms). Not only that, Access helps to process a large bunk of information and manages them effectively and efficiently.

Microsoft Access saves data in its format based on the Access Jet Database Engine. It can also link or import directly to the data stored in other applications or databases.

Just like every other Microsoft application, Access also supports the use of Visual Basic for Application (VBA)

To use Microsoft Access, you will need to follow the procedures below.

- Database Creation: The first thing to do is create a database and indicate what type of data to be stored in the database
- Data Input: After creating a database, the next thing to do is enter the data into the database.
- Query: This is a process of retrieving information from a database
- Report: This is where information from the database is organized in a nice and presentable manner that can be printed out in an Access report

Why Should You Use Access?

There are many benefits attached to the use of Microsoft Access and some of them will be outlined below.

- Cost Of Development: One of the benefits of using Microsoft Access is that it is less expensive compared to the larger database systems like Oracle, SOL server, etc., which require a huge amount of set up and high maintenance costs
- Software Integration: One of the notable features of Microsoft Access being a product of the Microsoft Office suite is that it can integrate well with two other apps in the MS office suite.
- Legacy Data: Microsoft Access can easily import many data formats, so the existing data is retained and not lost. It does not only save hundreds of hours of input time but can remove potential human input errors.
- Distribution: Microsoft Access has its Jet Database format that contains both the application and data in one file. With the ability to have the application and data together in one place, it is convenient to distribute the applications to many users, who can, in turn, run the apps in disconnected environments.
- Microsoft Access provides a fully functional, relational database management system in a few minutes.
- Microsoft Access can function well with many of the development languages that work on Windows OS.
- With Microsoft Access, you can create tables, queries, forms, reports, and connect using the macros.
- Microsoft Access allows the users to link data from its existing location and manipulate it for viewing, updating, querying, and reporting.
- Microsoft Access allows for customizing according to personal and company needs.
- Microsoft Access executes any challenging office or industrial database tasks.
- Access in its uniqueness can function with the most popular databases compatible with Open Database Connectivity (ODBC) standards, including SQL Server, Oracle, and DB2.
- With Access, software developers can use Microsoft Access to develop application software.
- Microsoft Access requires less code to get work done unlike SQL server and some other client-server databases).

- Microsoft Access is a very good tool for creating database applications with many readily available functionality.
- Another reason you need to use Access is that it is flexible, i.e., it allows you to put together a custom database and later change as needs are likely to change as needs arise.
- Access can be used alongside VBA, a programming language. Developers can create a custom solution for their database using the VBA code. This effective programming language contains codes or commands for specific programs.
- Microsoft Access allows users to choose any of the four ways to view reports:
  - Report view
  - Print view
  - Layout view
  - Design view
- Microsoft Access is a simple desktop application that does not need any particular hardware or license to function. Thus, making it more suitable and cost-effective for individual users and smaller teams who do not need larger and more complicated databases for an extra price.

Access users do not need to undergo any special training to get the skills needed to use this application. In a nutshell, Access is easy to master especially for users who are conversant with the use of Excel.

Chapter 1: **What is a Database**

A database is simply a tool for collecting and analyzing information. A database can store information about anything, be it people, objects, activities, and so on. Imagine working in a company where you have to keep information about the employees, their dates or births, dates of appointments, salary, the products they manage and many other things, a software tool like Microsoft Access will not only help you keep the information, but also analyze and arrange it in such a way that it will not be difficult to use, and any information will be easily accessed. The way in this Microsoft Access collects, analyzes, and keeps this information is known as a database.

Database Models

Relational Database

A relational database management system (RDBMS) stores data using a relational table structure. A relational table structure organizes data in tables made up of rows and columns. Tables are linked by related fields called keys. Keys are used to uniquely identify records and link records between different tables.

Example of a one-to-many relationship that avoids data duplication

As you can see from the image above, each order is linked to the employee that processed it. However, we only need to store employee information once in our system and use the employee key (EmployeeID) to establish the link between the two tables.

Below are some benefits of organizing your data in different related tables:

- **More efficient data storage**

In a relational data structure, you enter your data only once. This can save a lot of space, especially when you have a lot of data

- **Greater accuracy and data integrity**

When you enter data more than once, you risk introducing errors. For example, we were entering customer names and addresses directly into records. Suppose, you make a mistake with the customer's name in one or more of the entries. In that case, it means you will not find all the records for that customer when you perform a search for records linked to that customer. Also, when you make a mistake or need to make a change, you only need to do it in one place.

- **Best way to capture transactions**

The relational table structure is the best way to capture more complex data, such as transactions. Transactions can have one main record and several related records. For instance, you can have one customer order that includes several items, making up several order lines. If you were to capture this with a spreadsheet, it would mean entering the customer details multiple times. This uses up more storage space, and repetition can introduce errors in your data.

Hierarchical Model

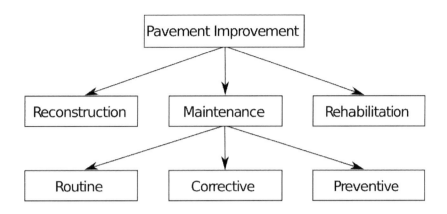

This model was developed in the 1960s to manage huge amounts of data for complex manufacturing projects like the Apollo rocket that landed on the moon in 1969. An upside-down tree characterizes its basic logical structure. The hierarchical structure contains levels, or segments. A segment is the equivalent of a file system's record type. Within the hierarchy, the top layer is perceived as the segment's parent. In short, the hierarchical model depicts a set of one-to-many (1:M) relationships between a parent and their children segments.

Final Assembly

Component A Component B Component C

Assembly A Assembly B Assembly C

The hierarchical data model yielded many advantages over the file system model. Many of the hierarchical data model's features formed the foundation for current data models. The hierarchical database quickly became dominant in the 1970s. It generated a large installed base, which, in turn, created a pool of programmers who knew the systems and who developed numerous tried-and-true business applications.

But, this model had limitations:

- It was complex to implement
- It was hard to manage
- It lacked structural independence.

Network

Network Model

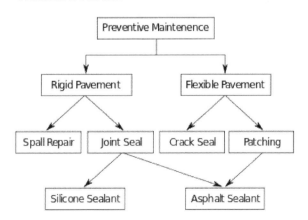

This model was created to represent complex data relationships more effectively than the hierarchical model, to improve database performance, and to enforce a database standard.

To help establish database standards, the Conference on Data Systems Language (CODASYL) created the database task group (DBTG) in the late 1960s. The DBTG was charged with defining standard specifications for an environment that would facilitate database creation and data manipulation. The final DBTG report contained specifications for three crucial database components.

- The schema. It is the conceptual organization of the entire database as viewed by the administrator. It includes a definition of the database name, the record type, and the components that make up those records.
- The subschema. It defines the portion of the database "seen" by the application programs that truly produce the desired information from the data contained within the database.
- A data management language (DML) defines the environment in which data can be managed to produce the desired standardization for each of the three components.

- A schema data definition language (DDL) enables the database administrator to define the schema components.

- A subschema DDL allows the application programs to define the database components that the application will use.

- A data manipulation language to work with the data in the database.

In this model, the user perceives the network database as a collection of records in 1: M relationships. This model allows a record to have more than one parent. In network database terminology, a relationship is called a set. Each set comprises of at least two record types: an owner record and a member record. A set describes a 1: M relationship between the owner and the member.

Information needs to grow as more sophisticated databases and applications are required because the network model has become too cumbersome. The lack of query capability puts heavy pressure on programmers to generate the code required to produce the simplest reports. The existing databases provided limited data independence. Because of the disadvantages of the network and hierarchical models, they were largely replaced by the relational data model in the 1980s.

Object-Oriented

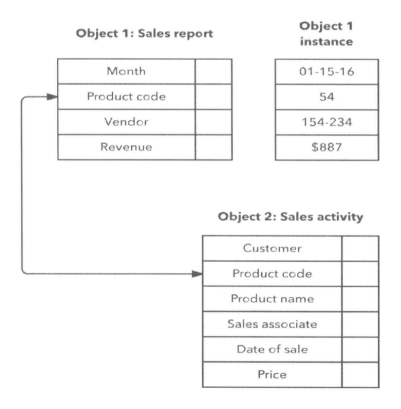

In the object-oriented data model (OODM), data and their relationships are incorporated into a single structure known as an object. Thus, the OODM is the basis for the object-oriented database management system (OODBMS).

Unlike an entity, an object encompasses information about relationships between the entities, and its relationships with other entities.

This model is based on the following components:

- An object is a conception of a real-world entity. An object may be considered equivalent to an ER model's entity.
- Attributes describe the properties of an object. For example, a PERSON object includes the attributes name, date of birth, address, etc.
- Objects that have similar characteristics are grouped in classes. A class is a group of similar objects with shared structure and behavior.
- Classes are organized in a class hierarchy. The class hierarchy resembles an upside-down tree in which each class has only one parent. For instance, the CUSTOMER class and the EMPLOYEE class share a parent PERSON class.
- Inheritance is the ability of an object in the class hierarchy to acquire the attributes and methods of the classes above it.

Unified Modeling Language (UML) is a language based on OO concepts that describes a set of diagrams and symbols that can be used to graphically model a system.

Chapter 2: Microsoft Access Databases

Access can carry out many activities , but a very important one is building big databases. These records run into hundreds and thousands, and management tools like Access will be important to monitor them. Normally, creating a type of database with these kinds of records will lead to a lot of errors. Still, with Microsoft Access, there is an elimination of the probability of error due to the automatic creation by the software. This database can be brought into existence within a maximum size of 2 gigabytes, now imagine how huge your creation can run into. You can also work around the size limitation created with this software by linking to tables in other Access databases or tables in multiple database files.

Using Microsoft Access to build your big databases will also make it possible for you to sort through them easily with the sorting, searching, and other creative tools that have been made available. Imagine how hard it could be going through hundreds of records to access a particular record, however, with Microsoft Access you can easily locate a particular record within hundreds, even thousands of records. Also, creating big databases using Microsoft Access ensures proper and insightful reporting. You can tailor the database to the activity you want to use it for, whether being left in digital form or printed out. If you are a project manager and you need the database for a presentation or to distribute amongst your team members, Access got you. Access will enable you to communicate effectively to your team members as the data created will be easy to understand.

Microsoft Access saves you from having to reenter all your collected data and allows you to keep multiple data sources consistent. It permits you to import and recycle all that you have entered into another software, for example, Microsoft Excel, when you wish to sort out using Microsoft Access.

In all that has been said, it can be deduced Microsoft Access is a very powerful software and a proper understanding of how to explore all its capabilities will make it an inevitable tool for you if you are a data analyst, or not but you deal with huge records. This tool will automatically record the most pleasant, easy-to-use, and navigated response.

Tables

Access stores your data in the form of tables, which are collections of data arranged in rows of records and columns of fields. With this arrangement, commonly used by spreadsheets, each table row contains one record, or complete sets of information, such as a person in a table of employees or one specific order in a table of customer orders. Each column of the table contains a separate field, or types of information, such as a person's street address or a dollar amount of a particular sale. The following figure shows a list of states and provinces in various countries, stored in a table in Access.

Queries

Once your data has been stored in tables, you can obtain specific subsets of that data by using queries. The word "query" literally means to ask, and Access queries provide a way of asking about your data. You can use queries to find a specific record (such as that of a person named Mary Smith), print mailing labels for all persons living in a Zip code, or display all employees who have not had a performance review in the past 12 months.

Queries let you select and work with data stored in multiple tables. When you design your queries, you'll identify which records should be included in the query results and which fields should be included. You can specify criteria, which determine what records of the underlying table appear in the query. The results of your queries can be used by the forms and reports you create. Access also lets you create **action queries**, which can be used to quickly modify or delete large amounts of data stored in tables. The following figures show an example of a query's design where the query retrieves data from an employee table, and displays only those records where an employees' job title is 'sales representative.' In the example, the first illustration shows the design of the query. In contrast, the second illustration shows the records selected by the query.

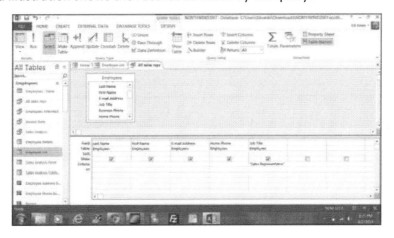

A query's design.

The resulting set of records (called a **record set**) is provided by the query.

Forms

In Access, you use forms to display the data stored in your tables or queries. Suppose, you haven't used forms in a computerized database before. In that case, you can think of them as being computerized equivalents of paper-based forms that are so familiar to businesses. Forms routinely are used for adding new data to a table and for editing or displaying existing data, usually in a one record at a time format, but occasionally in a spreadsheet-like arrangement. The following figure shows an example of a form in Access.

Using the form wizards provided with Access, you can quickly create many variations of forms. Forms can be designed to work with data from more than one table simultaneously. In the above figure, the form shown is based on a relationship between multiple tables, displaying one record from a table of members and all detailed records showing contributions made by each member.

Reports

The desired result of any database is to provide information in the form of reports, and Access is no slouch in this area. You can print reports from tables or queries in virtually any desired format. An example of an Access report is shown here.

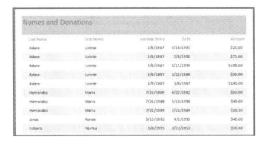

You can design reports manually or use the report wizards to help you quickly design reports. And reports in Access are not limited to mere text; they can also contain graphics, such as photographs of employees, or hyperlinks, such as addresses of websites.

Chapter 3: **Starting Access**

The workspace in Access 2022 is very similar to the previous version, although, as expected in every upgrade, there are some changes, and going through this section will introduce you to these changes. If you are familiar with Access, you will find the workspace very familiar.

Starting with the File tab, you would see a vertical list of commands that creates context-sensitive changes to the main workspace. This main workspace represents everything to the right of that left-hand menu panel essentially. Follow these procedures to carry out any of the activities mentioned in each bullet.

- If you want to start a new database, click "New" in the File tab's menu of options found on the vertical pane. Starter templates show up and the Blank Desktop Database button. In most cases, you'll be clicking on the Blank Desktop Database button so you can begin a new database.
- If you've opened an existing database, right-click on the database and select "Info" to get relevant statistics similar to the open database. Two big buttons and a link will show up, from which you can click on any of these commands - "Compact & Repair" to compact and repair the database files, "Encrypt" to create a password for the open database to deny access to others apart from you, or click on "View and Edit" to see the properties of the database.
- There are also "Save", "Save As", "Print" and "Options" commands. Each of these commands operates directly or leads to a dialogue box. For example, the "Save" command will automatically save your work, whereas the "Save as" command will open a dialogue box from which you can select what you want to save in the database and maybe create a new name.

Working With The Onscreen Tools In Access

Opening an existing database or a blank space in Microsoft Access changes the workspace, offering the Ribbon and its tabs shown here (Home, Create, External Data, and Database Tools). These tabs however are not to be confused with the context-sensitive tabs that appear when numerous database objects (the forms, tables, reports or queries that make up your database) are created or edited.

The ribbon tag at the top of the screen contains the tools you can use while working with your database. Although the tools here are dimmed if you have not used any of these tools, making use of even one of these tools will make all the other tools available for use and the buttons that are relevant to what you have opened and active in your database are available when you need them.

Moving From One Tab To Another In The File Tab

The red ribbon at the top of the screen displays the file tab and clicking on this ribbon will highlight the particular tab that is in use. You can move from one tab to the other by simply moving your mouse buttons.

Working With The Buttons

The Onscreen buttons in Microsoft Access are either action buttons - this means they perform an action when clicked, or they are buttons that represent lists or menus of choices. Each view in an Access app displays the specific predefined action buttons in the Action Bar that can be performed from that view. These buttons are found on the Action Bar and although predefined, they can be customized and you can add or remove the buttons. The buttons that represent lists or menus can be represented in two ways: drop-down list buttons that, like a small triangle, appear when clicked, a list of options appears, or the menu button that displays a list of menus.

The File Tab In Microsoft Access

At the top of the screen in Microsoft Access is a red ribbon, and on this ribbon is the File tab. The File tab gives you access to the file functions when you open a particular file. These functions include - Open, Save, Properties, and Close. Opening a database and clicking on the File tab opens information about the file you have opened.

The Quick Access Tools In Microsoft Access

Quick Access Tools in Microsoft Access is a toolbar. It can be customized and consists of commands not dependent on the tab at the ribbon on top of the screen. This tool can be customized in the sense that you can shift the location, and you can also add and remove tools that perform specific functions. Quick Access Toolbar is in the uppermost left of the workspace. Clicking the small triangular shape at the right corner of this tool will allow you to edit the tool by adding or removing specific commands to suit your style.

Using The Panes, Panels, And Context-Sensitive Tools In Microsoft Access

A very nice thing about Microsoft Access 2022 is being offered tools based on what you are creating. Microsoft Access offers the tools you need for the file you are working on or the feature you are using. A relevant onscreen panel will be shown at the top of the screen and you can choose whatever option you want to complete your task.

Customizing The Workspace In Access

Like many other softwares, you can customize the workspace when using Microsoft Access. There are three main components in the Access workspace - the ribbon, the backstage view, and the navigation pane. The ribbon contains the Quick Access Toolbar and you can customize this tool to suit your style. You can customize your workspace by working on any of these three elements. We will discuss how you can customize the Quick Access Tools in the next section.

Changing The Position Of The Toolbar Of Quick Access

The Toolbar of Quick Access is in the uppermost left corner of the file explorer window but if you wish to change this position because you don't like it, you can do so. Follow these steps to carry out this action.

1.) Select the arrow located at the home screen's bottom left corner.

2.) Select the "File Explorer" under the windows section to access the file explorer.

3.) After you have opened the file explorer, open a folder and select any of the files you want.

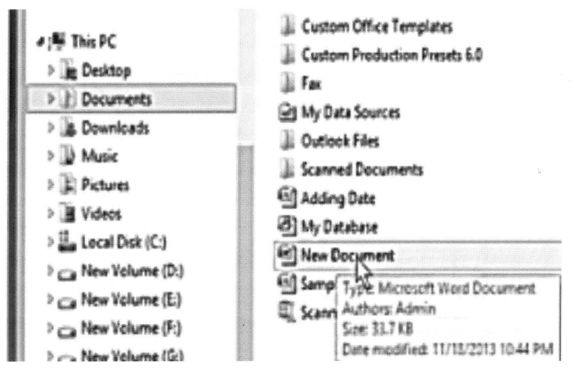

4.) To change the position of the Toolbar to the right-hand side of the ribbon, click on the down arrow to the right of the Toolbar and then click on "Show below the ribbon."

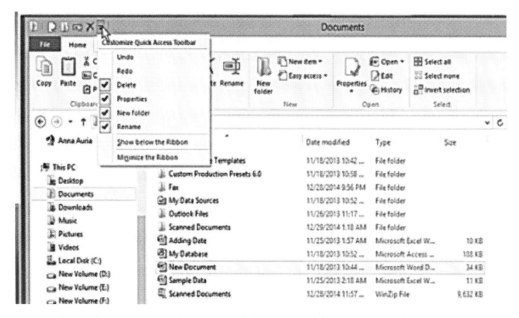

5.) You will see that the Quick Access Toolbar is just below the ribbon. Look at the position of the ribbon in the image represented below.

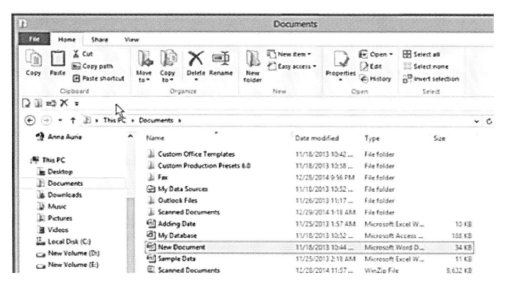

6.) You can take it back again to on top of the ribbon by clicking on that down arrow to the right of the Toolbar and then clicking on "Show above the ribbon".

Adding Tools To The Quick Access Toolbar

There are default tools that come with the Quick Access Toolbar, but the good thing is you can add to these tools, although the tools you want to add must perform specific functions. Now, follow these steps to add a command to the Quick Access Toolbar.

1.) Click on the drop-down button by the right of the Quick Access Tool.

2.) Clicking on any of the commands that appear will make a checkmark appear on the command and this means this particular command has been added to the Quick Access Toolbar.

Removing Tools From The Quick Access Toolbar

It is very easy to remove commands from the Quick Access Toolbar, and just like how these commands have been added, they can be removed. To remove a command, simply follow these steps.

1.) Click on the drop-down button by the right of the Quick Access Tool.

2.) Uncheck any of the commands you want to remove by clicking on them.

Minimizing And Maximizing The Ribbon In Access

The Ribbon at the uppermost part of your window contains the commands you require to carry out common tasks while using Access. It has multiple tabs, each with several groups of commands. The red ribbon that appears at the uppermost part of your screen in Microsoft Access can be minimized. If you feel the ribbon is taking too much space on your screen and you wish to minimize it, simply click the arrow in the lower right corner of the screen. To make the ribbon reappear, click a tab and when the ribbon is not in use, it will disappear again. To maximize the ribbon, click on a tab, after this, click the pin icon in the lower-right corner. The Ribbon will appear at all times.

Working with Screen Tips

ScreenTips in Access 2022 are the little names and brief descriptions of onscreen tools that appear when you put your mouse pointer over buttons, commands, menus, and many of the other pieces of the Access workspace. You can show or hide the screen tips when working with your Microsoft Access.

To show or hide screen tips, follow these steps.

1.) Click on the File tab.
2.) Select "Options."
3.) Click on "General."
4.) Under the options that display the User Interface, click the option that you want to be based on these self-descriptive options.

Show feature descriptions in ScreenTips: This option turns on ScreenTips and Enhanced ScreenTips and this will allow you to be able to view more information about a command, and this includes the name of the command, keyboard shortcuts on your desktop, art, and links to Help articles. This is the default setting.

Don't show feature descriptions in ScreenTips: This option turns off Enhanced ScreenTips and this way you will be able to see only the command name and maybe a keyboard shortcut. Don't show ScreenTips: This option turns off ScreenTips and Enhanced ScreenTips and this way you will only be able to see the command name.

Navigating Access with Shortcuts on Your Keyboard.

For some people, navigating Access with their keyboard makes them work more efficiently. The most frequently used shortcuts include:

- Alt or F10: To select the active tab and activate the Key Tips.
- Alt plus H: To use the home tab.
- Alt plus Q: To view the "Tell me" Box.
- Shift plus F10: To view the shortcut menu for an item you have selected.
- F6: If you wish to move the focus to another part of the window.
- F11: Use this to make the navigation pane visible or not.
- F2: To change Edit mode to Navigation mode.
- F4: If you want to hide or show a property window.
- F5: If you are in the Design view and you wish to switch to the Form view.
- Ctrl plus O or F12: If you want to open an existing database.
- Alt plus F5: to go to a specific record.
- Alt plus F4: To exit Access.
- Ctrl plus P: If you want to print, and you want to open the print dialogue.
- Ctrl plus F: To open the Find tab in the Find and Replace dialogue box when you want to search for a specific record.
- S: To open the page set up a dialogue box.
- Z: To zoom in or zoom out of a page.
- Ctrl plus H: To open the Replace tab in the Find and Replace dialogue box.
- Ctrl plus + (plus) sign: To add a new record in Datasheet view or Form view.

F1: To view the Help window.

Chapter 4: **Creating a Database**

There are several ways you can create a new database in Access. We'll go through the three methods below.

Creating a Blank Database from Access

To create a new blank database:

- Click Start (or press the Windows key on your keyboard to display the start menu.
- Click Access (Access should be listed in the group of applications under A)
- The Access Home screen is displayed.

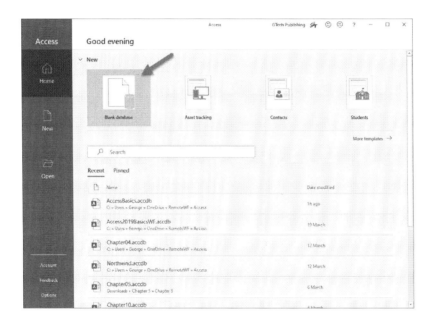

- Click Blank database.

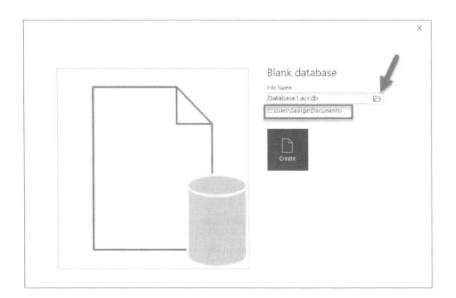

- The default file location will be your Documents folder on your C: drive. Click the folder icon and select a new location from the **File New Database** dialog box to change the folder location.

- In the File New Database dialog box, navigate to the folder where you want to save the database.
- In the **File name** field, enter the name of your database.
- Click **OK**.

Access takes you back to the previous dialog box, where you'll notice that the file name and location have been changed to the values you entered.

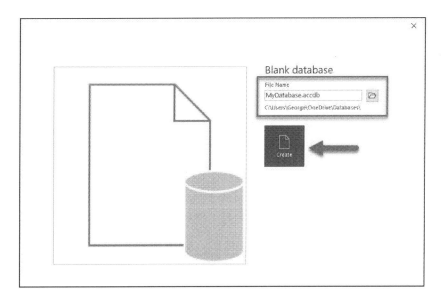

- Click the **Create** button to create the new database.

Creating a Blank Database Using File Explorer

One of the first things you need to do to create a new blank database in Access is select the database's directory. Navigating to the correct folder through the New Database dialog box can sometimes be confusing. One quick way to create a new Access database is to do it in File Explorer.

To create a new Access database using File Explorer (in Windows), do the following:

- In File Explorer, navigate to the folder where you want to create the Access database.
- Right-click any blank area on the right pane of the File Explorer window and select **New** > **Microsoft Access Database** from the pop-up menu.

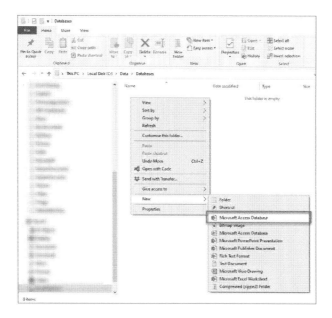

- Windows creates a new database file in the folder and selects the default name, enabling you to type over it.

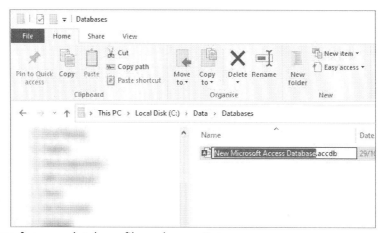

- Type in the name for your database file and press **Enter**.
- To open and use the database, double-click the file in File Explorer.

That's it. You now have a new blank database created in the location you want it.

Create a New Database from a Template

To create a new database from a template, after launching Access, click **New** on the menu on the left of the screen to display the **New** dialog box.

You'll notice a couple of Access database templates that you can use as a starting basis for your database. You can select one of the categories listed under **Suggested searches** to filter the list. These categories include **Business**, **Logs**, **Industry**, **Lists**, **Personal**, and **Contacts**.

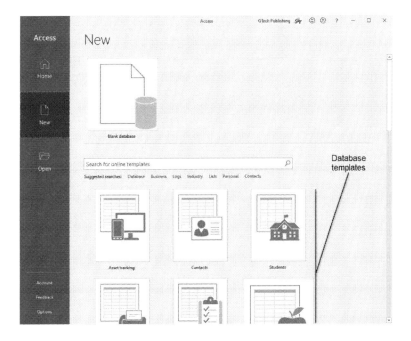

- Click the template that's the best match for the type of database you want to create. For example, if you want to create a contacts list, select Contacts.

The next dialog box has a brief description of the template, which gives you an idea of how suitable the template is for your requirements.

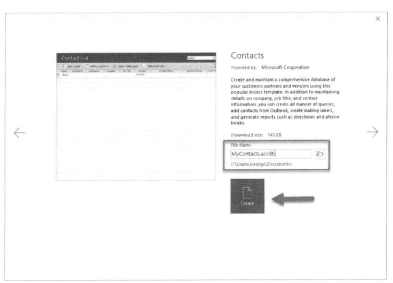

Note: You can view descriptions for the other templates by clicking the right arrow (to go forward) and the left arrow (to go back).

- Enter the file name. Click the folder icon to change the directory if you want to save the database in a different location from the default.
- Click **Create** to create the database.

Note: As this database has a macro to display a welcome screen, you'll get a security warning just under the Ribbon telling you that some content was disabled. Click the **Enable Content** button to start using the database.

Chapter 5: **The Ribbon**

The Ribbon can be described as the main replacement for the menus and the toolbars and offers the main command interface in Access. One of the main advantages of the ribbon is that it is said to consolidate, in a single place, all the various tasks or points of entry that formerly do require menus, toolbars, task panes, and some other UI components to display. With this, you have just one place where you can search for commands rather than going through different places.

When a database is opened, the ribbon will be displayed at the top of the main Access window, showing the commands in the active command tab. The ribbon has many command tabs with commands embedded in them.

Access's main command tabs are File, Home, Create, External Data, and Database Tools. Each of these command tabs has groups of commands that are quite related. These groups show some of the newly added users' interfaces like the gallery, a new type of control that displays choices visually.

The File Ribbon

The file tab is the first tab you see when launching your Microsoft Access software. It is a common tab built into other Microsoft desktop applications like Word, Excel, PowerPoint, and others. Microsoft Access File tab is a section on the Office Ribbon that allows users access to file functions. When you click the File tab, you will see the tools/commands. The photo below shows the tools in File tab.

The tools in the file tab are Home, New, Open, Info, Save, Save As, Print, Close, Account, Feedback, and options. You need to click the **File** tab and select the **Save As** option to save the Access file. With **Print** tool, you will print any Access file physically.

The Home Ribbon

The **Home** tab is the second tab of Microsoft Access when you launch the application. When you select the Home tab, you will be shown the tools available. The photo below shows it.

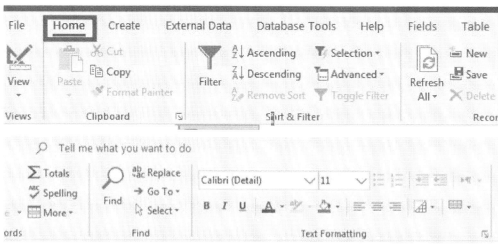

Among the tools you will find in the Home tab of Microsoft Access are view, copy, cut, format painter, Ascending, Descending, Selection, Advanced, Refresh All, New, Save, Spelling, Formula and Text Formatting tools.

So, if you want to make the text in your fields and records bold, you will find the tool in the Home tab under the Text Formatting. The bold tool is written with the capital "**B**" symbol. And to make text bold, just select the field or record containing the text and the click the bold tool.

On the other hand, you can change how the data you have in your Access object appear. By this, I mean you can change whether you want the information arranged in either ascending or descending order. Suppose, for instance you have some names listed in the fields of your Access arranged in alphabetical order. In that case, you can have them rearranged in ascending or descending order using a tool at the **Home** tab.

First select the words to have the text arranged in ascending or descending order. As the words are selected, click the **Home** tab of your Microsoft Access. If you want the text arranged in ascending order, select the tool named **Ascending**. On the other hand, if you want the data arranged in descending order, select the tool names **Descending**. That is all you need to do to get the job done. You can play around these tools to see the result you will get.

The Create Ribbon

The tab number three on the Microsoft Access interface is **Create** tab. When you select the create tab, you will be shown some available tools. As the tab's name reads, so are the functions you can perform through the tab.

You can add tables, table designs, SharePoint lists, query and forms in your database through the create tab. By default, a table is made available in your database. If you want other forms of documents, you can do that through the create tab of your Microsoft Access application. The photo below shows the tools available in the create tab.

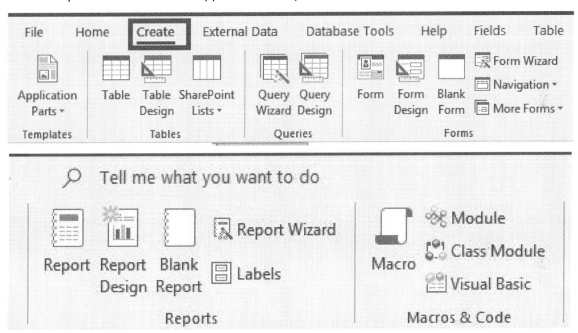

If, for instance, you want to add form to the database you are creating, all you have to do is click the **Create** tab and select the **Form** tool. But before you can add a form to your database, ensure you first saved the table that was added to the database by default. It is from the information available in the table that forms are created.

The External Data Ribbon

The External Data tab is the fourth tab of Microsoft Access software when you count from the left to the right. As the name of the tab sounds, you can integrate external document existing in your computer through the tools available in the External Data tab. The photo below shows the tools in the External Data tab.

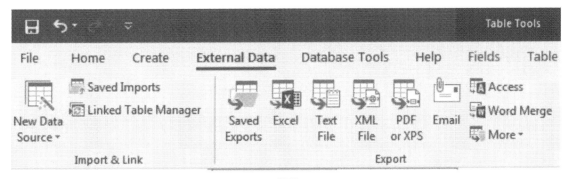

Look at the above photo, the tools in the External Data tab are New Data Source, Saved Imports, Linked Table Manager, Saved Exports, Excel, Text File, XML File, PDF or XPS, Email, Access, Word Merge and More. There are many things you can do with these tools.

Suppose, you want to import an Excel file you saved in your computer into the Access file for instance. In that case, you are to select the **External Data** tab followed by **Excel**. With this, a new window is opened on your computer. Locate the Excel file you want to import into your database and get it imported. On doing that, the excel file will be available in your database file.

Also, you may have a PDF file in your computer which you want to have in your Access database. That is something simple to do. Just select the **External Data** tab first. You will see the tool that reads **PDF or XPS**. Just select the tool, located the file in your computer and get it uploaded into your file database. That is all and you are done with the job.

The Database Tools Ribbon

The Database Tools tab is another great tab Microsoft have in their Access software. This tab comes after the External Data tab, and there are many things you can do with the tools that are inside of it. There are related commands in the database tools tab. These related commands (tools) include Compact and Repair Database, Visual Basic, Run Macro, Relationships, Object Dependencies, Analyze tools, Access Database, SharePoint, and Add-ins. The photo below shows the tools.

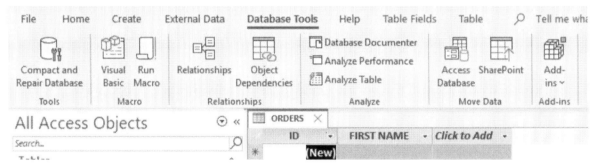

Let me explain few of the tools found in the Database Tools tab. **Compact and Repair Database** tool can make your database file smaller. It does not delete any data from your file but removes unused space. This improves the performance of your database by making it less bulky.

The **Compact and Repair Database** tool also helps repair any of your database files that encountered issue. The file might corrupt, but the Compact and Repair Database tool fixes the issue. It is an important tool that usually applies its impact when need for its use arises.

The **Run Macro** tool allows you to run Macro on your database. With Macro tool, you can automate input sequence that imitates keystrokes.

The relationship tool makes the difference between Microsoft Access software and Microsoft Excel. It is a unique tool that Microsoft developers took time to create. It allows you to relate the data in a table with that in another table you created. Also, you can relate the data in a table with that in a report.

The add-ins tool is a helpful one. With add-in, you can add extra features to your database. Add-ins are software that can be added to your Access to give it extra functionality. When you click the **Add-ins** tab, you will see text that reads "Add-in Manager". Select the **Add-in Manager**. You will be shown some available add-ins. You can select one and get it added. Just experiment with it.

The Help Ribbon

The Help tab contains tools you can select to get help from Microsoft Access team. When you select this tab, you will be shown some tools I have in the photo below.

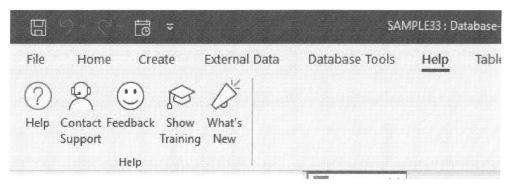

With the Help tab, you can access the helpful materials you need to become a better user of the Access software. Click the **Help** tool in the Help tab to see all the articles written by Microsoft to make you better user of the software.

With the **Contact Support** tool, you will be shown the channels you can follow to reach the team for any help you need. **Feedback** is the tool you need to select if you have any feedback to give to Microsoft regarding their application. **Show Training** is another helpful guide you may like to go through. And the last of the help tools is the one name **What's New**. It will show you something new with Microsoft Access software.

Chapter 6: **Creating Tables**

The database tables are the foundation or building blocks of a database. These are what contain or hold the raw data that are later manipulated. In this chapter, you will learn how to create database tables from scratch or the template.

Creating A Database Table

One of the most vital things to learn while using the database is how to create tables, and how the data are entered. In few minutes, we will be learning how to create a table using the three methods

- Creating a database table from scratch
- Creating a database table from a template
- Creating a database table by importing database table from another database

Creating A Database Table From The Scratch

To create a database table from the scratch, follow the steps

- Open **Access,** go to the **Create tab,** and click on the **Table Design button**
- **Click on the** Save button **on the** Quick Access toolbar
- In the **Save As** dialog box, input the descriptive name of the table and then click on **OK**

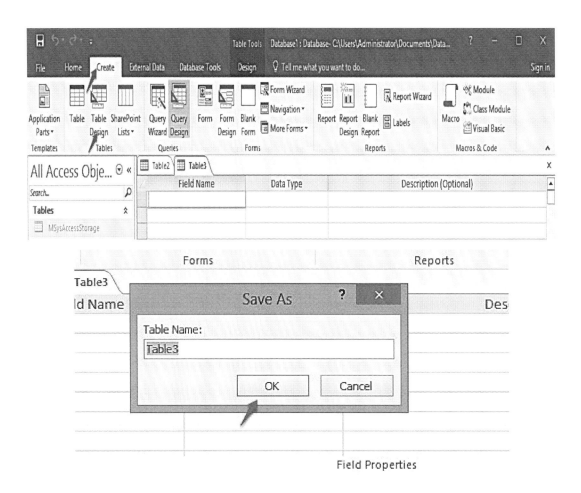

Creating A Database Table From A Template

Access provides four templates' types to create a table which are

- **Contacts:** This is used for storing contact addresses and phone numbers
- **Issues:** For prioritizing issues
- **Tasks:** This is used for tracking projects and their status
- **User:** For storing email addresses

Just like using a template for tables. Access also offers ready-made queries, forms reports.

To create a table using a template, follow the procedures below

- Open **Access,** go to the **Create tab,** and click on the Application Parts button
- In the drop-down list, under Quick Start; you can select **Contacts, Issues, Tasks, or Users**
- **In the** Create Relationship **dialog box**, **click** "There is no relationship" **and then click** Create.

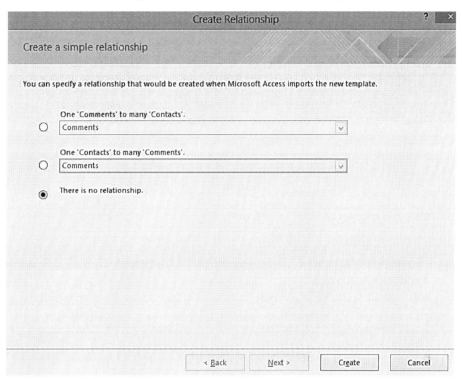

- On the Navigation pane, right-click on the name of the table you created and then select **Design View** (The Design view displays the names of the fields in the tables)

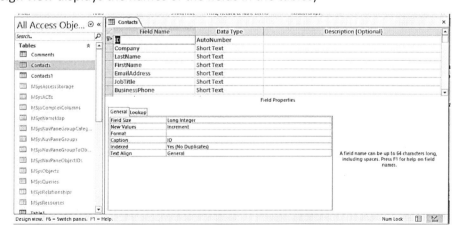

NOTE: *Before you create a database table using a template, ensure that all objects that are opened are closed*

Importing A Table From Another Database

Assuming the records, you need have been inputted in another table and you need to input them in a new table, follow the steps below

- Open **Access,** go to the **External tab,** and click on **Access**
- **In the** Get External Data – Access Database dialog **box, click on Browse.**
- In the File Open dialog box, select the Access database with the table, and then click on Open
- Select the first option button (Import, Tables, Queries, Forms Reports, Macros, and Modules) and click Ok
- Select the database table you want from **the Tables tab** and then click **on Ok**

Opening And Viewing Tables

To open a table, you will need to go to the Navigation pane and to view the names of the database table you created, you will need to select the Table group.

While opening and viewing tables in the database, there are two keywords you need to know

- **Datasheet View**: This is used for entering and checking data in a table
- **Design View**: This is used for creating fields and giving details about their parameters

To open and view the tables in the database, there are several ways to go about it. Below, are the ways to open and view tables

Opening Table In Design View

To open the table in the design view

- Select the table in the **Navigation Pane** and right-click on it
- In the shortcut menu, select **Design view,** and the objects in the table open as a tab on the work surface

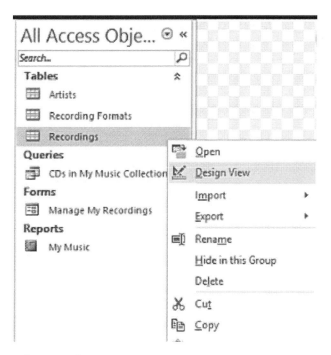

Opening Table In Datasheet View

To open the table in the Datasheet View

- Select the table in the **Navigation Pane** and right-click on it

In the shortcut menu, select **Open** and the objects in the table opens as a tab on the work surface

Chapter 7: **Relationships Between Tables**

Building Database Tables Relationship

Table relationships indicate the connection between two selected database tables following the same information they have in them. Major means of creating the relationship is to use one table's primary key field against the other's foreign key fields. Commit these two rules to memory any time you want to create a relationship between two tables:

- A relationship is only permitted within two related tables in the same database table, for instance, the number field can't be compared with the text field that they are not related with it has to be the related field.
- You are the one to tell Microsoft Access how the two tables will be related by using Primary keys and foreign keys.

Categories Of Relationships

Database relationship is of three categories, each category depends on the number of the field you want to relate with other in both tables, the following are the categories of database table relationship:

- **One-to-many relationship:** this is the most used relationship among the categories of tables relation. It is carried out by connecting one unique record (primary or indexed field key) field in one table against many records in other tables, for instance, you will see ID number is displayed in the student field only once while at the same time that student ID displays multiple times in examination field because the same student will do many examinations with the same ID number. Connecting these two tables is called the "One-to-many" relationship by using one field record of one table against the corresponding records in other tables.
- **One-to-one relationship:** it means linking tables with one field in each table. People don't usually relate tables in this way because such occurrences hardly happened.
- **Many-to-many relationship**: This is the establishment of a relationship in both tables with more than two fields in each table; none of these fields is the primary field key.

Managing Tables Within The Relationship Window

A relationship window is a window where a relationship is being established between the tables, and it starts by adding the tables into the window, then you can perform one or more activities on the table and finally establishing a relationship among the tables. To access the Relationship window, kindly:

- Open any table in **Design View** and click on the **Relationship** button in the relationship section to open the relationship window.

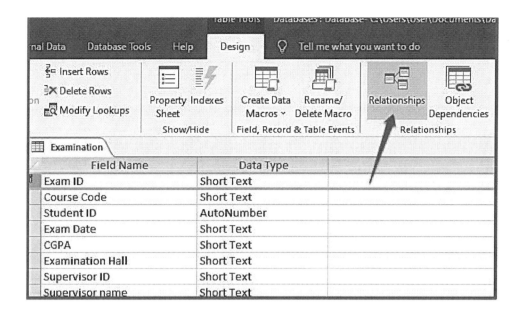

- Immediately you open the relationship window, the window will still be empty, then you can carry out the following activities aside from creating a relationship.

Add tables to the relationship window: click on the Add tables in the ribbon, and select the tables you want in the relation window from the show table dialog box, Use Ctrl-click to select multiple tables. Then tap on add button and lastly click the close button.

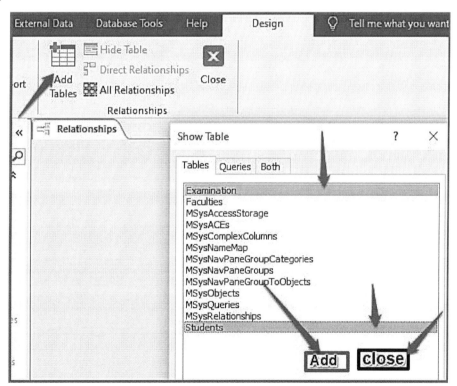

Arranging and resizing the tables: tap on the table title's window and drag to another position to change its location, click on any of the table's window border side to adjust the size of the table's window.

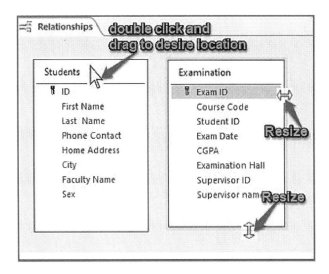

Removing a table from the window: select the concern table and tap on the Hide table.

Removing all tables from the window: tap the clear layout button and confirm it with Yes in the confirmation box.

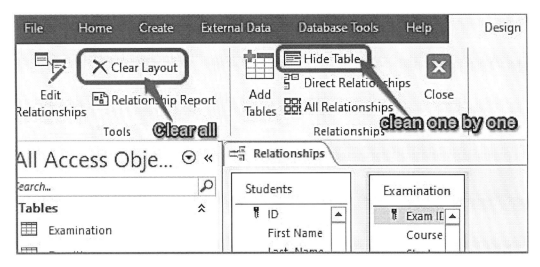

Putting one or more tables back to the window: tap on Add button and select the tables you want back, then click on add button and close the show table dialog box as usual.

Chapter 8: Creating Relationships

Establishing Relationship Between Tables

This is the major business of opening the relationship window. After you have gotten your tables added with the show table dialog box into the relationship window, then the next action that remains is to establish a relationship between those tables. To establish a relationship, kindly.

- Double-click and drag the **Primary Key Field** of the first table known as the parent table to the **corresponding field** which mostly has a similar name as the primary key field in the child table. As you are dragging, you will see a **plus icon** moving to the corresponding field. (if you are dealing with a very large table endeavor to bring the primary and corresponding field to the top of the table to make the relationship between both tables easier and avoid too much scrolling).

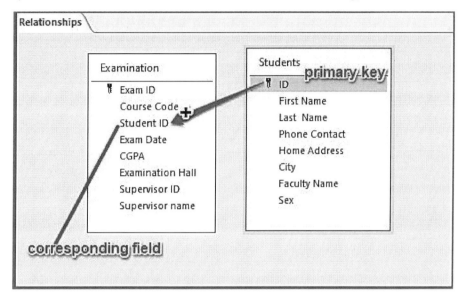

- If you drag the relationship between the primary key in the parent field to the corresponding key in the child table correctly you will immediately see the **Edit relationship dialog box**, then Place a **tick-mark** beside **Enforce referential integrity** check box to confirm the relationship as a one-to-many relationship to restrict it from being indeterminate relationship which simply means the relationship is not recognized and lastly click on **Create**.

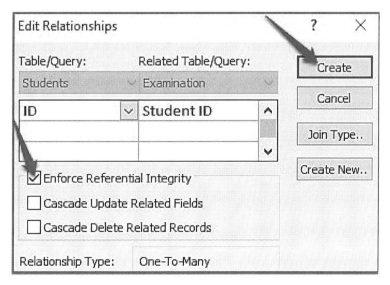

- Access must have created the new relationship between your tables in the window relationship with these two notes:
a. The presence of a line between the tables indicates there is a relationship between the tables.

381

b. You will see 1 beside the parent table and infinity beside the child table to give you a hint of the relationship, which will be visible only if you place a mark beside Enforce referential integrity tick box in (2) above.

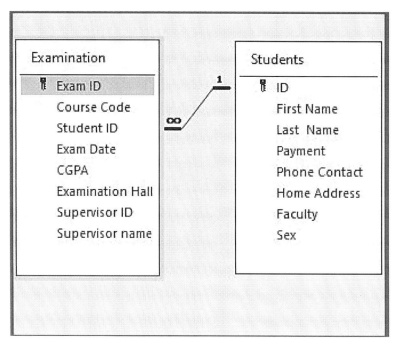

Note: you may continue to relate other tables in the database table by repeating the step (1-2). You may as well pick either of the parent or child tables above and relate it with another table either parent field or child field depends on how they are related with other tables you are comparing them with.

Modifying Table Relationship

After the table relationship has been established, you can move further to carry out one or two modifications on it, which is known as editing, to modify the relationship between tables, kindly:

- Right-click the **relationship line** that connects the two tables and pick **Edit relationship** from the drop-down list to access the Edit Relationship dialog box.

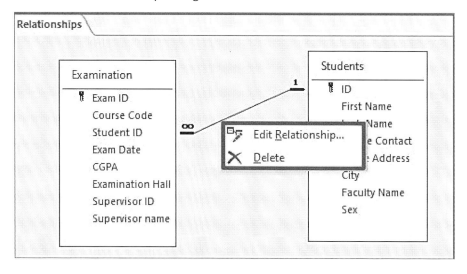

You can then perform any modification on it, you change the fields you link in each table before or anything you want to edit.

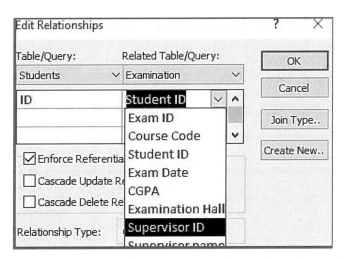

- Pick **Delete** from the Relationship drop-down list and pick **Yes** from the confirmation box to delete the relationship between two tables.

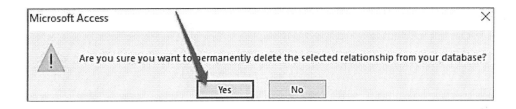

383

Chapter 9: **Entering Data**

Adding Records

To make an addition of a new record to a table or field, follow these steps.

1.) Open the table that you wish to add or remove one or two things by adding a record not already existing using "Datasheet View," or if it is a form, open it using "Form View".

2.) In the Records group found in the home tab, click on "New", or you can simply press Ctrl + Plus Sign (+).

3.) Locate the record that has an asterisk in the record selector and enter your new information.

4.) Click on the field that you want to use to enter this new record, and then input your data.

5.) To move to the subsequent field in the same row, press the TAB key on your keyboard. You can also use the Right or Left arrow keys, or simply take the cursor to the cell in the next field and click on it.

6.) To move to the subsequent field in the same column, use the Up or Down arrow keys, or simply click the cell you want.

Deleting Records

There will be many times when you wish to delete a record that you have entered. To do so, follow these steps.

1.) Open the table in "Datasheet View" or if it is a form, in "Form View".

2.) Select the record or records, if it is more than one record that you want to delete. To select a record, click the record selector next to the record.

3.) To extend or reduce the selection, drag the record selector if the record selector is available, or press SHIFT+DOWN ARROW or SHIFT+UP ARROW, if the record selector is not available.

3.) You can then delete the record by Pressing the DELETE key on your keyboard, selecting Home > Records > Delete, or pressing Ctrl + Minus Sign (-).

Chapter 10: **Forms**

Creating Forms

Learning how to create forms broadens your knowledge in the world of Access databases. Also, when you create a form, it adds to the files that make up your entire database. With respect to that, you will see the form appear in your Access navigation pane among other files you have already built.

Just like query files, forms are built from the data you already have in your table. Creating a form can save you a lot of time in the long run. It makes it easy for you as a user to import data into one or more tables you have in your database. See a form as a mirror through which you see all the information you have in a table and make the necessary correction if there is a need to do so. In a form, you have a clear view of the information you previously entered in your table.

Also, I will walk you through how you can give your form a name and also save it so as to appear as one of the files that make up your Access database. So, there are some good things you will learn from this section.

To create a form, you must have first of all built your table. It is from that your built table that you can create form. In the sample I will use, I named my created table "AUGUSTCUSTOMER". Select that table by just clicking or double-clicking on it in the navigation pane.

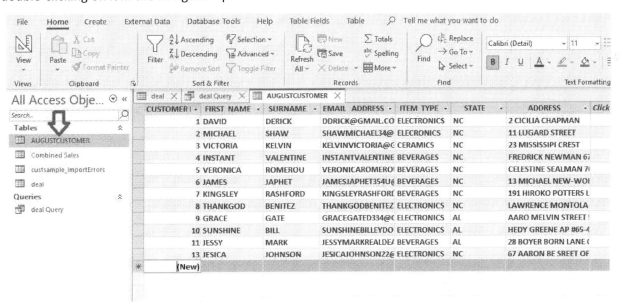

From the above photo, the table has already been created. So, the next step is to start building/creating the form from the table.

Select the **Create** tab which will then show you all the tools you have in this tab. Under the tools group, you will see the one named form. Click that **Form** tool which I indicate in the photo below.

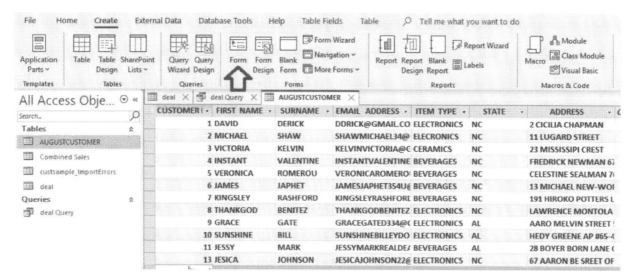

Immediately after you click that Form tool, a new Window opens showing each of the records and fields you have in your table in a clear and viewable state. It shows all the data in a way that you can easily make any correction you want to make from that form view. An example is the photo I have in the photo below. If you want to see the other records that are in that form, click the forward symbol which I also indicate in the photo below.

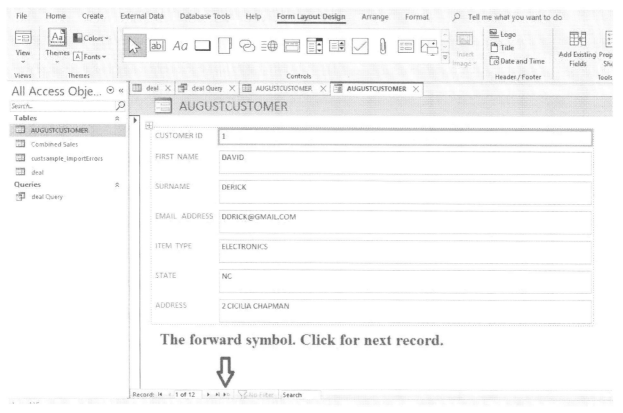

After viewing the information and making corrections where that are needed, you can save the new form file. To save it, click the **Save** icon at the top right-hand corner of the quick access toolbar section. The **Save** icon is indicated in the photo below.

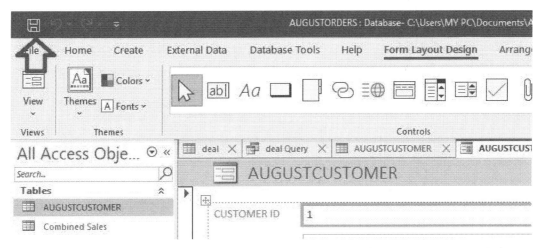

Give the form name. For me, I will give mine "AUGUSTCUSTOMERSFORM". You can give your form any name you can use to remember it based on the data you have in it. The name to be given to the Form is to be entered in the **Form Name** which will popup when you click that Save icon. After you have entered the name, click the **OK** button for it to be saved. Once this is done, you will see the saved form appear as one of the files that make up the database in the navigation pane. I hope with this teaching, you can easily create as many forms as you want in your database.

How To Insert Images In A Form

Even as you create a form, you can still give that form a unique additional design. If for instance the form contains data about your customers, you can decide to add the photos of those of your customers if you have them. Something like this adds extra beauty to your form.

To add an image in a form, right-click on that form file first as it appears on your Access navigation pane. The photo below shows the options shown when I right-clicked my form I named "AUGUSTCUSTOMERSFORM". Know that I right-clicked the form at the navigation pane.

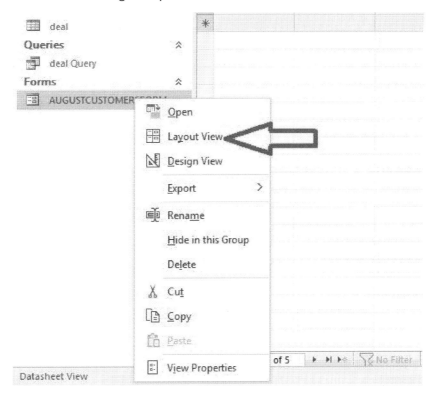

In the above photo, an arrow points at the **Layout View**. So, select the **Layout View** for you to be able to take the necessary actions that will allow you to upload an image. The photo below is what you will see when the Layout view opens. That data is based on what I have in my own sample form.

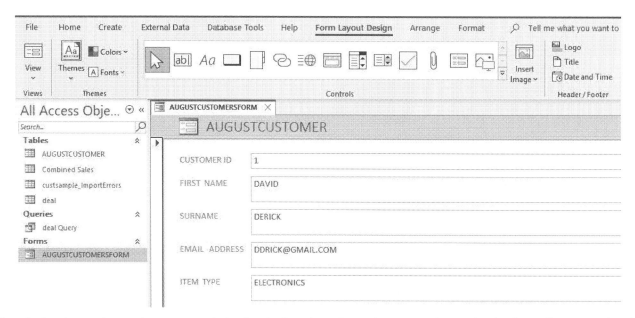

The photo above shows the commands in the design view. So, to insert any image in the form (for example, the one shown above), first click out of the record of the form so that the Insert Image tool will be made clickable. The next is to select the **Insert Image** command which is in the Controls group of the Form Layout Design.

This will open a new Window. You are to find the image you want to insert from a folder on your computer and double-click it. You will be taken back to the form record section. Drag your cursor to the part of the form where you want the image inserted and click at that spot. The image will be placed there. An example is the one I have below. It is assumed to be the photo of my customer that has that detail.

And lastly, click the **Save** icon at the quick access toolbar section for the image you inserted in the form to be saved. This adds beauty to your form in a great way. If your form contains your customers information for instance, having their images in the form will make it easy for you to recognize them when you see them.

Note: From the **Layout View**, you can insert logo, title, date and time, attachment, subform/subreport, check box, list box, combo box, navigation control, web browser control, links, tab control, button, label, and text box into your form. Just take your computer cursor to each of the command/tool in the Layout View and you will be informed what you can do with each. Experiment with each of them and see the result you will get.

388

Forms Wizard

The Form Wizard gives you more flexibility in terms of what fields you want to place on the form. The Form tools simply create a form with all the fields from the chosen data source. On the other hand, the Form Wizard allows you to select specific fields that you want on the form. Once created, you'll find that the form also provides more flexibility in terms of changing the size and positions of the textboxes and the labels.

I would recommend using the Form Wizard over one of the Form tools if you want more flexibility in the size and position of your textboxes.

To create a form using the Form Wizard, do the following:

- On the Ribbon, click the **Create** tab. In the **Forms** group, click **Form Wizard**.

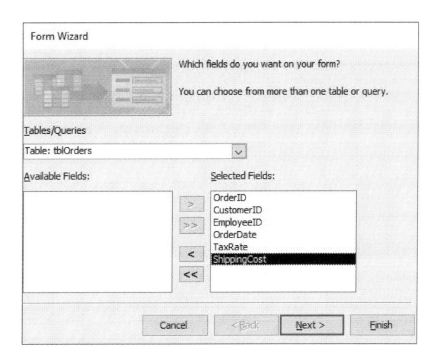

- Select the table or query that the form will be bound to from the **Tables/Queries** dropdown list.
- Select the field you want in the **Available Fields** list box and click the **Add** button (>) to add it to the **Selected Fields** list. Do this for all the fields you want to add to the form. To add all the fields, click the Add All button (>>).
- If you're creating a form/subform combination, after selecting the fields for the first table, you need to repeat the process for the second table. Select the second table in the **Table/Queries** drop-down list, and then add the fields you want for the subform to the **Selected Fields** list. Then click **Next**.

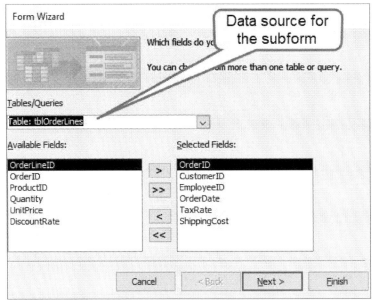

5.

- On the next page, select how you want to view the form and subform. In a one-to-many relationship, the subform will be bound to the child table. Ensure **Form with subform(s)** is selected, then click **Next**.

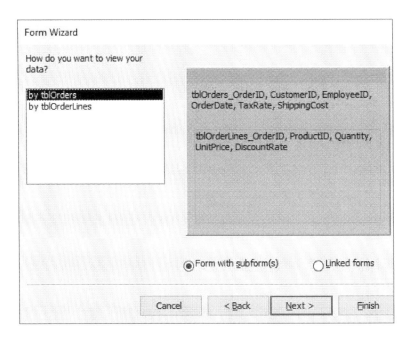

- Choose to display the subform as a **Datasheet** on the next page, then click **Next**.

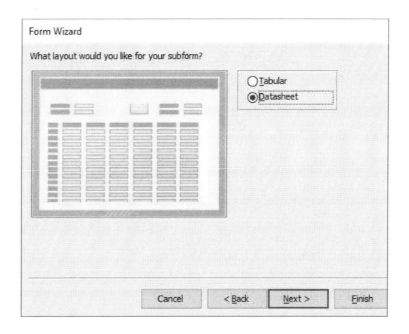

Note: If you're creating a single form (with no subform), you'll get the option to choose between Columnar, Tabular, Datasheet, and Justified layouts. If you want the fields next to their labels going down the form in a column, then select Columnar.

- On the next page, enter meaningful names for the form and subform so that they're easily identifiable in the Navigation Pane. You can choose to open the form in Form view so that you can determine what changes are required to finalize the form. On most occasions, you'll need to do some design fine-tuning after creating a form with the Form Wizard.

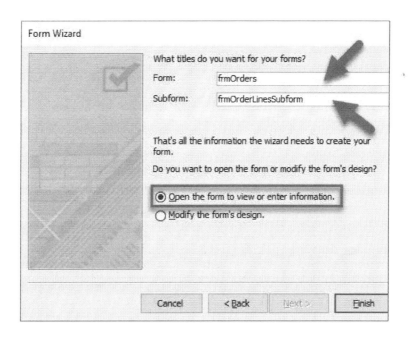

- Click **Finish** when done.

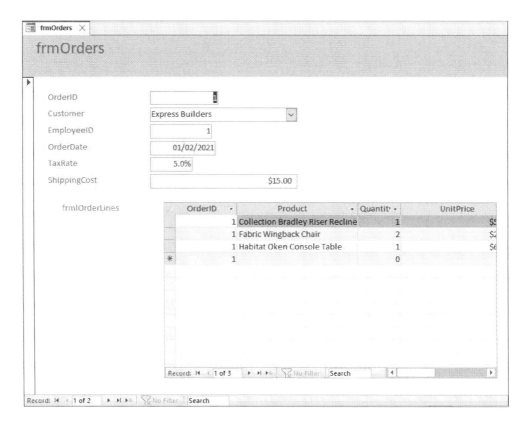

Access will display the form in Form view. As you can see, we need to make a few design changes to make the form more user-friendly.

Chapter 11: **Creating Queries**

In this chapter, I will guide you through on how to create query from a single table. A query is an answer to question based on the data you have in your prepared table. It is a means of sorting some data from the overall data in a table.

Take for instance that I am a business owner and I have list of customers names, locations (that is their individual states), email addresses, kinds of products they bought, and their address. These are the data in the table. A sample is the table I prepared which I have its photo below.

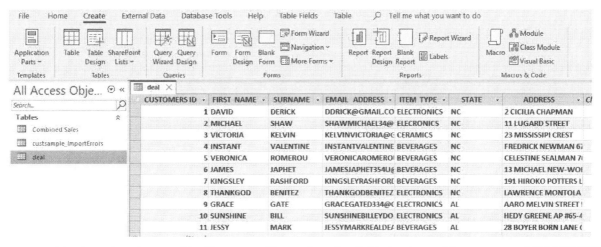

Taking a good look at the above table file, you will see that the fields in that table are named CUSTOMERS ID, FIRST NAME, SURNAME, EMAIL ADDRESS, ITEM TYPE, STATE and ADDRESS. These are my customers information that bought items from my supermarket store recently.

Let me assume that there is a new beverage product in market and I already have them in my store. I want to send email across to people that recently bought beverages from my supermarket store. I want to do so because I believe they are likely to buy the new brand of beverage. I can then use query to ask question on people that previously bought beverages from my store based on that my prepared table.

I will include some field information in the query form and lastly request that those that previously bought beverages from my supermarket store be sorted. Let me take it on step by step.

First, select the table file that you want to build your query form from the Access navigation pane. Example is the photo I have below where I selected the table file I named **deal**.

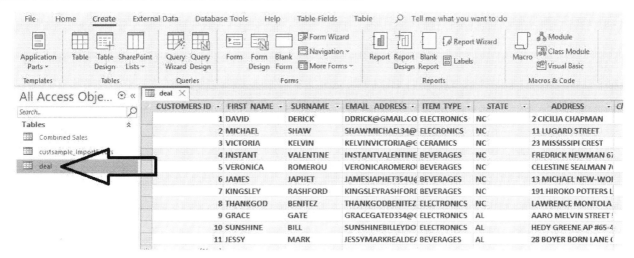

The next step for you to take is to select the **Create** tab. Under the Create tab, you will see some tools. But our interest is on creating query, so select the tool named **Query Wizard** which is indicated in the photo below. The

Query Wizard tool is in the group called Queries. You can still select Query Design tool instead of Query Wizard but I assume in this section that you have not used query on Microsoft Access before now.

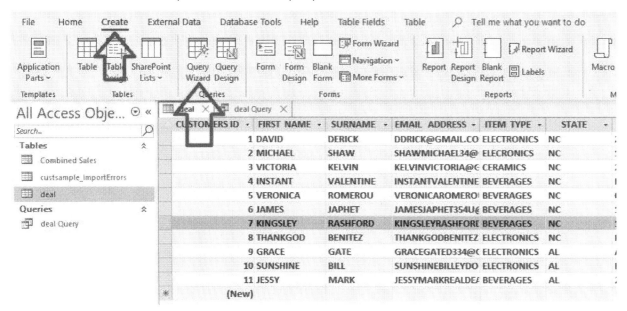

Immediately you click the **Query Wizard** command, a new interface will open in your Access. Example of the interface is the one I have in the photo below.

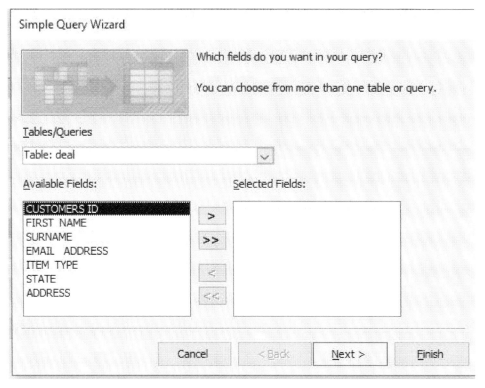

The above screenshot is called the Simply Query Wizard. The next action you have to take is to start adding the file you want moved from your table to the query file. To do that, select the filed name on the **Available Fields** section and then click the forward symbol (**>**) for it to be added to the **Selected Fields** section. The photo below explains this.

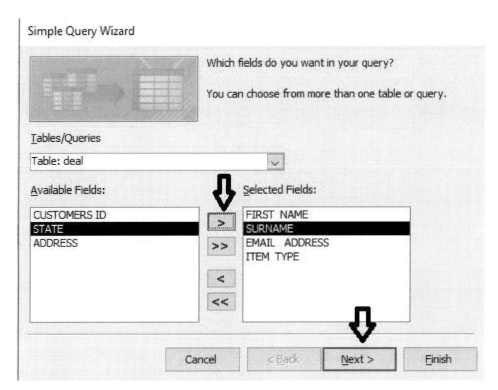

Add as many fields as you want. From the above photo, I just needed the fields I named FIRST NAME, SURNAME, EMAIL ADDRESS, AND ITEM TYPE. Therefore, I selected those fields and clicked the "forward icon" until they are added in the Selected **Fields section** which will then appear in my query.

The next step you need to take is to click the **Next** button which is at the bottom part of the Simple Query Wizard dialog box. This action will open a new page in the dialog box which I show in the photo below.

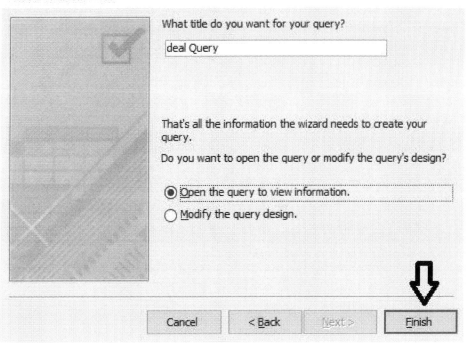

When you take a good look at the above photo, you will see that an arrow points at the **Finish** button. So, what I want you to do is to click the **Finish** button.

At this point, you have succeeded in creating query file in your Access database. The photo below shows the query I created from that data I select.

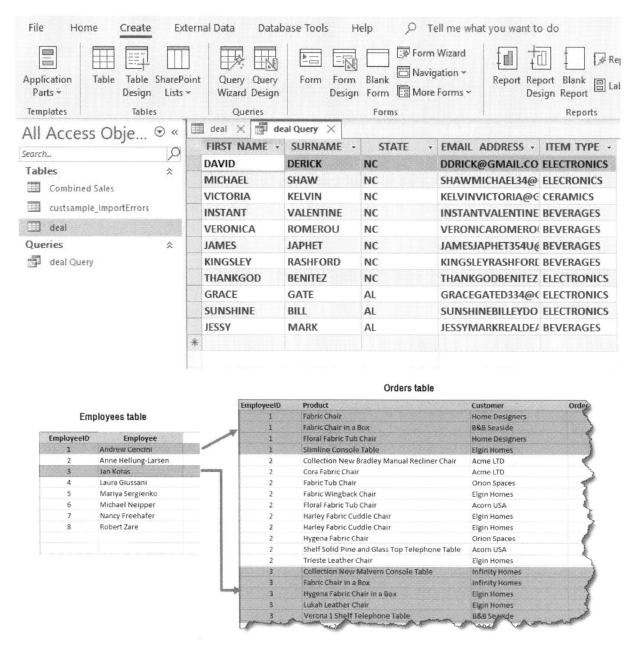

There is something I want us to do extra on query. This is one of the things query is known for. It is nothing else but asking the query question that will give us an answer. From the details of my customers, I want query to sort my customers that bought beverages based on the information in the above picture. This will lead us to the next subheading.

Modifying the Query Design

I want to modify my query by asking the program to give me the information of those that bought beverages from my supermarket. So, these are the steps you need to take to get that answer to the request.

Go to the Access Navigation pane and right click the query you just created. Select the option **Design View** from the options and this will show you an interface where you can start your modification for you to be able to run your query at the end of the task. Below is my own interface after I selected the Design View option.

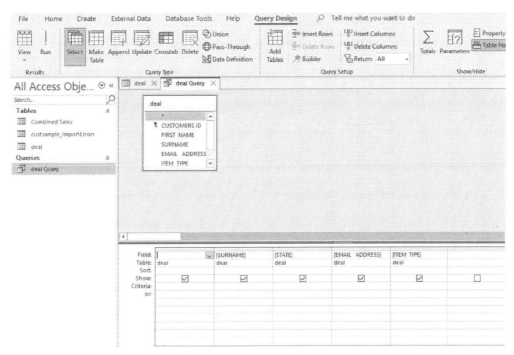

If you look at the first box, you will find out that it contains the field names I used when I first created my query file. In the second section with respect to the above photo, you will see that the same fields are ticked.

As I have stated before, I want to use this query to sort customers that bought "BEVERAGES" from my supermarket. In the **Sort** line, choose how you want the information sorted. I prefer using Ascending but you can still choose not to sort.

In the criteria line, type the data you want to have sorted. In my own sample, I want to sort the customers that have bought beverages before now. So, I will type "BEVERAGES" in the **Criteria** but under the **ITEM TYPE**. The photo below explains what I am talking about.

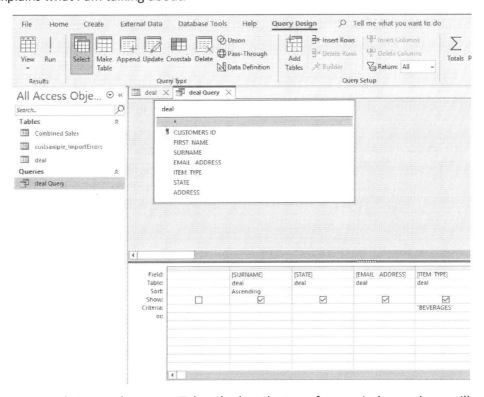

At this point, you are ready to run the query. Take a look at the top of your window and you will see that you are in the **Query Design** section. Among the commands that are their, click **Run**. The photo below shows the **Run** tool I said you should click.

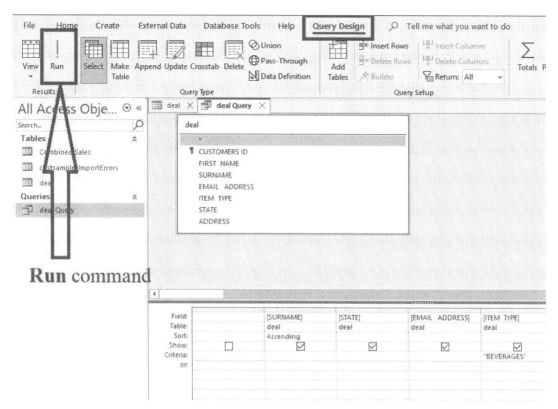

Run command

Immediately you click that Run command, query will give you answer to the instruction you gave to it. In my own sample, I gave it the instruction to show me customers that have bought beverages from my supermarket before and below is the answer.

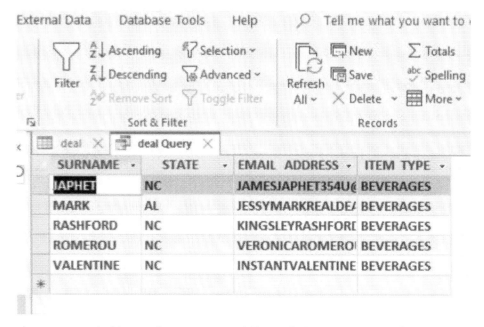

At this point, you have succeeded in running a query on Microsoft Access. Congratulations to you.

Query Parameters

With the parameter Queries you can be informed of criteria before you execute the query. A parameter query can come in very handy when you have a need to query various questions with the use of different criteria anytime you perform an execution.

When you make use of a parameter query, you will be able to build conditional analysis which is one that is based on various variables you choose to indicate each time the query is executed.

To build a parameter query all you have to do is;

398

- Replace **the hard-coded** criteria with text that you must have enclosed in square brackets.
- When you execute a parameter query, it will force open the Enter Parameter Value dialog box and prompt it to ask for a variable. Note that at this point, the text you must have typed inside the square brackets will be displayed in the dialog box.

How Parameter Queries Work

When you run a parameter query, Microsoft Access attempts to change any text to a literal string by enclosing the text on quotes. Note that if you place squares in brackets around the text, Microsoft Access will assume it is a variable and will attempt to bind some variable to the variable with **the use of the following series of tests:**

- Microsoft Access will check if the variable field inserted is a name. If it is identified as a field name, the field will then be used in the expression.
- If the variable is not a field name, Access will check to be sure that the variable is a calculated field. If Access determines the expression is a calculated field it will carry out the mathematical operation.
- If the variable is then not a calculated field, Access will check to see if the variable is referencing an object like the control on an open form or an open report.
- If all of the above options fail, the option left will then be to ask the user what the variable is, with this, Access will display the Enter Parameter Value dialog box, displaying the text you inserted in the Criteria row.

Ground Rules Of Parameter Query

Parameter queries also have their own ground rules that should be followed so you can make use of them properly;

- The name of a field cannot be used as a parameter. If this is done, Access will replace your parameter with the current value of the field.
- There is a need to place square brackets around the parameters. If this is not done, Access will automatically change text into a literal string.
- The number of characters in your parameter must be limited. When you insert a parameter prompt that is too long it might result in the prompt being cut off in the Enter Parameter Value dialog box.

Working With Parameter Queries

It is actually very innovative for you to get around with your parameter queries and learn how to make the best use of them, it will be very useful and will better help to solve your data analysis properly. This section throws more light on the various ways in which you can make use of the parameters in your queries.

Working With Multiple Parameter Conditions

You are free to work with as many Parameters as needed in a query. When you execute a query you will be prompted to insert some information that will enable you to filter on two different data points without the need to rewrite your query.

Combining Parameters With Operators

Combination of parameter prompts can be done with the use of any operator that you normally would use in a query. When parameters are used in conjunction with standard operators it enables you to either expand or contract the filters in your analysis without having to recreate your query.

Combining Parameters With Wildcards

One of the major problems often encountered with the use of a parameter query is that anytime the parameter is left blank when the query is being executed, the query will not return any records.

A proven method to solve this issue is the use of wildcards, this way even if the Parameter is blank, all records will be returned. Note that when you use the *wildcard alongside a parameter, it allows users to insert an initial parameter and still get results.

Using Parameters As Calculation Variables

Parameters can be used at any point where a variable is used and not only using it as criteria for a query. Parameters can also be of great importance when it has to do with calculations.

Using Parameters As Function Arguments

Parameters can be used as arguments functions. When the query that has the parameter is being executed, you will be promoted to a start date and an end date. Those two dates will in turn be used as arguments in the DateDiff function. You can also choose to indicate new dates anytime you run the query without having to recreate the query.

Note that the values inserted into your parameters must be a perfect fit with the data type that is needed for the function's argument.

Chapter 12: **Creating Reports**

Welcome to the last phase of the database object, where the result of the table you constructed and the query result you generated will be presented in the form of a Report. Don't be afraid of creating a report because it is not as complicated as you think it may be, you only need to take a tour of simple steps in creating a report. The report gives you a brief view of certain parts of the database information you needed professionally for easy reading and comprehension.

Creating A Professional Report

Access offers diverse techniques for creating a report, and those techniques offer different report appearances, though all the techniques are presenting the same information but in a different form. The easiest and best means of creating a report is through a report wizard, report wizard shows the exact information you want from your database table and query either by making use of the query information or by starting the query inside the report itself though that may be worrisome.

I will be taken you through the simplest means of creating a report with the report wizard via the query result you have saved into your database file. Let us get started with report creation with the following steps:

- Tap on the **Create** tab and click on **Report wizard** to access the Report dialog box.

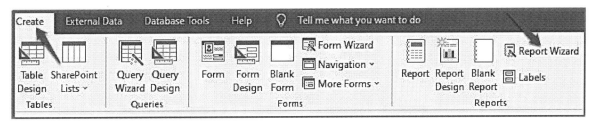

- Click on the **Table/Query** drop-down menu to choose the **Query** that has the result information you want to use in creating a report which will give you the list of fields it has and send it to the available fields box.

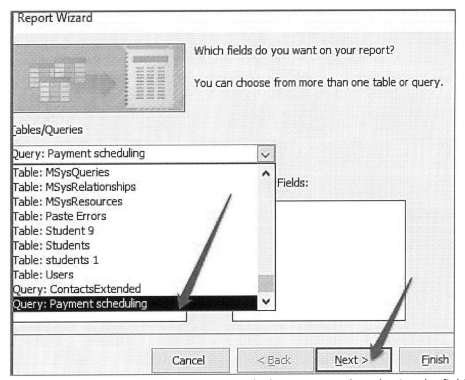

- Select the **Fields** you use in creating the query result that you want by selecting the field and clicking on greater than **">"** to send it to the selected field or this symbol **">>"** for sending all the fields to the selected box once, then select the next button.

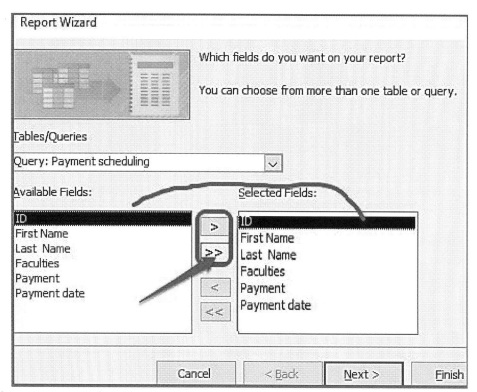

- If you desire you may select a **Field** and click the greater than > button to make it subgrouping head, then click the **Next** button.

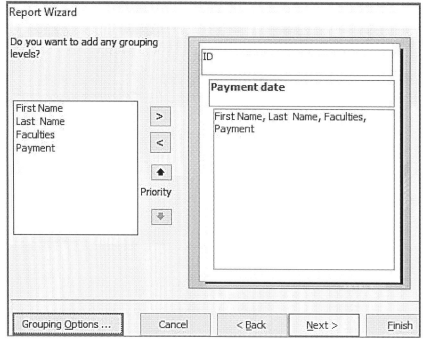

- Decide the **Sort** you want for your report result, you have the chance of choosing about four fields and sort them, kindly select the **field** and tap on **ascending** to change to descending order. if you don't want it simply click on the **Next** button.

- Select the report **Layout** and **Orientation** you want for both layout and orientation and click on the **Next** button.

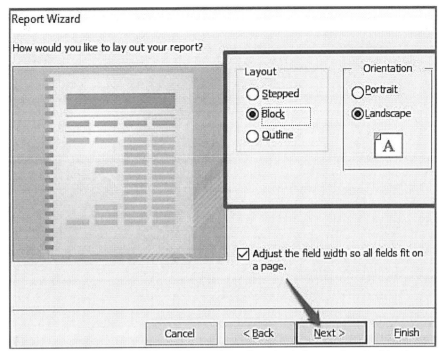

- Give your report a **title** that should be able to describe the information inside the report and which you will use to open the report next time you want to view the result inside the navigation by double-clicking the report name to open it.

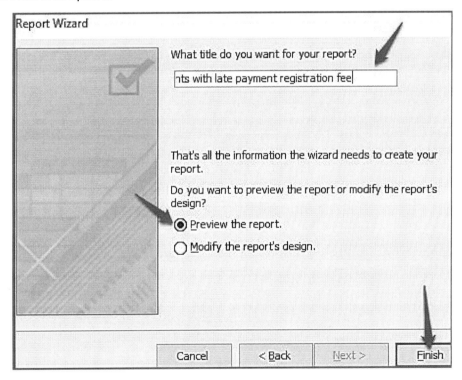

- Then select **Preview the report** option and click on the **Finish** button to generate a preview for the report.

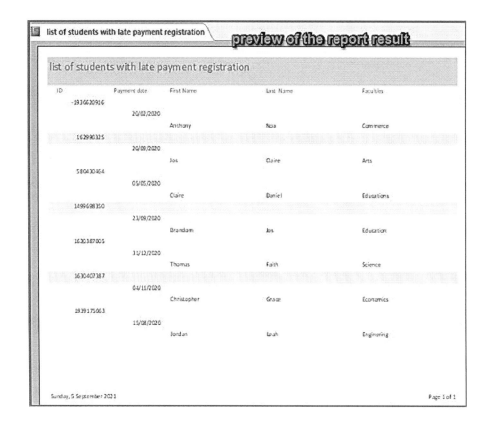

Opening And Inspecting A Report

The report is created for proper cross-examination and to carry out necessary activities, kindly observe the following instruction to open and inspect your report result:

- Move to the report group in the navigation pane, and look for the name of the report you want to open.

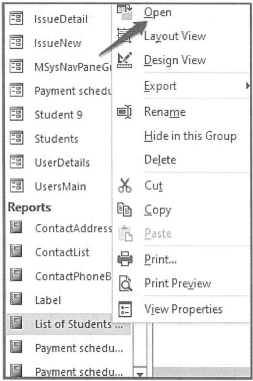

- Then double-click the **Name** of the report you want to open for inspection or right-click the **Name** and choose open in the fly-out menu to open the report in report view.

list of students with late payment registration				Monday, 6 sept, 2021
ID	Payment date	First Name	Last Name	Faculties
-1936620916				
	20/02/2020			
		Anthony	Noa	Commerce
162990325				
	20/09/2020			
		Jos	Claire	Arts
580430464				
	05/05/2020			
		Claire	Daniel	Educations
1499698350				
	23/09/2020			
		Brandom	Jos	Education
1630387005				
	31/12/2020			
		Thomas	Faith	Science
1630407387				
	04/11/2020			
		Christopher	Grace	Economics

Note: if you update your database table, the query result will be affected, and you need to update the report as well, to do that click on Refresh All button under the Home tab to update the report as well.

Refining The Appearance Of Your Report

You don't have to ignore your report when you notice the appearance is not up to the standard you want, you can go ahead and manipulate some tools to change your report look and layout. To refine the appearance of your report, kindly open it in layout view and then perform one or more modifications on it, to achieve that, do well to:

- Right-click your **REPORT** and select **Layout View** in the fly-out menu to open your report in the layout view.

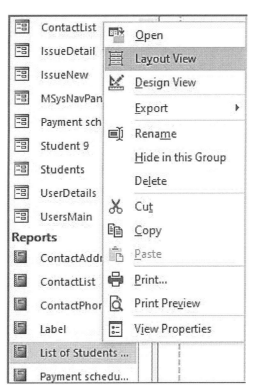

- For **Layout Modification,** select **Arrange** tab and move to the table section then click on the **Grid** menu and pick the **Layout** you want from the drop-down list, you may as well select **tabular or stacked.**

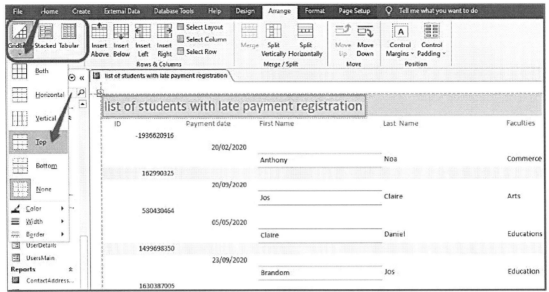

- For **margin modification**, click on **the field, record, or data** which its margin needs to be changed, click on the **Control Margins** menu and pick **any option** as it is shown below under Report Layout tools (Arrange).

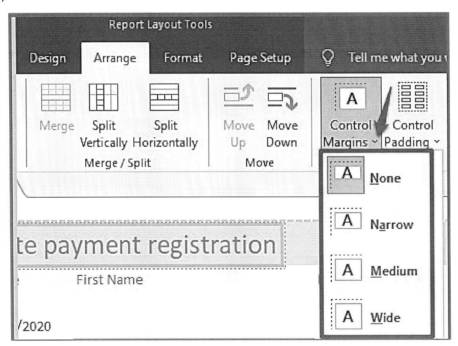

BOOK 7: MICROSOFT OUTLOOK

Introduction

Whether for personal or professional usage, everyone must be organized. Being organized in the modern world entails keeping track of email messages and appointments, preserving essential people's names and contact information, and establishing to-do lists to help you finish different sorts of personal or professional work.

Microsoft Outlook 2022 is a popular utility for managing email, appointments, tasks, and contacts in a single application. This book will teach you how to use Microsoft Outlook 2022 for Windows, which can be purchased alone or as part of a Microsoft 365 subscription.

You will discover how to save, manage, and read email messages. Create appointments and reminders to ensure that you never miss an important date! Create task lists to help you progress on various tasks, save and search through crucial people's names and contact information. By the conclusion of this course, you will be able to handle Outlook's four primary features: Mail, Appointments, People, and Tasks, with ease.

In addition to learning how to generate email messages, appointments, task lists, and contact information, you will also learn how to search for and locate information and organize and categorize data. Whether you need to manage your personal or professional life, this guide will help you learn Outlook for usage at home or work.

Chapter 1: **Geting Started**

Electronic communications keep us in touch with coworkers, customers, friends, and family. Outlook 2022 is a perfect choice for workers who rely on electronic communications, especially those who work in organizations that utilize Microsoft Exchange Server, SharePoint, and Skype for Business to handle collaboration. You can easily create, save, organize, manage, and retrieve messages, address books, calendars, and task lists from a single location. Moreover, Outlook makes this information accessible whenever and wherever you need it.

The pieces that determine Outlook's appearance and how you interact with it are referred to collectively as the user interface. Some parts of the user interface, such as the color palette, are purely aesthetic. Others are useful, such as toolbars, menus, and buttons. You may customize the aesthetic and functional features of the user interface to fit your tastes and working style.

How To Open Outlook

How you launch Outlook 2022 depends on the operating system on your computer. For instance: Outlook can be launched in Windows 10 through the Start menu, the All Apps menu, the Start screen, and the taskbar search box.

In Windows 8, you can launch Outlook from the Apps screen or search results on the Start screen.

Outlook can be launched via the Start menu, the All Programs menu, or the Start menu search results in Windows 7. You may also have an Outlook shortcut on your desktop or Windows taskbar.

When you launch Outlook, it examines your computer's default application settings. If Outlook is not the default email application, it shows a notification and the choice to make it the default so that any email generated outside of Outlook, such as from a Microsoft Word document or File Explorer, is created in Outlook using the main Outlook account.

To launch Outlook on a Windows 10 system:

1. **Select the** Start button**, followed by the** All applications option**.**

2. In the app list, select any index letter to see the alphabet index, then hit O to browse to the apps beginning with that letter.

3. ***Scroll the list as needed, then pick Outlook 2022 to launch the application.*** (NB: If Outlook 2022 is not shown, it may be located in a Microsoft Outlook folder in the M area.)

To launch Outlook on a Windows 8 system:

1. Display the Apps screen from the Start screen.

2. Click any index letter to view the alphabet index after sorting the Apps screen by name.

3. **Click O** in the alphabet index to see the list of applications beginning with that letter. Click Outlook 2022 to launch the application.

Manage Office And Outlook Settings

You can access application settings via the Backstage view, notably the Office Account page and the Outlook Options dialog box. This subject describes the configuration options available on the Office Account page of the Backstage view.

The Office Account tab of the Backstage view provides information on your installation of Outlook (and other Office applications) and the resources to which you connect. This information consists of:

- Your Microsoft account and management connections.
- The window's current backdrop and theme.
- Storage locations and services (such as Facebook and LinkedIn) to which Office has been linked.

- Your subscription information and links to manage it, if you have Office through an Office 365 subscription.
- The version number and update choices for the app.

Microsoft Account Options

You already have a Microsoft account if you use Office 365, Skype, OneDrive, Xbox Live, Outlook.com, or a Windows Phone. (Many non-Microsoft products and websites use Microsoft account credentials.) If you do not already have a Microsoft account, you may register any existing email account as a Microsoft account, establish a free Outlook.com or Hotmail.com account and register it as a Microsoft account, or create an alias for an Outlook.com account and register it.

Numerous websites and applications validate transactions using Microsoft account credentials. It is thus advisable to register a personal account that you manage as your Microsoft account, rather than a corporate account that your company controls. Thus, you will not risk losing access if you quit the organization.

You may rapidly customize the appearance of your Outlook app window by selecting a backdrop and theme from the Office suite. *(NB: These are Office-specific and have nothing to do with the Windows theme or desktop backdrop.)* The title bar of the application window has a backdrop with a modest style. There are 14 backdrops from which to pick, or you may choose for no background.

At the time of this writing, three Office themes are available:

- **Colorful:** Displays the app-specific color for the title bar and ribbon tabs, with light gray for the ribbon commands, status bar, and Backstage view.
- **Dark Gray:** Displays the title bar and ribbon tabs in a dark gray color, while the ribbon commands, status bar, and Backstage view are shown in a light gray color.
- **White:** Displays the title bar, ribbon tabs, and ribbon commands in white, while the app-specific color is used for the status bar.

From the Connected Services part of the page, you may link Office to your Facebook, Flickr, and YouTube accounts to view photos and videos, SharePoint sites and OneDrive storage locations, and LinkedIn and Twitter account to share information. To connect Office to one of these services, you must already have an account.

Outlook does not provide access to storage sites unless you have established a connection with them. When entering a photo into an email message, for instance, you will have the choice of inserting a locally saved image or searching online for an image. After connecting your Facebook, SharePoint, or OneDrive account, you may insert images from those sources.

Changes made on the Office Account page are applied to all Office applications installed on all machines linked with your account. For instance, changing the Office backdrop in Outlook on one computer affects Outlook on all other computers that are linked with the same Office account.

Some of the options on the Office Account page are also accessible through the Backstage view's Outlook Options dialog box. This dialog box includes hundreds of choices for configuring Outlook's behavior. It is advisable to familiarize yourself with the dialog box's content so that you are aware of what may be modified.

To view Office account configurations

1. Open **Outlook**.

2. In the application window or any item window, select the File tab to see the Backstage view, and then click **Office Account**.

To manage the connection to your Microsoft account:

1. Display the Office Account page in Backstage.

2. Click any of the links in the User Information section to start the desired procedure.

To change the backdrop of all Office program windows

1. Show the Office Account page in Backstage.

2. In the Office Backgrounds list, point to any background to get a live preview in the application window, and then select the desired background.

To alter the color palette of all Office program windows

1. Show the Office Account page in Backstage.

2. In the Office Theme drop-down menu, choose **Colorful, Dark Gray, or White**.

To link to a site for cloud storage or social media service

1. Show the Office Account page in Backstage.

2. Pick **Add a service** at the bottom of the Connected Services section, then click the kind of service you want to add and then the individual service.

To modify or delete a link to a social networking service:

1. Show the Office Account page in Backstage.

2. In the Connected Services section, click the **Manage link** to the right of the desired service. A web page opens and shows account-specific and account-accessible information.

Modify or delete the connection, or dismiss this page to return to Outlook

To cut ties with a cloud storage location:

1. Show the Office Account page in Backstage.

2. *In the Connected Services section, to the right of the storage location, you want to alter, click the Remove option.* (NB: You cannot deactivate the storage service connected with the Microsoft account that owns the Office 365 subscription if you have Outlook via an Office 365 subscription).

3. **Click Yes** in the confirmation message box.

To manage your Office 365 account:

1. Show the Office Account page in Backstage.

2. Select the **Manage Account button** in the Product Information section to reveal the sign-in page for your Office 365 administration interface.

3. Enter your account information and sign in to view your choices.

To administer Office Upgrades/Updates

1. Show the Office Account page in Backstage.

2. Select the **Update Options button**, and then choose the desired action.

Chapter 2: **The Ribbon**

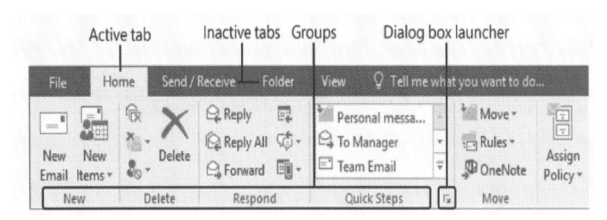

Unlike other Office applications, Outlook features several program window ribbons: one for each module and one for each item type window. (There are several item type windows, such as those for generating messages, appointments, meetings, contact records, and so on, as well as another set for modifying each of these item kinds.) The content of each item window ribbon corresponds to the content of the corresponding item type. The fundamental functioning of each ribbon is the same.

Each item type may have its Quick Access Toolbar and ribbon customized. This is more prevalent in Word, Excel, and PowerPoint than in Outlook, since Outlook includes separate ribbons with item-specific instructions.

The Home Ribbon

Contains the commands required for generating calendar items, showing certain calendar views, managing other calendars and calendar groups, and sharing the calendar.

The Skype Meeting group appears on the home page only if Microsoft Skype for Business is part of your organization's collaborative ecosystem. Skype not only allows you to initiate a real-time text, voice, video, and collaboration sessions with colleagues inside your business but also allows you to invite both internal and external participants to online meetings.

This folder contains instructions for generating and manipulating calendars. This page allows you to create a new calendar, modify an existing calendar, share a calendar with other Outlook users and define what each user may do with the shared calendar, access a calendar to which you are not presently connected, and modify a calendar's behavior behind the scenes.

A calendar is structurally nothing more than a folder that stores calendar items. When you designate a folder as Calendar type, it is subject to the display choices allotted to calendars and is handled with other calendars.

The Send/Receive Ribbon

Contains instructions for syncing Outlook data with mail server data. You may configure how Outlook sends and receives messages, whether Outlook automatically downloads whole messages or merely message headers, and if downloads are performed manually. You may also disengage Outlook from the current Internet connection if you operate offline, for instance, if you wish to cease sending and receiving messages while connected to the Internet.

The View Ribbon

Includes commands for viewing and rearranging calendar items, modifying the Calendar module's layout and look, showing missed reminders, launching additional calendars in separate windows, and dismissing open calendar item windows. *(NB: The Send/Receive tab is the same across all modules)*.

Fill BackStage

Outlook's Backstage view, shown by choosing the File tab at the left of the ribbon, contains commands relevant to administering Outlook rather than item content. The accessible Backstage commands are grouped on named pages, which may be seen by selecting the tabs in the left pane. The current Outlook module and the ribbon are re-displayed by clicking the Back arrow positioned above the page tabs.

On the remaining tabs of the ribbon, buttons reflect the commands associated with working with items and item content. By default, the Home tab comprises the most commonly used commands.

When a visual element like a photo, table, or chart is chosen in an item window, one or more tool tabs may appear at the right end of the ribbon to make instructions associated with that object readily available. The Tool tabs are only accessible when the corresponding item is chosen. the Tools heading above the tab name distinguishes them from other tabs.

Email Message Ribbon
Working In The Mail Module

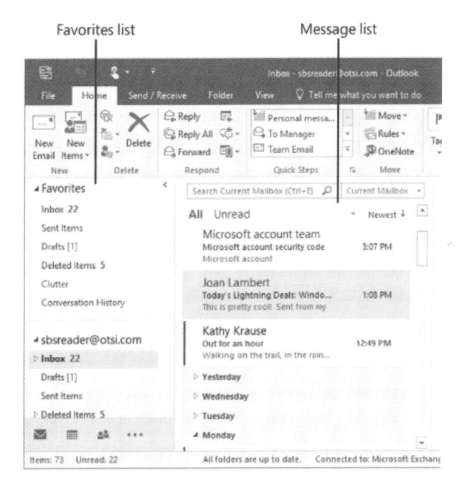

By default, the Mail module is shown when you launch Outlook. The Favorites list at the top of the Folder Pane and the message list in the content area comprise the Mail-specific content. The Home tab contains instructions relating to message management.

Folder Pane Content

The Folder Pane shows the Favorites list and the folder structure of your inbox in the Mail module (or mailboxes, if you have set up multiple email accounts). The folders you add to your Favorites list are shown at the top of the open Folder Pane and on the minimized Folder Pane.

When you are linked to a Microsoft Exchange account, the Inbox, Sent Items, Drafts, Deleted Items, and Clutter folders are immediately added to the Favorites list. Suppose Outlook is set to connect to many email accounts. In that case, you will find it helpful and reasonable to add the Inbox folders of each account to the Favorites list so you can view all of your messages from a single spot. Suppose, you have connectivity troubles with an account. In that case, you may add the account's Outbox folder to the Favorites list so you can readily determine whether messages are being delivered.

When you log in to any form of email account, each mailbox has the following nine folders:

- **Inbox:** Outlook distributes new messages to this folder by default.
- **Drafts:** Outlook maintains temporary copies of unsent messages in this folder, generated when you save a message without sending it for the first time. Outlook may also produce a draft for you while you work if you do not send the message immediately.
- **Sent Items:** Outlook maintains a duplicate of each communication sent in this folder. Change this setting if you want to save sent messages elsewhere or if you don't want to keep them at all, but the safest choice is to remain with the default.
- **Removed Items:** Deleted Outlook items from other folders are stored in this folder. They are not permanently removed until the folder is emptied.
- **Clutter:** Outlook tracks the messages you habitually discard and the ones you reply to. Based on these patterns, Outlook sends to these folder communications that it believes you will ignore.
- This folder is where Outlook places messages blacklisted by the spam filter.
- While establishing a connection to your mail server, Outbox Outlook stores outgoing messages in this folder.
- **RSS Feeds:** This folder contains the website information feeds to which you've subscribed. When you initially launch Outlook, Microsoft-recommended information feeds may appear here.
- **Search Folders:** These folders include the most recent results of your searches for messages matching certain search parameters.

The default installation of Microsoft Skype for Business provides a Conversation History folder where you may search, analyze, and resume instant messaging interactions (and other Skype communications). Your email service provider or third-party email security applications may have added additional folders. You may examine more folders by showing the Folder list in the Folder Pane of the current module.

The Folder list displays the whole folder structure for an Exchange account, which is substantially more sophisticated than the regular Mail module view. The Folders list for Exchange account mailboxes provides the following extra folders:

- **Calendar:** Contains the Outlook Calendar module's content.
- **Contacts:** Contains the Outlook People module's data.
- **Journal:** Contains the Outlook Journal module's content.
- **Notes:** Contains the Outlook Notes module's content.
- **Sync Problems**: This contains a list of communication failures and email server conflicts.
- **Tasks:** Contains the Outlook Tasks module's content.
- Folders created by users Contains any created calendar, contact, and task folders

The folders in the Folder Pane are shown in an order that is partially based on priority, or maybe simply a programmer's concept from the past that persisted. If desired, the folders may be shown in alphabetical order.

In addition to the account folder structure, the Folder list shows the Groups, Group Calendars, and Public folder nodes if your business uses Office 365 and Exchange.

Connect or subscribe to Microsoft SharePoint lists or Internet calendars. Connections to these groups will show on the same level as your inbox.

To include a folder in Favorites

1. Show the Mail module and then do any of the below actions:

- Dragging the folder to Favorites.
- Right-click the folder, and then **choose Show** in Favorites from the context menu
- Click the folder, and then click the **Show in Favorites button** in the Favorites group on the Folder tab.

To show the Folder list in any module's Folder Pane.

1. Perform one of the subsequent:

- In the Navigation Bar, click the **Options (...) icon**, followed by Folders.
- If the Folders button has been added to the Navigation Bar, click the Folders button.
- Enter Ctrl+6.

To show folders alphabetically:

1. Select **Show All Folders A to Z** in the Clean Up group on the Folder tab,.

To organize subfolders alphabetically

1. Select the folder containing the subfolders by clicking on it.

- Right-click the folder, then choose **Sort Subfolders by Name**.

The Message Ribbon

The four tabs on the ribbon of a task window are titled **Task, Insert, Format Text, and Review**. The Task tab contains the commands used to create and manage most tasks. There are commands for managing and assigning the job, sending it to a OneNote notebook, and toggling between the task pages. This tab also has options for assigning a task's category or follow-up flag, blocking other Outlook users from reading the task's information while linked to your account, and adjusting the notes pane's magnification level (not the task window).

The Insert, Format Text, and Review tabs are the same as those found on other item windows. The actions for adding, updating, and formatting items only apply to information in the Task window's notes pane.

Chapter 3: **Sending Email**

Regardless of your email account, if you have an Internet connection, Outlook allows you to send email to anyone inside your business and throughout the globe. Outlook is capable of sending and receiving email messages in three formats:

- HTML supports paragraph styles (such as numbered and bulleted lists), character styles (including fonts, sizes, colors, and weight), and backgrounds (such as colors and pictures). The majority (but not all) of email applications support HTML. Programs that lack HTML capabilities render these messages as plain text.
- Rich Text has more formatting possibilities for paragraphs than HTML, including borders and shading. Still, it is only compatible with Outlook and Exchange Server. Outlook transforms Rich Text messages sent outside of the Exchange network to HTML.
- Plain Text does not allow the formatting options found in HTML and Rich Text messages, although all email clients support it.
- The content of email messages is not restricted to plain text. Email messages may include practically any material created in Microsoft Word documents. Since Outlook 2022 and Word share similar commands, you may already be acquainted with numerous content formatting procedures.

You can give a professional touch to your communications by including your contact information in the form of an email signature and utilizing a certain font style or color. (Other formatting options, like themes and page backgrounds, are available but might not always display as intended and can make your correspondence look less professional).

You can also arrange the text of your message to make it more understandable by using headers, lists, and tables. You can also visually display information by incorporating charts, images, and other forms of graphics. You may attach files to your message and link to additional information, including files and websites.

Creating an email is a reasonably straightforward procedure. Typically, you will enter information in the following fields:

- Enter the email address(es) of the message's principal recipient(s) in this space. This is the sole mandatory field to send a message.
- Subject In this section, provide a summary of the message's content or purpose. It is crucial to offer a topic, while it is not needed, so that both you and the receiver can identify the message and that the message is not banned as spam by the recipient's email application. Outlook will alert you if you attempt to send an email without a topic.
- **Message body:** In this section, which is a huge text box, enter your message to the recipient. The message body may include several sorts of information, including structured text, hyperlinks, and images.

Create Messages

Simply enter the intended recipient's email address (or name, if he or she is in your contact book) into the address box in the message header of the message composition window to address an email message.

There are three address fields where you may insert email recipients:

- To Use for principal receivers. These are often the individuals you want to reply to the message. Each message must have a minimum of one address in the To field.
- Cc Use for receivers of **"courtesy copies."** You often want to keep these individuals updated about the email topic but do not expect a response.
- Bcc is Used for receivers of a **"blind courtesy copy."** You want to keep these individuals updated but wish to conceal them from other message recipients. Bcc receivers are not visible to other message recipients and are thus not included in message replies unless explicitly included in one of the response message's address fields.

- The To and Cc fields are consistently presented in the message header. By default, the Bcc address field is not visible. Clicking the Bcc button in the Show Fields group on the Options tab of the message composing window will show it in the message header.

Suppose your email account is part of a Microsoft Exchange network. In that case, you may send messages to another user on the same network by typing their email alias, such as Joan; the at symbol (@) and domain name is optional. Suppose you input the name of a person whose email address is in your address book. In that case, Outlook resolves the address before sending the message. This procedure is known as resolving the address.

Depending on how you input a message recipient's name or email address into an address field, Outlook either resolves the name or address instantly (if you selected it from a list of known names) or resolves it after you send the message.

The resolution procedure for any name or address yields one of two outcomes:

- An underline appears underneath if Outlook resolves the name or addresses correctly. Suppose, the name or address matches one in an address book. In that case, Outlook replaces the original item with the value of the **Display As field** in the contact record and highlights it.
- If Outlook cannot resolve the name or address, the Check Names dialog box will appear, prompting you to choose the desired address.

In the Check Names dialog box, you may choose one of the pre-selected alternatives or any of the following:

- **Select Properties** to get further information about the chosen choice.
- **Select Show More Names** to show the address book by default.
- **Select New Contact** to create a new contact record immediately from the dialog box in your default address book.

To launch a message composing window for an email

1. Perform one of the following:

- Under any module, on the Home tab, click the **New Items button** in the new group, followed by the Email Message button.
- Select the **New Email button** on the Home tab of the Mail module's New group.

To put an email address in a box

1. In the message composing window, click the **To, Cc, or Bcc box**, followed by one of the following:

- Complete the address.
- Enter a portion of a previously used address and then choose it from the list.
- Select the address box's label to open the Select Names dialogue box, where you can choose one or more addresses from your address book (s).

To input an email message topic

1. In the Topic field of the message composing window, enter the email message's subject.

To insert content for an email message

1. In the message composition window's message body field, input the message's content.

To format an email message's content

1. Select the material to format in the message composing window's message body area.

2. Apply basic font and paragraph formatting using the Mini Toolbar or the Basic Text group on the Message tab.

Save And Send Messages

Outlook stores a duplicate of the message in the Drafts folder at regular intervals (every three minutes, by default) while you're drafting a message (every three minutes). This is meant to prevent you from losing in-progress communications. Outlook allows you to save a draft when you end a message for which no draft has yet been created.

You can manually save a message draft at any moment and continue editing it in its window or immediately in the Reading Pane. The unread message counter to the right of the Drafts folder in the Folder Pane grows when you save a draft. If the draft is a response to a message received, [Draft] will show in the message header.

Outlook deletes the message draft, if one exists, and temporarily transfers the message to the Outbox when you send a message. After the message has been successfully sent, Outlook transfers it from the Outbox to the Sent Items folder. If a problem with the connection stops Outlook from sending the message, it stays in the Outbox.

Send From A Specific Account

If Outlook is set to connect to several email accounts, a From button appears in the message composition window's header section. The current account is shown next to the From button.

By default, Outlook thinks that you plan to send a message from the current account. Suppose you begin drafting a message while viewing the Inbox of your work account. For instance, Outlook will choose your work account as the message-sending account. If you respond to a message received by your account, Outlook uses your account to transmit the message.

To change the active account while writing a message, click the **From button** and the account you want to send the message from.

If you have the authorization to send messages from an account you haven't set in Outlook, such as a generic Customer Service email account for your firm. Select **Other E-mail Address** from the list, enter the email address you wish to send the message from, and **click OK**.

Respond To Messages

You can react to most incoming email messages by clicking a response button in the Reading Pane, the message window, or the Respond group on the Message tab. You may react to a message by responding to the sender, all message recipients, a meeting invitation, an instant message, or by forwarding the message.

When you choose one of the following choices, Outlook produces a new message based on the original. It automatically populates one or more of the address fields:

- **Reply:** Creates an email message containing the original message text, addressed to just the original message sender.
- **Reply to Everyone:** Creates an email message containing the original message text, addressed to the message sender and any recipients indicated in the To and Cc boxes. The message is not intended to blind courtesy copy recipients (Bcc recipients).
- **Reply with Meeting:** Creates an invitation to a meeting that is sent to all message recipients. The message text is included in the content pane of the meeting window. Outlook offers the current date and the next available half-hour for the meeting.

Message responses include the original message's header and body, followed by a space for your response. None of the attachments from the original message are included in replies. Before sending a reply email, you may add, modify, or remove recipients.

Carefully observe proper email etiquette while replying to an email. For instance, if your answer is not relevant to all the original receivers of a message, do not respond to the complete list of recipients, particularly if the message was sent to a distribution list that may have hundreds of members. By addressing the message to yourself and putting additional recipients in the Bcc field, you may prohibit anyone from responding to all recipients of a message you send. The recipient list will after that be hidden from view.

You could forward a message to any email address (regardless of whether the receiver uses Outlook) if it was not sent with limited access. Outlook 2022 provides the following options for message forwarding:

- **Forward:** Create a new message that includes the original message's content and attachments.
- **Forward as Attachment:** Creates a blank message that includes the original message as an attachment but has no content. The new receiver has access to the original message content and any attachments when he or she opens the attached message.
- Both forwarded messages have the original message's header and body, followed by a blank line where additional information may be entered. Include attachments from the originating message in forwarded messages.
- Outlook does not automatically complete the recipient fields when you forward a message.
- Suppose, you respond to or forward a message from inside the message window. In that case, the original message stays open after sending your answer. You may direct Outlook to close original messages once you answer them; at that point, you are likely through with the communication.
- If your firm has the requisite infrastructure for unified communications, you may additionally have the following response options:
- Call or Call All initiates a Voice over Internet Protocol (VoIP) call from your computer to the phone number of the original message sender or the original message sender and additional message recipients.
- Reply with Instant Message or Reply All with IM Opens an instant messaging window with the message sender or the message sender and additional recipients as conversation participants. You must input and send the first message to initiate the instant messaging session.

The answer choices available in your installation of Outlook may differ from those listed below. The response choices for your installation may be accessed through the Respond group on the Message tab of the message window and the Home tab of the program window.

Alternative response choices exist for nonstandard messages, such as the following:

- A request for a meeting has choices for responding to the request.
- An assignment of a task comprises acceptance and rejection alternatives.

If a message has voting buttons, you may react by opening it, selecting the Vote button in the Respond group on the Message tab, and then choosing the desired answer. Alternatively, you may click the InfoBar (labeled Vote) in the Reading Pane and then choose the desired answer.

Responding To An Email Message

1. Do one of the following at the top of the Reading Pane or in the Respond group on the Message tab:

- **Click the Reply button** to generate an already-addressed answer to the original sender. If the communication was sent to anybody else, they would not be included in the reply.
- **Click Reply All** to produce a response that is already addressed to the original sender. If the message was sent to additional recipients, their addresses are also included in the reply.
- The RE: prefix occurs at the beginning of the subject line to signify a response to a previous message. The old message, including its header information, is shown in the content window, divided by a horizontal line from the new text.

Note that a Reply or Reply is considered a Response. Even if attachments were included in the initial message, none of the responses included attachments. (There is no evidence that the original communication included any.)

1. Input your reply's text at the top of the content window.

2. Click the **Send button** in the response header to send the reply. The original message stays visible.

Resending And Recalling Messages

If you wish to send a new version of a message you've previously sent, such as a weekly update to a status report, you may resend the message. Resending a message generates a fresh version of the message without any attachments that may have been included in a forwarded message. To resend a message, do the following steps:

1. Open the message you want to resend from the Sent Items folder. (Or, if you forwarded the mail to yourself, you may access it from your Inbox.)

2. On the Message tab, under the **Move group**, click the **Actions button** (the ScreenTip for this button reads More Move Actions), and then select **Resend This Message** in the list.

Outlook generates a duplicate of the original message form. You may modify the recipients, topic, attachments, and content of the message before sending the updated version.

You may recall a message by asking Outlook to delete or replace any unread copies. Once a receiver opens a message, it cannot be recalled.

The message recall feature is only available to recipients with Exchange accounts. Recipients with Internet-based email accounts or who have already seen the original message will get both the original message and the recall notice or replacement message. *(NB: You can test the message recall feature inside your business before using it so that you are confident in its operation)*.

To remember a message, do the following steps:

1. Open the message you want to remember from your Sent Items folder.

2. On the **Message tab**, inside the Move group, select the **Actions button**, followed by Recall This Message. The Recall This Message dialogue box provides choices for dealing with the recalled message.

3. In the Recall This Message dialogue box, choose whether you want to delete or replace the delivered message and if you wish to get an email notification of the success or failure of each recall. Next, click OK.

If you opt to replace the message, a new window for messages will appear. Enter the desired content for the replacement message, and then send it.

Attachments

Attaching a file to an email message is an easy method to transmit a file (such as a Microsoft PowerPoint presentation, Excel workbook, Word document, or image). Recipients of the message may preview or open the attachment from the Reading Pane, open it from the message window, forward it to others, or save it to their PCs.

When Outlook is the default email client, you may send files using a variety of methods:

- **From Outlook:** You can compose a message and then attach the file to it. If the attached file is kept in a shared place, such as a OneDrive folder or SharePoint library, you have the option of sending a link to the file rather than a copy.
- **From Office software:** You can email a Word document, Excel spreadsheet, or PowerPoint presentation while you are working on the file. You have the choice of sending a copy of the file as a mail attachment or a link to the file if it is kept in a shared place.
- **From File Explorer:** Any file may be sent as an attachment simply from File Explorer. When transferring images from File Explorer, you have the option to resize them to minimize file size.

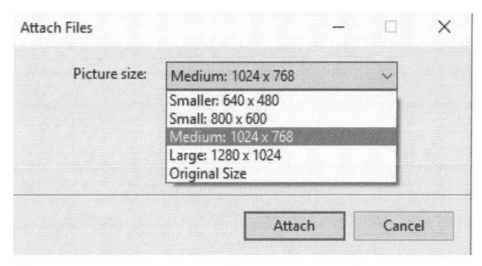

After attaching a file to an email message using any of these ways, you may alter or delete the attachments before sending the message. When you attach files from shared locations, a cloud icon next to the file icon shows that the attachment is a link to the file rather than a copy. You can simply email a copy of the online file if you so want.

You may transfer Outlook things, such as email messages and contact details, in addition to files.

To attach a file to a message sent by email

1. Do one of the following in the message composing window to reveal the Attach File menu:

    -   In the Include group on the Message tab, click the **Attach File button**.
    -   Click the **Attach File button** in the Include group on the Insert tab.

The Attach File menu contains a list of recently accessed files stored in places to which Outlook can connect.

On the Attach File menu, choose one of the following options:

-   Click the file you want to attach if it appears in the list.
-   Select **Browse Web Locations** at the bottom of the Insert File menu, and then click a connected online storage place to reveal the storage structure of that location in the Insert File dialog box. Select the file you want to attach, then click the **Insert button**.
-   Click **Browse This Computer** at the bottom of the **Insert File option** to open the Insert File dialog box showing your local storage structure. Select the file you want to attach, then click the **Insert button**.

The associated file or files are shown underneath the message header. If the file you uploaded is saved online, the symbol for the file will have a cloud.

To generate an email with an attachment from inside an Office document

1. Click the **File tab** inside the document, spreadsheet, or presentation to see the Backstage view.

2. **Click Email** on the Share page of the Backstage view to reveal email choices.

3. Click Send As Attachment, Send a Link, Send as PDF, or Send as XPS in the Email window to generate an email message and attach the desired file format.

If you have an account with a fax service provider that allows the sending of faxes through email, you may select the Send As Internet Fax option and enter the fax number to address the message in the format needed by the fax service. If your fax service provider is Contoso and the fax number is (425)555-0199, you might send an email to 14255551212@contoso.com. The fax service electronically transmits the message to the recipient's fax number.

To compose an email with an attachment using File Explorer

1. Select the file(s) you want to send.

2. Right-click the file or files you want to send, then choose to Send to, followed by Mail recipient.

3. If the files are images, the Attach Files dialog box will appear, allowing you to minimize the file size. Clicking a size in the Picture size list will provide an estimate of the total file size of the images at the specified maximum dimensions.

4. After specifying the image size, if required, click Attach to compose the message.

To attach a duplicate of a file stored online

1. Include the file attachment in the email message.

2. In the Attached section, point to the file attachment, click the arrow that appears and then click **Attach** as a copy to download a temporary copy of the file and attach it to the message.

To exclude/remove an attachment from an outgoing email

1. In the Attached section, click the arrow next to the file attachment, and then click **Remove Attachment**.

Attaching an Outlook item to an outgoing email

1. To launch the Insert Item dialog box, perform one of the following in the message composing window:

- In the Include group of the Message tab, select the **Attach Item button**, followed by Outlook Item.
- Click the **Outlook Item button** in the Include group on the Insert pane.

Preview Attachments

Each time you launch Outlook and connect to your email server, any new messages received since your previous connection are shown in your inbox. Depending on your settings, Outlook either downloads the full message to your computer or merely the message header, which contains basic information about the message, including:

- The product type (message, meeting request, task assignment, and so on)
- Who sent it?
- The date of receipt
- The subject
- Icons placed in the header of a message represent optional information such as:
- The most recent action taken in response
- Whether attachments exist
- If the message's digital signature or encryption has been verified
- If the sender designated the communication as urgent or not urgent

The message list shows the header information for each message. You may see message content in the Reading Pane or by opening messages from the message list.

Display Message Content

The content of the communication may be seen by opening it in a messaging window. You may save time, though, by reading and interacting with emails (and other Outlook objects) in the Reading Pane. The Reading Pane may be shown to the right or below the module content pane.

If a message includes external material, as many marketing email messages do, the external information will only be downloaded automatically if your security settings enable it. Otherwise, you must provide download permission for the external material.

If you find it difficult to see the text in the Reading Pane at its default size, you may adjust the amount of magnification by using the Zoom controls found at the right end of the program window status bar. Changing the Zoom level is transitory and only lasts till another message is selected. The Zoom controls are only accessible for message content; attachment previews in the Reading Pane are not supported.

To show a message's content

1. In the Mail module, you may do any of the following:

- Open a message in its window by double-clicking the message's header in the list of messages.
- Read a message without opening it by clicking the message's heading in the message list to show it in the Reading Pane.
- Using the Preview function, display the first three lines of each unread message beneath the message header.

To navigate message content inside the Reading Pane

1. In the Reading Pane, do one of the following steps:

- To scroll at your own speed, move the vertical scroll bar on the right side of the Reading Pane.
- Utilize the scroll arrows to advance or regress one line at a time.
- To advance or regress one page, click above or below the scroll box.
- Use the Spacebar to advance or reverse one page at a time. When you conclude a message using the Single Key Reading function, hitting the Spacebar again shows the beginning page of the subsequent message. This option is highly useful if you like to read many consecutive messages in the Reading Pane, or if you prefer to use the Spacebar over the mouse.

Display Attachment Content

Attachments to a message can be opened or downloaded from the message window or Reading Pane. Outlook is also capable of displaying interactive previews of several attachment formats, including Word documents, Excel workbooks, PowerPoint presentations, Visio diagrams, text files, XPS files, and picture files.

Outlook will not be able to preview a file of a certain kind in the Reading Pane if the corresponding preview software has not been installed. You may show the applications used to preview files on the Attachment Handling page of the Trust Center window, which you can get from the Outlook Options dialog box by clicking the Trust Center button.

When you click on certain kinds of attachments, you are prompted to certify that the material originates from a reliable source. You can accept the content on a case-by-case basis, or you can authorize Outlook to ignore the warning alert for files of this sort.

Previewing a file may save a substantial amount of time. Additionally, you can engage with the preview in several ways, to the point where you may not even need to open the file.

If you believe an attachment may contain a virus and have a trustworthy anti-malware tool installed, you may want to download the file and scan it for viruses before opening it.

To preview the content of an attachment in a message

1. Click the attachment once in the message window or Reading Pane that is now active. The attachments tool tab appears on the ribbon, and an attachment preview displays in the message content window or Reading Pane.

To work with attachment content in the preview

1. Show the preview of the attachment, and then perform any of the following:

- Scroll horizontally and vertically across stuff.
- Point to the comment markup in a Word document to see the remark in its entirety.
- To navigate between worksheets in an Excel workbook, click the tabs at the bottom of the preview area.
- To go across slides in a PowerPoint presentation, scroll vertically or use the Next button. The preview section supports both transitions and animations.
- When previewing a PowerPoint presentation, click the slides in the preview area to watch the presentation with all transitions and animations, or click the Next button (the arrow) at the bottom of the vertical scroll bar to view the presentation without the animated components.

- Click hyperlinks to view online sites or files, or links to compose email messages.

To go back from the attachment preview to the message body

1. Perform one of the following:

- **Click Back** to message in the message header's upper-left corner.
- **Click the Show Message button** in the Message group on the Attachments tool tab. (Return to Message shows as a ScreenTip when the button is selected.)

To open a file attachment using the default application

1. In the message window or Reading Pane, do one of the following steps:

- Double-click the attachment in the message's header.
- Click the attachment in the message header to see a preview. Then, under the Actions group on the Attachments tool tab, **select Open**.

To save a file attachment on a storage device

1. Follow one of the steps below from the message window or Reading Pane:

- Place the cursor over the attachment, click the arrow that appears, and then **click Save As**.
- **Click the Save As button** in the Actions group on the Attachments tool tab.

2. In the **Store As dialog box**, choose the location where you would want to save the file, and then **click Save**.

To save multiple attachments to a storage drive

1. From the message window or Reading Pane, perform one of the following to view a list of all attached files:

- To save all attachments, point to a file attachment, click the arrow that appears, and then **select Save All Attachments**.
- In the Actions group on the Attachments tool tab, select the **Save All Attachments button**.

2. By default, all attachments are chosen in the Save All Attachments list. If you want to save just a subset of the files, select the file you wish to save and then either:

- **Use Shift+click** to choose adjacent files.
- **Hit Ctrl+click** to choose files that are not contiguous.

Sending Email to Groups
Creating Contact Groups

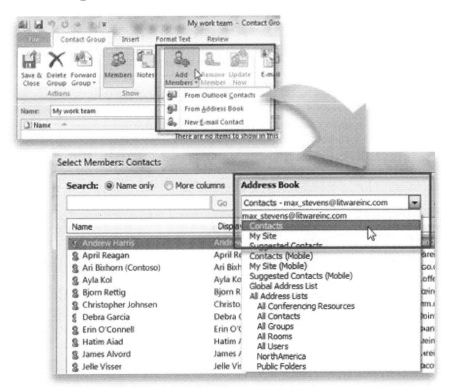

Users can create a contact group that includes all group members if you routinely send messages to a certain set of individuals, such as members of a project team, club, or family. Then, by sending a message to the contact group, you may reach out to all of the group members.

Contact groups are similar to private distribution lists. A distribution list is accessible to everyone on your Exchange Server network, but a contact group is only accessible via the local address book in which it is stored. However, you may send a contact group to others for their own use.

Individual persons, resources, distribution lists, public folders, Microsoft SharePoint site libraries with email capabilities, and other contact groups may all be added to a contact group.

You may either choose an existing contact record from an address book or provide a name and email address to add a member to a contact group. When you utilize the latter technique, you can also establish a contact record for the individual at the same time.

When you send a message to a contact group, a copy of the message is sent to each member of the group. If you wish to send a message to the majority of a contact group's members but not all, extend the contact group in the address field to include the whole list of members, then delete individual receivers from the particular message before sending it.

To begin building a contact group:

1. To start a new Contact Group window, perform one of the following:

- Click the **New Contact Group button** in the People module's Home tab's New group.
- On the Home tab, in the New group, click **New Items**, click **More Items**, and then select **Contact Group** in the Mail, Calendar, or Tasks module.
- Press **Ctrl+Shift+L** in any module.

2. Give the group a name in the Name field.

To create a contact group from existing contacts

1. Open the window for the contact group.

2. In the Members group of the Contact Group tab, click the **Add Members button**.

3. Select one of the following options from the Add Members list:

   - Select the Members dialog box, which displays your default contact book, by clicking From Outlook Contacts.
   - Click From Address Book to launch the Select Members dialog box, which will reveal the address book that was selected as the first to be checked.
   - Open the Address Book window from any module, choose **Options** on the Tools menu, adjust the order, and then click OK.

4. If you wish to choose contacts from a different address book, expand the Address Book list in the Select Members dialog box, and then click the address book you want to use.

5. In the Select Members dialog box, add each contact you wish to add to the contact group to the Members box by doing one of the following:

   - Select the contact, then click the **Members button** in the lower-left corner of the dialog box.
   - *Click twice on the contact.* (NB: By holding down the Ctrl key while choosing numerous names and then clicking the Members button, you may swiftly add multiple entries to the Members box)**.**

6. Click **OK** to add the contacts to the contact group when you've finished adding contacts to the Members box.

7. Click **Save & Close** on the Contact Group tab in the contact group box.

To add new contacts to a group of contacts

1. Open the window for the contact group.

2. Click the **Add Members button** in the Members group on the Contact Group tab, then click New E-mail Contact to open the **Add New Member dialog box**.

3. Type the name you wish to show for the contact group member in the Display name box.

4. Type the email address of the contact group member in the E-mail address field. You're unlikely to change the E-mail Type or Internet Format settings. If you want to send plain text versions to a single recipient but wish to make rich text messages for the contact group, you may choose plain text from the Internet Format option.

5. Clear the **Add to Contacts check box** if you don't want a contact record for the new contact group member in your default address book

If that option was chosen, click OK to add the new contact to the contact group and create the contact record.

Creating Folders

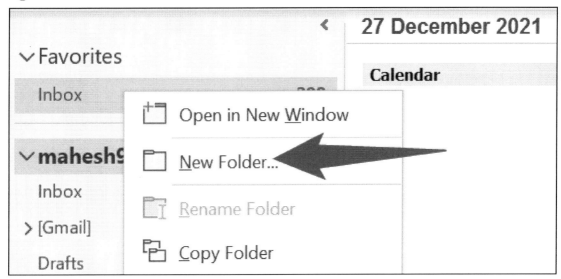

There are a few ways to create folders in Outlook.

The first way is to right-click on the "**Inbox**" and select "**New Folder**".

A new window will pop up, and you can type in the name of your new folder.

To create a subfolder, right-click on the folder you want to create it in and select "**New Folder**". Type in the desired name for your subfolder.

The second way is to go to **File > New > Folder**. A new window will open where you can type in the desired folder name. You can also make a subfolder by doing this same process within another folder.

Once you have created your folders, it's time to start using them. To move an e-mail message into a specific folder, drag and drop it from your Inbox (or any other mailbox) into the desired folder(s).

You can also use keyboard shortcuts: Ctrl+Shift+N for creating a new message; Ctrl+Up arrow or Down arrow key moves messages one level up or down; Alt+F4 closes Outlook completely).

You may want to apply some rules so that certain e-mails are automatically sorted into specific folders (e.g., all meeting invitations sent from certain people go into my Meeting InvitationsFolder).

To do this, go to **Tools > Rules & Alerts**. The Rules Wizard will open where you can set various criteria for incoming messages (e.g., sender address, subject line content, words found within the body of the e-mail) and specify what action should be taken when that rule is triggered (move the message to a specified folder(s), play sound notification, etc.).

Using Microsoft E-mail Folders

E-mail folders are an important part of e-mail management in Microsoft Outlook. They allow you to organize your messages into specific categories, making it easier to find what you need when you need it. In this section, we will discuss the various types of e-mail folders available in Outlook and how to use them effectively.

Outlook provides users with a variety of tools for managing their e-mail correspondence. One of these tools is the ability to create folders to organize messages. We will discuss what folders are and how to use them in Outlook.

Folders also allow you to group related messages. For example, you might create a folder called "**Invoice**" and move all your invoices into that folder. You can then open the folder to view all the invoices at once or filter the messages by date or sender.

How Do I Create An E-Mail Folder

To create a new e-mail folder:

Step 1: In Outlook, **click File > New > Folder**. The Create New Folder dialogue box will appear.

Step 2: Type a name for your new folder in the Name text box.

Step 3: Click OK. The new folder will be created and added to your Navigation Pane on the left side of the screen.

Step 4: To move e-mails into this newly created folder, drag them from your Inbox (or any other mailbox) onto the new folder's name in the Navigation Pane.

The first type of e-mail folder is the **Inbox**. This is where all new messages are delivered by default, and it serves as a central location for managing your incoming mail. You can create additional folders under the Inbox to help organize your mail further. For example, you might create a folder for "**Work**" and another for "**Personal**".

Another type of e-mail folder is the **Sent Items** folder. This stores copies of all messages that have been sent from your account, including those that were deleted after being sent. It's a good idea to archive old messages in this folder; they're not taking up space in your mailbox anymore but are still accessible if needed later on.

The next type of e-mail folder is called **Deleted Items.** As its name suggests, this stores any e-mails that have been deleted from your mailbox either manually or automatically by the Outlook rules engine. It's important to empty this folder regularly so that it doesn't get too cluttered and cause performance issues with Outlook.

Organizing Messages

The message list by default sorts the email messages you receive by time and date of receipt (from newest to oldest). In Outlook, you can organize, categorize, and sort messages to keep discussion threads together and to help you quickly evaluate which messages are the most essential, which can be discarded, and which need urgent attention.

Assigning categories to similar things helps make the process of organizing Outlook items of all types easier. The objects in Outlook may then be arranged, sorted, filtered, and searched by category.

How To Display And Manage Conversations

A conversation is started when a receiver responds to an email message with numerous messages. Conversations with several receivers and answers might include a lot of information. A conversation view is a different way of grouping messages by topic. All messages with the same topic show under one discussion heading in your Inbox (or other message containers).

The discussion header contains information about the messages in the conversation, such as the number of unread messages and if one or more messages include an attachment, are categorized, or have been highlighted for follow-up.

Within a chat, you may show several levels of messages as follows:

- To show the most recent message in the Reading Pane and all the unique messages in the conversation (the most recent message in each thread) in the message list, click the conversation header or the Expand button once. Only reading these messages will provide you with all the information available in the discussion.
- To see all messages in the discussion, including those from your Sent Items folder, click the Expand button once again.
- When more than two persons are involved in an email discussion, especially if the email was sent to a wide distribution list, several people typically react to the same message, and additional people respond to each of those messages. Branches are many dialogues that develop from the main discourse.

The following are some of the advantages of showing messages as conversations:

- When you get a message that is part of a discussion, the whole conversation is moved to the top of your Inbox, and when you click the conversation header, the new message displays.
- Unread messages are indicated by a blue vertical line and a bold blue topic in a chat. If there are several unread messages, the number is shown after the topic in parentheses. Below the topic, the senders of the unread messages are shown.
- From inside the chat, you can access sent messages. (They stay in the Sent Items folder, but they may be viewed and opened from the Inbox.) This is particularly useful if you need to view email attachments that aren't included in the answers.
- All of the texts in a chat may be managed as a group. When you click the discussion headers, all the messages in the conversation are selected. You may move or sort all the messages together.
- You may change how the Conversation view shows messages to fit your workflow by turning on or off the following display settings:
- Messages from Other Folders will be shown. Conversation view by default shows messages from any folder, including sent messages from the Sent Items folder. (Sent messages are shown by an italic typeface inside an extended chat.) This feature may be disabled to only see messages from the current folder.
- Above the subject, show senders when a discussion is collapsed, the conversation header shows all the conversation participants' names above the conversation topic by default; when the conversation is completely enlarged, the conversation header just displays the subject. The names of the discussion participants are shown above the conversation topic in this configuration, which flips the order of the information in the conversation header. The topic may not be seen in certain instances, such as when Outlook shows a message on the second line.
- Always broaden your conversations. When you click the Expand Discussion button or the conversation header once in Outlook, it displays all messages in the conversation.
- Use the Indented Classic View. Outlook uses this parameter to indent older messages inside individual mail threads to illustrate the thread's evolution. Since a message might be at the root of numerous branches yet only show once in the message list, this option is less effective than the default setting for presenting divided conversations.

Whether or whether the messages are shown in the Conversation view, Outlook monitors discussions by topic. To manage discussions, you can use the following features:

- **Ignore the Discussion:** This command sends the specified discussion, as well as any future connected messages, to the Deleted Items folder. When using the Ignore Conversation command, be careful. Message topics help Outlook identify conversations. You will not get any irrelevant communications in the future that have the same message topic as a discussion that you have opted to ignore.
- **Cleaning Up Discussion:** This command removes superfluous messages from a conversation or folder (messages whose content is entirely included inside subsequent messages). Outlook does not automatically clear up classified, marked, or digitally signed communications by default. When you clean up conversations on the Mail page of the Outlook Options dialog box, you may change the conversation clean-up settings.

To make the messages in a discussion visible

1. To see the unique messages in the chat, click the conversation header or the Expand button once.

2. To see all the messages in the chat, click the Expand button once again.

To choose all of a conversation's messages

1. Make a single click on the discussion header.

To alter the appearance of discussions in the message list

1. Click **Conversation Settings** in the Messages group on the View tab. A checkmark in the Conversation Settings menu indicates that an option is enabled.

How To Arrange Messages By Specific Attributes

Outlook organizes messages by date, from newest to oldest, by default. You may also sort objects by any of the following characteristics:

- Account Messages are organized by the email account they were sent to. This is handy if your Inbox contains messages from many email accounts (for instance, if you receive messages sent to your POP3 account in your Exchange account mailbox).
- Attachments Messages are categorized first by whether they include attachments, and then by the date, they were received.
- Category Messages are organized into categories that you create. Messages with no category are shown first. Messages that have been allocated to several categories appear in each of the category groupings.
- Set the start or due date. Messages that haven't been marked and messages with no particular timetable are displayed first. Messages with particular start or deadline dates that you've added to your task list are organized by date.
- From Messages are sorted alphabetically by the display name of the message sender. Messages sent from two distinct email accounts or two different email programs (for example, Outlook and Windows Mail) will not always be grouped together.
- Importance The priority of messages is denoted by a red exclamation point, Normal (the default), or Low (indicated by a blue downward-pointing arrow).
- The major recipients are listed alphabetically in the To Messages section (the addresses or names on the To line). The arrangement of addresses on the To line is precisely reflected in the group name.
- Size Messages are categorized according to their size, including any attachments. Huge (1–5 MB), Very Large (500 KB–1 MB), Large (100–500 KB), Medium (25–100 KB), Small (10–25 KB), and Tiny (10–25 KB) are the different types of files (less than 10 KB). If you work for an employer that restricts the size of your Inbox, this function is handy since it allows you to quickly discover huge messages and delete or transfer them to a personal folder.
- The Subject Messages are organized alphabetically by subject, then by date. Organizing by discussion is similar, only the messages aren't threaded.
- Type Messages, encrypted messages, message receipts, meeting requests and meeting request answers, tasks, Microsoft InfoPath forms, and server alerts are all put together in your Inbox (or another folder).
- After you've arranged the items in your message list, you may modify the sort order. The message list header shows the message list's current sort order and layout.
- By default, each arrangement's messages are organized into groups that are unique to that category. When communications are organized by date, for example, they are divided into groups: current week, last week, two weeks ago, three weeks ago, last month, and older. There is a header for each group. You may pick and process messages by group, or collapse a group so that just the header is shown.

(NB: You can sort messages by any visible column in Single view or Preview view. You can add a column to the view if you wish to sort by an attribute that isn't visible).

To arrange messages by a specific attribute

1. Complete one of the following tasks:

- In any view, click the message attribute in the Arrangement gallery on the View tab.
- In Compact view, click the current arrangement in the message list header, then click the message attribute.
- Right-click any column header in the Single or Preview view, **choose Arrange By**, and then select the message attribute.

To reverse the message list arrangement's default sort order

1. Complete one of the following tasks:

- In any view, click **Reverse Sort** in the Arrangement group on the View tab.
- In Compact view, click the current sort order in the message list header.

- Right-click any column heading in Single or Preview view, then **choose Reverse Sort**.

(NB: By clicking the column header in a list view, you may sort by any column and reverse the sort order by clicking the column header again)**.**

Group or ungroup messages

1. Complete one of the following tasks:

- In any view, click Show in Groups in the Arrangement gallery on the View tab.
- In Compact view, click the message list header, then Show in Groups from the menu.
- Right-click the header of the column you wish to group by in Single view or Preview view, then choose Group By This Field.

To choose a set of messages

1. Select the group's title.

To expand the current message group

1. Complete one of the following tasks:

- Select the left-hand arrow in the group heading.
- Select Right Arrow from the keyboard.
- Click the **Expand/Collapse button** in the Arrangement group on the View tab, then click Expand This Group.

To make the current messaging group disappear

1. Complete one of the following tasks:

- Select the left-hand arrow in the group heading.
- Use the left arrow key to navigate.
- Click the **Expand/Collapse button** in the Arrangement group on the View tab, then click Collapse This Group.

To collapse or expand all message groups

1. Click the Expand/Collapse button in the Arrangement group on the View tab, then Expand All Groups or Collapse All Groups.

To reorganize the message layout (and other view settings)

1. Click the **Reset View button** in the Current View group on the View tab.

2. **Select Yes** in the Microsoft Outlook dialog box.

Creating Rules

Microsoft Outlook offers users the ability to create rules to manage their e-mail. Rules can be used to automatically move, delete, or reply to e-mails based on certain criteria that you specify. This is a good way to keep your Inbox organized and under control.

To create a rule in Outlook, go to the "**Home**" tab and select "**Rules.**" Then click "**Create Rule.**" You will then be prompted with a series of questions about how you want your rule to function. Let's look at each of these options:

1. **From:** This is where you specify who the e-mail needs to come from in order for the rule to apply. You can choose an individual or use specific keywords or addresses within the e-mail message itself. For example, if you only want work-related e-mails sent directly to you, you could add your work e-mail address as the "**From**" address here.

2. **To:** This is where you specify who should receive any messages that match this rule's criteria. For example, if certain people always send spammy messages that you don't want cluttering up your Inbox, add their e-mail addresses here, and any messages from them will automatically be deleted without ever appearing in your Inbox folder; at all!

3. **Subject:** If there are specific words or phrases included in an e-mail's subject line that trigger action for this rule (e.g., deleting all messages with 'Vacation' in the subject line), then enter those words/phrases into this field.

4. **Folder:** If there are certain folders inside Outlook where particular types of e-mails should always go (e g., moving all incoming receipts into a Receipts folder), then select it from this drop-down menu.

5. **Actions:** Here is where you decide what actions should happen when an e-mail message matches this particular criterion set up by your rule. The available actions include Moving Message To A Folder; Deleting a Message; Copying Message To Another Folder; Forwarding Message As an Attachment; Responding With A Template; Redirecting a Message; Playing An Audio File. When The E-mail Is Received.

Conditionals: These allow for more complex rules involving multiple conditions (AND/OR statements). For example, if someone sends an attachment as well as text within the body of their message, AND both meet some other specified condition(s), THEN one action may occur while another would not.

Dealing with Junk Mail

MS Outlook is a personal information manager. It can be used as a stand-alone application or can be connected to a Microsoft Exchange Server, which enables shared access by multiple users.

Outlook provides several ways to access your junk and spam e-mails. The first way is to go to the Junk E-mail folder in the **Navigation Pane** and select the message you want to view or delete.

The second way is to click on the **Junk E-mail** button on the Standard toolbar and then select either:

The **Show Messages** option displays all messages that Outlook has classified as junk mail in your Inbox, regardless of whether they are currently hidden from view.

This option also includes any messages that were previously deleted from your Inbox and then moved back into it by outlooks automatic filtering process

The **Hide Messages** option hides all messages that have been classified as junk mail by outlook's automatic filtering process.

Chapter 5: **Contacts**

There are a few different ways that you can access your Microsoft Outlook contacts. The first way is to open Outlook and click on the Contacts tab. This will bring up all of your contacts in a list on the left side of the screen. You can also search for a specific contact by typing their name into the search bar at the top of the window.

The second way to access your contacts is by clicking on the Address Book link in Outlook's main toolbar. This will open a new window with all of your contacts listed alphabetically. You can also browse through them by category or group.

The third way to access your Microsoft Outlook contacts is by exporting them to an external file format like CSV or vCard. To do this, go to **File > Export** and select either **CSV** or vCard from the drop-down menu. Then choose where you want to save the file and click Export.

Microsoft Outlook contacts are available for both Windows and Mac users. To get started, you will need to download Outlook from this Microsoft website. You can download it from both desktop and web versions. Outlook Contacts features are available for all versions of Outlook.

Contact Booking

You can use Outlook's Contacts feature to keep track of everyone you interact with. You can use Outlook contacts to manage your business meetings and holidays.

To add a person to your contacts list, simply right-click on a contact's name and click on "**Add to contact list**". Similarly, you can remove a contact from your contact list by clicking on "**Remove from contact list**". You can also assign a custom name to contact by right-clicking on contact and clicking on "**Change name".**

You can assign a color to your contact's name to make it easy for you to identify them easily.

Calendar Sync With Contacts

After adding a contact, you can use the calendar to set a meeting or appointment in Microsoft Outlook contacts. You can easily find the contacts whose calendars you are going to set an appointment or meeting from the contact book.

You can also set an appointment in your calendars using Microsoft outlook contacts.

Adding New Contacts

Start from scratch or use information from an email message to build a new contact record. When you need to establish a new contact record, you can do it quickly and effortlessly from any module or from an address book. The contact record shows in the contact list when you save it.

You may also establish a contact record with only one piece of information (such as a name or business name) or as much as you wish. By copying the business information from an existing record to a new one, you may easily establish contact records for numerous persons who work for the same firm.

How To Save And Update Contact Information

Create a contact entry in an address book to preserve contact information for a person or business. General, Details, Certificates, and All Fields are the four content pages for contact records. The General page contains the most often used contact information and is frequently the only page you see.

You can store the following sorts of contact information on the General page of a contact record:

- Name, firm, and position title
- Addresses for business, home, and alternative locations
- Phone numbers for your business, home, mobile, pager, and other devices
- Fax numbers for business, home, and alternative locations

433

- URLs, IM addresses, and email addresses are all examples of addresses.
- A picture, a corporate logo, or another distinguishing picture
- Text and images such as pictures, SmartArt diagrams, charts, and shapes may be used in general notes.

You may save extra personal and organization-specific information on the Details page of a contact record, such as the following:

- Professional details, such as department, office location, occupation, manager's name, and assistant's name
- Personal data, such as a nickname, spouse or partner's name, birthday, anniversary, and title (such as Mrs., Miss, or Ms.) and suffix (such as Jr. or Sr.) for use in communication

The Certificates page shows any digital ID certificates you've saved for conversations with that individual, while the All Fields page shows all the fields in the selected category of information.

How To Create Custom Contact Record Fields

You can add a custom field to store information that doesn't match any of the built-in contact record fields. Text, numbers, percentages, currencies, Yes/No responses, dates, times, durations, keywords, and formulae may all be stored in a custom field.

Follow these steps to create a custom field:

1. **Launch the** Contacts window.

2. **Select All Fields** from the Show group on the Contact tab.

3. On the All Fields page, in the lower-left corner, **select the New button**.

4. In the New Column dialog box, type the column name and choose the type and format of the field.

How To Print Contact Records

The People module allows you to print an address book or individual contact records on paper or to an electronic file (such as a PDF or XPS file). Contact records are printed from the Print page of the Backstage view, just like any other Outlook item.

Outlook provides a range of print formats depending on the view:

- **Card Design** In two columns, the contact information is shown alphabetically. The top of each page and the beginning of each letter group include letter images. You may fill out extra contact information on the final page of the printout. (This is referred to as a blank form in Outlook.) This design is offered in three variations: Business Card, Card, and People.
- Small and medium booklet styles are available. It's configured to print eight numbered pages (Small Booklet) or four numbered pages (Medium Booklet) per sheet and displays contact information alphabetically in one column. A contact index at the side of each page identifies the location of that page's entries in the alphabet, and letter visuals appear at the top of each page and at the beginning of each letter group. These designs are offered in three different views: Business Card, Card, and People.
- **Memo Style:** Displays contact information under a memo-style heading with your name and is prepared to print one record per page. This design is offered in three variations: Business Card, Card, and People.
- **Style of Phone Directory** In two columns, the names and phone numbers of contacts are shown. The top of each page and the beginning of each letter group include letter images. This design is offered in three variations: Business Card, Card, and People.
- Contact information is shown in a table that fits the on-screen arrangement. In both Phone and List views, this design is accessible.

Most of the preset print styles may have their layouts changed and saved as custom print styles. The preview pane on the Print page of the Backstage view shows how the chosen contact records will look when printed.

Printing contact information from an address book

1. Select the address book you wish to print from the People module.

2. Select the view from which you wish to print:

- Display the module in Phone or List view to print contact data in Table Style.
- Display the module in Business Card view, Card view, or People view to print the contact records in Card Style, Small Booklet Style, Medium Booklet Style, Memo Style, or Phone Directory Style.
- Select the first contact record you wish to publish if you simply want to print one or a few.

To add another contact record to the selection, hold down the Ctrl key and click each one you wish to print.

1. Open the Backstage view's Print page, and then perform the following:

- Select the printer you wish to use from the Printer list.
- Select the desired print style from the Settings menu.
- **Select Print** from the drop-down menu.

Chapter 6: **Calendar**

When you travel with your portable computer to sites in different time zones, you will likely adjust the computer's time zone to reflect the local time. The timings shown in the Outlook window, such as appointment times and email message reception times, adjust to the new time zone when the time zone is changed.

If your computer is running Windows 10 and has GPS capabilities, you may configure Windows to automatically adjust the time zone to match your location. Display the Date & Time page of the Settings window, then toggle the **Set Time Zone Automatically button** to the On position.

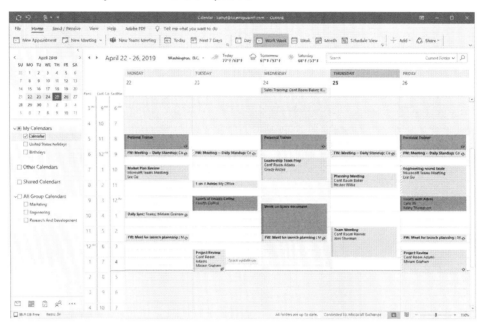

The Calendar module shows the time beside each time slot in the Day view, Work Week view, and Week view. The Outlook may be configured to show any time zone or two time zones, and the time zones can be labeled. If you have coworkers or customers in a different time zone or are traveling, showing various time zones might help you schedule meetings or just keep track of the time in another area.

When displaying two time zones, the time zone to the left of the calendar time slots is the main time zone.

To specify the time zone shown on the calendar

1. Click the **Arrange button** on the Home tab to see the Calendar page of the Outlook Options dialog box.

2. In the Time zones area of the Calendar page, pick the desired time zone in the first Time zone list.

3. Enter the column's label in the first Label box if you want to label the time column.

4. **Click OK** in the Outlook Options dialog box.

For the calendar to show two time zones

1. **Select the Arrange button** on the Home tab to see the Calendar page of the Outlook Options dialog box.

2. In the Calendar page's Time zones section, choose the Show a second time zone checkbox.

3. Click the desired time zone in the second list of Time zones.

4. If you want to label the time columns, fill out the first and second Label boxes.

5. Click OK in the Outlook Options dialog box.

To swap the main and secondary time zones

1. Show the Calendar page of the Options dialog box for Outlook.

2. Click the **Swap Time Zones button** in the Time zones area of the Calendar page.

3. Click OK in the Outlook Options dialog box.

Specify Appointment Time Zones

You have the option to define the time zone when scheduling an appointment or meeting, both for a start and finish time. If you travel regularly, you may find that this is time well spent. Here is an illustration of why you would want to do this:

Imagine you are a resident of Dallas, Texas (in the Central Time Zone). You have a weekly meeting on Wednesdays at noon. One week is spent in Seattle, Washington (in the Pacific Time Zone, two hours ahead of Central Time). When you arrive in Seattle, you set your computer's time zone to Pacific Time. Appointments in your calendar are adjusted to account for the time zone shift. Your Wednesday meeting has been rescheduled to 10:00 a.m. You join the conference call at the appointed time.

During the meeting, you hear that a customer presentation will take place the following Tuesday at 2:00 p.m. You schedule the presentation in your calendar for Tuesday at 2:00 p.m., but you do not specify the presentation's time zone.

When you return to Dallas, you set your computer's time zone to Central Time. You examine your schedule on Wednesday morning and see that you must attend the client presentation. The lecture is scheduled at 4:00 PM on your calendar. When you arrive at the client's location, the presentation is over. Due to your failure to mention the appointment's time zone, the appointment time changed by two hours when you returned to Dallas.

How To Work With Multiple Calendars

The Calendar button or link in the Navigation Bar opens your default email account's calendar. Additionally, you may show the following calendar kinds using the Calendar module:

- Other Exchange email accounts' calendars Outlook shows a calendar called Calendar for each connected Exchange account. Outlook appends the linked email address to the calendar name in the Folder Pane so that you can distinguish between numerous accounts.
- **Custom calendars:** In the same manner that you build mail folders, address books, and task lists, you construct a calendar as a folder that stores calendar entries.
- Calendars of your organization's personnel Individually or in groups, you may show the availability of your coworkers inside an Exchange-based company without specific authorization.
- **Integrated calendars:** The calendars of other Outlook users may be shared with you.
- Site calendars for SharePoint Microsoft SharePoint calendars may be linked to Outlook.
- **Internet calendars:** You may import or subscribe to calendars from the Internet.

The Folder Pane in the Calendar module offers a list of available calendars. You can store numerous calendars in a calendar group so that they can be shown or hidden concurrently. Each calendar is allocated a certain hue. When numerous calendars are presented, the colors of each calendar are displayed in both the Folder Pane and the content pane.

Connect To Other Calendars

Coworkers inside a company that utilizes Exchange can share the whole or a portion of their calendars. Even if they do not, you may see a colleague's availability by opening his or her Outlook calendar. The default settings allow coworkers to see the availability (Free, Busy, Out Of Office, or Working Elsewhere) of other members of their Exchange organization without showing appointment specifics. This data, which is also used by the Scheduling Assistant, allows you to discover convenient meeting times with coworkers.

There are several specialty calendars accessible online, including ones that monitor professional sports schedules, holidays, entertainment, and scientific data. (For instance, your local school system or sports team may have an Internet calendar that you can import or subscribe to on their website.)

Internet calendars are represented by files with the extension.ics. You may discover Internet calendars via a web browser search, links on the websites of certain organizations, or a calendar-sharing service.

Internet calendars may be used in one of two ways:

- **Sign up for the calendar:** You get periodic updates from the calendar publisher, but you cannot modify the calendar data.
- **Import the schedule:** Outlook allows you to interact with a local copy of the calendar. You may edit the calendar's information, but you will not get any updates from the calendar's publisher.

Numerous online calendars have a link or button that initiates the subscription or import procedure. If the Internet calendar you want to connect to does not give a straightforward solution, you can connect manually.

To see a colleague's calendar in your Outlook Calendar module, follow these steps:

1. Show the Calendar component.

2. In the Manage Calendars group on the Home tab, click **Open Calendar**.

3. Click From Address Book on the Open Calendar option to open the Select Name dialog box.

4. **Select Global Address List** in the Address Book list to view the members of your Exchange organization.

5. Locate the individual whose calendar you want to show and double-click the individual's name to enter it into the Calendar box.

6. Click OK to open the chosen calendar in the Calendar module content area and add it to the Shared Calendars list in the Folder Pane, even if the calendar's owner has not formally shared it with you.

Share Calendar Information

When scheduling meetings with you or viewing your calendar using Outlook, coworkers may see your available working time. You have various alternatives if you wish to share additional information with coworkers or others outside of your organization:

- By sharing your calendar with chosen coworkers, you can enable them to access calendar item information.
- By delegating management of the calendar to chosen coworkers, you may enable them to see your complete calendar, schedule appointments, and reply to meeting requests on your behalf.
- You may share your calendar with everyone who has access to the Internet by publishing it to the Office.com website or a corporate web server.
- You can transmit a professional visual depiction of your appointments over a specified time period to anybody who utilizes an HTML-capable email application (not only Outlook users), such as coworkers, friends, and family members.
- The Share group on the Home tab of the Calendar module has options for emailing, sharing, and publishing calendar information.

Share Calendars With Co-Workers

Your coworkers can see your availability from your default calendar to schedule meetings with you if your email address is part of an Exchange network. You may share a calendar (or any other Outlook folder) with others on your network and allow them to view, alter, or create entries. You can share your default calendar as well as a secondary calendar you've created, imported, or subscribed to. The permissions you provide each coworker determine the degree of access he or she has.

You may also adjust the default access level to allow coworkers to see more information without having to share the calendar explicitly. When you share a calendar with someone, you provide them access to a limited amount of information about each appointment, meeting, or event on the calendar.

The following are the detailed options:

- Limited availability Free, Busy, Tentative, Working Elsewhere, or Out Of Office time blocks are shown. This is the default degree of detail.
- Limited information Time blocks containing the appointment, meeting, or event topic and availability are shown.
- Complete information Shows time blocks identified with the topic of the appointment, meeting, or event, the location, availability, and all meeting information.

How To Print A Calendar

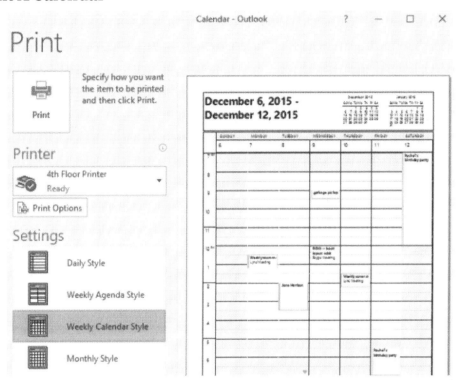

If you're traveling without a laptop or want to have your weekly schedule readily accessible in your briefcase, you may find it useful to print a day, week, month, or other period of your calendar. Any time span of your calendar may be readily printed.

Outlook comes with various print styles, and you may add more if you desire. The print styles offered differ depending on the view you're in when you choose Print.

The following are the default print styles:

- Everyday Look Prints one day per page for the given date period. The date, day, TaskPad, reference calendars for the current and forthcoming months, a description of working hours in 30-minute chunks, and a place for comments are among the printed items. You may select whether to print the TaskPad and notes sections from the Page Setup dialog box.
- Weekly Agenda Format Prints one calendar week per page for the given date range, including reference calendars for the current and next months. You may choose how to organize the days and whether or not to print the TaskPad and Notes sections from the Page Setup dialog box.
- Style of Weekly Calendar Prints one calendar week per page for the given date period. Each page offers a reference calendar for the current and upcoming month, as well as a date range and time increments for working hours. You may pick a vertical or horizontal layout, divide the week over two pages, include a task list, add a space for handwritten notes, define the range of hours to print, and only print your specified work week rather than a typical seven-day week from the Page Setup dialog box.
- Monthly Fashion Each month in the given date range gets its own page. Each page displays the current month, as well as a few days from prior and upcoming months, as well as reference calendars for the current and following months. You may choose whether to print a single month over two printer pages and whether to show the TaskPad and Note areas from the Page Setup dialog box.

439

- Tri-fold design Each day in the given date range is printed on a separate page. The daily schedule, weekly schedule, and TaskPad are all included on each page. You may choose which calendar element shows in each section from the Page Setup dialog box.
- Style of the calendar Your appointments for the given date period are shown, along with the appointment information.

To see and print a calendar:

1. Show part or all of the time period you wish to print in the Calendar module.

2. Switch to Backstage mode. **Click Print** in the left pane to see the printing choices and a preview of the current period's calendar as it would look when printed. Outlook chooses a print style that is appropriate for the present time.

3. On the Print page, choose one of the options:

- Select the printer you want to use from the Printer list.
- Select the desired print style from the Settings menu.
- To print the current date range and print settings, click the **Print button**.
- Choose one of the following options to adjust the sample display:
- To see a different page of a multipage calendar, use the Page Navigator to input the page number or use the Previous or Next arrows.
- Click the **Actual Size button** to enlarge the calendar page entries.
- Click the **One Page button** to see one page at the largest size that fits in the preview window.
- Click the **Multiple Pages option** to see more than one page (if printing a multipage calendar).
- Scroll up or down through the material if the vertical scroll bar is activated.
- Scroll left or right across the page if the horizontal scroll bar is activated.

4. To make further adjustments, enter the Print dialog box by clicking the Print Options button.

5. Select one of the options in the Print dialog box:

- Expand the Print this calendar list, then click the calendar you wish to print.
- To print just certain pages of a multipage calendar, click **Pages** in the Page range area, then enter the pages you wish to print.
- In the Print range area, pick or input the Start and End dates to print a date range.
- Select the Hide details of private appointments check box to only show availability for items tagged as Private.

Select **Print** to print the calendar with the current settings, Preview to save the settings and return to the Backstage view's Print page, or Cancel to print the calendar without saving the settings.

Add Appointment

Appointments are blocks of time that you reserve exclusively for yourself (as opposed to meetings, to which you invite other Outlook users). A scheduled appointment has a beginning and ending time (as opposed to an event, which befalls for one or more full 24-hour periods).

Events are day-long blocks of time that you arrange on your Outlook calendar, like birthdays, payroll days, or anything else that occurs on a certain day but not at a precise hour. Setting an event is equivalent to creating an appointment in all other aspects, including the option to choose a location, indicate recurrence, indicate your availability, and attach other information to the event item.

You can arrange an appointment by entering a topic and time in an appointment window or on the calendar directly. The basic appointment window also contains a field for the appointment location and a notes box for storing general information, such as formatted text, internet links, and file attachments, so that they are quickly accessible at the time of the meeting.

If you add an appointment that immediately precedes or follows another, the InfoBar at the top of the window will show that the two appointments are nearby on your calendar. If you make an appointment that overlaps with an existing appointment, the InfoBar will show that there is a time conflict.

To plan an event, simply the date is required. You may arrange an event inside an appointment slot or on the calendar itself.

When the Calendar view is shown, events are presented in the date section of the calendar, while appointments are displayed in the time slots.

To create a new appointment window

1. In the Calendar module, do one of the following actions:

- On the Home page, click **New Appointment** in the New group.
- Enter Ctrl+N.

Or

In any module, do one of the following:

- On the Home tab, under the New Items section, **select Appointment**.
- Press Ctrl + Alt + A.

To schedule an appointment

1. Create a new appointment window.

2. In the Subject field, provide a descriptive name for the appointment.

3. In the Location box, put the location of the appointment, if applicable, or any other information you want to have accessible in the appointment header.

4. In the Start time row, enter a day and time or pick one from the drop-down menu. The End Time in Outlook is automatically set to a half-hour after the Start Time.

5. Enter or pick a date and time in the End time field. An appointment may last overnight or many days.

6. On the Appointment tab, click the **Save & Close button** in the Actions group.

Or

1. Show the calendar as Day, Work Week, or Week in the Calendar view.

2. Perform one of the following actions in the calendar pane:

- On the day of the appointment, click the time window in the calendar corresponding to the appointment's start time.
- Drag between the appointment's start and finish times.

How To Define Your Availability Time

Outlook's calendar distinguishes between working and nonworking hours. The calendar time slots during your work hours are colored differently from those outside your work hours, and are the only timeslots accessible to your coworkers when they plan meetings with you using Outlook.

By default, the Outlook work week is set as Monday through Friday, 8:00 a.m. to 5:00 p.m. (in your local time zone). This may be modified to suit your specific work schedule. You may define a start and finish time for your typical work day, the days of the week that you work, and the day of the week you want to show first when just the work week is displayed in your calendar.

To show your work week

1. Click the **Work Week button** in the Arrange group on the Home page.

To alter your work week settings

1. Click the **Arrange button** on the Home tab to see the Calendar page of the Outlook Options dialog box. ***(NB: The Work Week options are shown in the Work Time area at the top of the page)***.

2. Perform one of the subsequent:

- In the Start time list, pick the start time for your workday.
- In the End time list, pick the end time for your workday.
- In the Work week area, mark the days you work and deselect the days you don't work.
- Select the beginning day of your work week from the option labeled First day of week.

(NB: You cannot set a work day that spans midnight or various start and finish timings for separate days in Outlook)**.**

BOOK 8: MICROSOFT PUBLISHER

Introduction

One may wonder what Microsoft publisher means, considering we already have Microsoft Word, enabling you to get your writing done. The difference lies in their functions, as we will see in the latter parts of this study.

Microsoft publisher is a publishing application on a desktop. Microsoft publisher is focused on the design and art of the written content. Just like the name implies, it is a tool used by small businesses or private individuals who might want to get handy and make designs themselves, as they may not have professionals at hand

From its initial release in 1991 and its subsequent series of upgrades through the years, Microsoft publisher, which is included in higher-end editions of Microsoft Office was developed to create visually rich and professionally looking publications without spending money and time on a complicated desktop publishing application.

It is fantastic to know that you can create simple designs like greeting cards, labels, flyers and programs, personalized birthday cards, professional business cards, and even more complex stuff like professional e-mail newsletters, postcards, brochures, yearbooks, and catalogs.

Microsoft publisher is, however, only included in some versions of Microsoft.

Difference Between Publisher and Word

Both Microsoft Publisher and Microsoft word are quite capable software programs in and of themselves. While there are numerous similarities between the two applications, they each serve a distinct purpose. The distinctions between Microsoft Word and Microsoft publisher will be discussed in this section.

Each place's importance on content and design distinguishes Microsoft word from Microsoft's publisher. Microsoft word puts content first, while Microsoft publisher puts design and layout first. Both software programs provide an immense number of feature-rich possibilities.

Microsoft publishers and Microsoft word have an enormous influence on today's computer users. In this book, the purpose of each program and what it excels at will be discussed. Then with the help of this book, you will find the distinction between the two to assist you in deciding which one to usefor your next job.

What Is Microsoft Publisher

Microsoft Publisher is a desktop publishing tool that allows you to make professional calendars, flyers, postcards, posters, newsletters, cards, certifications, and even websites.

Microsoft Publisher is appealing because it allows you to create professional-looking content without learning a program designed exclusively for designers. It comes with a large number of pre-installed templates, as well as additional templates that can be downloaded for free from within Microsoft Publisher. You may even use it to deliver articles to a list of consumers using mail-merge features.

You can develop almost any type of publishing project you wish. You can construct something from the ground up if you so desire. You can also choose one of the hundreds of predefined free themes accessible within the program if you prefer simplicity and quickness.

What purpose did Microsoft Publisher serve? It, too, made the playing field more level. Design firms no longer enslaved businesses. People didn't have to pay much to receive high-quality brochures, flyers, or other marketing materials.

History of Windows Publisher

On September 16, 1991, Microsoft Publisher was initially announced. It was created with the novice computer user in mind. Microsoft Publisher was built primarily for folks who did not want to spend a lot of time messing around with their computers, and Windows 3.0 had just been released.

Microsoft Publisher is an excellent low-cost option for anyone who wants to create something that appears professional while still saving money.

The Uniqueness of Windows Publisher

Microsoft Publisher's primary goal is to make the content seem good.

If Microsoft Word's goal is to focus on content, Microsoft Publisher's goal is to make that content appear attractive and succeed.

"Content Sells," you may have heard, and although that is true, there is something to be said about how that content is delivered.

Microsoft Publisher's most exciting feature has to be this. You can make what you say look beautiful with minimal effort... literally. People are drawn to high-quality eye candy and will read what is offered if presented appealingly.

Consider the last time you received a flyer. If you took it from their hands, the only thing that would entice you to read what was written on it would be its attractiveness. If it were merely printed on white paper with no pictures, images, or text placement, it would be a bore to read. However, if the text was strategically put, with color and visuals in just the right places, there's a good chance you would read it.

The concept of "Page Wizards" was initially presented by Microsoft Publisher. Page Wizards were created after Microsoft noticed that many users lacked the requisite design abilities to create a visually appealing page. In reality, software engineers felt dissatisfied when they made tools to perform the job, but customers didn't know how to utilize them. The software engineers came up with the idea of employing Wizards to help users jump-start their projects, essentially doing a lot of the design work.

Professional design firms still scoff at using Microsoft Publisher to develop any project, but it's not about the tool; it's about making quality design accessible to the average user who has no idea what good design is.

Today, Microsoft makes software available to everybody, regardless of whether or not they are professionals in that sector. This is why you'll find what amounts to "Page Wizards" in every Microsoft Office program now available. This philosophy drives every Microsoft Office product, allowing individuals to accomplish more than they previously imagined possible.

Varieties of Publications One Can Create Using Microsoft Publisher

One of the things I like about Microsoft Publisher is that it can be used at home and in enterprises. The Real Estate industry, out of all the industries that utilize Microsoft Publisher, is the one that has benefited from it the most.

One can use Microsoft Publisher to make business cards and flyers for their open houses. They can even design high-end, professionally designed brochures without paying a professional design agency a dollar.

Real estate agents are not computer nerds, and they don't have to be to get the most out of publisher. They merely need to turn on their computer, open Microsoft Publisher, choose a layout they believe will work well for their potential client, and click PRINT. Microsoft Publisher is cost-effective and facilitates providing high-quality projects by any standard.

Another feature of Microsoft Publisher that I appreciate is that it is not limited to business use. You can use Microsoft Publisher to make flyers to advertise a local yard sale or to put images of your lost pet on telephone poles with your phone number that can be quickly removed by tearing the flyer off.

Students can use Microsoft Publisher to create school projects that look fantastic. The list goes on and on, and your only limitation is your creativity. Microsoft Publisher probably has a template for anything you can envision. If it doesn't, you can create it from scratch with Microsoft Publisher.

Microsoft Publisher and Microsoft Word have a lot of similarities. The built-in templates available to you are perhaps the most evident. The built-in assistance system is another crucial aspect that is sometimes ignored when comparing the two.

If you're unsure how to perform something, write your question into the search box, and each product will respond with suggestions. Each product's help system is fantastic; you should check it out if you haven't already.

The most straightforward approach to distinguishing Microsoft Publisher from Microsoft Word is to demonstrate which software you would use in a specific situation. I've listed various projects I'd use in Microsoft Publisher and Microsoft Word below.

For instance, I'd use Microsoft Publisher to complete the following tasks:

- A printed calendar
- A flyer
- A poster
- Banners
- Business cards
- Brochures
- Greeting cards

Each of the topics described above is focused on the visual and design aspects.

There are several things you can do in both Microsoft Publisher and Microsoft Word, but that does not imply you should.

You could, for example, make a business card in Microsoft Word, but it would be wiser to do so in Microsoft Publisher because this project focuses on design. And, as I previously indicated, when it comes to design, Microsoft Publisher should be your go-to software solution.

Similarly, you could write a newsletter in Microsoft Publisher, but it would be quicker to do so in Microsoft Word because the project's focus is on content. And as I previously indicated, when it comes to content, Microsoft Word should be your go-to software solution.

On Your Next Project, Which Application Should You Use?

How do you know which software solution is best for the project you're working on? When choosing the tool to employ on your next project, start by asking yourself, "What is the primary purpose for this project?" Microsoft Word is the way to go if it's all about the content. Microsoft Publisher is the way to go if the style and layout are more critical.

Features of the Microsoft Publisher Application

Microsoft Publisher helps you easily create, customize and share a wide variety of professional quality publications and marketing material. With publisher, you can easily communicate your message in different publications, saving you time. Whether you need to create brochures, newsletters, postcards, greeting cards or electronic newsletters, you can get high-quality results without having experience in graphic design.

- **Create visually appealing posts**

Publisher offers a wide selection of new and improved tools that will make you look like a design genius and help you create content that will definitely impress you. Use the improved image editing tools, including the ability to use panoramic movements, the zoom feature and crop images and image markers, which allow you to replace images and simultaneously preserve the page layout instantly. Easily adjust each image so that your publication looks optimal.

Design and reorganize the pages like a professional, thanks to the new object alignment technology. This technology offers visual guides to help you align and locate your content effortlessly, although the final design is always in your hands. Create dynamic publications quickly by inserting and customizing blocks of default content, both integrated and from the Publisher community, directly from publisher. Choose from a range of page elements (for example, sidebars and articles), calendars, borders, ads and more.

Give your text a professional typography appearance with the new OpenType typography. Publisher 2010 offers compatibility with ligatures, stylistic sets and other professional typography features available in many OpenType fonts. Use integrated or custom OpenType fonts to create text that is as shocking as images with just a couple of clicks.

- **Manage your posts better with easy-to-use tools**

Creating and managing publications is much easier when you can work the way you want. The extraordinary new printing experience built into publisher allows you to preview print the entire page with a series of page layout tools and adjustable print settings. The new printing experience is just one of the many features available in the new Backstage view, an alternative to the File Menu in Microsoft Office.

Microsoft Publisher is a program that provides a simple editing history like that of your sister Word product, but unlike Adobe InDesign and Adobe InCopy, nobuilt-in) XML code management. It provides an integrated possibility. It helps to create, customize and easily share a wide variety of publications and marketing material. It includes various templates installed and downloadable from its website to facilitate the design and layout process. Before starting to use this application, we will know what the main features are and how you can use them. The first thing you should know is that everything is within a frame since the frames make it easier to move around the parts of the publication to create a design.

- **Full-text editor**

The options to transform the text are as many as we can find in Microsoft Word. This allows us to make the most varied creations.

- **Business identity**

If what you want is to give an image to your business, with Microsoft Office Publisher you have the option to do all the stationery, such as letters, cards, posters, catalogs, forms, etc., and everything is generated automatically from the design you want.

- **Website creation**

With the advancement of technology, the Internet has gotten into most homes. Now you can design your own web page with countless options.

- **Communication Effectiveness**

Suppose your goal is to reach customers in an effective way. In that case, Microsoft Office Publisher offers you hundreds of templates to make all kinds of publications, each made by professionals in image.

- **Most attractive e-mails**

Microsoft Outlook complements Microsoft Office Publisher so you can use the projects and make your e-mails more presentable.

- **Diversity of cards**

You may just want to use the software to make personal presentations. If what you want is to make beautiful cards, the application offers you hundreds of different reasons for the best-known occasions, such as Mother's Day, Father's Day, Valentine's Day, etc.

How To Buy Publisher

There are three different methods of purchasing publisher on your PC. The **first method** is the most preferred one and here is what you need to do: Visit **http://www.office.com**, select **Get Office**, and it will drop you to a page where you can obtain Microsoft Office for Home or business.

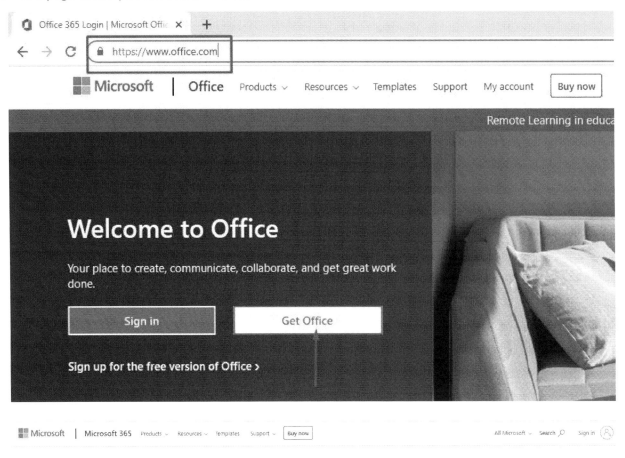

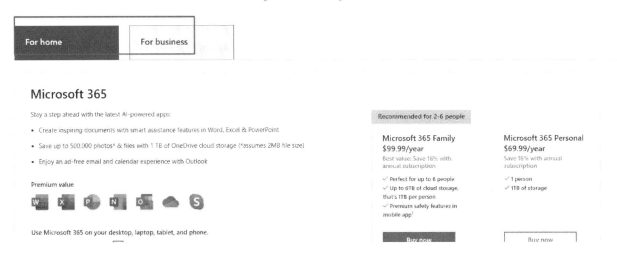

Also, you will discover multiple subscription plans that offer Microsoft Publisher when you scroll down. The subscription plans include Microsoft 365 Family, which goes for $99.99, Microsoft 365 Personal, which goes for $69.99 and Office Home and Student 2019, which goes for $149.99.

Compare Microsoft 365 with Office

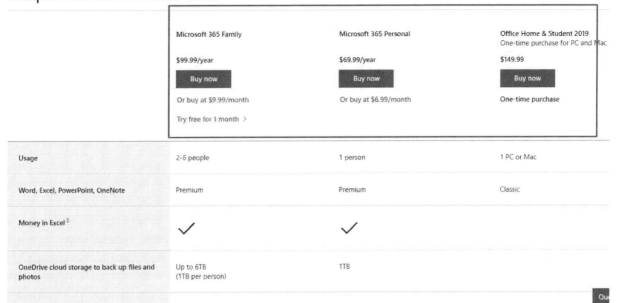

	Microsoft 365 Family	Microsoft 365 Personal	Office Home & Student 2019 One-time purchase for PC and Mac
	$99.99/year	$69.99/year	$149.99
	Buy now	Buy now	Buy now
	Or buy at $9.99/month	Or buy at $6.99/month	One-time purchase
	Try free for 1 month >		
Usage	2-6 people	1 person	1 PC or Mac
Word, Excel, PowerPoint, OneNote	Premium	Premium	Classic
Money in Excel [3]	✓	✓	
OneDrive cloud storage to back up files and photos	Up to 6TB (1TB per person)	1TB	

Alongside Microsoft Publisher, you will also be entitled to Microsoft Word, Microsoft Excel, OneNote, PowerPoint, Outlook, and others, which can be shared with others.

Secondly, if you would prefer to purchase Microsoft Publisher as a standalone application and pay a one-time fee, simply move to **http://www.microsoft.com**, search for publisher, and select the option to purchase Microsoft Publisher (This works best if you are purchasing Microsoft Publisher alone).

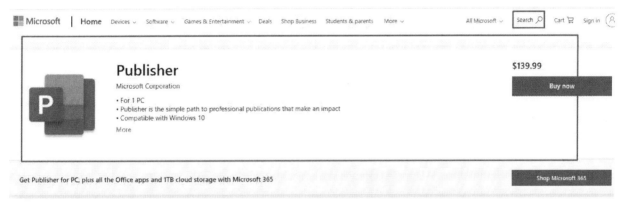

The **third method** is to visit third-party websites like eBay, Amazon, and other related sites to purchase publisher. It goes for similar prices, and you can get it on your PC with just a few clicks. Meanwhile, the only downside to purchasing publisher on third-party websites is that you might purchase an older version, and some functionalities might not be there.

How To Install Publisher

After showing you how to purchase Microsoft Publisher from Microsoft Office and other third-party websites, it is inevitable that we also discuss the process of installing Microsoft Publisher on your PC.

All you have to do to install Microsoft Publisher on your PC is to visit https://www.office.com and select the sign-in button (This should be done if you have a Microsoft account and if you don't have one. And if you do not have an account, select **Sign up** instead.

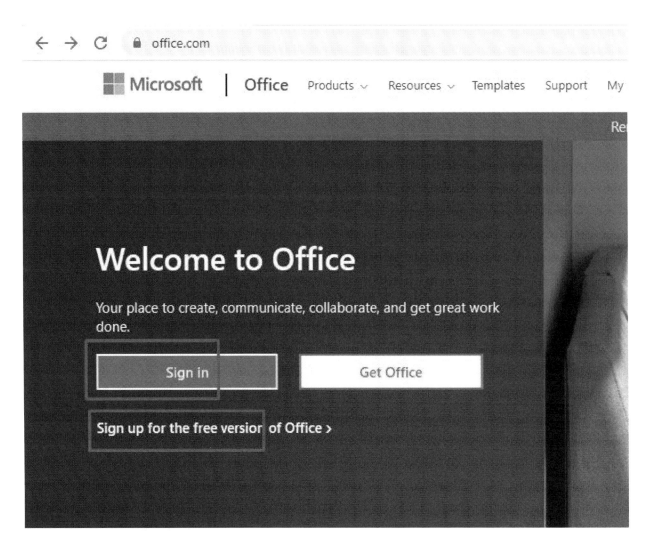

Now, after signing in, you will be taken to another page where you will find an option at the top right-hand corner of your screen that says **Install Office**. Proceed to install Office, and if you do so, you will also be installing Microsoft Access, Microsoft Word, and Microsoft PowerPoint among others.

How To Start Publisher

Microsoft Publisher is a desktop app that must be downloaded before using it. There is no online way of accessing Publisher like Word, Excel, PowerPoint, etc.

So, after the installation process is completed, locate the search field on your PC (The search field is dependent on the version of Windows you are using). *For Windows 10, the search field is located on the taskbar.*

Then, type **Publisher**, click on it to open, and you will be taken to the Microsoft Publisher start page.

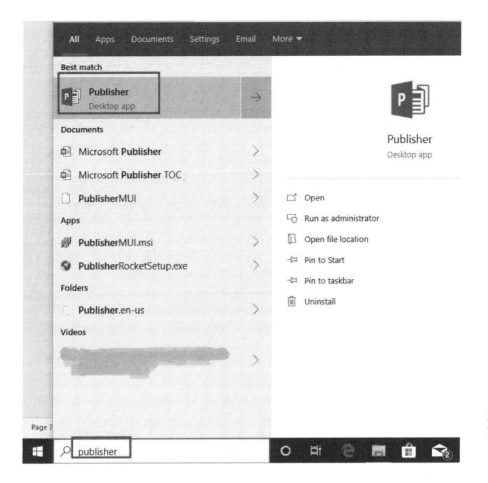

If this is an application you would often use, right-click on publisher in the taskbar and select **Pin to Taskbar**. This will add publisher to the taskbar and you can then easily open it by clicking on its icon in the taskbar.

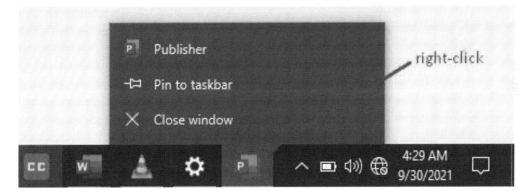

- ***Start Creating A Publication In Publisher***

Immediately when publisher is opened, the choice of various types of templates will be opened as a Catalog. In creating a publication using a template most likely the one you prefer most, all elements as graphics, fonts colors, and others can be changed. Also, in creating a new publication, you can re-use the templates without re-applying your customization.

Templates can be made from any of the publications when you save the such publication as a Publisher template file. When you select a new template intending to start a new publication, a copy of the template file will open. By this, the original template will not be mistakenly altered. Any time you need to make changes to a template, what you need is to open a copy of the template file, make the required changes you want and make sure you save it again as a template.

Designing a master publication can save time to show your company brand and its identity but make sure that you save it as a template so that any time you need a new version, this template can be used and addition can

451

also be done to the information that matches the version. Using the template of the publication, you regularly produce creates room for quantity and continuity of the publications.

- ***Creating Publication Using a Template***
- Click File
- Go to New
- The template gallery will open. Now select a publication type of your choice, like Greeting cards.
- Scroll through designs by using the left and right arrows, then find the template of your choice
- Click create.

- ***How Do You Find a Template***

You can find a particular template for your publication by browsing using templates based on keywords. For instance, if a tri-fold format brochure is what you want to create, then browse through the format options instead of taking yourself through the Brochures category. In the search box, you can type tri-fold brochure templates in the available tri-fold format.

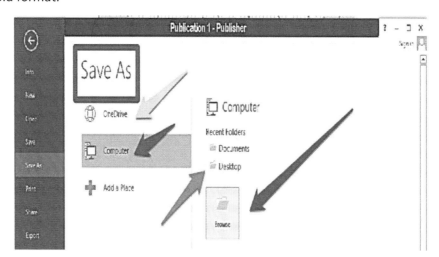

- ***How to Change Your Template***
- From File
- Click on New.
- Click on PERSONAL. Now double-click the name of the template.
- Any changes you want to make, you can do it.
- Click File.
- Click on save as.

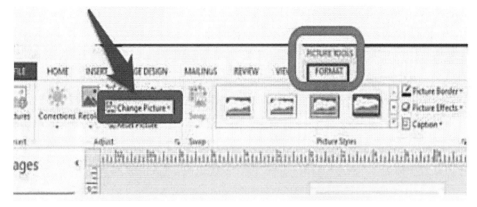

- Go to drive C on your computer
- Click Publisher Template in the Save As type box
- Type a name for the template
- Click save
- ***Publication Customization***

The object will be made up of any publication that is created, even if such publication is created from the beginning of a given template. Any picture you insert serves as an object. If a table is also inserted in a template is equally an object. However, text inserts are contained within an object. An object will be customized through the selection of the object to make changes. Therefore, abound box will appear around it.

The Backstage View

After launching Microsoft Publisher, you will arrive at the start page, which is also the backstage view. This is where you will carry out some of your Publisher functions, including creating a new design, opening an existing one, and editing an unfinished one.

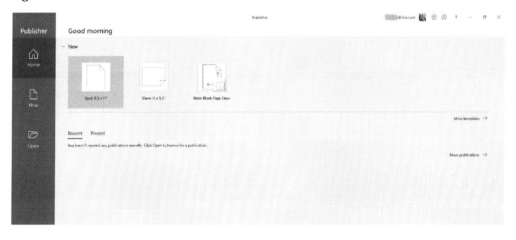

On the left-hand corner of the start page, you will find options including **Home**, **New**, and **Open**. Also, you can open a **blank page** or a blank Publisher file on the start page. And at the right-hand corner is the option for getting templates, which says **More templates**.

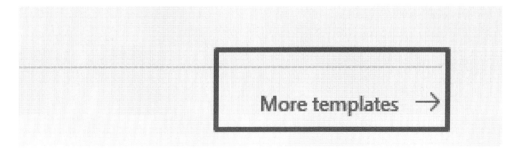

453

Good morning

New

Below the blank pages option, we have **Recent** and **Pinned**. The Recent tab allows you to view your past or recently worked design, while the Pinned tab allows you to pin documents you have formerly worked on.

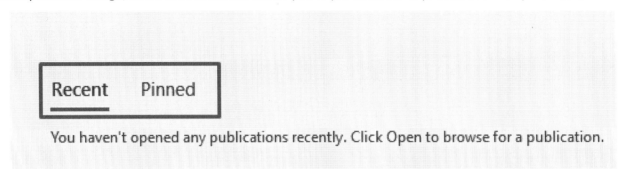

Recent   Pinned

You haven't opened any publications recently. Click Open to browse for a publication.

If there are numerous designs you have done before, you can simply use the search field to locate a particular design work. This saves you from the stress of having to search numerous design files to locate a design work you completed weeks or months back.

Search

Recent   Pinned

When you select the **New** option on the left-hand corner of your screen, you will be presented with numerous available templates. Additionally, you can also search online for new templates if you are not satisfied with the ones Office presents to you.

The provided templates are beautiful and useful depending on the type of design you want to make. For instance, if there is an available birthday template, you can easily edit the birthday template to fit the exact birthday celebration design you want to create. As mentioned earlier, this saves you from the stress of having to create a new birthday template from the beginning. These templates also apply to other works, such as creating a book cover and so much more.

Also, on the left-hand corner of your screen is the **Open** function. Clicking the Open function will show you a list of your recently opened Publisher files. Furthermore, it will also allow you to navigate through OneDrive and your local PC to locate Publisher files you have recently opened.

However, you should be able to do almost everything you need from the **Home** function.

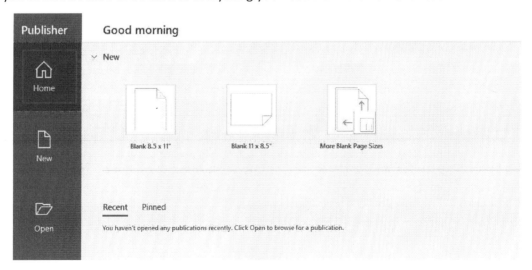

The Interface

The Microsoft interface is the Publisher publisher's main area where all publications' activities are being executed, such as creating, modifying, and designing of Publication. It is the next screen after the opening screen on

Microsoft Publisher. The interface has certain components that you need to know to make the work easier for you. Those components are described below:

- **Ribbon**: Ribbon is the control drive of publisher where all the tools reside. It comprises tabs and commands. When you click on a tab, all the commands in that group will spring out.
- **Navigation Pane**: this is the pane where each of the pages you created for the publication can be located. Each page is represented with a thumbnail in the navigation pane. Click on a thumbnail to move to the corresponding page in the Publication window.
- **Publication Window:** this is the current page of the publication you are designing on publisher. When you click a page in the Navigation pane, it will be the one that will be displayed in the publication window.
- **Rulers**: these are located at the topmost and left side of a publication window which you can use as a yardstick to measure the vertical and horizontal dimensions to make it easier to place objects accurately on the page.
- **Status bar**: this gives you certain information about the activities you are carrying out on the screen. It also contains zoom and view buttons on the right side of the status bar.

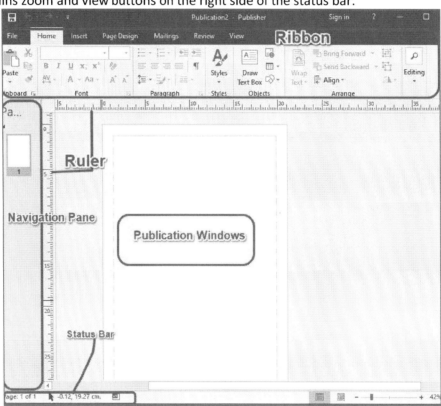

- ***The Ribbon Tabs In Microsoft Publisher***

The main tool on your Microsoft publisher is the ribbon. This object allows you to perform all the commands that are available in the program. The ribbon is divided into different tabs; within these are different groups of commands. The commands in each group allow you access the use of the button's menus, and boxes available within each group. There are also advanced options available for all the dialogue boxes. You can also double click on your active tab within your ribbon to either hide or reveal the content on your ribbon. It helps you to gain more workspace for your publication. To switch on the buttons of groups being displayed, just switch or click on each button on your ribbon. The tabs on your ribbon are; file, Home, insert, page design, mailings, review, view and help.

- *The File Tab*

The File tab is a component of the Office Ribbon in Microsoft Publisher and other Microsoft Office programs that offers you access to file functionality. For example, the Open, Save, Close, Properties, and Recent file options are all accessible from the File tab.

- *The Home Tab*

The Home tab is the default tab in Microsoft Office products such as Microsoft Publisher, Microsoft Word, Microsoft PowerPoint, and others. The Home tab in Microsoft Word is seen in this illustration.

Characteristics of the Home tab

Users can access a variety of functions using the Microsoft Publisher Home page, including the ones listed below.

- Change the font's size, color, and type.
- Make text vivid or underlined.
- Change the color of the text highlighting.
- Align the page's text to be left-aligned, centered, or right-aligned.
- Contains bulleted or numbered lists.
- You can increase or decrease the space between lines and paragraphs.
- Indentation can be scaled up or down.
- Frames can be added, edited, or deleted via text, text fields, and tables.
- You can add or change the title type.
- Draw a horizontal line in the center of the page.
- Replace or search for text.

- *The Page Design tab*

The web page layout tab is the primary vicinity to move in deciding on a background in your publication.

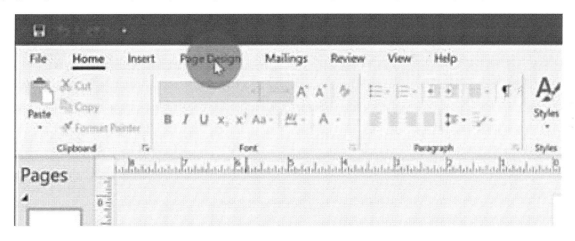

On clicking on the web page layout tab, it opens up the web page layout ribbon, and a number of alternatives open as much as assist you in adjusting what the layout web page appears like.

The web page layout tab lets you extrude the residences of a web page such as; its margins, orientation, and size. In addition to this option, this tab consists of instructions associated with color schemes, font schemes, and additionally converting the background of your page.

Changing The Background in Publisher

- In changing or applying a new background, you must click on the **background** option on the right-hand side of the ribbon.

- This opens up a variety of different options which you will pick from. If you choose to, select a **solid background** or a **gradient background. B**etter still, you could select the **more background** option if you do not want a plain solid background.
- After selecting the **more background** option opens up the **format background** dialogue with a few more options.

- Within the **Picture or texture fill** option, there, you should see a button giving you the chance to insert a picture.
- Go ahead and click on that.
- After selecting that, the **insert pictures** dialogue opens up.

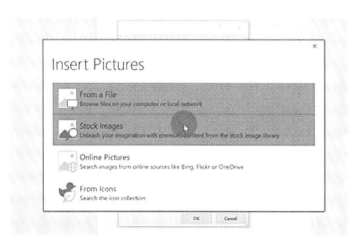

- You could select an option that fits your preference. In this case, we will go with stock images.
- This opens up the **stock images** dialogue

- Select an image that best fits your product
- Click on **insert**
- This calls you back to the **format background** dialogue. Since we already have the image selected, click **OK**.
- You now have a beautiful background on your flyer
- *The Insert Tab*

To insert a picture into the publication you are making; the insert tab is the way to go.

The **insert tab** gives options of commands for inserting objects within the publication you are developing. Aside from inserting objects, you also have the freedom to insert pages or catalog pages.

On selecting the **insert tab,** you will find all sorts of different items you could bring into your publication.

You can insert:

- Tables
- Pictures
- Shapes
- Calendars
- Borders & Accents
- Advertisements

Inserting and Adjusting Text

- To add text, you can go to the **home tab.** Within the home tab, you will find an option to draw a text box.

- Click on that. And from there, you will notice that you can now place your text box wherever you want the text to appear on your design. It is also resizable.

- Type in your text into the text box. You can increase the text, change the font, or adjust the color.

- *Mailings Tab*

The **mailings Tab** embodies the **mail merge** tool. The Microsoft Publisher mail merge tool allows you to send bulk e-mail messages to many subscribers in a contact list, such as e-newsletters. You must first construct an address list in publisher before using the mail merge wizard tomerge your publication.

What you can do with **mail merge** is you can use it to send out a holiday card or greeting card. You can use mail merge to customize every single card. For example, if you have a hundred different friends that all have different names. You can customize the cards with their names on them.

It greatly simplifies creating customized messages for a large number of people.

- *The Review Tab*

It is Ribbon's sixth tab. This page provides you with several useful commands for modifying your document. It assists you in proofreading your text, adding or removing comments, tracking changes, and so on. Proofing, Comments, Tracking, Changes, Compare, and Protect are the six groupings of linked commands on the Review tab.

The review tab includes spell-checking commands, accessing the web for dictionaries, using the thesaurus, and translating material into other languages.

- *The View Tab*

The View tab is next to the Review tab on the toolbar. You can toggle between Single Page and Two Page displays using this tab. You can also manipulate layout tools like limits, guides, and rulers. Its main goal is to provide you with a variety of methods to view your content. Document Views, Show/Hide, Zoom, Window, and Macros are the five groupings of related commands on the View tab.

When we select the view tab, we can examine master pages and reveal or hide items on the page such as guidelines, rulers, the scratch area, and baselines. You can adjust how you view your document with the zoom feature, as well as how to handle numerous publication windows that are open at the same time, all from the View tab.

Chapter 2: **Working With Images**

How To Insert A Background Image

To change your background, follow the steps below:

Select the page design option within your ribbon and click the page background option under the page design within your ribbon to display a dropdown menu of your default background choices

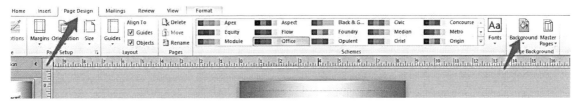

Select the background picture of your choice, and drag your mouse on each to see what it looks like in your background. To apply any of them just click on it. To remove the background 've applied, click on the no background option under the background drop-down menu button and remove the previous background you selected and change it to the normal white background.

If you want to create a custom background, go back to the background option, and from the dropdown menu, select more background options and it will bring you this dialogue box below

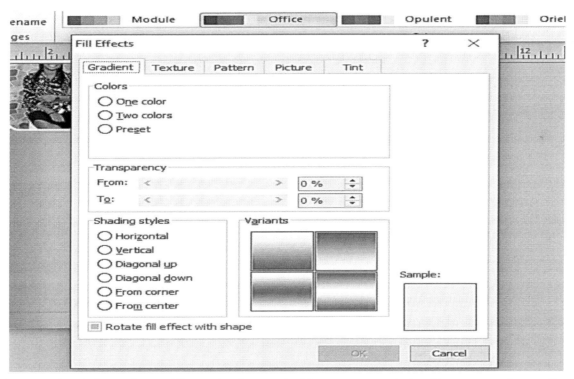

You can then use this dialogue box to fill your background with any custom design. You can use the gradient option, or texture, or pattern, and even import pictures from your computer to use as a tiled page background or the tint option from the dialogue box and click the ok button. It will apply any of the options you choose.
You have many options to select from when applying your page background in Microsoft publisher.

How To Insert Online Pictures

You could again use the built-in function called Insert Online Pictures under the Insert Illustration group in publisher to insert online images, pictures, or Clip Arts.

- Locate the Online Pictures button on the Insert tab.
- To find an image or Clip Art, start typing a description of what you are searching for, such as "cookie."
- Select the image you would love to use, then click the insert button.
- You can now alter the image after inserting it.

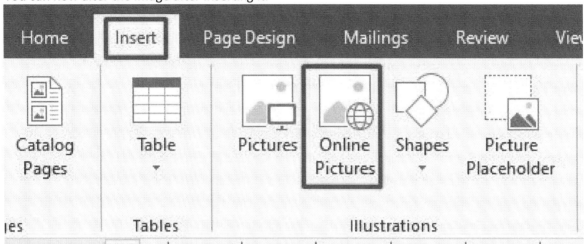

How To Adjust Size, Crop Photos, And Align

This section shows you how best to size your photos, align your photos and crop your images by either reducing or increasing their size.

Now, we have a newly dropped photo on the canvas, but it does not look nice because it is too big. Let us go ahead to **adjust the size** to our need.

For a start, click the image, move to the photo's edges, and drag to increase or decrease its size, whether length or width.

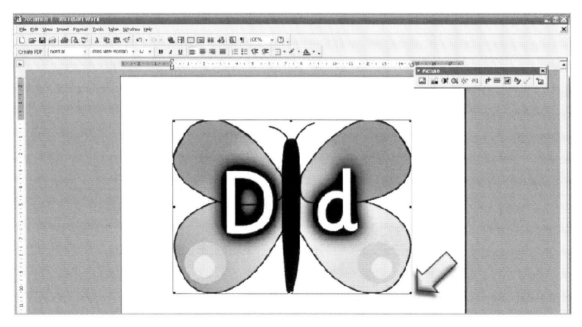

Also, click the image and click the **Format** tab. Here, we have several options we can use to format photos. For instance, you can apply Corrections, Recolor, Crop, and many more to your images.

To **crop a photo**, click the **Crop** button on the right-hand side of the **Format** ribbon.

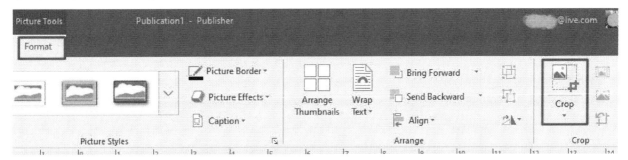

Then, move the edges inside and that part of the photo will be cut off.

To **align your photo**, select the photo and click the **Format** tab. Then, click **Align** on the Format ribbon and choose **Relative to Margin Guides**.

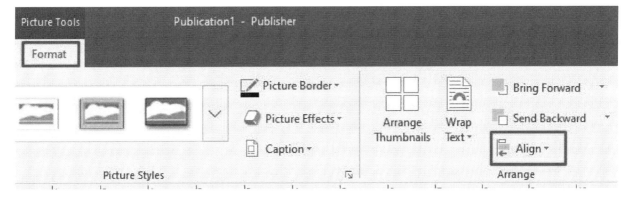

Click the Align button again and align the photo to the left, center, right, top, middle, bottom, distribute vertically or horizontally.

Chapter 3: Working With Text and Shapes

How To Insert And Modify Text

Each text frame on the publication page needs to be replaced with your text. You have two ways of inputting text into the publication depending on how voluminous the text you want to enter into the publication. Suppose it happens to be a few words, you can do that on publisher while multiple texts will be convenient on the word processing application (Microsoft Word). For convenience, you will have to type those text into the Microsoft Word program and then import it into the Microsoft Publisher.

Let us quickly check how to insert text to Microsoft Word and import those text into publisher as stated below, especially when the text you want to replace is more than thirty words:

- Navigate to the **Word** program, enter the text, save the file with a simple name, and close that particular file.
- Move to **publisher** and select the **text you want to replace** and click the Home tab, then click the **Style** menu and jot down the name of the **built-in style** for the text in that placeholder so that you can apply the style to the text you want to import later on.
- Then click the **Insert** tab and tap on the **Insert File** button to access the "**Insert Text dialog box**".
- Choose the **file** that you want to replace with the text in the selected placeholder text **{the file you created in (i)}**. The imported text will be replaced with the text in the selected frames. If the imported text is more than the text frame, the publisher may ask you to fit the flow of the text into different placeholders kindly click No. There are better methods of dealing with text that does not fit the frames later in the next section.
- You can now select the text in the text frames and click on the **Style** menu on the **Home** tab, then select the style you have **jotted down in (ii)** above to apply it to the imported text or leave it untouched if you prefer the style you apply to it in the Word application.
- *Fitting Text Into The Text Frames*

Whenever you notice **red selection handles** around the text frame, for example, an indication that the text does not fit into the text frame.

Also, whenever the text frame **holds a story or text,** there will be a "**Text in Overflow**" icon at the bottom-right of the concerned text frame. Each time you see any of these two signs on a text frame, you have to adjust the fitness of the text into the text frame. Microsoft publisher provides various means of dealing with text-overflow, which we will address in this section.

- *Fitting Overflow Text Inside A Single Text Frame*

To fit the text-overflow into a single text frame, either the heading or paragraph, you can try any of these three procedures:

- **Enlarge the text frame:** click **any of the selection handles** to increase the text frame size so that it can hold the whole text conveniently.
- **Shrink Text On Overflow:** you can shrink the overflow text. All you need to do is to click on the **Text Box** tab and tap on the **Text Fit** menu, then select "**Shrink text On Overflow**" from the drop-down menu, though this command does not care if the text is big enough for people to see and therefore you have to be vigilant when using this command because it will reduce text size automatically to fit into the text box.

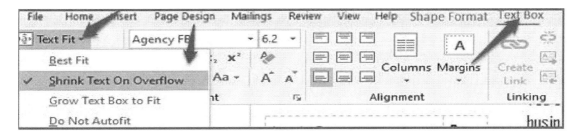

- **Adjusting the text frame margin:** this at a time works wonders by default text frame always has space to keep text from touching the box which the text frame margin. All you need to do is to reduce the text frame margin to make it smaller to create more space for the overflow text. To shrink the text frame margin and create more space for the text, kindly click the Text box tab, tap on the Margin menu, and then choose **Narrow** from the drop-down menu.

- ***Transferring Overflow Text From Frame To*** *Frame*

Perhaps you don't want to fit the text-overflow into a single box, or maybe the text can't conveniently fit into a single box, then you have to direct it into another frame. As discussed in the next section, there is a way to flow overflow text from frame to frame.

- ***Directing Text To Another Frame***

You should know the indication of overflow text by now, that is the text frame with red selection handles or the one text frame with the "Text In Overflow" icon (...) at the bottom right of the text frame. Now it is time to move the overflow text into another text frame. The first assignment is to find the text frame where you will move the overflow text into or create a **new text box** by clicking on **Draw Text Box** and dragging the **icon over the page** to draw a new text frame.

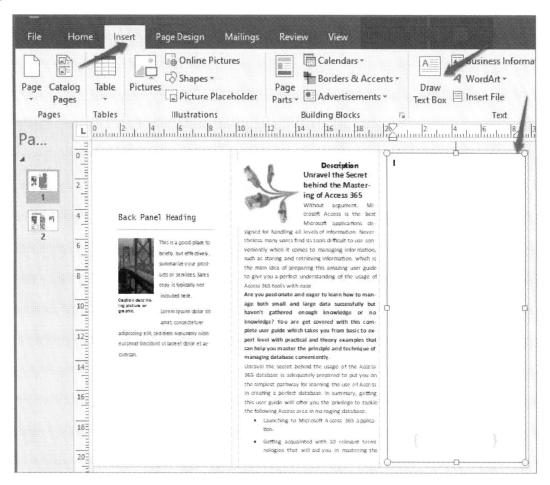

Then follow the instructions listed below to move overflow text from one frame into another text frame:

- Select the **text frame** that has the overflowing text and click on the **Text Box tab**, then click on **Create Link** button.
- Navigate to the text frame where you want to move the overflow text into the **mouse pointer like a pitcher**, then click the **receiver text box frame** with the pitcher pointer to direct the overflow text inside it. If the receiver text frame is on another page click on such **page** on the **Navigation Pane** and click on the **empty text box** to move the overflow text into it.

466

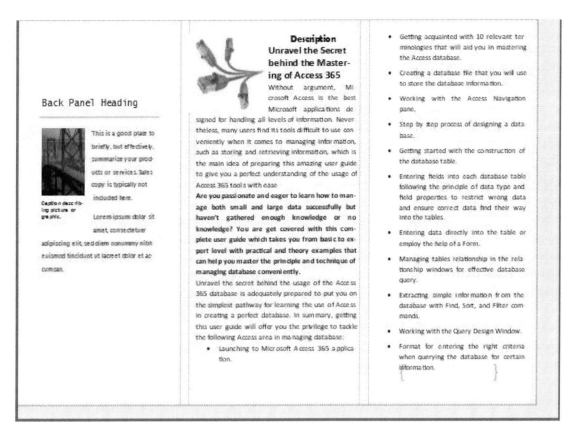

- *Managing Text Frames With A Story*

When text frames have a link, it means they share certain information in common, and such is referred to as Story in Publisher. There are various ways of dealing with text frames with a story link. Below are various ways of managing story links in publisher:

- **Moving from one text frame to the other:** click the Text Box tab, then select **Next** to move to the next frame or Previous to move to the previous frame.

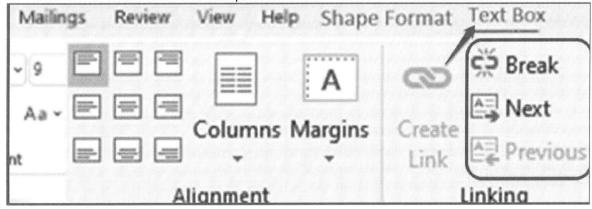

- **Remove the link between frames**: remove the link simply means to discontinue the link between two frames, kindly choose the frame that will be the last frame on the chain and click the **Text Box** tab, then click on the Break button.
- **Select the text in all the text frames:** click the **Home** tab and tap on the **Select** menu, then choose Select All object or use the shortcuts key by pressing (Ctrl + A).

- *Filling Up A Text Frame*

At times you will have much space inside a text frame. This is the direct opposite of text-overflow, where text is much more than what the frame can contain. You can use any of these procedures to manage a text frame that has a lot of space after you have imported the text into it:

- **Best Fit**: click the **Text Box** tab and tap on the **Text Fit** menu, then select Best Fit on the drop-down menu. This will increase the text inside the text frame to make it fit into the text frame.

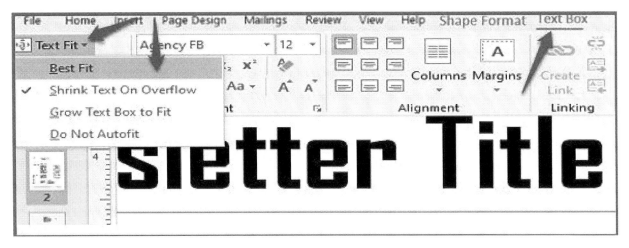

- **Add Word, graphic, or art**: try to add some words to the headings or subheadings. You can add a small graphic or artwork to fill up the space.
- *Formatting Your Text*

As time goes on, you may feel like changing the format of your text; use any of these two techniques to format your publication text:

- **Using Home Tab commands**: click on the Home tab and navigate to Font and Paragraph headings. Use any of the buttons in both headings to change the appearance of your text by selecting the text and applying the format.

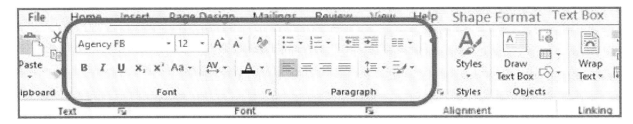

- **Styles**: select the text you want to format and click the Home tab. Click the Style menu on the style headings and select the desired style format you want on the text. Kindly use the undo command to redo your action if you have played wrongly with the Style.
- *Wrapping Text Around Graphic, Picture, Word Art, And Frame*

Wrapping text around an image, frame, word arts, and other graphics show you are a competent Publisher and such will create a sense of good impression in the mind of the targeted audience. These are the guides for wrapping text around the image, word arts, and other graphics:

- Select the **objects** that you want to wrap the text with.
- Click the **Format** tab and tap on the **Warp text** menu to select a desired warping option from the drop-down list.

468

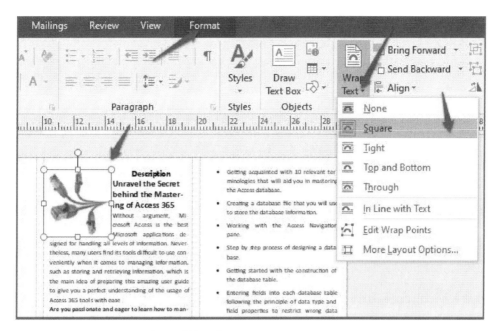

• Inserting New Frames On The Publication Pages

The frame is an essential part of the publication page. This is the only way of adding any elements into the page, such as text, graphic, image, word art, and so on. frames are simply what makes up a publication page without a frame the publication page will be empty. Stay tuned in this section to fully understand working with the frame.

• Inserting A New Text Box Frame

To insert a new text box frame, kindly find your way to either Home or Insert tab, then:

- Click the **Draw Text Box** and move to the page where you want to place the new text box.
- Drag the **Plus** icon over the page to create the text box.

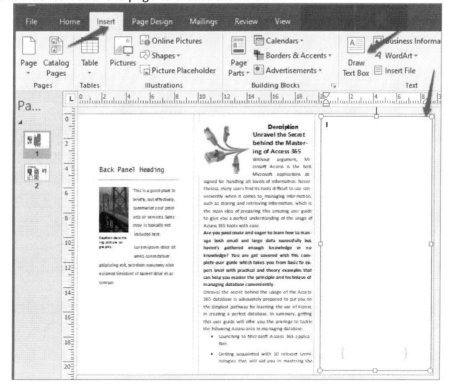

How To Insert And Modify Shapes

- *Inserting Shapes*

One great way to induce some flavor and interest in your publication is by applying shapes. There are numerous shapes available for your use and you have the freedom of customizing them using your colors.

- To get started, locate the **Insert tab** and select it.
- After that, you would have successfully opened it and you will have to select the **shapes** option

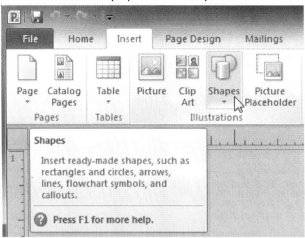

- Scroll through the plethora of shapes to find a fitting one.

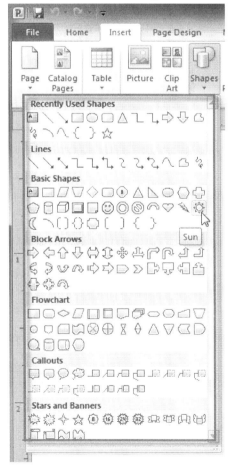

- Select the shape you intend to use.
- At this point, after selecting, you can begin to move your cursor to fix the size and location of the shape.

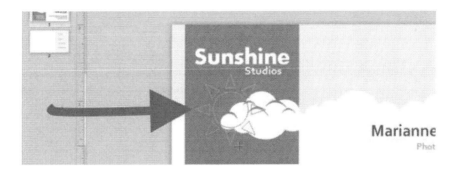

- *Borders*
- *Adding A Border to A Master Page*
- Select Page design and click on master pages
- Select your master page, and locate Edit Master Pages
- Click home, select shapes. Getting to the basic shapes section, there you can select a rectangle
- Place your cursor on the page and drag it to draw the page border
- Right-click on the border; next, click on format auto shape
- Locate the colors' and the lines tab, then choose a color and line type, next, select OK.
- On the master's page tab, select the option titled close master page.
- ***How to Add A Line Border Unto A Single Page***

With a page selected, click **home.** Locate **settings** and click.

In the **basic shapes** category, select the **rectangle.** Next, drag to bring the page border. Take the rectangle to the rear if there are subsisting elements on the page, such as pictures or text boxes, by choosing the rectangle and clicking Send Backward > Send to Back. As a consequence, everything will be piled up on top of the rectangle.

On the border, do a right-click next, click on **format auto shape.**

Select a color and line type from the **Colors** and **Lines tab**; next, select **OK.**

- ***How to Add A Pre-designed Pattern Border To A Page***
- Select the page and then go to **Home > Shapes**.
- Click the Rectangle Button pictures located within the Basic Shapes area. Next, pull to bring out the page border.
- Right-click the periphery and select **Format Auto-shape** from the menu.
- Then select BorderArt from the **Colors, Lines tab.**
- Select the desired border from the ready-to-use Borders list, then select **OK.**
- ***How to Create A Custom Border***

Include a custom border made from an image file, scanned image, or a drawing software picture for more flair. Publisher border art will be utilized to store your custom border.

- Click **BorderArt**, then Create Custom in the dialogue box that displays.
- Select a picture by selecting it with the cursor.
- Locate the image you would like to use in the **Insert Pictures** dialogue box, whether on your system or using Bing's Images search.
- Next, click on **Insert** after selecting the image.

471

- Locate the **Name Custom Border** dialogue box, name your custom border, then click **OK**.

How To Set Text Margins

Layout guides help to arrange your publication elements accurately. If you refuse to set up your publication layout, you might encounter improper arrangement or layout of graphics, text, and objects on your publication pages. An object may overlay or rest on another object, text frame may stumble over the margin, text in one column may spill to the next column and various wrong alignments.

Microsoft Publisher provides four apparatuses for setting an accurate and systematic layout for publication pages they are **margin guides, ruler guides, grid guides, and baseline**. Using these four layout guides effectively directly results from a tidy and nice publication.

- *Margin Guides*

Margin guides are the blue border lines that indicate the start and end of the margin. It is a great tool for keeping the objects within limits by restricting them from going beyond the margin.

If you can't find margin lines or indicators on the pages of your publication, you should call it back by clicking on the **View** tab and placing a checkmark on the Guide check box.

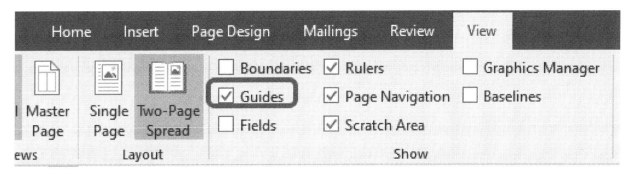

You can change the measurement of your margin (click on the **Margin**s menu and select the margins option for your publication or select the **Custom Margin** to specify the margin measurement inside the Layout Guides).

- ***Ruler Guides***

Ruler guides are the green lines that you can draw horizontally or vertically on the page of your publication to make aligning of graphics, text, and other objects convenient. You can draw ruler guides on your publication when it is required and remove them immediately after you are done if it stands as a distraction to the next action you want to carry out.

Let me quickly show you two ways of placing ruler guides on your publication page:

- **Built-in Ruler Guides**: click the **Page Design** tab, tap the Guides menu, and select any **ruler guides** format you want from the drop-down menu.

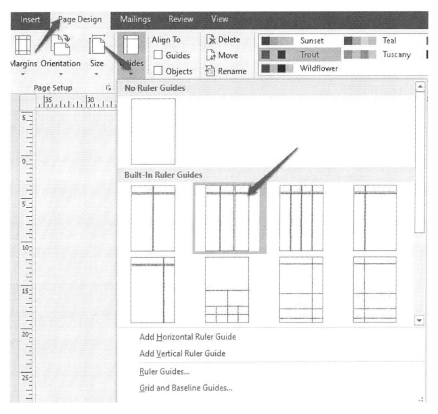

- **Drawing ruler guides**: click the **Page Design** tab and tap the **Guides** menu, then select **Add Horizontal Ruler Guides** or **Add Vertical Ruler Guides**. The horizontal or vertical ruler guide will be placed on the page. **Click and drag it to the desired spot** within the publication page.

Note: when you are done using the ruler guides, you can remove the guides by selecting **No Ruler Guides** from the **Guides** drop-down menu.

You can shift or copy the ruler guide by holding the **Ctrl key** and hovering the mouse over the ruler guide until you see a two-headed arrow with a plus icon, then double-click and drag the **ruler** to another position to shift a ruler guide to another location or double-click and drag to another position by left-clicking to copy a ruler guide to another location.

To remove Ruler guides in the meantime, click the **View** tab and remove the **checkmark** on the **"Guides"**.

- **Grid Guides**

Grid guides are the grid of blue lines that appear over the publication page. Grid guides are ideal for aligning frames and objects squarely across the page.

To specify grid guides for your publication, kindly click the **Page Design** tab and tap the **Guides** menu, then select **"Grid and Baseline Guides"** from the drop-down menu to access the **"Layout Guides"** dialog box with Grid Guides being selected at default, then adjust **the Grid guides** settings as described below:

- Specify the number of **rows and columns** of the grid you desire.
- Specify the **Spacing interval** to control the nearness of the object to the grid. It is always **0.2** by default. You must not set the Spacing below 0.2 unless you want frames and objects to brush each other.
- (Optional) place a checkmark on the **"Add Center Guide between Columns and Rows"** check box to draw a line between row and column of the grid you created.

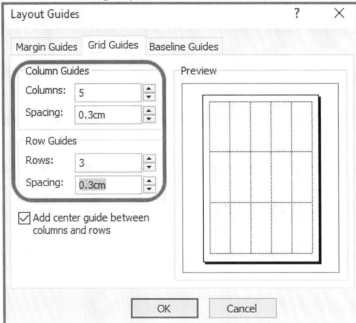

Note: you can remove the grid guides by finding your way to the **Layout Guides** dialog box with the Grid Guide tab selected and enter 1 into the column and row text boxes and click Ok.

To remove Ruler guides in the meantime, click the **View** tab and remove the **checkmark** on the **"Guides"**.

- **Baselines**

Baselines are the horizontal dotted brown line that shows up on the publication page to make aligning objects, frames, and text lines easier.

You can specify the interval of the baseline on the **Page Design** tab, then click the **Guides** menu and select **"Grid and Baseline Guides"** from the drop-down menu, then click on the **Baseline Guides** tab and enter the **Spacing** measurement to decide the space interval of the baselines and the **offset** values into the offset textbox to decide the offset margin settings lines.

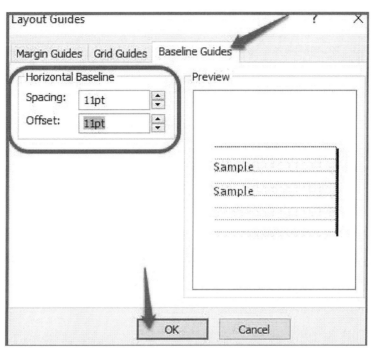

To make the Baseline visible on the page, click on the View tab and place a checkmark on the "Baseline" check box.

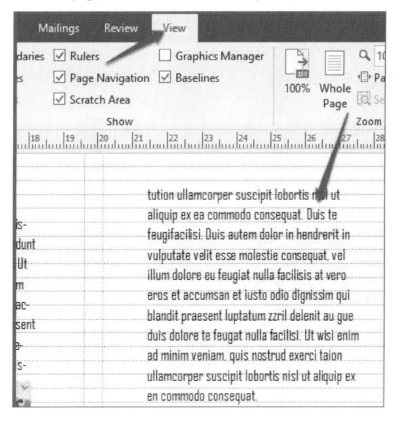

- *Aligning Objects To Snap To Guide And Other Objects*

Aligning object to ruler or grid guides make frames and object queue up accurately on the page. To make this alignment work, kindly click the **Page Design** tab and place a **checkmark** on the **"Guide"** check box to enable the objects to align to the ruler or grid guides. You can place a **checkmark** on the **"Objects"** check box to enable the object align to other objects on the publication page.

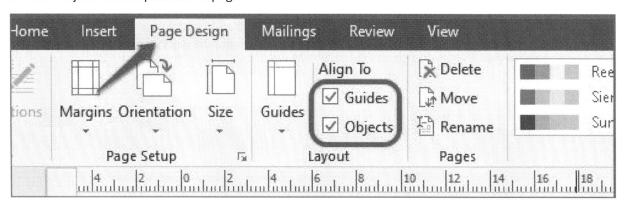

How To Add Business Information

Instead of typing to add business information as we just did, you can use the **Business Information** feature to easily add things like company name, address, e-mail, phone number and more to your design.

To add business information to your design, click the Insert tab and click Business Information.

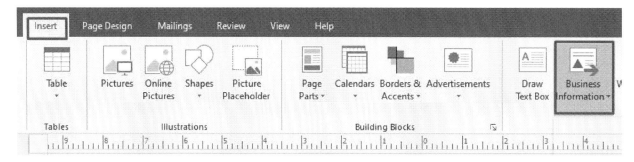

A field then opens and you can click on the information you want to add. For instance, you can click on **Address**, type the address, increase the font size, change the color to a befitting one, and move the text box to the right place in your design.

How To Insert An Object From A PC

If you seek to improve your design work and make it a lot more attractive than it is, you can choose to insert or add images from your PC. Perhaps, you already have a company logo to add to your design, for instance.

To **insert an object from a PC, click the Insert tab and Pictures**.

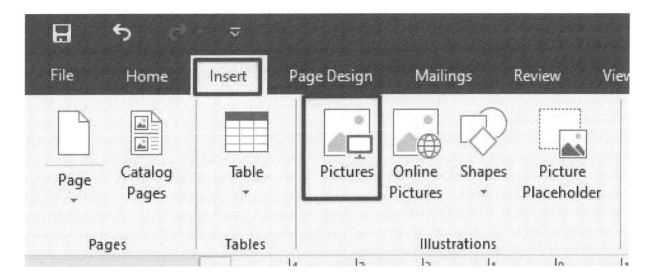

It then launches a file picker, where you are expected to locate and choose the particular image/logo you want to insert from your PC.

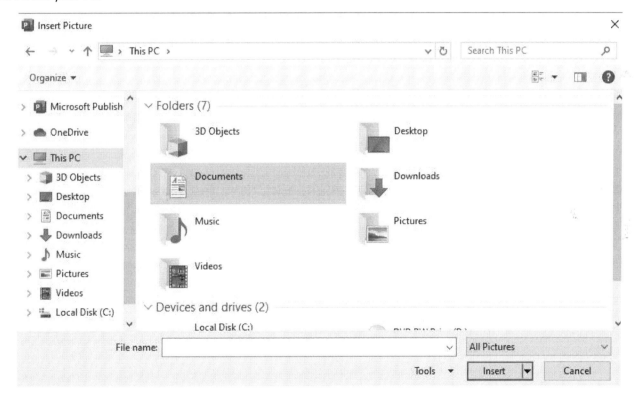

After locating and selecting the image/logo you want to insert into your publication, click **Insert** and the image will appear on your design.

Once added, you should adjust it (make it smaller or larger), so it will fit perfectly into your design.

How To Arrange Object Layer

This is professional means of laying one frame on another frame. When you intentionally lay a frame on another frame, it makes the publication look more professional than the frame that is wrongly and roughly overlaps over another. Follow these instructions to creatively lay the frame on one another and decide which one comes to the top:

- **Text Wrapping:** click the **Format** tab and tap on the **Wrap Text** menu, then select **None** from the drop-down menu.

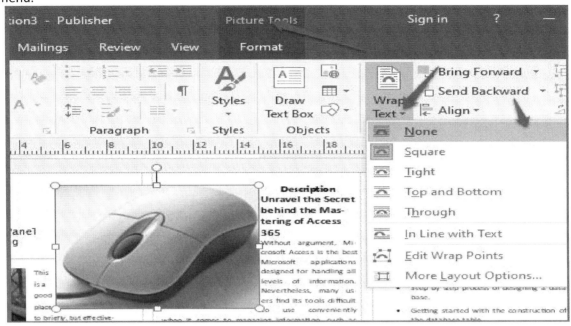

- **Fill Color:** you have to remove the fill color from the frame you want to place above to allow the frame below to show through them. You can do that by selecting the concerned frame, clicking on the Format tab, then clicking on the Shape menu and selecting No fill from the drop-down menu.

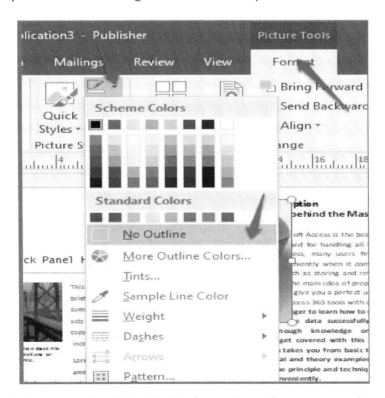

- **Dictating the Stack Order**: you should decide the frame that will come on top between the two overlapping frames. To do that, click the Format tab and tap on Bring Forward or Send Backward, depending on the frame you selected.

478

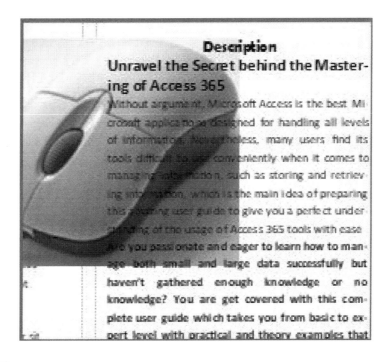

How To Zoom In And Out

By default, you will be able to see your entire publication on your screen, but whenyou're working, you will want to view your publication a little bit bigger because, by default, your text will be very small. Hence, you can zoom in and out of your publication using the zoom slider that is located in the bottom right-hand corner of your screen.

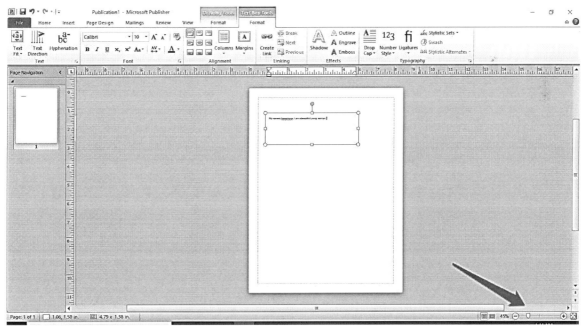

Moving the **vertical bar** on the **zoom slider**, you can zoom either in or out. You can also choose the **plus or minus** sides to the left and right of your zoom slider.

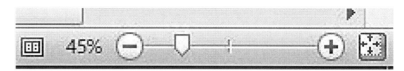

As you click the plus or minus sign, you can either zoom in or out in ten per cent increments (your text will be increased or decreased by ten per cent).

Also, you can zoom in and out within your document on your keyboard using a mouse as a scroll wheel. To zoom in using your keyboard, hold down the **ctrl key** while you move the **scroll wheel** on the mouse up, you'll be zoomed in.

To zoom out, also hold the control key on your keyboard while you move the control key and the mouse down; you will be zoomed out. Using the keyboard option zooming in or out, your zooming will be increased by twenty per cent increments.

Additional zooming options can also be seen on the view tab within your ribbon. Click on your **view tab**. You will see a zoom group display. You can quickly move to a hundred per cent zoom, click on the button to do so.

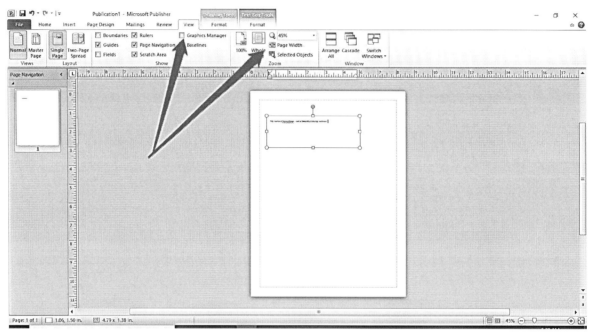

To view your whole page screen at any percentage you desire on your screen, click the **whole page** button. You can also zoom to a specific percentage by clicking on the drop-down menu and then choose the percentage you want. Your **page width** button will allow you to automatically zoom in on the document as far as possible so that the width of your publication will take up the entire screen.

Chapter 4: **Managing Your Publication**

While working on any project, it is of the utmost importance that you save your document frequently to prevent loss if your program closes unexpectedly. Unexpected program closures, accidental shutdowns, power outages and other numerous disasters might leave you frustrated and waste your efforts and time. This chapter will discuss how to save, share, print, and export your publications.

How To Save Your Publication

To save your publication:

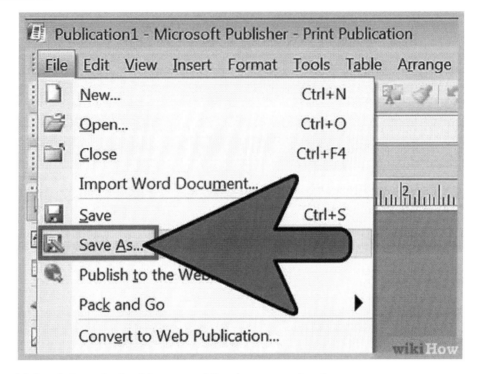

Ensure your publisher is launched, with your publication opened on it.

Select the **file menu** on your ribbon

Click **save as** .

In the save as dialogue box choose the destination you want your publication to be saved to.

In the **file name**, type in the name you want it to be saved as that you can easily remember.

Once you're done, select the **save** button

If you're done with the publication you can close your current project without closing the whole program; if you want to work on another project, or peradventure you still want to work on it, just continue and click save intermittently

How To Print, Share, And Export Your Publication

After you have successfully done creating the publication, the next activities are sharing it to the appropriate quarters that need it and printing it for public use. This section will show you the process of sharing and printing a publication for the target audience or public consumption.

- ***Sharing Your Publication***

The major method of sharing publications is via e-mail. These are step-by-step processes of sharing your publication work:

- Click the file tab to access the backstage view and tap on the Share button from the backstage drop-down list.
- Tap on the E-mail option and select any of the sub e-mail options for sharing the publication as it soothes you, such as PDF, Attachment, or XPS.

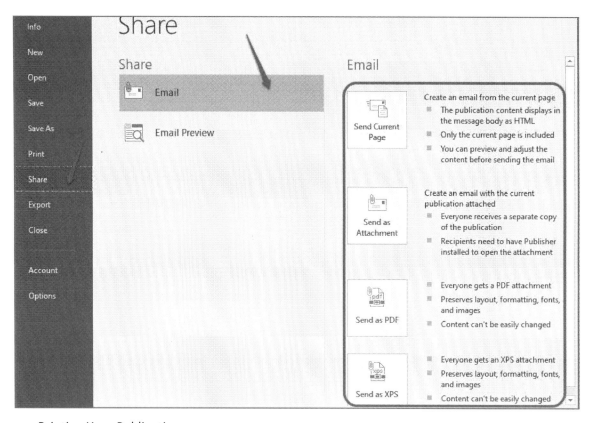

- *Printing Your Publication*

Print Preview

Before printing your publication, make sure your work is set up using the page dialogue box. When that is done, the next thing is to preview your work, so you don't have to waste paper by printing several different copies before you get it right. Publisher allows you to view your publication as it will be printed, called **print preview.** In print preview, you can see how your publication will be on paper, with the publications you've set up in your page dialogue box. To use print preview:

- Open the file tab within the ribbon
- Click the print option
- In the section to the right of the backstage of your work, you will see the print preview.

Note: three buttons will appear on the far lower right side of your screen. You can use the slider to increase or decrease your viewing page.

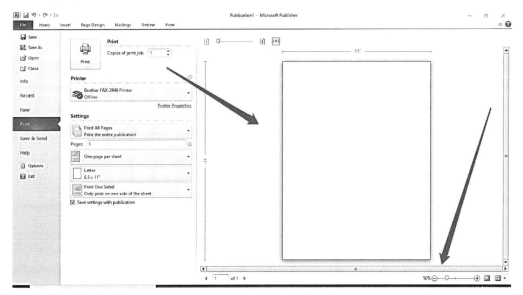

You can also double-click on your page to zoom in or out

Printing

You can print your publication ordinarily from the printer by studying the following instructions:

- Click the **File** tab and select **Print** from the backstage drop-down list.
- Specify the settings you want for the publication printing, such as the **number of copies, printing, one-sided and double side per print, and other settings.**
- Quickly glance through your work by navigating to each publication page with the navigation page at the bottom, then click on the Print icon at the top left to print the publication.

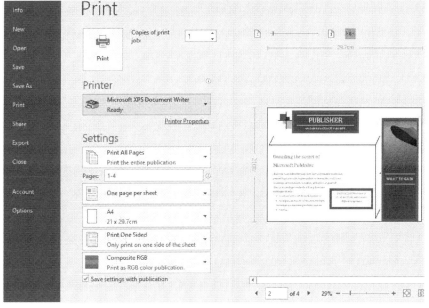

- *Exporting Your Publication*
- To export your work, go up to the left-hand of the screen and click on the **File tab.**

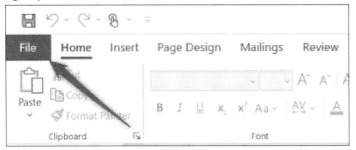

- This opens up what is known as **backstage.**

- Within that screen, click on **export.**

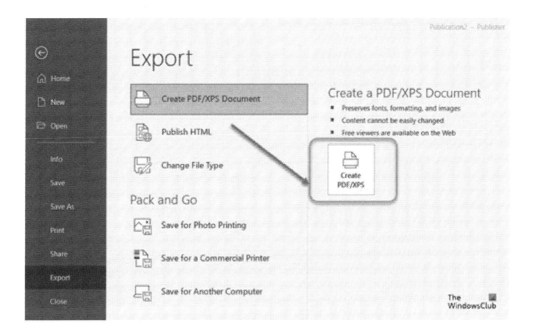

- Within the **export menu,** you will see different options for sending out as a PDF/ XPS, HTML, or a chance to alter the file type.
- When you export the publication in a PDF/XPS format, it will maintain the same look as what you have within your publisher
- Within the **change file type** option, you can export it into a publisher file, a PNG, a GIF, and many more.

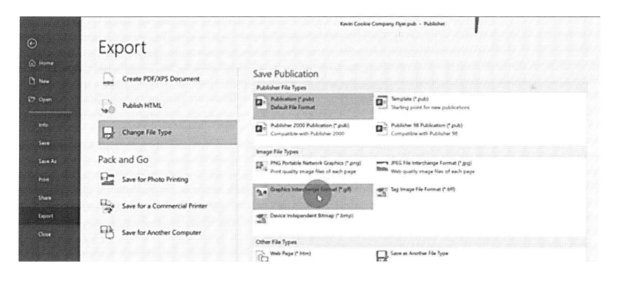

BOOK 9: MICROSOFT ONENOTE

Introduction

O neNote is a free digital note-taking app from Microsoft that you can use to capture ideas and thoughts. It is a tool that automatically syncs and saves your notes so you can access them anywhere on your phone, PC or any type of device that has access to the web. So if you're using it on a computer and accessing it across any of your devices, you could go to your phone, install the app, log into your account and access the same information.

You can use it to create notes and add content to them and it stores your notes in the cloud. So you can use them on whatever device you happen to be on. It's very similar to other note-taking tools like Evernote and Google Keep.

This is great if you're probably in a classroom taking notes, if you are in a business meeting, or just for your everyday life, family life, or planning a vacation. You just want to put all these ideas in one spot.

There are different versions of OneNote like OneNote 2013 and OneNote 2016. Still, the official version of the app now is just called OneNote. It is available in Windows and also Mac. Plus, you get it for free, and it syncs across all your devices. You can also install the OneNote app on IOS and Android devices, and there's a web version that works on almost any modern browser. So, you see, there are many ways you can use OneNote to be more organized and productive.

How To Get OneNote

You may be thinking of how to take advantage of OneNote and how to get to OneNote. Well, the good news is OneNote comes with Windows 10, so if you have a Windows 10 device, you already have one note.

How do you get to OneNote? You can simply go down to the search field and just type in "OneNote" and what you'll see happen is OneNote will show up as the best match on the list. You can now click on it and the OneNote app will open up. If you are a Windows 11 user, unfortunately, this application doesn't come pre-installed. For that, you just need to visit Microsoft Store and there, you can find OneNote.

Another way you could also get OneNote is from your web browser. You could simply open up your web browser and then go to office.com. This is how you're going to access OneNote. Click on sign-in and if you have a Microsoft account you sign in with your Microsoft account. If you don't have a Microsoft account you could create one for free by clicking on the create one button.

OneNote stores all your notes in the cloud, and because they're in the cloud it can sync those notes between all the devices you're using. So if you create a note on your phone, you'll immediately see it on your desktop. For the syncing to work you need to log into OneNote and to do this you need a Microsoft account. This could be one that you use at work or school with office 365 or another Microsoft service like Outlook.

Once you sign in you'll land on office.com and see that you can access OneNote by clicking on the OneNote icon. In addition to OneNote, you could also get Word, Excel, and PowerPoint through office.com. If you have a phone whether an Android device or an iOS device, you can also download the OneNote app from the App or the Google Play Store. You can install that on your phone.

Chapter 1: **Getting Started**

Knowing what kind of tools are hidden in each ribbon right from the start will make your note-taking much easier. But first, it's important to know that an MS Office program can communicate with the other Office programs. While we will see these integration tools in the ribbons, they might also be hidden in the ribbons of Word and PowerPoint.

The Home Ribbon

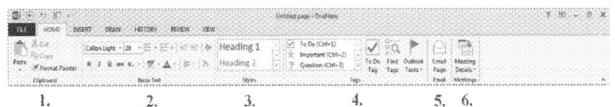

Many of the tools in the Home ribbon might be familiar to you. The Clipboard, Basic Text, and Styles groups are the usual suspects in all Microsoft programs and work the same. To the right of the Styles group, you'll start with the new stuff.

Clipboard Group

Paste, Cut, and Copy: The usual buttons common to all Microsoft programs.

Format Painter: Also a usual tool, it lets you take formatting from one item in the document and "paint" it on other items in the document.

Basic Text Group

Formatting: These basic formatting options like font type and size, bulleted lists, and background color are nothing new and will not be covered here.

Styles Group

Styles list box: This tool has options similar to the Styles group in MS Word but with a fewer choices. Many different headings can be selected, including the page title style, citation, quote, code, and normal styles.

Tags Group

Tag Box: This is a list box of tags you can scroll through. Clicking the More arrow will cause the entire list of available tags. There are many tags to choose from, like: Critical, Remember for blog, and Idea. You can customize tags by creating new ones based on a chosen tag or modifying an existing one.

To Do Tag: The first tag in the list box. Use this tag to indicate a "to do" item which can be checked on completion.

Find Tags: Use this tool to search for tags in your notes. It comes in handy especially if you use a lot of tags.

Outlook Tasks: If you use Outlook for your email and to keep track of tasks, this tool is helpful if you want to add tasks to Outlook while taking notes in OneNote or vice versa.

Email Group

Email Page: As the title suggests, this tool launches Outlook using your default email address and inserts your current notes page into the new message. All you have to do is type in the email address of the person you want to give the page to and click send!

Meetings Group

Meeting Details: This tool also uses Outlook. Clicking it brings up a list of meetings for the current day from your Outlook Calendar. You can also go through past or future meetings. Once the correct meeting is selected, OneNote will pull out all the details and attach them to your notes.

The Insert Ribbon

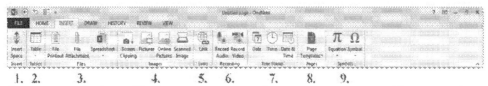

This ribbon contains many tools that will allow you to customize your notes by attaching as much external content as you desire. Many are self-explanatory and similar to those in the Word and PowerPoint Insert Ribbons and will be covered only briefly.

Insert Group

Insert Space: This tool lets you create a space as large as you want. Simply select the tool and then click and drag where you want the space to go. Insert Space is useful if you find you need some extra space to include additional information like drawings or pictures.

Tables Group

2.3: Creating a table in OneNote and the layout option ribbon that appears.

Tables: Create a table in your notes to insert information in a more orderly format. This tool will allow you to create a table with the number of cells you indicate on the drop-down menu, draw your table, or make a table with an Excel spreadsheet. A new Table Tools Layout ribbon appears with options if you decide to make your table. You can even sort your table or convert it to an Excel spreadsheet if you'd like.

Files Group

File Printout: This tool prompts you to choose a file from your computer which it will then create a "printout" of. It inserts a link to the file and the actual file into your notes in a format that looks like a printed or scanned document image. This "printout" cannot be edited, but you can click on the link to open the original file for editing. Note: by default you may only use File Printout with Microsoft Office Program files.

File Attachment: Similar to File Printout, File Attachment prompts you to select a document to attach to your notes. However, there are no limitations to the type of file you can attach. This tool only provides an icon of the type and name of the document you have attached and does not attach a printout of the document.

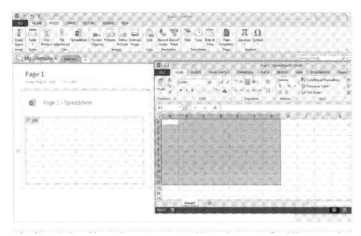

Spreadsheet: Clicking this tool gives you two options: Existing Excel Spreadsheet and New Excel Spreadsheet. Choosing an Existing Excel Spreadsheet will prompt you to choose the Excel file from your computer. At the same time, New Excel Spreadsheet will insert a small spreadsheet into your notes. Choosing New Excel Spreadsheet is the same in this and the Tables tool.

Images Group

Screen Clipping: This brings up the most recently viewed screen where a clipping can then be taken and inserted into notes. Be sure to open the page you want to take a clipping of before going back to OneNote because once this tool has been chosen it will not let you change the screen to be clipped.

Pictures: As with all other programs with this tool, it opens the computer's file browser so an image can be selected and inserted into notes.

Online Pictures: Clicking this will open a window where you have a few options: Office.com Clip Art, Bing Image Search, your OneDrive account, Facebook, or Flickr. If you choose Facebook or Flickr, it will prompt you to enter your account information so it can access your photos.

Scanned Image: Choosing a Scanned Image will open up your computer's program associated with an attached scanner. You may scan a document or photo to be inserted into the notes.

Links Group

Link: When writing notes, you might have information from external websites or from within other notes you have taken. That's when the Link tool may be used. To link, highlight the text you want to link and then click the Link tool. The "Text to display" will automatically be the highlighted text and then you can copy and paste a link, search the internet (it will use your default browser), search your computer to link a file, or even search through your other notebooks and notes.

Recording Group

Record Audio: Be ready when choosing this tool! On click three things happen, the toolbar changes to an audio recording studio, automatically begins recording audio, and an icon of a .WAV file named after the page will be inserted into your notes. This comes in handy if you are an auditory learner or you want to speak your thoughts to be typed at a later date. Record Audio is useful for students to record lectures to listen to later.

Record Video: Extremely similar to Record Audio, Record Video simply takes video from your computer's webcam.

Time Stamp Group

Date: Clicking Date will simply enter the current date.

Time: Similarly, Time will enter your current time.

Date & Time: This tool will enter today's date and time.

Pages Group

Page Templates: Page Templates can be a huge time saver, if you do anything requiring a common format, such as taking notes daily for college classes. Clicking the Page Templates tool will open a drop-down menu where you can choose from various template types.

Note: Choosing a template will make a new page. The last option, Page Templates…, will open up a sidebar that breaks down each template group into a list of templates to choose from.

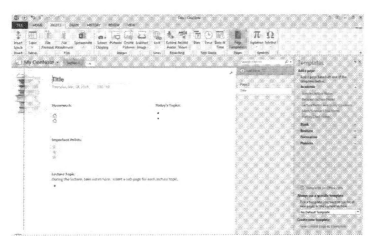

The example template shown above is "Detailed Lecture Notes". It includes homework tags, bullet points for the topics covered during the class, tags for important points of the lecture, and even tips for making a new sub-page for each lecture topic covered.

Symbols Group

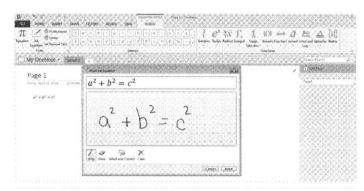

Equation: With this tool you have a variety of common math equations to choose from such as the area of a circle and the Pythagorean Theorem. They will look like this: $A = \pi r^2$ or $a^2 + b^2 = c^2$, respectively. Once you're working with the Equation tool, you have many options to choose from to either customize an equation or create new equations. Each of the Equation Tools in the Design Tab can take some getting used to, but come in handy for anything needing easily-readable equations. In addition, you can write equations by hand or with your mouse and OneNote will create typed equations for you!

Symbol: Clicking the Symbols tool opens a drop-down box of common and recently used symbols and the ability to choose from various additional symbols.

The Draw Ribbon

The Draw ribbon makes your notes stand out by pointing out information, drawing diagrams, or highlighting PDFs.

Tools group

Type: The default way of taking notes is by typing them, so this should be selected unless you take notes differently. Remember to reselect this option when you want to return to typing your notes.

Lasso Select: This tool allows you to select things by drawing around them and makes an easier alternative to holding down the Shift key and clicking on items to select things. After selection, you may drag the items around the screen to organize your notes better.

Panning Hand: The panning hand allows you to click and drag to pan to another part of your page, which is particularly helpful if your page(s) are long. It becomes too much hassle scrolling through.

Eraser: Selecting the Eraser tool opens a dropdown menu so that you can choose the size of the eraser you would like. Then simply click and drag over shapes and/or drawings to erase. You can also use the Stroke Eraser which lets you erase entire stroke marks made by the pen and highlighter tools. Note: Eraser does not erase type, only drawings and shapes.

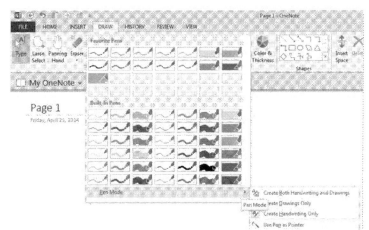

Drawing tool list box: The default list box has a few choices of pen color, thicknesses, and highlighter colors. Opening the dropdown menu gives you even more choices of sizes and colors. Use the Pen Mode to indicate what you will use the drawing tools for: handwriting and drawing, drawing only, or handwriting only. Another option is to use the pen as a pointer. This allows you to draw an arrow to parts of your notes that will disappear after a short period. This is useful if your notes are part of a presentation or you are explaining your notes to a colleague or fellow student.

Color & Thickness: easily customize pens and highlighters to the color and thickness you want

Shapes Group:

Shapes: Draw basic lines, shapes, and even graph axes. You can enter "Drawing Mode" if you will be using the drawing tools and not typing text for long periods. This removes the possibility of accidentally clicking on a text box and switching functions. If you're drawing shapes, you can snap them to the grid for a nicer layout.

Edit Group

Insert Space: This is the same tool from the Insert Tab, Insert Space tool. Click and drag to create a space between your notes.

Delete: Clicking this simply deletes drawings, highlighted text, or selected note boxes.

Arrange: Arrange your drawings into layers on the page. That is, bring a specific drawing to the front or send it backward related to other drawings on the page.

Rotate: Rotate your drawing or shape in many different directions or you can choose to flip it.

Convert Group
Ink to Text: If you're taking notes on a touch screen during a class or meeting, select the hand-written notes and then click on the Ink to Text tool. It will convert your handwriting into typed notes instantly. However, if your notes are messy you may have trouble deciphering them.

Ink to Math: Similar to Ink to Text, it will convert handwritten math formulas into nicely organized equations.

Shape drawing is available in OneNote, and you can even draw freehand shapes.

To draw:

1. Simply select the **Draw tab**. Here, you will find all the options you need to sketch.

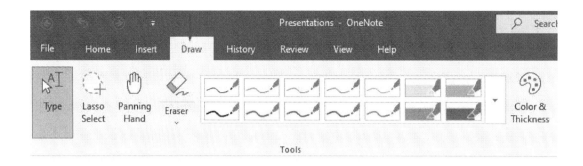

2. Choose a drawing pen from the **Tools group**.

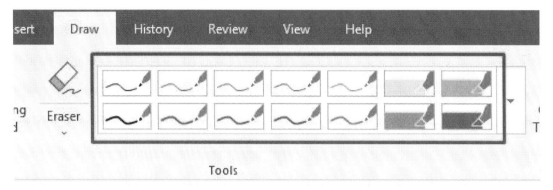

3. Click **Color & Thickness** in the **Tools group** to choose a color and thickness for your sketch.

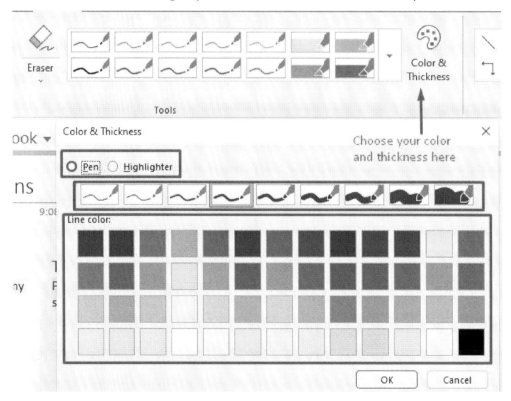

4. You can then draw with your mouse or stylus. And do not forget that you can undo your actions as you draw, provided there is an error by pressing Ctrl + Z on your keyboard.

5. When you are done drawing, switch back to the Type mode by clicking the **Type** button in the **Draw tab**.

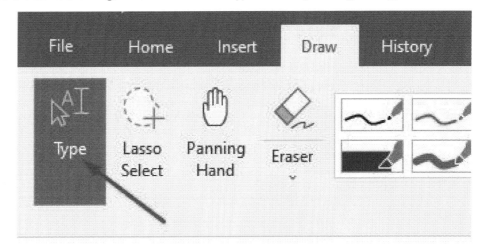

Drawing shapes

You can draw various shapes, ranging from oval to rectangle and rectangle to a straight line. There are no restrictions on what you can draw. However, what is drawn is determined by what is required and known. As a result, fundamental technical knowledge, as well as practice, are needed.

To draw:

1. Select a shape from the **Shapes group** in the **Draw tab**.

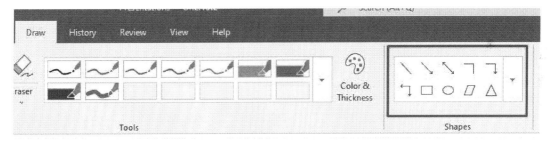

2. Now, your cursor should change to plus. Click, hold, and drag on the position you want your shape.

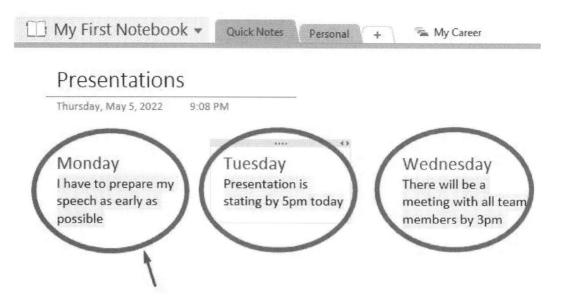

3. You can change the color and thickness of your shape by right-clicking on it and selecting **Pen Properties**.

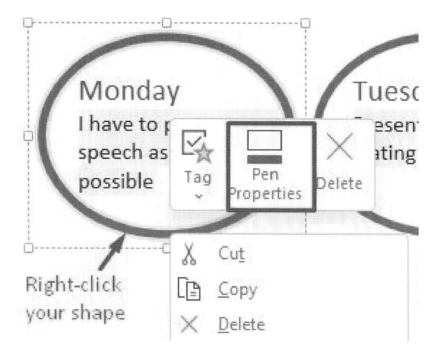

4. Proceed to choose a color and how thick you want your shape to be. You can switch between **Pen** and **Highlighter**. Then, click **OK**.

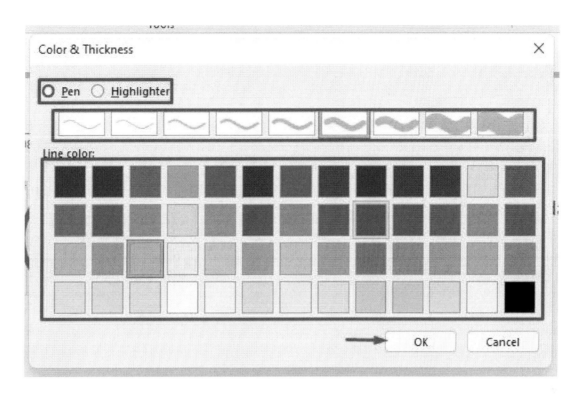

5. To be good at drawing, you must keep practicing and learning from experienced artists. There will be many mistakes here and there, but you can always use the **Undo button** or **Ctrl + Z** to reverse your actions.

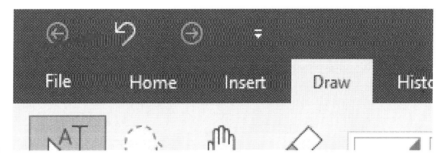

4.

The Review Ribbon

1.   2.   3. 4.

The Review ribbon doesn't have many options, but 4 out of 7 of them should be familiar to you. Spelling, Thesaurus, Translate, and Language are all tools found in the other MS Office Programs. You might have also seen the Research tool depending on which programs you frequent because surprisingly, it's not to be seen in Word.

1. **Spelling Group**

Spelling: The normal spellchecker tool.

Research: It is very intuitive even if you have never seen or used the Research tool. Clicking it will bring up a sidebar that lets you conduct searches using sources in the dropdown menu (the default is Bing search). If you highlight text before clicking on the tool, it will automatically insert the highlighted text into the search bar.

Thesaurus: Selecting the Thesaurus tool opens a sidebar where you can enter a word to check for synonyms. Alternatively, you can highlight text and then click the tool, which will automatically search for synonyms.

2. **Language Group**

Translate: The Translate tool allows you to translate your notes into another language. You can choose the language you want your notes translated to by going to the option at the bottom of the drop-down menu.

Language: Similarly, the Language tool lets you choose what language you want OneNote to proof (spellcheck) your notes and the language to use when translating handwritten notes to text.

3. **Section Group**

Password: This tool allows you to password protect things. More specifically, it will bring up a sidebar where you can create a password to secure the currently selected section tab. Please read the instructions though, as some functions are not allowed. For instance, the information contained within a protected section is unsearchable and must first be unlocked.

4. **Notes Group**

Linked Notes: The last tool in this ribbon, Linked Notes, is used while the page is docked to the desktop. Its purpose is to attach notes to the window currently open other than OneNote. This is particularly useful if you're taking notes on PDF documents or digital books.

The View Ribbon

This ribbon lets you customize your note-taking experience with a variety of different options. For instance, you can reduce distractions or allow split-screen. You can also make your digital notebook appear similar to a traditional printed notebook. Here, make the notebook comfortable.

1. **Views Group**

Normal View: This is the default view and because of this, the tool is highlighted in purple.

Full Page View: Clicking this will bring you into full page view. This removes all tabs, ribbons, and sidebars. Think of it as a "no distraction" view. Return to normal view by clicking the double-sided, diagonal arrows on the top right corner of the screen.

Dock to Desktop: This view is perfect when your notes are based on information taken from the web or another program. Dock to Desktop docks the current notes page to the side or bottom of your computer screen so that you may take notes while viewing another window simultaneously. Note: Click and drag the ellipses (...) symbol at the top of the docked notes page to change where it docks on your screen. Additionally, this view links the notes taken to whatever window it is that you have open while typing the notes. The first time docking notes, OneNote will warn you that it is doing this. You may stop taking linked notes or go to the linked notes options by clicking on the link icon on the top right-hand side of the notes page. Similar to Full Page View, click on the double-sided, diagonal arrows on the top right corner of the screen to return to normal view.

2. **Page Setup Group**

Page Color: Change the color of your pages using this tool. All colors are a light pastel so they don't distract your writing.

Rule Lines: Select this tool to open a dropdown menu that will let you give your page rule lines and make the page feel like a real notebook. Choose from the wide rule, college rule, small grid, large grid, and others. If there are rule lines on the page, you can change their color. You can also decide if you want to set rule lines as a default for all new pages opened.

Hide Page Title: Clicking this tool simply removes the title, date, and time from the page. Click again to bring it all back.

Paper Size: The Paper Size tool opens a sidebar where you can choose from a standard paper size or enter a specific height and width. For printing purposes, you may also indicate print margins. You may also save your paper size as a template.

3. Zoom Group

Zoom Out: This tool makes your page zoom out so you can see more of the notes you have entered.

Zoom In: In contrast, this tool zooms in on your page so you can look at the finer details of certain notes.

Page Width: Clicking this will zoom your page to the full width of all notes taken. For instance, if your page is wider than it is long, this tool will zoom your notes to where you can see all notes spanning the entire width of the page.

4. Window Group

New Window: This tool opens up a new window identical to the current OneNote window, which includes notes and all. You might use this if you want to take notes on multiple pages at once or create two versions of the same page. Remember that these versions can be viewed with the History tab.

New Docked Window: This tool also opens up a new window identical to the current window. Only the new window will be docked to your desktop and take linked notes.

Send to OneNote Tool: One of the most useful tools is Send to OneNote. By default, this window opens when OneNote starts. What it does is give you the ability to take screen clippings, insert a printout of a document, and create new quick notes to put into OneNote. We have already covered screen clippings and printouts, but not quick notes. Quick notes opens up a notepad-style window where you can easily type notes on the go. On exit of the window, a pop-up will let you know where they were saved: to a special Quick Notes folder which can be found at the bottom of your list of Notebooks.

Always on Top: Clicking this will keep your OneNote window on top of any other window you might have open. While not very useful in full page or normal view, it works well if you need to have OneNote and another window in a split screen situation.

Chapter 2: **Taking Notes**

Pictures

This feature enables you to add pictures to your work. Images can be added directly from your computer storage or the internet.

To insert pictures:

- On OneNote, click the **Insert tab** and choose either **Pictures** or **Online Pictures**. Clicking **Pictures** will enable you to upload pictures from your computer storage while clicking **Online Pictures** will enable you to upload pictures from the internet.

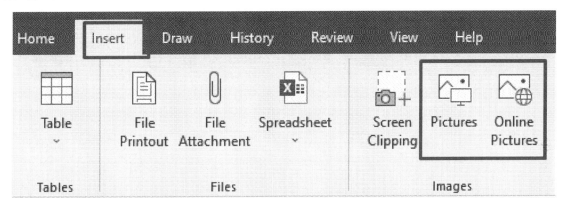

- Click on either depending on where you want to insert the picture. Then, locate the picture.

Adjusting Image Size

After inserting a screen clip or picture, you might need to resize it. Adjusting your image to the correct size makes your note look clean and friendly.

To resize an image:

- Click the uploaded image once.
- With the bounding box around the image, you can extend by simply clicking, holding, and dragging one of the small boxes.

Screen clipping taken: 5/4/2022 11:11 AM

Conversion Of Images To Text

Have you ever come across an image that you fell in love with the text on it, then decided to go through the stress of typing these texts not minding how lengthy it is, thereby wasting precious time that could have been invested in more profitable ventures. With your OneNote app, this particular action could be accomplished within a split second by utilizing the OneNote app feature of Optical Character Recognition (OCR).

To perform this unique task, follow these simple steps:

- Insert the image having the text you wish to copy in your note.
- Right-click the image, then select **Copy Text from Picture**.

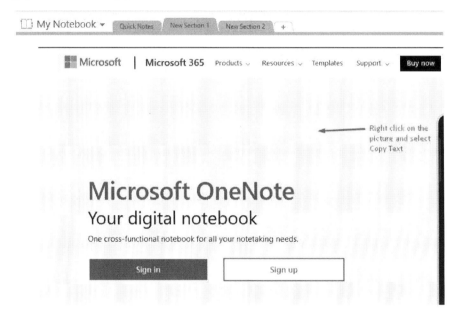

- Finally, right-click any space on your screen and select **Paste** to reveal the text content you just copied.

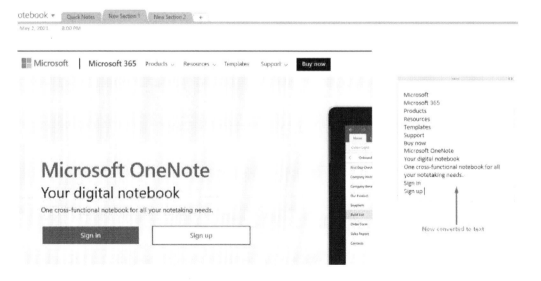

502

- It doesn't just end there. You can also search for text on an image. After you must have uploaded the photo containing the text, on your **search bar**, type the text content you are looking for in the uploaded image. OneNote highlights the search content as you type.

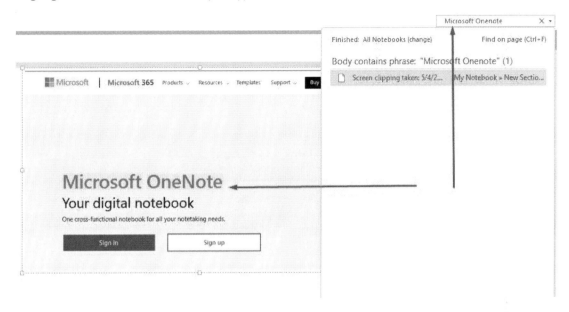

Tables

OneNote is designed for quick and easy content capture, and that philosophy extends into tables.

To insert a table, you can click on the " **Insert**" tab from the menu, click on the "**Table**" tool and draw out the width and height of your table. Please note that this is not an Excel spreadsheet, so there's no calculation in there.

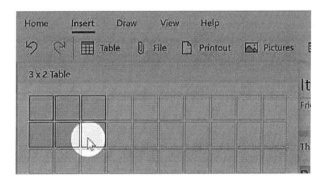

Oftentimes, you don't know how big the table is going to be until you start to work with it. However, there's a quicker and easier way to create a table in OneNote. Simply type a word and then press the **tab key**; OneNote will automatically turn what you typed into a table. Type something into the second cell, then press the tab again to add another column to your table. Keep doing that until you've defined all of the headings on your table, and once you're ready, press the "**Enter**" key to insert a new row, and you can keep adding new rows by pressing enter from the last cell of the last row.

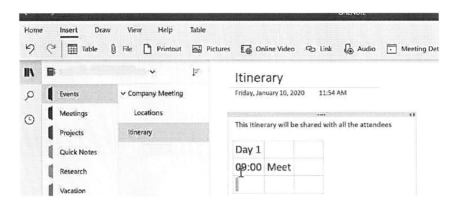

When you click on a table, the table toolbar appears. Click on it to add more columns or rows, to delete columns, rows, and even the whole table at once. You can also add a background color to individual cells.

The table tools in OneNote are simple and easy to use but not as advanced as tools like Excel and Word. If you want to share a live excel spreadsheet that can be edited by multiple contributors in real-time, we recommend sharing the excel file via team SharePoint or one drive.

If you have a table prepared somewhere else, such as Microsoft Excel, for example, you can just copy it from Excel and paste it here, and you will have that table created. However, this will appear as a table with no calculation here, even though it came from Excel, but you can use it to store your finished calculations in OneNote just by copy-pasting it.

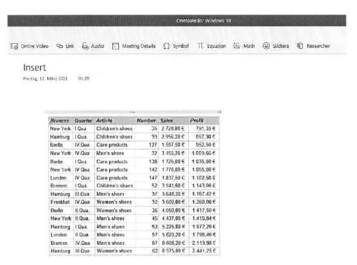

Please note that OneNote 2019 has the functionality of using excel tables within OneNote, but the OneNote for windows 10 version doesn't.

Converting A Table To An Excel Spreadsheet

You can utilize the Convert to Excel Spreadsheet tool to give yourself greater flexibility when dealing with tables in OneNote.

To convert a table to an Excel spreadsheet:

- Click anywhere on your table to activate the **Table tab**.
- Then, click the **Table tab** and click **Convert to Excel Spreadsheet**.

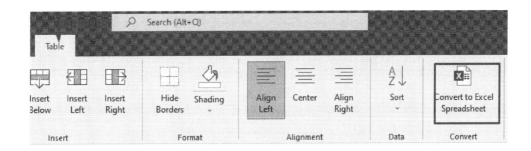

- You are then shown an Excel spreadsheet. Click **Edit** on the spreadsheet to fully open Excel.

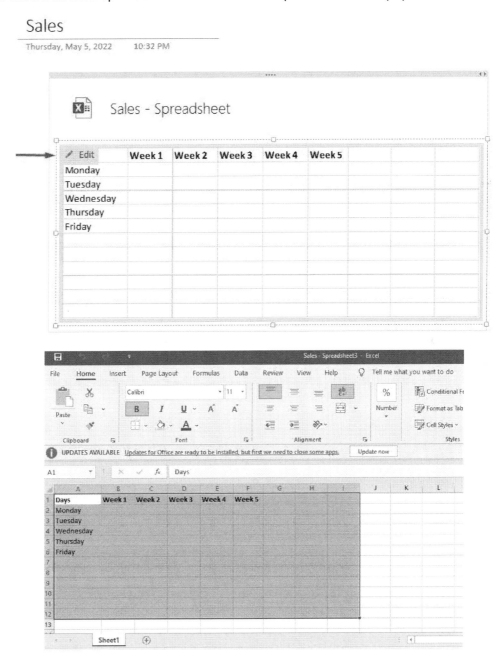

Write Notes

Working with Notes

Your notebook is unlike the conventional notebook, where you can only write notes. Think of your notebook as an electronic noticeboard where you can pin pictures, sticky notes, and other media. The block where you add a note is called "Note Container." You can click outside it too, in fact, anywhere to add a new note.

You can perform a lot of functions by selecting the notes. You can resize the notes if you feel that the current ones are taking up more than the required space. Just point to the right side of the Note Container, and when you see the resizing handle (double-headed arrow), hold and drag the mouse left or right to make it smaller or bigger.

You can get to a point where you might feel that the work is looking messy. At this point, you can also change the note order to reorganize your notes. Simply right-click on the note, and select from the list of options you'll see under "Order" to adjust the order of your notes.

Moving and Copying Pages and Sections

If you only want to move a page within the same section, it is as simple as dragging and dropping it where you would like to move it. If you need to copy it to a different section or entirely different notebook, the process is slightly more complicated.

Select the pages you want to be copied or moved by clicking them while holding Ctrl on your keyboard. Then, from the File menu, select 'Move or Copy.' You can also right-click (tap and hold on touch screen devices) and select an option from the drop-down menu.

A window will appear that you will be able to choose where you want to move the page(s) to. There will be a list of sections with the current notebook as well as a list of all available notebooks with a '+' sign next to their names. You can click the '+' to expand the list of sections in every listed notebook and select the final destination for the page(s).

When you have found the appropriate location, click either 'Move' or 'Copy' in the dialogue box to confirm the action.

In a similar fashion, you can move the sections. Right-click the title tab of the section you wish to move or copy and select the 'Move or Copy' option. A very similar window will pop out, and you can select the destination notebook.

Merging Sections

You might realize at a later time that you need to merge similar sections to make your work more organized. This can be done easily, but you need to be careful as there is no way to reverse it, and you'll have to segregate it later on manually. If you ever want to merge two sections, right-click the name of the tab of the section you want to combine and select 'Merge into Another Section.' The window with the same structure will appear, and you will be able to select another section you want to merge the original one with. The pages of the merged section will only appear in their new location, and you'll have to delete the copy of the section you merged.

How to Manage Unfiled Notes

Sometimes, you may take notes in a hurry and jot down information randomly; these make unfiled notes (also known as quick notes or side notes). This can also include information OneNote has saved from Web browsers.

These notes are available separately in a section called "Quick Notes" (It was called "Unfiled notes" before the 2013 version). You can either leave the notes there or move them to a more meaningful location of your choice.

To check if you or OneNote have saved any unfiled notes, follow these steps:

1. By clicking on the name of your current notebook, open the notebook pane. You will be able to see it on the left side, right below the ribbon. (This step can be skipped if the Notebook pane is already docked to the screen).

2. Click "Quick Notes," at the bottom of the Notebook pane.

3. Click the page tabs on the right in the Quick Notes section to browse through any notes collected in that section.

If you don't want to organize the notes in this section just yet, you can always browse through and search for any notes you might need. The Quick Notes section works just like any other section of OneNote. But leaving random pages in this section will not make your work look organized, so you would need to eventually move these notes or some of the notes to their relevant location.

The process of moving and copying unfiled notes is the same as those of other notes. You can simply discard the notes which you made in a hurry and no longer feel the need for them. The process of deleting data is explained below.

Deleting Data

If you ever want to delete an entire notebook completely from your local drive or online storage, you will have to do it outside of OneNote. The program itself doesn't offer this option, so you will have to locate the physical folder in which the notebook is stored and delete it manually, just like you would delete any other folder.

Removing sections and pages is simple and straightforward. Right-click the name tab and select delete. After the confirmation, these will be moved to the OneNote Recycle Bin and can be restored for the duration of 60 days.

Handwriting Notes and Conversion to Text

You can handwrite notes if you have a touch-enabled computer, pen device, or tablet. You can even write all your notes in the handwritten form if you so prefer. In order to handwrite, select a pen, and then drag your finger or pen device on the screen or pad. The mouse can also be used to draw, but the results are often unsatisfactory.

You can handwrite by following these simple steps:

4. Click on the Draw tab on the ribbon.

5. Select a pen in the Tools group from the Pens gallery.

6. You can now use your finger, pen device, or mouse to handwrite a note by dragging.

You have two modes to choose from; Create Handwriting Only mode or Create Both Handwriting and Drawings.

Converting your handwritten note to text is fairly simple. All you have to do is select the note you want to convert to text. Select "Ink to Text" in the Convert group, and your note will be converted to text. A quick way to convert the complete page is to make sure that no notes on the page are selected. Clicking the "Ink to Text" button will convert the complete page in this case.

Constructing Outlines

Outlines are a list of important topics on a particular subject. In an outline, the topics are divided into different levels. The first-level topics are not shown as being subordinate, whereas the sublevel topics are shown as subordinates. OneNote 2013 offers the paragraph handle to help construct outlines. The paragraph handle appears when you move the pointer over a topic in the outline list (on the left). You can follow these steps to construct an outline:

Changing outline level (indentation): You can change the topic's outline level by dragging the paragraph handle to the left or right. Dragging it to the right will lower the outline level while dragging it to the left will raise it. This can also be done through shortcuts. Pressing Tab or clicking the Increase Indent Position button on the Home tab will move the topics to the lower level. In order to raise a subtopic to a higher level, you can press Shift+Tab or click on the Decrease Indent Position button.

Moving a topic up or down in the outline: Dragging the paragraph handle up or down will move it accordingly.

Selecting a Topic or Its Subtopic: Just click on the paragraph handle

Collapsing or expanding a topic's subtopics: Double-click the paragraph handle. Pressing the Alt+Shift+Plus sign to expand subtopics or the Alt+Shift+Minus sign to collapse.

Selecting Topics at different levels: Click on Select from the shortcut menu that will appear after you right-click the paragraph handle. A submenu will appear, and you can choose the level. You can now select all the topics on the same level to format them.

Working with Subpages

Subpages help a lot in organizing your work. For example, you can write the details of a project in subpages and maintain a summary on the main page. Subpages can be maintained at two levels. You can simply add new Subpages or convert the current pages into subpages. Right-clicking on the page in the page list will give an option to "make subpage." You can do this with either the new pages you might have created or the existing ones. Since the subpage is always added below an existing page, the first page of a section can't be made a subpage. Subpages can be renamed just like pages.

When you right-click on a subpage, options will appear, which you can use to rearrange subpages. The "Make subpage" option (which you earlier used to make a subpage) will make the subpage go down to the lower level. "Promote Subpage" will make it go to a higher level until it becomes a page. "Collapse Subpages" will make the subpages hide in a selected page. Clicking the arrow that will appear alongside it will expand the subpages again.

Preventing Auto Syncing

OneNote is programmed to sync the notebooks stored online automatically. This means that changes made on one device will be auto-imported to another device as soon as you log into the software, ensuring you have the same copy across the board. However, there are times when this can be counterproductive for you, and in such situations, you can prevent the program from performing automatic syncing.

To do this, right-click the tab of the notebook name and select 'Notebook Sync Status.' The window will appear featuring two radio buttons. One that is marked by default enables automatic syncing. Beneath it, there is the option for manual syncing. Mark 'Sync manually' and click close. Now you will only be able to sync that particular notebook manually by right-clicking its name tab and selecting 'Sync This Notebook Now,' or you can also use the previously described window.

Exporting Notes

While OneNote does not have a 'Save' option, there is an 'Export' option under the File menu. You begin by selecting pages, sections, or an entire notebook you wish to export and then clicking the option.

A new window appears, allowing you to select the format that your data will be exported. There is a difference between exporting entire notebooks as opposed to exporting pages or sections.

For the notebooks, you will be able to choose between the OneNote package file, XML Paper Specification, and Portable Document Format (.pdf).

For sections and pages, apart from these three, you will also have additional options: OneNote 2010-2013 Section, OneNote 2007 Section, Word Document (.docx), Word 97-2003 Document (.doc), and Single File Web Page (.mht).

Understanding and Configuring OneNote Options

Not unlike other Office applications, OneNote also has a rather extensive Options section that can be accessed from the File menu. These options mostly relate to general program settings (appearance) as well as language options and some more advanced settings.

In the 'General' section, you will be able to setup a default font type, size, and color, as well as your name, initials, etc.

'Proofing' section offers options for handling typing errors, auto-correction, and similar options. The window is quite like the one found in MS Word.

Under 'Save & Backup,' you can change the default saving locations and handle how often the data is auto-saved.

Using the 'Send to OneNote' section, you can decide if you'd like the content from other applications and your screenshots to be imported into OneNote without asking automatically or if you'd prefer to be asked by the program every time (this is the default option).

'Audio and Video' tab will let you adjust recording settings. These options will be discussed in depth later.

Under 'Language,' you can switch between different installed languages and determine how and when they are used.

Finally, the 'Advanced' section allows you to set up some more complex options that are a bit too detailed to describe but include things like battery optimization (for battery-powered devices), handling passwords, text recognition, etc.

Note: If you ever want to protect any particular section with a password, you can do this by using the Review tab and selecting 'Password.' A window will appear, asking you to input your password twice (they have to match). After inputting your password and clicking 'OK,' you will be asked if you want to delete the old backups not protected by the password. Select 'Yes' for maximum protection. All backups created afterward will be protected.

You can remove the password using the same process and click 'Remove Password.' You will need to input the password to confirm, and after that, the section will no longer be protected.

Some Other Useful Options

You have the option of changing the color of your notebook (or some pages or section) depending on what you're creating the notebook for. This can also help you organize the book as you can highlight some of the pages you feel are most important. Go to the section of the notebook and page which you want to change the color for. Click the View tab, and you'll see the option of "Page Color" in the Page Setup Group. You can select any background from the list and following the same steps, can revert back to the white background.

You can also change the color of the Section tabs to organize your notebook. You will see an option of "Section Color" once you right-click the section you want to change the color for. You can then select from a series of options, and your section tab will change color accordingly. You can change the color of all the sections or some selected ones, as per your preference. The default color of the section tab is light grey.

Screen Clippings

This feature enables you to take a screenshot of your screen. While working on your computer system, it is often possible to come across pieces of information that could be important for future use. These pieces of information can range from a notification that pops up to a web page; it could even be breaking news and many others. With your OneNote app, a screenshot of such pieces of information can be made and stored until it is needed.

To screen clip:

1. Open and set the information you wish to capture in a good view on your computer screen.

2. Open OneNote and click the **Insert tab**. Then, click **Screen Clipping** in the **Images group**.

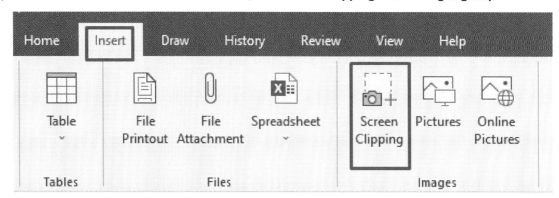

3. OneNote then minimizes itself and brings you back to the pieces of information which you have already set up for capturing in step 1 above.

4. Now, click, hold and drag the cross-cursor to select the screen area you wish to capture.

Finally, your screenshot appears as an image on your note and, at the same time, is automatically copied to the window's clipboard. You can also use the screenshot on another page of your note or an entirely different app. This is achieved by simply pressing **Ctrl + V** on your keyboard to paste your screenshot on another page of your note or any other app.

Audio And Video

Here is another unique feature of your OneNote app. It enables you to add audio and video files to your work. With this feature, you could express yourself better and differently uniquely.

To record:

1. On your **Insert tab**, click one of these; **Record Audio** or **Record Video,** depending on which you wish to add to your note.

2. A new tab then comes up, **Recording Tab**, which contains all the tools you need as you record; you have a play, pause, stop, rewind, fast forward, and the counter.

510

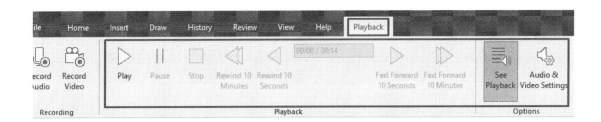

3. As you record, the counter reads. Once you are done recording, press stop, and the record will be added directly to your note.

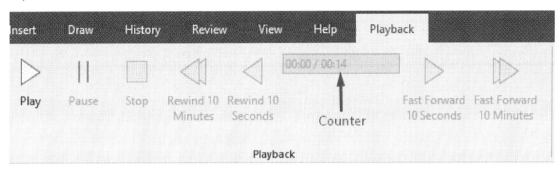

Using Tags

Tags are visual markers that can be added to any part of your note to keep you reminded of an essential part of the content when browsing through it. The best part of these tags is that they don't have limits; you can use them to your best abilities.

It can also be used to line up items in your note. We have different tag styles, and each of them serves different purposes.

To use tags:

1. Select the **Home tab**, then go to the **Tags group**. All the tags we have here are for different uses.

2. Click the **To Do** tag in the Tags group. This brings up a box where you can add some text about the task you want to do. Type some text; press **Enter** on your keyboard to move to the following line, where you can add more tasks that you wish to do. You can add as many tasks as possible to your To-do list.

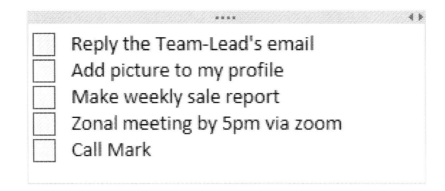

3. You can prioritize each of those tasks when you tick/untick the boxes in front of these tasks you already entered.

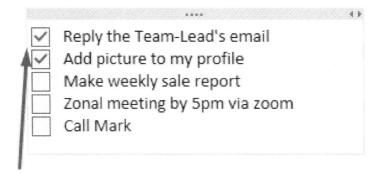

4. You can change the icons in front of your task to a different one from the Tags group.

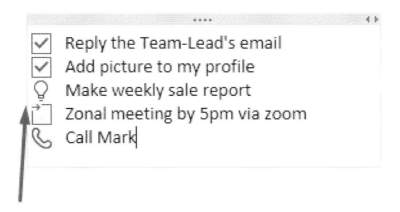

The Outlook Task

This type of tag on your OneNote app enables you to organize an outlook task that can be used to track tasks in your outlook and get you reminded of such tasks. With this feature, you are sure to manage deadlines for different works with ease and still remember things on your To-do list. Quite interesting how your OneNote app can perform vast complex tasks to make your work easier.

To set your outlook task:

1. Ensure your cursor is in the front of the task.

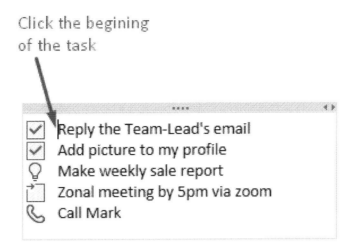

Click the begining of the task

☑ Reply the Team-Lead's email
☑ Add picture to my profile
♀ Make weekly sale report
↱ Zonal meeting by 5pm via zoom
☎ Call Mark

2. Click **Outlook Tasks** in the **Tags group**. You can then select a date from the list or choose **Custom** to set your date.

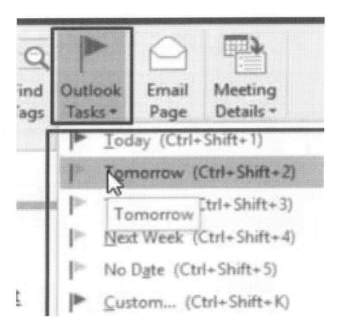

How do you ascertain that your tasks have been successfully scheduled on Outlook? This is what you do:

- Open your **Outlook** application.
- Click the **Task View** button to display recently created tasks on the OneNote app.

Removing Tags

You can easily remove tags when you place your cursor in front of the task; then, you press the **Backspace key** on the keyboard.

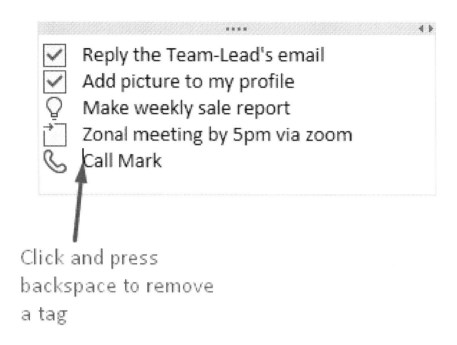

Click and press
backspace to remove
a tag

Finding Tags

How do you find these tags without looking through pages by pages or sections by sections on OneNote? Your OneNote app was designed to pop your search results in a very easy-to-read and summarized manner. In this way, you do not need to waste your precious time scrolling through pages word by word, looking for tags. This means that you have successfully evaded the manual method of searching to locate tags.

To locate tags very promptly:

1. On the **Home tab**, click **Find Tags**.

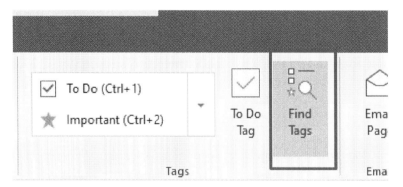

2. On the right-hand side of your OneNote, the **Tags Summary** pane pops out. Click on the **Group tags by** the box. Then, select how you want your tags to be sorted.

514

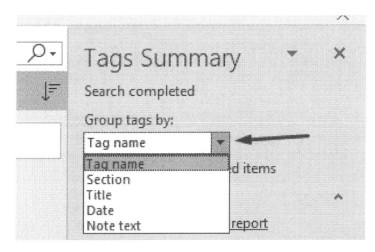

3. You can also use the **Search** option in the **Tags Summary** pane to narrow down the tag(s) you are finding.

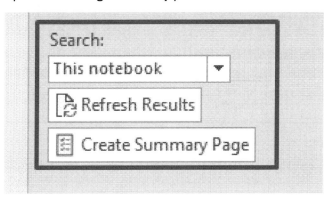

To-do List

To-do lists are reminders of things that need to be accomplished within a certain timeframe. Team to-do lists are very useful in keeping all team members apprised of tasks and deadlines.

This is another of the great features of OneNote. It has built-in functionality that enables the creation of To-Do lists that are not only actionable but can also be accompanied by a message or a link, or an attachment.

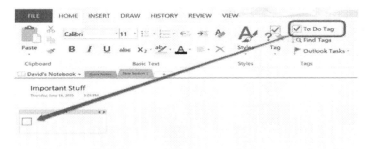

Place the cursor where you want the To-Do list to begin, head to the Home tab, and click on the To-Do button. Start adding tasks to your list.

For every particular task on the checklist, you can list the actions that need to be taken to accomplish it and then tick it as done.

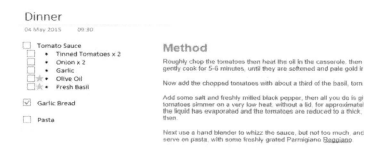

To create the bulleted list within a checklist, press Control +. Control +2 will add a star, while Control + 1 will pair a test like the one above with a check box.

You can also embed files on OneNote to save time when you are doing the task. Rather than going back to your PC and locating a document or file, you may need just embed it within the To Do list, and you will just have to click on it when you require it.

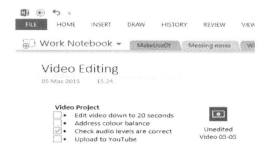

There is so much you can accomplish with the To Do lists, including integrating with the Outlook and Calendar apps for efficient management of tasks and reminders of when they are due.

Note Templates

What do you do with your page templates? These templates are designed in such a way that it enables you to do the following;

- Give your notebook a better background.
- Apply colors to the pages of your notebook.
- Give your notebook a more uniform layout and a consistent look.

To use these templates:

1. Click the **Insert tab,** then click **Page Templates**.

2. The template pane pops up on the right-hand side of your screen. To expand each category of the individual templates to see more options, click on the small arrows next to the category.

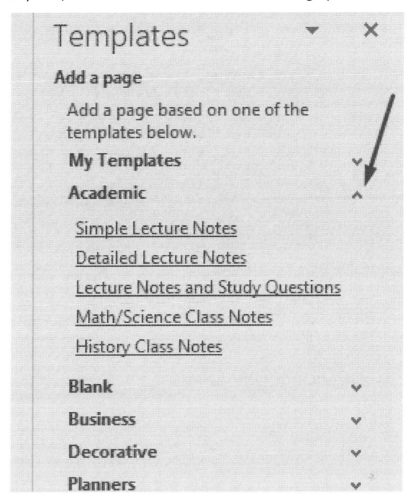

It is pertinent you know that there are several templates on OneNote that can be used in different areas of life. Clicking on any of these templates requires you to work on a separate new page that would be automatically created. In summary, all you have to do is to:

1. Click on the section you want your template to be applied to.

2. Click on the template you want to use, after which a new page automatically comes up.

3. However, you might mistakenly select a template you don't wish to use; all you have to do is choose another template and delete the formerly created page.

4. Explore all these templates to see how they can be helpful to you.

Also, you might be too good and would want to make a template of your own; all you need to do is;

1. Create and design a page the way you want it.

2. Finally, click **Save the current page as a template** in the template pane. This automatically creates a new template titled **My Templates**.

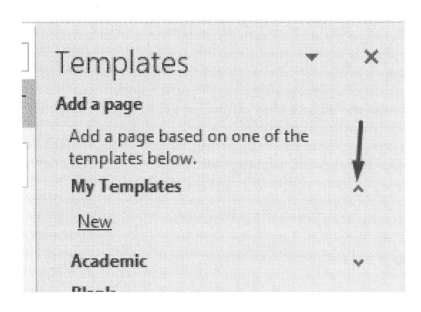

Click on it to select your newly created templates whenever you want to use them.

BONUS
MICROSOFT TEAMS

Introduction

Microsoft Teams is a collaborative communicational network, integrated with continuous workplace conversation, video meetings, data storage (including file sharing) and application. It's a platform that brings together interactions, ongoing chat, phone calls, meetings, file information, and applications in one location. Users should use any enterprise-grade security tool so that they can work efficiently with others.

Teams are nothing more than an application that lets users gather a team, work together and use chat (discussions) instead of emails; and networks instead of just files and directories. The software integrates with the Office 365 branch management platform and features plugins that can be incorporated with non-Microsoft apps. Microsoft Teams is a rival to products like Slack and is an improvement and upgrade course from Microsoft Skype to Enterprise.

Microsoft unveiled Teams at a conference in New York and released the software globally on March 14, 2017. It was developed during the company's internal hackathon and is currently headed by Brian MacDonald, Microsoft's corporate vice president.

Teams have a workspace that allows users and their team members to edit their work files safely at the same time likes, mentions, and reply with just one button. Teams provide a forum where users and their teams can make their own workspace by inserting notes, connecting websites, incorporating apps, and customizing their experience in the cloud without location boundaries. Microsoft Teams makes users more successful by providing them with all the features they need, including chat, audio/video calls, files and directories, meetings, and more.

Microsoft Teams makes use of a directory called Azure Active Directory (Azure AD) to store identity information. Teams also connect with other programs inside Office 365; e.g. when you build a team, a SharePoint Online site and an Exchange Online Group mailbox are given to each member. Persistent chat functionality is supported by a chat interface that communicates with the Office 365 substrate and provides several of the built-in Office 365 features, such as archiving and eDiscovery, for data sharing in teams. Teams will have a call and meeting interface built on the next generation cloud-based platform already used by Skype and Skype for companies.

Chapter 1: **Understanding Microsoft Teams**

Installing Microsoft Teams

You can use Teams in three significant ways: using a web-based app, installing a Client on your PC or laptop, or installing a Teams mobile app on your smartphone or tablet. Irrespective of whether you use Teams, the principles remain the same.

First, let's log in through the web-based system. Now, install the application on your desktop.

To sign in to the Teams web-based version, follow these steps:

1. Log in to your most preferred browser and type in this URL ***https://teams.microsoft.com***.

2. Sign in using the account details you used when you were registering for the Office 365 trial.

3. When you see the option to download Teams, or use the Web App, select 'Use the Web App Link' instead of the initial option. Many people are only using this web-based platform to access Teams, yet I prefer the Teams Client that I downloaded and installed on my Personal Computer. I discover it's a lot more functional and better blends with several devices like my phone call headset and my video call webcam.

To install a Teams application on your Windows laptop or desktop, execute these processes:

1. Log in to your most preferred browser and type in this URL (***https://teams.microsoft.com)***. If you have not signed in to the web service from the previous set of measures, you will be prompted to sign in. If you've already signed in, the Teams web app will be displayed on your browser.

2. Sign in to the Teams site by entering the password you created if you are not already signed in. When you sign in to the Teams site for the first time, you will be presented with the choice of installing a Teams client or proceed with the web app. We continued with the web app in the previous set of steps. Here, we're going to install the mobile client.

3. Select the profile icon that shows at the upper right corner and select Open the Mobile App.

4. Save the file on your computer. You can set the destination on your hard disk where files are downloaded from your internet browser. By default, files are typically set to download to the Downloads folder where all downloads are saved. If you can't find the file you downloaded, confirm your web browser configuration settings to see where the files you downloaded are located.

5. Once the Teams configuration file has been downloaded, launch and execute the script. After a couple of moments, a pop-up box requesting you to log in will appear .

6. Type your username and press the sign-in button. If you've already signed in to the Teams with your internet browser, you won't be asked for your password anymore. The Teams Client loads and let you know that there's an ultimate phase in having Teams set up and linked to the Office.

Select 'Let's Do It' to start, then press yes to enable Teams adjust your machine. Teams must work in the background to connect to the Office on your system and then load the Teams program. Congratulations to you! Now you've got teams working on your local machine.

Setting Up Microsoft Teams

To create a new team, you must have the right to create Microsoft 365 groups. For governance reasons, in most organizations, the permission to create a team is granted only to a group of people. If you can execute the following steps, this means you've got the applicable rights:

1. Open **the** Teams window**;**

1. **Click** on the **Join or create a team** link or alternatively on the **gear** icon (⚙);

2. **Click** on the Create a team button.

At this point, the team creation window will open:

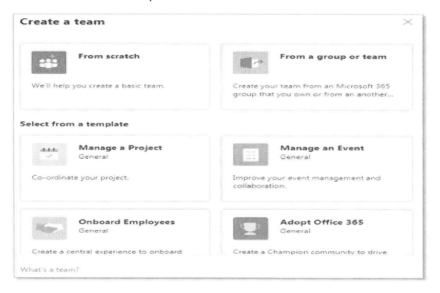

Let us create a team *from scratch* first. We will get back to *From a group or team* option later. As shown in the figure, Microsoft Teams also offers several ready-to-use templates from which we can create a team. When we choose the first option, we are presented with the following window:

522

What kind of team will this be?   ✕

Private
People need permission to join

Public
Anyone in your org can join

Org-wide
Everyone in your organisation automatically joins

Private teams are restricted to a specific group of people. For example, the 'Corporate Communications' team is open only to employees from the Communications Department. To access the team, the owner must add you as a member.

Public teams are open to everyone in the organization.

Org-wide teams are essentially global teams, where everyone is automatically made a member. These teams can be used as an extension of the corporate intranet, or when the intranet is down, to communicate with all the employees.

For now, we are going to create a private team:

1. Give a name to your **team**. For example, if you choose to name your team "Microsoft Teams Deployment Project," the associated Microsoft 365 group would be "MicrosoftTeamsDeploymentProject@YourTenantDomainName," and the SharePoint website URL would be "https://YourTenantName.sharepoint.com/sites/MicrosoftTeamsDeploymentProject." Note that accented characters and spaces are simply deleted from the group name and the SharePoint URL;

2. Enter **a** description**;**

3. Click on the Create button;

Setting Up Your Account

Once the Teams layout file has been downloaded, open and run the file. After a few moments, a dialog box requesting you to sign in will pop up, as shown below.

1. Enter your username and click **Sign In**. If you have signed in previously to Teams using your net browser, you won't be asked for your password again. Once you click on Sign in, the Teams user loads, showing that there is one more step to set up Teams with Office, as illustrated below;

One more step to set up Teams with Office

Click **Let's do it**, then click **Yes** in the next screen to get everything hooked up.

Let's do it

2. Next, click on Let's do it, and then click Yes on the next screen to permit Teams to make the changes to your computer.

   Teams then work in the background to connect with Office, after which the Teams application

loads, as shown. Now, the Teams user runs on your PC.

Setting Up Video Conferencing In Microsoft Teams

This is another feature available on the Teams app where you can video call. This feature requires the Google chrome app, internet explorer or any browser to function.

- Open the team's app and go to the team or channel you want to hold the video call with.
- Select the camera icon at the bottom of the compose text bar.
- You can add a subject if you want to.
- Click Meet now to begin your conferencing (it would ask for permission to make use of your camera and microphone. Do well to grant these access).

From the toolbar, you can turn on/off your microphone and share your screen with other members of your team.

Join Meeting On Microsoft Teams

Joining a Teams meeting is a straightforward process. You can decide to join the meeting via your Outlook calendar or via your "Meeting" tab on Teams. If you are joining from the Outlook Calendar, just click on the link "Join Microsoft

Teams meeting", or if enabled, dial the toll-free or local number and type in your given conference ID number when requested.

If you are joining the meeting directly from Teams, all you need do is locate your "Meetings" tab, then click on the meeting, and finally, click the "Join" tab at the top-right corner of your screen.

Creating A Channel

Normally, teams would automatically create a general channel for you and your members but you might create some more.

- Click on the three dots besides the team name you want to create a channel for, then Tap **Add Channel**.

A window will come up. From there, input the channel name, description, and also set other privacy options you deem fit for the channel. Once you are done, click **Add** button to successfully create a channel.

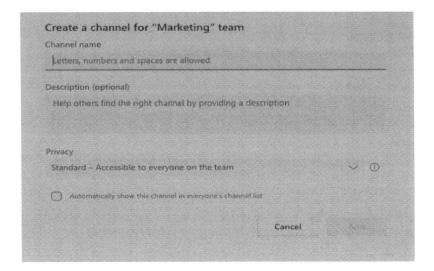

Joining By Channel

Discover the meeting you want. When a meeting is on a channel, you'll see an encouragement or an invitation to join, important substance, and who's in the meeting directly on the channel. Essentially, pick Join and afterward select **Join.**

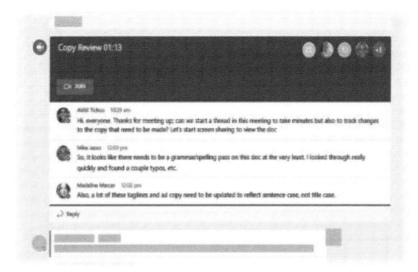

When a meeting is held on a channel, you will see an invitation to join relevant content and the host directly on the channel. Just choose **Join**.

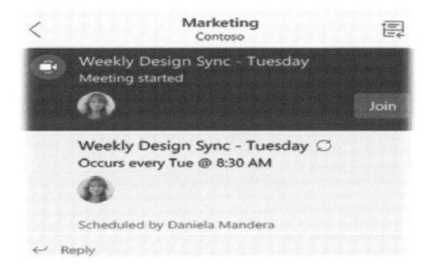

Teams Navigation Buttons

Microsoft Teams user interface may seem, at first glance, challenging for new users. Where to begin? What to do with all these icons, tabs, hyperlinks, etc.? Worry not, as we explain the function of every part of the *Teams* in the following chapters, and dive into every feature that enables effective communication and collaboration.

1. **Teams**: These are all the teams that you have been added as a member. You can click on any of them to communicate and collaborate with your colleagues.

2. Every team has **channels**. The *General* channel is created by default. You can add channels according to the topics or objectives relevant to your team.

3. Display **more options** to manage the team.

4. **Filter** your teams or channels to display only those that match the entered text in the filter text box.

5. The **Command box** and **Search box** helps you search for messages, files, and people, or type a command using the forward slash (/) character.

6. Every channel has **tabs** to help you pull together all the conversations, files, apps, and services related to the channel.

7. Access Microsoft Teams **settings** menu.

8. Manage your **profile**, add a photo, set your availability and status message, manage notifications, etc.

9. Call an instant meeting (**Meet now**).

10. When you click on the **Channel Info** icon, you can see the description and view those who are members of the channel, among other information related to the channel.

11. Display **more channel options**, such as managing channel notifications and obtaining the link to the channel.

12. In a channel, to get things going, you can **post** messages to your colleagues, or reply to existing ones (to post a new message, start a new conversation. See item #16 on this list.)

528

13. You can **react** to a message posted by someone. When you hover with your mouse over the message, many emoticons appear, from which you can choose.

14. You can **attach a file** to your message.

15. You can **reply** to a message post on the channel.

16. Start a **New Conversation**, and add an attachment, gif, or emoji to it. If you just want to reply to a message, kindly use the Reply link (see item #15 on this list).

17. The Gear icon lets you **manage your teams**, access analytics about their usage, or create a new team.

18. *Teams*' Apps store: where you can find all the **apps** available to add to your teams.

19. Here, you can find popular apps to add to your teams.

20. Manage all the **files** you shared in Microsoft Teams, and see where they are stored.

21. Manage your contacts, your voicemail, and add speed dial or make a **call**.

22. View your **calendar** and schedule, or join a meeting.

23. View and organize your **teams**.

24. See the history of your **chat**, chat with a colleague, or make audio/video calls.

25. Here, you can find all your **activities** in *Teams*

Go back to your last activity or just hover over the **back arrow** to see your recent activities.

Add Or Remove Members And Owners

1. **Add members** you want to work with on your new team. You can add up to 10,000 members;

2. **Add guests** you want to invite. If you enter email addresses with a different domain than your ***tenant***, Microsoft Teams will consider them as guests. You can add up to (number of your licensed users x 5, that is 5 guest users per licence, for your ***tenant***);

3. **Click** on the Add button;

4. **Click** on the Close button;

By now, you've seen your newly created team alongside all the other teams:

Removing Owners, Members, Or Guests From A Team

Removing members and guests happens in the same "Manage team" window:

1. Open **the** Teams window**;**

2. **Click** on the **3-dot menu (...)** (More options) to the right of the team's name;

3. Click **on** Manage team**;**

4. Open **the** Members tab;

5. Search **for the** member **you want** to remove**;**

6. **Click** on the **X sign**, to the right of the rectangle containing the member's name, to remove her/him. There is no warning message before actually removing a member. So, you have to be sure to remove the right person.

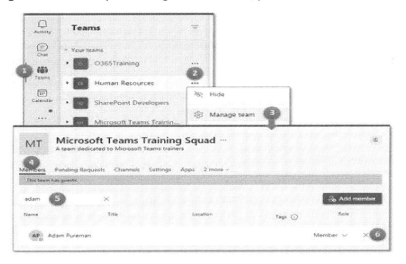

Make Changes To Teams

As a team owner, if for a reason, or before you make the team available, you need to change its name, its description, and/or the way it is accessed, follow these steps:

Open **the** Teams window;

1. **Click** on the **3-dot menu (...)** (More options) to the right of the team's name you wish to edit;

2. **Click** on the **Edit team** option;

3. Enter **the** new name;

4. Enter **the** new description (optional);

5. **Choose** the **type of privacy** (private or public);

6. **Click on** the "Done" button to complete the task.

Troubleshooting Microsoft Teams

Since the release of Teams, there have been some common issues and simple steps to resolve them:

- The Office version issues
- Turn it OFF, then ON again

Sometimes, the simple solution is the best one, and in most cases, simply removing the Teams product license for such a person, saving, then re-using the license will do wonders.

- Clear up the cache

Removing a cache when you want to get Teams performing is never a bad idea.

Simply Close the Teams app, and ensure the process will stop in the Task Manager.

- Run credential manager

This is the final tip that will help if you notice authentication errors when people try to access the desktop app.

- Click Start, then type Run
- Put in rundll32.exe keymgr.dll,KRShowKeyMgr

In the stored passwords and usernames, find themsteams_adalsso credentials and click "remove" on each username or password.

View Meetings

Pick a calendar to see your meetings and appointments during the day or week of work. Such appointments will stay synchronized within the Outlook calendar.

Pick a meeting invite to view what such a meeting is all about, who will attend and respond to the meeting.

Schedule A Meeting

Follow this procedure to schedule new meetings:

1. **Open** the **Calendar** window;

2. **Click** on the + New meeting button;

3. Enter **a** meeting title**;**

4. **Add** required **attendees**. To add **optional attendees**, **click** on the **+ Optional** link. To invite people outside of your organization, **enter** their **email addresses**;

5. **Set** a **date** and **hour** for the meeting;

6. **Enter** a **description** for the meeting;

7. Set *to* True *or* Flase *the* response options*:* Request responses *and* allow forwarding*.*

8. **Set** the *Require registration* option to *None* if you want to schedule an ordinary meeting. For a meeting with registration (webinar), set the option to either *for people in your org* or *Everyone*.

9. **Click** on the Send button to send the invitation.

To see people's availability, **click** on the **Scheduling Assistant** at the top of the **New meeting** window:

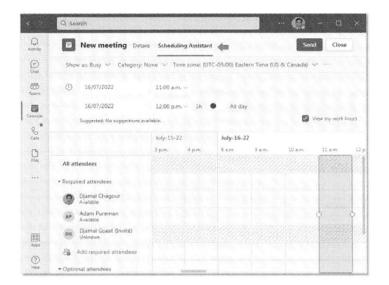

How To Record Your Teams Meeting

Recording a meeting can be extremely useful. You can review what was discussed, or just make it available to colleagues who could not attend.

Your Microsoft Teams administrator has to have already turned on the **Allow cloud recording** option in **Teams** Admin Centre. You will then have to join the meeting to record it:

On the meeting control bar, **click** on the **3-dot menu (…)** (More options);

1. Click **on** Start recording**.**

When you start recording, a red-filled circle appears to the left of the meeting's duration, and a notification bar is shown below the controls toolbar, letting you know you're recording the meeting:

The other participants will as well receive a notification, informing them that the meeting is being recorded:

To **stop recording**, **click** again on the **3-dot menu (…)** (More options), then click on the Stop recording button.

- Cloud recording must be enabled in Microsoft Teams admin centre in order to make any recording;

Guests and participants from other organizations cannot start the recording of a meeting.

Chapter 3: **Other Microsoft Teams Operations**

How To Customize Microsoft Teams

Changing Microsoft Teams' Themes

For the time being, ***Teams*** comes in three flavours: default, dark, and high contrast. To change the application theme, head to your profile picture and perform the following steps:

1. **To open the menu, click** on the **three dots** to the left of your profile picture;

2. **Click** on the **Settings** option;

3. In the settings window, **click** on **General**;

4. **Choose** a **theme** to apply;

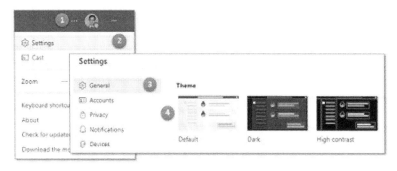

Here is what the dark theme looks like:

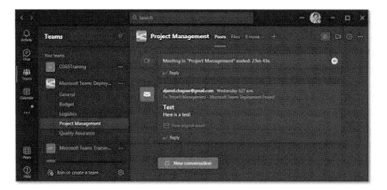

*Changing **Teams'** Desktop App Language*

There are times when we need to change the language the ***Teams*** displays. For instance, bilingual people, especially Canadians, may have to switch between English and French, depending on whether they are working with colleagues in Québec or in the rest of Canada. To change the app language, follow these steps:

1. **Click** on the **three dots** to the left of your profile picture and open the menu;

2. **Click** on the **Settings** option;

3. In the settings window, **click** on **General**;

4. **Select** your **language** in the ***App language*** combo box;

5. **Click** on the Save and restart button to apply the chosen language.

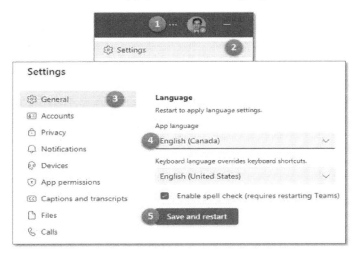

Understanding The Application Settings

In the general settings of **Teams**, under the "Application" section, there are several useful configurations that need to be understood and applied according to each user's preferences:

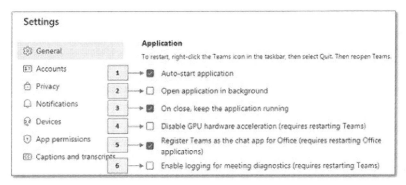

6. **Auto-start application**: Enables/disables **Teams** auto-launch when Windows starts.

7. **Open application in background**: When Windows starts, **Teams** does not show but runs in the background. This way, you will not see the **Teams** window but will still receive desktop notifications from it.

You can open the **Teams** application by clicking on its icon on the system tray:

1. **On close, keep the application running**: In this case, even if the *Teams* window is not open, you can still receive notifications.
2. **Disable GPU (Graphics Processing Units) hardware acceleration**: This is used in *Teams* especially to enhance video visualization. To reduce the CPU/ RAM usage by *Teams*, check this box.
3. **Register Teams as the chat app for Office**: This sets *Teams* as the chat app to chat with teammates, while co-authoring an Office document.
4. **Enable logging for meeting diagnostics**: This adds meeting diagnostic entries to the log file. *Teams*' desktop logs can be accessed by right-clicking on the *Teams* icon in the system tray and selecting "Get logs":

Or by opening the text file:

C:\Users\UserName\AppData\Roaming\Microsoft\Teams\logs.txt

Managing Audio And Video Devices

Audio and video devices used in Microsoft Teams for calls and meetings are managed and tested through the profile menu in the "Settings" window:

1. **Click** on the **three dots** at the left of your profile picture to open the menu;
2. Click **on** Settings;
3. In the settings window, **click** on **Devices**;
4. **Selec**t and configure the **audio** and **video devices** you wish to use in *Teams*.

Setting Your Status Message

Status messages are usually used to inform people of our status, especially when we are out-of-office. In the Microsoft ecosystem, we can set status messages in *Teams*, as well as in *Outlook*. The two applications are well integrated.

First, let's see how to set a status message in *Teams*:

1. Click **on your** profile picture;

2. Click **on the** "Set status message" **hyperlink;**

3. **Enter** a **status message**, e.g. when you want the out-of-office message to appear;

4. **Choose** if you want the **message to be shown above the Compose box** when people message or @mention you;

5. **Set** a **date and time** after which the message has to be cleared;

6. Optionally, you can **set** an **"out of office"** message;

7. **Click** on the "Done" button to set your status message.

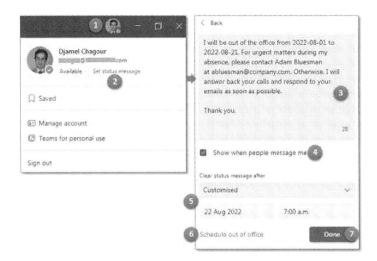

A status bar appears under the title bar of Microsoft Teams application to remind you that your status message is now on:

Now when people try to message or mention you, they will see your status message as shown below:

When people hover over the profile picture, they will see the status message:

In Outlook, we can set automatic replies when we are out-of-office and not available to respond to emails. When a person sets an automatic reply in **Outlook**, **Teams** becomes aware of it, and displays it when you open your chat window with that person and when you @mention here:

Additionally, when we hover over the profile picture, we can see the automatic reply:

540

Notice the arrow inside a circle added to the picture and the background colour of the message. To conclude, we must bear in mind that automatic replies in **Outlook** are for responding automatically to emails when we are not available, while status messages in **Teams** are to inform people about our status or about an important fact inside **Teams**.

Upload A File

Uploading a file means putting files into your team's channel from your system. Read the following steps to know how to do that.

1. Open the **file tab** at the top of the window of the channel.

2. Click on upload; an option will come up.

3. Click on **file.**

Choose the file you want from your system, click on open, or double click on the file you want from your system. Once you click, the file starts uploading.

Create A New Folder

Sharing information is at the heart of an effective collaboration. It is for this reason that every channel in a team has its own **Files** tab. Members can create, upload, edit, and co-author documents within the channel.

To create a new Office document or a new folder:

1. Open **the** Teams window**;**

2. **Locate** the **team**, and **click** on the **channel** in which you want to create a new document or a new folder**;**

3. **Click** on the Files tab to open it**;**

4. **Click** on the **downward arrow** to the right of the **+ New** option**;**

5. **Click on Folder** to create a new folder, or on any type of new document**;**

6. **Enter** the **name** of the new folder or document**;**

7. **Click** on the Create button.

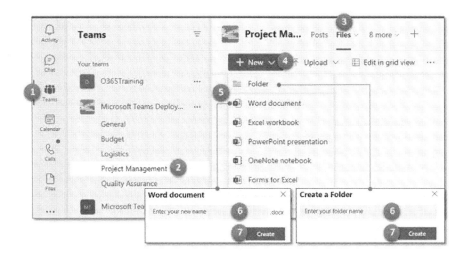

Download The File

To download files or folders:

1. **Select** the **files** or **folders** to download;

2. **Click** on the **Download** link;

3. Find **the** downloaded files **in your** Downloads **folder.**

Open The Files Tab On Your Channel

In every channel, there is a file folder where you can share files for that precise channel. To access this folder,

1. Go to the Files tab above the conversation box and click on it.

In the library, you either upload an existing file or create a new one. When a file is uploaded, it creates another copy in teams.

How To Use Teams Features

Here, we'll explore how to use the features on Microsoft teams. Once you're inside the Microsoft Teams, you'll see the interface containing Activity, Chat, Teams, Calls, Files amidst others. Now, let's delve into these features one after the other.

Activity

The Activity feed is where all the interactions with other team members you're collaborating with will be.

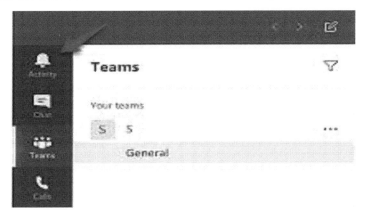

Teams User Activity Report

In the Microsoft Teams user activity report, you have access to the Microsoft Teams activity in your organization. The Teams user activity report gives you a sight of the most mutual events that users perform in Teams. This includes the number of people involved in a conversation on a channel, how many users interconnected via private chat message and how many partook in calls or meetings. You can see these pieces of information for your entire group, as well as for each user.

Chat

The chat area is where you can manage private messaging with individuals in your team. Chats can be one-on-one or

in a group.

You might be using **Microsoft Teams** because it encompasses your group's Office 365 subscription, or you decide to use it yourself. Irrespective of how you started using Microsoft Teams, you may use your initial communications to send mails to other people in your team.

Immediate mails in Teams occur in **channels**. Channels are a domicile where people can type emails, add files, and share links. You can go to **Channel** to converse with colleagues, learn and share conversation, and generally stay in tune with your communal circle.

Channel is inside a team, and a team can have many channels. You can give any name to your channel. Using a name that pronounces the reason for the channel is more preferable. For example, if you are creating a channel for your team to discuss Engineering Practice, you can name it "Engineering Practice."

Teams and Channels

This is where you will collaborate as a team. Here, you can post content to your team and also have specific group documents that you can keep in one area. To start your teamwork cooperation, you need a team. Setting up Teams is easy and done in a few clicks, requiring a team name and a depiction after which you can invite or add team members.

Below are two types of Teams:

Public Team

A public team is exposed to anyone in an organization. A user can freely invite another user to join. Here, up to 10,000 people can join and they don't need the owner's approval to join.

Private Team

Private Team is only for users that are invited. A user's access is possible only if the owner approves it. The Team owner can also add and remove users. Currently, a private team is not detectable to everybody in an organization.

Teams are made up of channels. Channel is the conversation platform between teammates and can be created in the Team tab.

Channels can be general or diverse. A General Channel is automatically created. You can have diverse channels within a team. For example, you can have a Marketing Team and then Channel it as "Social Media", "Product Launch" and "Blogs" etc. Or a company could be a team while channels can be related to units in the company. You can choose whatever fits into your organization's way of working.

Calendar

Microsoft Teams features a variety of tools to increase productivity and upgrade communication between staff, one of which is the Calendar feature. Microsoft Teams has one calendar in common, which allows team members to create meetings directly within the Teams app, specify details, and add other members so that they are not only informed of the event but have it added to their synced Microsoft Teams calendar as well.

Calls

The Call feature helps to keep track of all the calls you have made. You can make one-on-one calls with anybody in your team directly from a chat without having to host a team meeting. Although entries for these calls will appear in your chat, these calls are isolated and won't show in any team conversation. You can also make group calls with this feature.

Files

The files area is where you can work on shared documents with your team. As your team works collectively, you will surely have the files that you want to share and cooperatively work on. Microsoft Teams make it simple to share files and work on them collectively. If you're working in Word, Excel, PowerPoint, or Visio files, your teammates can view, edit, and collaborate on them through Teams.

Setting Up And Managing Channel Moderation

The administrator of each private channel has control over the channel's settings, which include the capacity to add and remove users, add tabs, and **@mention** the entire channel. The parent team settings have no influence on these parameters. A private channel inherits settings from its parent team when it was first created; however, settings can subsequently be altered for the private channel without affecting the parent team configurations.

The owner of a private channel can add or delete users and change settings by clicking the Manage channel, followed by the Members and Configuration tabs.

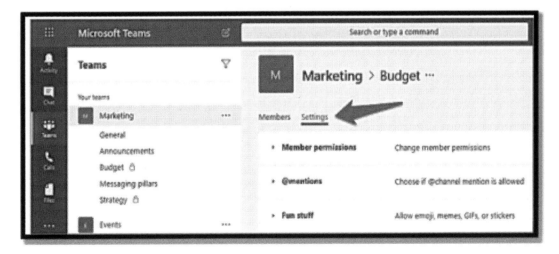

Tabs

Tabs are web pages that are inside the Microsoft Teams. Tabs can be included as sections of a channel found in a team, a group chat, or as a private app for individual usage. A tab can be illustrated as the likelihood of adding essential information to either your private chat, group chats, or even a team channel.

How To Add A Tab To Your Team

1. To add a tab, click on the channel you want to add a tab to

2. Click on **Add Tab**

3. Click on any of the options (tabs) below. This is used in adding PDF tab, Word Tab, Excel Tab, and so on. You can also search for the tab you are looking for using the **search bar.**

4. After selecting a tab, select the file and click on **save**

Note: You can only create a tab if you have attached a file of that specific type of tab.

What Is Wiki Tab

A wiki tab is a tab used for different purposes, like drafting notes, editing, and chatting. It is automatically created by MS teams. Check the picture below to find where the Wiki tab is placed.

How To Create Tabs For Pdf, Word, Excel, PowerPoint

This is similar to adding tabs in a channel. Follow the procedure of adding tabs, and click on the PDF, Word, Excel, PowerPoint tabs.

How To Rename A Tab

1. Click on **word** tab, click on the arrow down button beside it;

2. A drop-down would be displayed, click on **rename;**

3. Type the new name.

How To Delete A Tab

1. Click on **word** tab, and click on the arrow down button beside it

2. Click on **remove**

Microsoft Teams Apps

To learn about the available apps, head to the ***Teams'*** App Store; open the Apps window:

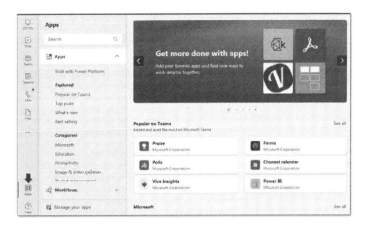

You can also explore installed apps, that you can use within your team, by opening the **Apps** tab when managing a team: go to the Teams window, select your favourite team and click on the 3-dot menu (...) (More options), then on "Manage team." In the **Manage team** window, click on the **Apps** tab, then on the **More apps** button:

You will be surprised by the number of apps that you can integrate into **Teams**.

We have already become acquainted with the **Who** bot. Here, for example, is the answer the bot provided when asked who knows about SharePoint:

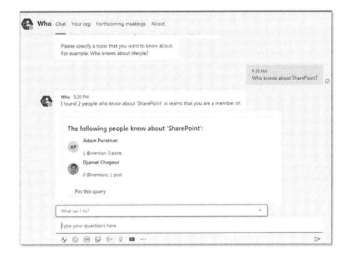

Chapter 4: **Conclusion**

Microsoft Teams is an excellent choice as far as connecting with team members online is concerned. With the several features of Teams that have been explained and illustrated in this guide — ranging from the Activity tab to the Files tab, to the use of other Office apps with it and several other features — I believe by now, you can effortlessly collaborate with your team members using Microsoft Teams and achieve more.

Ensure you practice the use of the various features of Teams as discussed and illustrated in this guide to make the most of it and become a professional Microsoft Teams user.

Made in the USA
Middletown, DE
15 October 2023

40871967R00305